(2007–8) and a sabbatical leave (2008–9) provided the time needed to devote to research and writing. Helpful comments followed presentations of the research at the Stern School of Business, New York University (2011), Booth School of Business, University of Chicago (2011), Harvard Business School (2011), Chinese Academy of Social Sciences (2011), Cornell University (2010), Tsinghua University (2010), University of Bamberg (2009), New School for Social Research (2009), Johns Hopkins University (2009), and Fudan University (2008). He also thanks those who offered probing questions and comments following presentations at the conference "1989: 20 Years After" at the University of California, Irvine (2009), the "Manufactured Markets" seminar sponsored by the University of Paris in Florence (2009), and a meeting of economic sociologists of the Italian Sociological Association in Sardinia (2009).

The Center for the Study of Economy and Society at Cornell provided intellectual as well as administrative support throughout the project. Participants in weekly Economy and Society Lab meetings provided an ongoing forum for discussion of ideas underlying this book. Other graduate students at Cornell read and usefully discussed the manuscript in seminar.

Chapters 2 and 9 draw on materials that have been published separately. We thank the publishers for permission to adapt and use portions of the following copyrighted articles: Victor Nee, "The New Institutionalism in Economics and Sociology," *The Handbook of Economic Sociology*, ed. Neil J. Smelser and Richard Swedberg (Princeton and New York: Princeton University Press and Russell Sage Foundation, 2005), 49–74; and Victor Nee and Sonja Opper, "Political Capital in a Market Economy," *Social Forces* 88 (2010): 2105–2135.

We gratefully acknowledge the help of graduate research assistants in the Department of Sociology at Cornell: Yujun Wang, Ningxi Zhang, and Zun Tang, as well as Christopher Yenkey, Li Ma, Mark Jacobs, and Paul Lee.

Many colleagues read the entire manuscript and contributed detailed comments and criticism: William Parish, Michael Macy, Walter Powell, Benjamin Cornwell, Lisa Keister, and Frank Young. Other scholars who commented on parts of the manuscript include Howard Aldrich, Fredrik Andersson, Wm. Theodore de Bary, Matthew Bothner, Susan Buck-Morss, Ronald Burt, Franco Cerase, Robert Ellickson, Joseph Galaskiewicz, Christer Gunnarsson, Ravi Ramamurti, Eric Siggia, Iván Szelényi, and Markus Taube. Glenn Carroll, Michael Hannan, Douglas Heckathorn, Håkan Holm, Jesper Sørensen, David Strang, Richard Swedberg, Anne Tsui, and Rafael Wittek contributed useful counsel at various stages.

Sonja Opper acknowledges the generous support of the Department of Economics at Lund University, which granted a teaching-free year (2009) to support research and writing at a critical stage. She also appreciates the lively and valuable discussions at seminars organized at Lund University (2010), Cornell University (2007, 2011), Fudan University (2007, 2010), the University of Duisburg-Essen (2008, 2010), Erasmus University of Rotterdam (2009), and the University of Trier (2008). Furthermore, she is grateful for valuable comments received from conference participants at the Annual Meeting of the International Society of New Institutional Economics (2011), the Conference on Endogenous Institutional Change at Lund University (2011), the Annual Meeting of the International Academy of Chinese Management Research (2010), the Annual Meeting of the Academy of Management (2008), and the Annual Meeting of the European Economic Association (2008). Over the years, student feedback also provided a constant stream of ideas. Most importantly, participants in the graduate courses on "China's Economy" at Lund University were among the first to listen to our argument and to discuss some of the key ideas developed in this book. Finally, friends and family provided invaluable support. In particular, Sonja thanks Björn Meyer for many fruitful discussions, for insightful remarks on part of the manuscript, and for his steadfast support and encouragement.

Victor Nee acknowledges Brett de Bary's unflagging interest and support and the feedback she has offered throughout. She and the Egyptian filmmaker Safaa Fathy joined us in Zhejiang, Shanghai, and Jiangsu to film and record onsite interviews and visits to firms. A John Simon Guggenheim Fellowship

Acknowledgments

A quest to explain institutional change that gave rise to a new economic order is complex and challenging. This book reports the results of a six-year (2005–2011) study that aims to do just that. The effort has had many moving parts, involving contributions of an international research team. Our intellectual debts are deep and extensive. Here we wish to thank the researchers, scholars, and staff who contributed to our study over the course of those years. David Su, Lu Hanlong, and researchers at the Institute of Sociology of the Shanghai Academy of Social Sciences shared with us their expertise and advice every step of the way. Without the dedication and efforts of Sun Bocheng and his entire staff at the Market Survey Research Institute, our firm-level surveys in the Yangzi delta region could not have been carried out. Colleagues in China helped us significantly: Shi Jinchuan, Justin Yifu Lin, Victor Yuan, Guo Li, and Lu Hanyin.

The John Templeton Foundation provided major funding for the project. We thank especially Barnaby Marsh, who took an interest in the project's aims from inception to completion. We are also appreciative of the support of the Swedish Research Council, the College of Arts and Sciences at Cornell University, Tetra Pak Corporation, and the Crafoord Foundation for funding the research.

We thank Michael Aronson, our editor at Harvard University Press, for his support and editorial input at each stage. Rachel Davis provided outstanding editing of the manuscripts, which clarified our arguments. Thanks also to Barbara Goodhouse, our production editor.

Tables

Figures and Tables

Figures

Contents

To
Margaret Nee (1919–2011) and Fanny de Bary (1922–2009)
Margret and Herbert Opper

Library of Congress Cataloging-in-Publication Data

Nee, Victor
   Capitalism from below : markets and institutional change in China / Victor Nee,
Sonja Opper.
        p.   cm.
   Includes bibliographical references and index.
   ISBN 978-0-674-05020-4 (alk. paper)
   1. Capitalism—China. 2. Entrepreneurship—China. 3. Industrial policy—
China. 4. China—Economic policy. 5. China—Politics and government.
I. Opper, Sonja. II. Title.
      HC427.95.N44   2012
      330.951—dc23   2011042367

CAPITALISM FROM BELOW

Markets and Institutional Change in China

VICTOR NEE
SONJA OPPER

HARVARD UNIVERSITY PRESS
Cambridge, Massachusetts, and London, England
2012

CAPITALISM FROM BELOW

CAPITALISM FROM BELOW

1

Where Do Economic Institutions Come From?

The emergence and robust growth of a private enterprise economy in China was neither envisioned nor anticipated by its political elite. In launching economic reform in 1978, the initial motivation was to address failures of central planning within the institutional framework of state socialism. The political elite approved reform policies in order to stimulate productivity in a command economy weighed down by years of lagging economic performance. With their continuing emphasis on public ownership, the post-Mao reforms seemed nothing other than an ambitious project to shore up the state-owned economy in the aftermath of a calamitous decade of political turmoil. Compared to the sweeping changes under way in other transition economies, the Chinese reform seemed overly conservative, committed to restoration rather than transformative change. Contrary to expectations of economists in the West, however, China's economic reforms gave rise to a thriving market economy.

Why did a dynamic private enterprise economy and institutions of capitalism emerge in China? How could entrepreneurs overcome formidable barriers to entry enforced by government? What are the institutions that allow private economic actors to compete and cooperate in a transition economy still dominated by government-owned firms? And where did economic institutions of capitalism come from? Standard economic theory does not offer ready solutions explaining China's path to capitalist economic development.

In implementing the party's reform policies, the central government sought to improve incentives by decentralizing and cutting back on state control of economic activity. In agriculture, reformers decentralized production to the peasant household through a land-lease system and promoted the gradual liberalization of rural markets. In industry, reform measures sought to strengthen material incentives for management and workers through retention of profits and more enterprise autonomy. In parallel, the state promoted foreign direct investments (FDI) to alleviate capital constraints and to speed up the country's technological catching-up process. Reform leaders implemented fiscal decentralization to strengthen economic incentives for provincial and local government through a revenue-sharing arrangement. Though lower-level governments have the obligation to submit a fixed proportion of fiscal revenues to the higher level of government, they retain the residual for their own budget.[1]

In Eastern Europe and the former Soviet Union, following the collapse of Communist Party–led governments, economists representing international economic agencies gathered in capital cities to advise the political elites of the newly established governments on how to design and build the economic institutions of capitalism. These political elites sought, through a rapid sequence of top-down reform measures, to promulgate the formal rules and regulatory structures of market capitalism in line with policies recommended by the International Monetary Fund (IMF) and the World Bank. The rationale for a "big bang" transition, emphasizing rapid, large-scale privatization, price liberalization, and currency reforms, rested on assumptions about the entrenched nature of central planning as an economic order. In the view of many economists in the West, only shock therapy would do the job of breaking away from the powerful entrenched interests and all-encompassing grip of central planning, rapidly providing a legal framework as the institutional foundation of a market economy.[2] China's piecemeal economic reforms appeared destined to fail, they thought, while the bold reform measures under way in Eastern Europe and the former Soviet Union promised in short order through "big bang" transitions to institute free-market capitalism.

Within thirty-odd years, however, China's per capita gross domestic product (GDP) calculated at current prices has increased more than thirty times in spite of rapid population growth. Starting out from a nominal per capita GDP of only $150 at the start of reforms—at that time ranked 131 in the world—China entered the group of upper-middle-income countries with a registered per capita GDP of $4,603 in 2010.[3] The effects for social and economic well-being were pronounced. Since the beginning of economic reforms, average life expectancy rose by five years to seventy-three years in 2009, even exceeding that in upper-middle-income countries.[4] Income inequality increased rapidly after an initial decline, and is on par with that in the United States; even so, economic reforms have benefited all income groups.[5] Between 1981 and 2005, more than 630 million Chinese left absolute poverty (based on the benchmark of $1.25 per day for consumption), which reduced the fraction of population living in poverty from 81.6 to 10.4 percent, establishing a record for poverty reduction in human history.[6]

The rise of a privately owned manufacturing economy has played a key role in wealth creation and has changed China's industrial landscape dramatically. By 2009, only around 20 percent of the gross industrial output value in domestic production was generated by fully state-owned and collective enterprises. Forty-one percent accrued to private companies registered as partnerships, limited liability companies, or shareholding firms. In addition, 25 percent accrued to limited liability companies of mixed ownership, and 13 percent to shareholding corporations of mixed ownership (including stock-listed firms.)[7] Private enterprises secured 40 percent of industrial profits, and employed 47 percent of the industrial workforce registered in domestic-funded companies.[8]

Why were China's economic reforms, envisioned as a restoration project, more effective in fostering market-driven structural change and economic growth than the sweeping reforms undertaken by political elites in Eastern Europe and Russia, which closely followed policy recommendations of the IMF and World Bank? Why did the private enterprise economy, initially so disadvantaged, not only survive but thrive in China's transition to a market economy?

The State Remaking Economic Institutions

Many observers point to the prominent role of central and local government to explain China's successful transition to a market economy, now in its fourth decade of transformative economic growth. Whether this is described as the helping-hand government, local state corporatism, or the developmental state, there is an underlying notion of the government's decisive role in devising and shaping the emerging institutions enabling and motivating China's economic miracle.[9] It is generally thought that China's development mainly rests on a state-directed process of institutional change, wherein efficiency-enhancing formal rules and policies are instituted by political elites.[10] Although the trial-and-error character of economic reform has been widely acknowledged, analysis interpreting the successes and failures of China's market transition tends nonetheless to focus on political actors in central or local government. Various studies document how local government officials used their regulatory and financial power to successfully advance local economic development through infrastructure investments or through local industrial or technology parks.[11] Even regional analysis of adaptive institutional change rarely focuses attention on initiatives by entrepreneurs and firms, but on the role of local governments, which, substituting for missing national legislation, provided temporary regulations that protected private firms against local state expropriation. Wenzhou Municipality, for example, a southern coastal city in Zhejiang Province that lacked a Maoist-era industrial base, responding to local commercial activities, put in place local private firm regulations already in 1987, one year before the central government launched a first official document to regulate private firms.[12] Wenzhou officials also established local policies guiding and promoting entrepreneurial activities, including a simplified taxation system. Local policies there and elsewhere fostering "adaptive informal institutions" suggest that the government's acquiescent attitude often played a supportive role in those localities, where the marginalized private sector could rapidly develop, in spite of missing formal institutions safeguarding private property rights.[13]

Building on the view that the polity, as the enforcer of the rules of the game, is "the primary source of economic performance," state-centered analysis underscores the role of political actors.[14] The idea that politicians play a key role is both substantively undeniable and intuitively appealing. With its monopoly of the use of legitimate violence, the state enjoys substantial cost advantages in institutional change. By contrast, the free-rider dilemma constrains the ability of economic actors to assume the cost of collective action to establish and enforce the rules of the game. The political elite's interest in revenue maximization motivates the exchange of public goods provision for tax revenue, which in turn aligns elite interest in sponsoring formal institutional change to promote economic growth.[15]

In departures from central planning, instituting the formal rules of a market economy necessarily comes first, in this view, because the polity can change formal rules virtually overnight. Informal constraints are not only slow to change, but also beyond the reach of the political elite.[16] They are seen as a source of friction working at cross-purposes to the political elite's effort to implement institutional change.[17]

The Limit of the State-Centered Explanation

The problem with the state-centered approach, however, is that it cannot explain the emergence and self-reinforcing growth of China's robust private enterprise economy, by now a central component of the manufacturing economy. During the first decade of reform, though the central government encouraged household businesses *(geti hu)*, it explicitly sought to restrict private commercial activities to a peripheral role. To the extent that the government implemented regulations to legitimize private firms, it was in a spirit of tolerance of a necessary concession, allowing marginalized social groups—rural households, the unemployed, laid-off and retired workers—to start up small-scale production, but not providing active support or a level playing field. If the political elite had had their way, the seeds of capitalism, sowed as an unintended consequence of reform policies, would have been contained by state-mandated rules restricting the size of private firms to individual household production, which would have stayed in the traditional mode of making small-scale commodities for the market. This form of household production flourished in all preindustrial societies, as in the traditional putting-out system in the West before the rise of modern capitalism. Both Karl Marx and Max Weber noted that it is a self-limiting form of traditional economic organization.[18] In their accounts, the modern capitalist enterprise did not develop from traditional household production.[19]

In the early 1980s, the political elite envisioned the household firm as an organizational form promoting self-employment for marginal economic actors at the periphery of an economy dominated by state-owned enterprises. Local government freely issued licenses to start up household-based private firms to farmers producing for urban markets, traditional merchants, artisans, peddlers, and educated youths returning to the city from years in the countryside. The political elite did not anticipate that large numbers of start-up firms would grow quickly into sizeable manufacturing enterprises even before the government formally acknowledged the registration of larger private companies in 1988.

In many areas, politicians surreptitiously allowed the larger private firms to register legally as collective enterprises formally owned by local government, though the founding capital was private and actual firm operations did not involve regular government participation in management. Such "red hat" firms laid the basis for a thriving private enterprise economy in Wenzhou, for example.[20] Local governments received in return a management fee, typically specified as a certain percentage of after-tax profits. Other entrepreneurs attached their business to established collective or state units as so-called hang-on households *(gua hu)*. Under these arrangements, entrepreneurs paid a fee for the use of the name, stationery, and bank account numbers of the registered public firm.[21] However, such disguised forms of private firms remained vulnerable to expropriation by local governments through special taxes and mandatory contributions to community projects. The predatory taxes and expropriation by local government and the looting of assets and wealth of peasant entrepreneurs highlighted the problem of insecure property rights.[22]

It was not until a decade after the start of economic reform, when private enterprise was already growing rapidly, that the first constitutional amendment (Article 11) in 1988 eventually conferred legal status to private firms. The corresponding national regulation—"The Temporary Regulations of Private Enterprise" (July 1988)[23]—governing private firms with more than seven wage laborers *(siying qiye),* however, still reflected the government's intent to limit the private sector to a subordinate if not inferior role, as the sector was officially viewed as a *supplement* to the socialist public-owned economy.[24]

The constitutional change recognizing the legality of private enterprise fell far short of conferring social legitimacy and secure property rights upon entrepreneurs. No explicit central government policy enhanced or facilitated the founding of private firms. Quite to the contrary, market entry remained costly. The Administration of Industry and Commerce (the formal supervisory bureau of private firms) in Beijing, for instance, required 443 approval items for registering a private firm.[25] The taxation system further deepened the sector's competitive disadvantage. While the maximum tax rate for collective enterprise was 55 percent, the corresponding rate for private firm income reached 86 percent.[26] Tax exemptions and tax reductions—typically offered to newly founded public firms—were generally not granted for private firms.[27] Unlike their collective competitors, private firms had no access to government-guaranteed start-up capital. Overall, the formal status of private enterprise remained insecure and subject to local political interpretation. Discrimination was widespread, particularly with respect to applications for export licenses, approval of international travel, or access to production material and qualified technical staff. Arbitrary local fees and taxes imposed heavy burdens on private firms, with up to eighty distinct fees levied on them. Oftentimes entrepreneurs faced illegal ad hoc increases of these fees, which in cases of nonpayment led to the confiscation of production material or products. Finally, the regulation constrained private-sector entrepreneurship by specifying production quotas and restrictions on allocation of after-tax profits.[28]

If the private enterprise economy had developed within the institutional framework of state-crafted formal rules, it would have been restricted to small-scale commodity production and "fake" collectives operated as private businesses, but legally owned by local government. In this structural position, the private economy could only have developed as an auxiliary sector subordinated to a dominant state-owned economy. Local government's response to competitive pressures from private firms was to protect local government-owned firms.[29] When in the 1990s conservatives in central government enforced policies aimed at safeguarding and developing large state-owned enterprises, private firms legally registered as township and village enterprises were readily shut down en masse. Through the decade of the 1990s, the central government's policy sought to contain the private enterprise economy as a peripheral, subordinate sector of the Chinese economy.[30] As Jiang Zemin, the general secretary of the Chinese Communist Party, emphasized as late as 1997: "State-owned or collectively-owned assets or property must continue to hold a position of advantage or superiority. . . . The state-owned economic sector must hold a dominant and controlling position with regard to the key sector and key spheres."[31]

Although in 2004 the government amended the constitution to confer to private firms equality with state-owned enterprises and formally guaranteed to "protect the lawful rights and interests of the private sector," private property remained vulnerable. Regulations concerning the creation, transfer, and ownership of property were put in place only with China's Property Rights Law, enacted in 2007 after years of political controversy. Critics claimed that the equal treatment of state-owned and private companies would violate China's principles as a socialist state. Even after formal rules extended equality of rights to private enterprise, many entrepreneurs remain skeptical that recent legal reforms provide substantive benefits. The local courts continue to be subordinate to local political interests and priorities of the Communist Party. Even when entrepreneurs succeed in court in litigating claims, often directed at local government, enforcement of court rulings is uncertain, especially in the less developed inland provinces. Recent figures indicate that only 53 percent of court rulings involving domestic firms are actually enforced.[32] Such problems of uncertainty faced by entrepreneurs are reflected in cross-national indicators of security of property rights, which rank China on par with Angola, Belarus, and Azerbaijan, and slightly lower than Russia.[33] These assessments are in line with the World Bank's evaluation of the quality of business regulations around the world. In 2011, China ranked 151 in terms of ease of starting a business, and 93 in terms of investor protection. For regulatory quality overall, China ranked seventy-ninth (behind Zambia and Vietnam).[34]

Insofar as the political logic of reform in China was aimed at safeguarding and promoting the public ownership economy, state-centered analysis has little applicability in explaining where economic institutions enabling the dynamic rise of a private enterprise economy come from. Focusing on state-mandated rules has little utility in understanding the dynamics of endogenous institutional change.[35]

Endogenous Emergence of Economic Institutions

In order to explain capitalist economic development in China, we focus not so much on the policies of the state as on institutional innovations of economic actors. While we agree that politicians played an important role in initiating the shift to market allocation, we argue that the rise of capitalist economic institutions rests on bottom-up entrepreneurial action. Informal economic arrangements enabling, motivating, and guiding start-up firms provided the institutional foundations of China's emergent capitalist economic order.

But how could entrepreneurs build from the bottom up the economic institutions needed to protect economic transactions? How did they overcome collective action problems? In an institutional environment characterized by weak property rights, how did entrepreneurs resolve problems of uncertainty to start up firms and invest in growth? How could they compete with government-owned firms that benefited from most-favored treatment in the state's industrial policy?

Our theory explaining endogenous institutional change focuses analytic attention on social mechanisms embedded in networks. Our study of the founding processes and entrepreneurial activities of private firms in the Yangzi delta region examines micro-level mechanisms enabling the rise of economic institutions supported by informal norms and social networks within close-knit business communities.

When the initial wave of entrepreneurs decoupled from the traditional socialist production system, motivated by a search for new profit-making opportunities in decentralized markets, the government had neither initiated financial reforms inviting a broader societal participation nor provided property rights protection or transparent rules specifying company registration and liabilities. Instead, it was the development and use of innovative informal arrangements within networks of like-minded economic actors that provided the necessary funding and reliable business norms. Entrepreneurs devised through trial and error the institutional arrangements that enabled them to start up and grow private manufacturing firms. Barriers to entry compelled and motivated entrepreneurs to build their own networks of suppliers and distributors, and below the radar of the state to develop competitive advantage in self-organized industrial clusters of producers, suppliers, and distributors. Despite the absence of formal rules safeguarding property rights of the capitalist enterprise, the emergence and diffusion of cooperation norms at the micro level enabled entrepreneurs to commit to a private enterprise economy and allowed them to survive outside the state-owned manufacturing system.

Thus, in the decades of economic reform, bottom-up institutional innovations played a crucial role in enabling and motivating capitalist economic development. Such institutional arrangements enabled the private sector to respond effectively to changing market incentives and opportunities, and thereby influence—from within the private enterprise economy—the emerging economic institutions of capitalism. In this perspective, the rules of the game are themselves the outcome of repeated interactions of economic actors.

Initially this was not a broad-based national movement. China's entrepreneurial development was spatially concentrated and grew through protracted bursts of entrepreneurial activity, similar to the "waves of creative destruction" that Joseph Schumpeter observed in other such dynamic periods.[36] Particularly the Yangzi delta region emerged as a center of entrepreneurial capitalism, and thus it lends itself as a natural laboratory to study the formation of capitalist economic institutions.

Through a bottom-up dynamics of cumulative causation, a fledgling private enterprise economy diffused and grew in the Yangzi delta and in other coastal regions. Situated in industrial clusters decoupled from the state-controlled economy, many start-up firms rapidly expanded; other start-ups continuously entered into play. Swarms of entrepreneurs who started up private manufacturing firms in these regions began to undercut the dominance of established collective firms. These were not the small household firms *(geti hu)* approved by the state, but a new organizational form of privately owned capitalist firms *(siying qiye)*. Despite a host of policies aiming to strengthen and modernize the state-owned and state-controlled manufacturing base in the 1990s,[37] a rapidly growing private enterprise economy cumulatively eroded the market share of government-owned enterprises.

Plan of the Book

Chapter 2 lays out the conceptual framework integrating ideas and insights from the new institutionalisms. There we introduce our theory of endogenous emergence of the institutions of entrepreneurial capitalism and proffer a multilevel causal model of institutional change. In our model, institutional dynamics operate in both directions, from institutional mechanisms embedded in macro-structures to micro-level behavior, and from micro-motives and behavior to macro-level institutional change.

The following chapters apply our multilevel causal model of institutional change to substantive fields of entrepreneurial action, in order to document the rise and operation of informal norms and economic institutions in an environment devoid of credible and enforceable formal institutions. With our analysis we hope to illustrate the underlying micro-level mechanisms that allowed China's entrepreneurs to successfully decouple from the existing system of state socialism. Chapter 3 describes the spatial and economic geography of the Yangzi delta region, our seven-city sample, our research design and the methodology of our quantitative surveys, as well as the use of face-to-face interviews. Chapter 4 examines the firm's founding processes and the corresponding norms explaining a rapid growth of the private firm population. How did entrepreneurs raise the initial founding capital? How did they manage to start up and expand firms in an environment without secure property rights protection and formal recognition of their firm's legal status? Where did they acquire the "soft skills" of opening and running a business? Chapter 5 turns to the closely linked question of the specific organizational strategies entrepreneurs employed to limit the individual costs associated with decoupling from standard forms of socialist production. Chapter 6 details how similar micro mechanisms guided the development of privately organized supply and marketing networks beyond the control of the state. Chapter 7 then discusses the rise of labor markets. What mechanisms enabled entrepreneurs to gain access to skilled labor in an environment where labor allocation and security are long-standing privileges of public forms of production? What helped private firms to gradually develop the norms and labor standards enabling them to compete with public and foreign companies for skilled and experienced professional staff? Chapter 8 shifts attention to the key question whether the development of workaday norms in entrepreneurial networks allows for dynamic firm development and innovative activity. Can informal institutional arrangements embedded in entrepreneurial networks actually enable private firms to move up the technological ladder if formal protection of intellectual property rights is only in its infancy? Or do we simply witness the rise of a parallel economy mainly consisting of fly-by-night businesses emphasizing imitation rather than innovation, not ready to compete with the government-sponsored public firm economy strongly supported by national innovation policies?

Analysis of these economic activities in China's state-controlled economy would be incomplete if we bypassed the important question as to what role political connections have played in the rise of a private enterprise economy. Chapter 9 brings the state back in, examining the role of government and the extent to which political connections facilitated the founding and economic performance of private firms. Chapter 10, in conclusion, reviews the core theoretical and empirical findings.

2

Markets and Endogenous Institutional Change

In the decades following the start of economic reform in 1978, despite the weakness of formal rules protecting property rights, the private enterprise economy emerged as the fastest-growing sector. By 2008, it provided employment for more than 100 million people, roughly twice the size of the workforce employed by all government-owned enterprises. Through bottom-up endogenous processes, entrepreneurs created a parallel economy of more than 5.5 million officially registered private firms with more than \$1.3 trillion of registered capital.[1] From outside the established economic order dominated by state-owned enterprises, entrepreneurs developed from the bottom up economic institutions that enabled them to compete and cooperate in spite of disadvantageous or simply absent state-mandated formal rules. These institutions allowed them to surmount formidable barriers to market entry and discriminatory policies of the state.

How could economic institutions develop from the bottom up within a relatively short period of time in China? The emergence of markets played a crucial role in enabling entrepreneurial activities. First, the gradual replacement of bureaucratic allocation by market mechanisms involves a *shift of power* favoring producers relative to redistributors.[2] Most importantly, the emergence of markets gives producers a greater set of choices. They can develop new organizational and ownership forms and can informally work out new institutional arrangements for cooperation and exchange outside the socialist system of state allocation. Almost imperceptibly, but accelerating following tipping points, self-reinforcing shifts in the institutional environment cause traditional state-owned enterprises to lose market share to hybrid and private ownership forms.[3] Second, marketization provides *incentives,* as in markets rewards are increasingly based on a firm's performance rather than the strength of political connections. The most effective way to stimulate productive entrepreneurial activity and innovativeness is to diminish relative rewards for unproductive or destructive rent seeking and increase payoffs for productive activity.[4] Finally, markets help to detect and assess new *opportunities.* Opportunity creation goes well beyond resource availability through market allocation. The market mechanism itself offers economic actors a means to assess potential opportunities from entrepreneurial action, as well as opportunity costs for failing to invest in productive activities.[5] The emergence of markets thus endogenously expands the opportunities for entrepreneurs and firms to identify new markets and prospects for profit making.

In sum, the greater autonomy afforded by decentralized markets enables and motivates entrepreneurs to develop informal arrangements that build from the ground up the economic institutions of a private enterprise economy.

Quite unexpectedly, the lack of corresponding legal and regulatory framework supportive of any private firms larger than seven employees and not registered as "red hat" firms did not pose an effective constraint on entrepreneurial action. Instead, China's experience shows that "economic activity does not grind to a halt because the government cannot or does not provide an adequate underpinning of law. Too much potential value would go unrealized; therefore groups and societies have much to gain if they create alternative institutions to provide the necessary economic governance."[6] The powerful incentives stemming from newly arising market opportunities cannot be overestimated.[7] "At that time, anyone starting a business made money" and "You have to grasp the opportunity, if you see it" are common remarks expressing the atmosphere of the early phase of market transition in China. Just as norms embedded in interacting individuals enable, motivate, and guide economic transactions in societies with well-established legal systems, informal norms develop to facilitate economic activity when economic actors cannot rely on the legal system to litigate the resolution of disputes over property rights and contracts. The informal norms that play such a pervasive and important role in launching private sector economic growth in transition economies seem to operate fairly effectively beyond the shadow of the law. As the general manager of a chemical company in Zhejiang Province noted, "There are so many problems with legal implementation. It is easier to get together a circle of friends who inform each other" and "Whoever dares to do something bad, everyone will know it."[8]

Role of Social Norms

During the first decade of economic reform, entrepreneurs who sought to expand their firm beyond the approved size of no more than seven employees for individual household production *(geti hu)* risked not only outright expropriation by local government, but a host of predatory actions in the guise of fines, taxes, and "charitable contributions" to government-sponsored projects. Even after the central government acknowledged the formal registration of private firms with more than seven employees in 1988, activities of private firms remained officially limited to certain sectors. Local governments also continued to erect barriers to entry, restricting entrepreneurs' market access to protect collectively owned rural industrial firms.[9] In the early 1990s, there was even a risk that private entrepreneurs would be accused of speculation or smuggling in case of long-distance transfers of goods and services.[10] Yet, despite the absence of legal institutions safeguarding property rights of private firms, despite weak formal enforcement of contracts, and despite the ever-present risk of predatory expropriation, China's private enterprise economy experienced explosive growth.

Such broad-based, robust entrepreneurial action supported mainly by endogenous economic institutions arising from interacting individuals is challenging to explain. It is well known that in small groups, social control is a by-product of everyday interactions. "The great bulk of controls over social behavior are not external but built into the relationships themselves, in the sense that either party is worse off if he changes his behavior toward the other."[11] Even so, control via norms becomes more problematic the larger the size of the group and community.[12] Whenever there are costs associated with monitoring and enforcing informal rules, actors will assume the costs only if doing so results in a greater benefit to themselves. Moreover, "somebody has to pay for the selective incentive, and paying for the selective incentive is, itself, a collective action in that it provides a benefit to everyone interested in the collective good, not just the people who pay for the incentive."[13] Thus, stable cooperation is likely to depend on a complex set of design principles. Social norms can enable close-knit communities to successfully avoid the "tragedy of the commons" problem in managing communal resources.[14] Such governance structures rely on long-standing social relationships and community sanctions rather than on external authority to solve the collective action problem threatening the depletion of communal resources.

A broad consensus across the social sciences agrees that informal norms are mainly effective in the governance of exchange in close-knit communities of economic actors. These typically involve tribal and peasant societies, or in advanced industrial societies, highly specialized markets with a limited number of market players engaged in repeated exchange. Detailed case studies highlight the variability of motivations and mechanisms of private ordering in close-knit networks. Diamond traders, for example, systematically reject formal rules as insufficient for the specific business risks inherent in the diamond industry. Traders instead rely on a sophisticated extralegal contractual regime including arbitration proceedings enforced by trading clubs designed to disseminate information about reputation among members.[15] A study of conflict resolution among cattle farmers in Northern California sheds light on less standardized procedures. Despite their differences, a common identity as ranchers of Shasta County sustains a live-and-let-live philosophy, which enables parties to practice mutual restraint. As long as accounts balance along multiple dimensions of interpersonal relations, parties in disputes settle informally.[16]

If the total gains from cooperation exceed the costs, private orders relying on informal norms can provide a stable framework for economic actors to sustain repeat transactions. Entrepreneurs in China's transition economy rely on informal norms within their networks to secure trust, acquire information, and make cooperation possible in a competitive economy. In spite of bureaucratic red tape and missing property rights protection, entrepreneurs have founded firms and built businesses on the basis of social norms without state-mandated contractual law guiding business behavior. They use small loans from friends and relatives for their start-up capital, develop supplier and sales networks outside the established distribution channels of the state, and resort to informal monitoring and mediation to resolve business disputes. The cooperation norms allowing for a continuous growth of the private enterprise economy include (1) the norm of reciprocity among firms in the same niche; (2) the expectation that successful entrepreneurs should help friends, relatives, and employees start up their own firms, either directly through financial resources or more indirectly with professional advice and on-the-job training; and (3) the norm that established entrepreneurs ought not continue to borrow money from friends and relatives, but instead rely on business loans and internal accumulation to fund new investments. Such norms constitute the sinews of endogenous economic institutions facilitating cooperation among entrepreneurs in the context of fiercely competitive markets.

In explaining the rise of capitalism, we thus turn on its head the causal priority asserted by new institutional economics.[17] However, assigning causal priority to the endogenous construction of informal economic institutions does not imply that we slight the importance of credible commitment by the state to formal rules protecting and legitimating private property rights. Informal property rights are claims based on de facto ownership, which by nature is weaker and more uncertain than de jure rights.[18] When challenged by competing claims, de facto ownership is always subordinate to de jure property rights. Hence, the more the scope and value of transactions increase, the greater the entrepreneur's interest in securing de jure property rights for productive assets. Our argument is that the bottom-up construction of endogenous economic institutions has *causal priority* over state-mandated rules and policies in explaining the rise of China's private enterprise economy. Only after the private enterprise economy was already well established as an irrepressible and powerful engine of economic growth did the state begin to enact, *ex post*, the formal rules and policies that cumulatively conferred legitimacy, formal legal rights, and equality to private firms.

This is consistent with the causal sequence in the rise of political and economic institutions in the West. Norms often precede laws, and only become formalized once a "norm becomes firmer" and once "there is growing support to formalize it through the promulgation of laws." Civil liberties, the very foundation of democratic systems, exemplify this: "The legal system can only protect free speech if there is substantial support for it among a population willing to tolerate dissent and willing to protect those who exercise it."[19] Congruence between legal rules and informal norms is therefore often the result of this sequence where laws simply support, maintain, and extend what is regarded as a just and appropriate social norm. As with political institutions, economic law often builds on established and widely accepted business norms. In Amsterdam, home of the world's first stock market and stock company (the East India Company, founded in 1602), formal shareholder rights were largely absent, and many of the financial transactions were even prohibited by law. Securities trading relied on self-interest and self-enforcement.[20] By the 1630s the Netherlands was already a "highly commercialized country with well developed and innovative financial markets and a large population of sophisticated traders,"[21] although it was not until 1851 that the Amsterdam Stock Exchange Association was founded to organize and regulate share trading. Likewise, the London Stock Exchange did not receive its first codified rule book until 1812, whereas organized securities trading had started as early as 1698. The Brussels stock exchange worked for more than one hundred years up to 1935 with minimal government regulation. Worldwide, the inception of securities markets was not usually preceded or even accompanied by formal state-mandated rules protecting shareholder rights. Company stocks were traded informally and transactions were treated as gentlemen's agreements, often conducted in local coffee houses or open marketplaces. Interest-based and self-governed "organizations—mainly in the form of corporations—were vital to Europe's political and economic institutions during the late medieval growth period as well as the modern growth period."[22] Good formal institutions have typically followed, rather than preceded, economic development.[23]

Our Framework

In recent years, a "sociological turn" in economics has led to a reappraisal of emphasis on the causal primacy of the state in innovating institutional change. Sociological institutionalism "departs from and complements the institutions-as-rules approach, which studies institutions as determined by economic or political forces," defining institutions more broadly as systems "of rules, beliefs, norms, and organizations that together generate a regularity of (social) behaviour."[24] The sociological literature on transition economies similarly has sought to direct research away from the focus on political actors of the state-centered perspective. Through in-depth interviews, observation of natural settings, and surveys, field research has uncovered societal sources of endogenous institutional change: "Far from trivial, this close attention to spontaneous processes in the everyday life of factories, villages, and neighborhoods raised important theoretical questions about the sources of change in communist societies as it reveals significant spheres of social action outside the direction and control of the party-state."[25] The sociological turn in economics and the new institutionalism in sociology are complementary; building on these approaches provides rich veins to mine for an explanation of endogenous institutional change.[26]

The definition of institution we use integrates the structural approach of sociology with the agency perspective of economics. We define institutions as systems of interrelated informal and formal elements—customs, conventions, norms, beliefs, and rules—governing social relationships within which actors pursue and fix the limits of legitimate interests. They are self-reproducing social structures that provide a conduit for collective action by enabling, motivating, and guiding the interests of actors and enforcing principal–agent relationships. It follows from our definition that fundamentally transformative institutional change does not simply involve politicians remaking the formal rules, but requires the realignment of interests, norms, and power. Our definition shifts analysis of the effectiveness of enforcement of contractual agreements to social mechanisms endogenous to the transaction between principal and agent.

Sociologists have long held the view of markets as self-reproducing social structures within which buyers and sellers transact across market interfaces. "However difficult it often is to account for all their detailed characteristics," market institutions "are at least the product of the very things economics disregards—the relatively permanent relationships between individuals or between groups, which form social structures."[27] Economists concur that repeated exchange is commonplace even in markets characterized by the ease and reliability of impersonal exchange. The market is defined, for example, as "a forum" for carrying out *"exchange that is voluntary: each party can veto it, and (subject to the rules of the marketplace) each freely agrees to the terms* [italicized in original]."[28] In such definitions, "the market" is generally differentiated from "a market" or "a marketplace," which refers to a specific physical place or cyberspace where goods are bought and sold: "By 'the market,' I mean the abstraction."[29] But economists have yet to find a fully satisfactory way to characterize the structure and process through which firms actually constitute a market. Indeed, as Harrison White has observed, "because the market is a tangible social construction opaque to tools familiar to economists, and because sociologists by and large have not looked, the market has remained a mystification."[30] In addressing how to characterize the market as a self-reproducing social structure, White proposed "embedding economists' neoclassical theory of the firm within a sociological view of the market" by integrating signaling theory.[31] In his model, firms are like organisms seeking out niches in an ecology. Markets develop as endogenous institutional constructs as firms watch signals emitted by their competitors and position themselves to compete in a niche.

The challenge to demystify markets calls for examining the relationship between norms embedded in informal social processes and the formal rules mandated and enforced by the state. Many economists now accept the view that social norms are likely to play a stronger role in explaining economic behavior than was commonly assumed.[32] Indeed, the formal rules that make up the institutional environment and informal norms embedded in ongoing social relations jointly interact to shape economic behavior in the marketplace.

In a generalized multilevel causal model (see Figure 2.1), top-down processes allow higher-level and more encompassing structures to shape—both constrain and empower—the structures and actions at lower levels. But "simultaneously, counterprocesses are at work by which lower-level actors and structures shape—reproduce and change—the contexts within which they operate." Top-down and bottom-up processes interweave "as they combine to influence institutional phenomena."[33] Causal mechanisms operate in both directions, from macro to micro and micro to macro levels.[34] Thus, state institutions not only impose formal rules on corporate and individual actors but also respond to accommodate interests mobilized from the bottom up. Economic actors can through collective action trigger changes in the institutional environment. The arrows pointing downward from societal institutions indicate constraints placed on social action through formal rules and the sanctions enforcing them. The arrows pointing upward indicate that the macro environment is constituted and modified by social action. This may involve mobilization or negotiation that utilizes channels in compliance with formal rules, as with formal types of lobbying. Or it may sometimes involve collective noncompliance and accompanying endogenous innovation.

Only if individual interests and preferences are well aligned with the incentives structured in the institutional environment will they reinforce compliance with formal rules through self-monitoring and mutual enforcement. Otherwise, if individual interests are not aligned with the structure of opportunity legitimized by the state, strategic interest may give rise to decoupling from institutionalized routines,[35] which may in turn lead to the formation of self-help opposition norms once a sufficient number of actors decide to decouple from the formal framework. Informal norms gain in importance as more and more actors find it rational to decouple from existing formal rules.[36] The collective action of economic actors imposes pressure on the state to respond initially by enforcing the existing legal and regulatory structures. Once a critical mass is reached, however, and collective action becomes self-reinforcing, the state can no longer effectively enforce compliance. Opposition norms may eventually spur changes in the formal rules, if a certain threshold level of noncompliance with state-mandated rules is reached and state actors see a need to adjust formal rules accordingly. In this way, social norms and group behavior are no longer relegated to a passive role of cultural filters, but comprise active forces of endogenous institutional change.

The bottom-up emergence of capitalism in China rests on the following causal factors. First, shifts in *market competition* provide incentives for economic actors to come up with bottom-up institutional arrangements to secure gains from emergent opportunity structures. Second, *entrepreneurial action* generates institutional innovations, and through a process of trial and error, successful solutions diffuse through the regional economy. Third, *mutual monitoring and enforcement* in crosscutting networks of like-minded actors

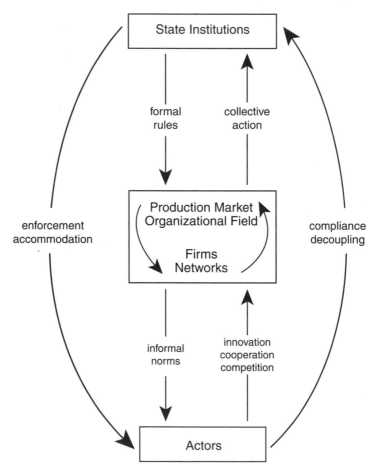

Figure 2.1. A multilevel model of institutional change.

reinforce novel behavioral strategies and norms. Fourth, through *mimicking*, swarms of followers pile in, and following tipping points, a self-reinforcing social movement dynamic evolves, which in turn facilitates local collective action to lobby for changes in the formal rules consonant with informal norms. Industry-based associations and lobbyists act as agents representing social interests. Politicians eventually respond to bottom-up innovations by changing formal rules to accommodate and regulate emerging economic realities.

Maintaining Social Norms

The structure of social relationships matters in explaining economic behavior. But what explains motivation for trustworthiness and abstention from opportunism in ongoing social relationships? Why is trustworthiness found more commonly in such relationships than in transactions between strangers?

The answer is found in specifying the mechanisms intrinsic to social relationships that develop and maintain cooperative behavior, enabling actors to engage in collective action to achieve group ends. These mechanisms are rewards and punishment in social exchange and their use in upholding norms: shared beliefs and expectations as to appropriate behavior.

Informal norms arise from the problem-solving activities of human beings in their strivings to improve their chances for success—that is, the attainment of rewards—through cooperation. These rule-of-thumb guidelines as to expected behavior evolve through trial and error and are adopted by members of a group when they result in success. In other words, "members of a close-knit group develop and maintain norms whose content serves to maximize the aggregate welfare that members obtain in their workaday affairs with one another."[37] Hence, norm emergence involves a collective learning process in which members gain experience through different strategies and gradually identify those that seem to have an edge over others.[38] Established norms have previously evolved through similar social learning processes.[39]

Numerous studies confirm the efficacy of social rewards and punishment in motivating trustworthy behavior and abstention from opportunism with respect to the norms of the group.[40] These informal standards of appropriate behavior are maintained when reward is expected to follow conformity, and punishment, deviance. Members of a group routinely reward conformity to norms by conferring social approval and status. Conversely, members punish failure to conform to norms through their social disapproval and, ultimately, through ostracism. Hence, the monitoring of norms is a spontaneous by-product of social interactions. Repeated interactions lower the cost of monitoring members, assuming they are in close enough contact with one another that information about members' conduct is common knowledge.[41] Reward and punishment in repeated exchanges—when actors take into account the weight of the future, as in ongoing relationships—motivate cooperative behavior. Community sanctions complement bilateral responses, applying also when transactions are infrequent. In sum, trustworthiness and reliability as forms of cooperative behavior arise from rational action responding to social rewards and punishment in ongoing relationships.[42]

A detailed account of interactions in a work group made up of a supervisor, sixteen agents, and one clerk illustrates how the self-interested action of individuals endogenously produces a pecking order through social exchange. Agents consulted fellow agents about the appropriate legal rules that applied to their case, rather than bring their questions to the attention of the supervisor who evaluated their work.[43] The interactions involved both gaining something and paying a price, as in market exchange:

> A consultation can be considered an exchange of values; both participants gain something, and both have to pay a price. The questioning agent is enabled to perform better than he could otherwise have done, without exposing his difficulties to the supervisor. By asking for advice, he implicitly pays his respect to the superior proficiency of his colleague. This acknowledgement of inferiority is the cost of receiving assistance. The consultant gains prestige, in return for which he is willing to devote some time to the consultation and permit it to disrupt his own work. The following remark of an agent illustrates this: "I like giving advice. It's flattering, I suppose, if you feel that the others come to you for advice."[44]

The importance of social rewards (e.g., status) and sanctions in the normative regulation of a social structure is highlighted here.

Members of social groups cooperate in enforcing norms because not only their interests but also their identities are linked to the group's success.[45] Rational choice theory emphasizes reputational effects on social behavior, but emergent principles of proper conduct embedded in identities are also important in norm compliance.[46] For example, there are many occasions when no one is monitoring closely, yet people comply with norms that are woven into their identity. This is because identity as well as interests explains the willingness to cooperate in a competitive environment.[47]

Routine social exchanges, especially repeated transactions, along with the potential for community sanctions, constitute glue for the bottom-up institutional arrangements that endogenously arise to sustain long-term economic relationships. Mutual dependence—on information flows, on access to scarce resources, on interfirm collaboration in technology development, and on privately organized supply networks autonomous from state-controlled sources—further reinforces long-term stability of contractual relationships, without reliance on third-party enforcement.

The social mechanisms guiding the action of firms within networks and industrial clusters are not dissimilar from those influencing strategic action of individuals in close-knit groups. When facing uncertainty under high stakes, intendedly rational actors satisfice by looking for successful competitors and making plausible guesses about the reasons for their success. Organizations tend to mimic other, similar organizations that they perceive to be successful. For manufacturers especially, mimicking entails learning by doing in efforts to internalize the technological and organizational basis of success of leading competitors.

Social Norms and Institutional Change

The behavior of economic actors frequently bears little resemblance to the legitimate courses of action stipulated by state-mandated formal rules. Instead, social groups based on personal connections serve to organize market-oriented economic behavior according to informal norms reflecting the private expectations and interests of individuals.[48] They often act at odds with the goals formulated by politicians.

Norms operating in the shadows of state-mandated rules can both limit and facilitate economic action. On the one hand, a decoupling of norms from these rules can give rise to inefficient allocation of resources when individual actors collude to secure resources from government for their group, resulting in structural rigidities and economic stagnation.[49] In Russia, mafia-like business networks operated to obstruct Boris Yeltsin's efforts at building a market economy. On the other hand, a decoupling of norms can also facilitate economic action and promote growth by providing a framework for trust and collective action. In China, informal privatization and local institutional arrangements have contributed to two decades of economic growth during the early stages of economic reform.

Given the variance of possible interactions between formal rules and social norms, it is a central task for theory development to better specify the nature of the relationship. Under what conditions will norms evolve into self-reinforcing opposition norms, which then undermine the effectiveness of formal rules? By opposition norms we refer to beliefs that enable, motivate, and guide collective action, decoupled from and not legitimated by state-mandated rules. Opposition norms are commonplace in all societies and span a wide range of activities, be they those of alienated minority youths in America and Europe or the untaxed economic transactions between buyers and sellers in the informal economy of established market economies. Especially in the early stage of norm emergence, opposition norms often involve "subterranean" activity below the radar of the state, and thus are not detected by law enforcers.[50] They can remain below the radar indefinitely, but at an inflection point, opposition norms can burst into the public arena to enable, motivate, and guide self-reinforcing collective action compelling politicians to respond. Political elites face a range of options in their response, from strengthening law enforcement and use of coercive force to adaptive institutional change.

To understand the link between opposition norms and endogenous institutional change, it is crucial to explore the role of private orders in allowing members of social subgroups to improve their welfare position, although the state is unwilling or unable to protect their economic transactions. Clearly, to the extent that social groups have interests and preferences independent of what politicians or organizational leaders want, informal norms and organizational practices will evolve to "bend the bars of the iron cage" imposed by formal rules. Whether decoupled norms operate only under distinct circumstances or more widely, developing into self-reinforcing opposition norms leading to endogenous institutional change, depends on whether a critical mass of societal participation is reached.[51] In all command economies it was commonplace that individuals and firms sought to alleviate shortages of the formal economy by resorting to black-market activities and barter trading.[52] While this practice was against the formal rules, it never gave rise to endogenous institutional change. Although company managers hoarded goods and repair parts to prepare for unexpected shortages, these activities remained limited in scope. In retrospect, the scattered occurrence of black markets and barter trading may have stabilized the system, as companies were better able to respond to temporary shortages. Black markets may also have helped to contain social discontent. As a thought experiment, assume now an alternative scenario: Given the beneficial effects of barter trading and black markets, a growing number of economic actors divert parts of their production to black-market activities. The informal economy expands and expands, and subsequently planned production and public revenues decrease. Once a certain tipping point is reached, the official economy collapses.

The reason why in socialist economies the informal norms of black markets and barter trading did not evolve into self-reinforcing opposition norms is fairly obvious. Institutional and organizational sanctions effectively suppressed these activities. Tight monitoring, high probabilities of detection, and costly sanctions made black-market activities risky and expensive. The above counter-scenario would be possible only if increasing numbers of actors could conveniently imitate the illegal activities at low cost without fear of sanctions or punishment.

The contrast between these scenarios underscores the conditionality of norm development. Evidently, to understand the different aggregate outcomes resulting from conflicting formal and informal norms, it is important to study the individual choices economic actors are facing. This moves individual utility expectations to the center of analysis. The key question is to identify under what conditions the total number of individuals who choose to deviate from the existing state-mandated rules reaches a critical mass and gives rise to a self-reinforcing opposition norm. Only in this case do informal norms evolve as an independent source of institutional change, even in the absence of a formal coordinator.

The individual choice either to follow state-mandated rules or to deviate can be illustrated using a Schelling diagram that links the expected individual utilities with aggregate, observable preferences in society.[53] Schelling's core insight is that utilities shaping an individual's behavior often depend on the observable behavior of others in the community or peer-group. For instance, a person might be much more inclined to employ a housemaid without paying social security taxes if it is common knowledge that all the neighbors do the same. Tax discipline also rapidly declines once tax evasion has become known as common practice. Of course the link between individual and aggregate behavior is not limited to cases of legal conflict but also is common in everyday situations. For instance, a dinner guest may find it perfectly satisfying to wear jeans and a sports coat for a dinner party if everybody else does the same. The perceived satisfaction is likely to be much lower, however, if everybody else is wearing dinner jackets or evening gowns.

Assume now an individual i facing a binary decision either (1) to follow and comply with a state-mandated rule or (2) to deviate and follow an alternative informal norm. It is sensible to assume that in any society there will always be a certain number of individuals who do not comply with given rules. Smoking in public spaces, speeding on highways, and evading taxes are common examples. Reasons for noncompliance may range from unexplained random behavioral mutations to rational calculation via shifts in ideology within a small social group. Through word of mouth and observation, such precedents will lead to imitation, if the particular behavior seems to have an edge. Since "rules that prescribe behavior . . . do not influence behavior unless people are motivated to follow them,"[54] it is sensible to further assume that the value to the individual actor of a distinct behavioral choice generally increases with the number of other individuals following the same rule or norm. In other words, it is the conformity to the norms of a social group that renders the behavior valuable and a form of capital.[55] The expected individual payoff of complying with either the state-mandated rule or the decoupled informal norm increases with the number of others making the same choice.

In the following graphical illustrations (Figures 2.2–2.4), C indicates the utility (u_i) an individual secures by choosing to comply with state-mandated rules. D indicates the corresponding utility if the individual deviates and his or her activity is guided by opposition norms. For simplification but without loss of generalizability, both functions are assumed to be linear. In reality, one will observe cases with decreasing marginal payoffs and a leveling off, once a certain proportion of society follows the respective norms. There will not be negative marginal effects, however. On the horizontal axis measured from 0 to N, X indicates the number of "others" in society who choose to deviate. Thus, in the far left at 0, all other members of society comply with state-mandated rules; in the far right corner, all N members of society deviate.

Scenario I (see Figure 2.2) captures the situation typically described by the legal-centrist tradition of the new institutional economics. Compliance with state-mandated rules always yields higher individual payoffs than noncompliance, independent of the total number of others who choose either to comply or to deviate. D begins below zero for two reasons: First of all, the individual behavioral choice will not yield any positive payoffs if that choice is not shared by other members in society. Second, even though state enforcement can never be complete, noncompliance is likely to be penalized, given the high detection risk in a fully rule-compliant society (as others may denounce noncompliant behavior). There is no point where expected benefits from decoupling are higher than benefits from rule-compliance. Even if all *N* members of society choose to deviate (the intersection of *D* with the right *y*-axis), the expected individual utility from deviation would still be smaller than if they complied (compare with the intersection of *C* with the right *y*-axis). This scenario is broadly consistent with the assumption of the state as the central arbiter of institutional change. In this view, there is no possible distribution between deviators (*X*) and compliants (*N*−*X*) where decoupling of norms promises individual advantages, which explains why institutional change is not initiated from below. Underlying reasons may be diverse. On the one hand, effective sanctioning through state agencies may explain the smaller payoffs connected with noncompliance. On the other hand, collective action problems associated with norm enforcement may explain this. In any case, under the expected utility functions, any rational individual *i* is likely to comply.

Scenario II (see Figure 2.3) illustrates the opposite case, where individuals who deviate enjoy consistently higher payoffs than individuals who comply with state-mandated formal rules—independent of the number of others who choose to deviate or comply. Even if only one other individual *i* out of *N* deviates as well, benefits from noncompliance are consistently (and increasingly) higher than those from rule compliance (*D*>*C*). This scenario would apply both where state-mandated rules are economically inefficient (no positive

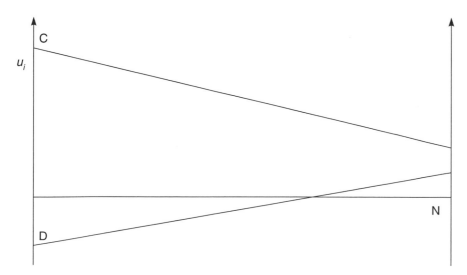

Figure 2.2. Scenario I: Dominance of formal rules.

payoffs from C) and where the state does not have the financial and administrative means (or political will) to effectively enforce state regulation. In reality, however, this case is unlikely to be found unless in situations of political
distress and disorder, where state power has almost fully collapsed.

Scenario III (see Figure 2.4) presents the most interesting case, as it incor-
porates the potential rise of opposition norms and exemplifies scope conditions under which institutional change may be driven by their spontaneous
development. In this case, C and D intersect. At the intersection, where X of
the other members of society deviate and $(N-X)$ members conform with
state-mandated formal rules, compliance and noncompliance promise the
same individual rewards. This point X represents a saddle equilibrium, however. If only one more individual joins the group of X individuals who deviate,
expected utility from noncompliance is higher than from rule compliance.
Thereafter, a self-reinforcing process will tend to evolve and draw in more and
more individuals.[56] Thus $(X+1)$ marks a tipping point. Individual noncompliance may thus turn into a self-reinforcing opposition norm.

Based on this scenario, it is fairly straightforward to identify the specific
set of scope conditions under which a decoupling of social norms may become
an independent source of institutional change. Let a specify the expected

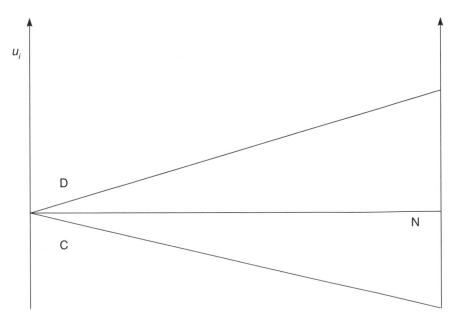

Figure 2.3. Scenario II: Inefficient and nonenforced state-mandated rules.

individual utility if all other members of society comply. Let b specify the marginal decrease in utility with every additional "other" who does not comply. Then, with X indicating the number of individuals choosing to deviate, the expected payoff C from norm compliance for any individual i equals $a - b\,X$.

Now let $e \leq 0$ specify the negative utility (costs) of noncompliance if no other member of society deviates. Whereas these costs will vary with local legislations, their level is defined by the detection rate and expected penalty (including legal costs and social sanctions). Negative values for e indicate that no individual i can expect positive rewards from deviation if no other individual out of N deviates as well. Of course, it is not even a norm unless shared with a group of others, so that no benefits are expected; in addition, risk of penalization through state and society are extremely high if everybody else follows state-mandated rules. In reality, enforcement of formal rules of the state may vary locally, depending on the capacity and interests of local administrators. Differences in the budgetary position, particularly, but also variation in political ideology can influence the quality of law enforcement. One should therefore think of Figure 2.4 as illustrating context-bound regional and local conditions rather than a general societal condition, for across a country one is likely to find variations of e. Variations may be particularly pronounced in transition and developing countries, where regulatory and administrative quality often differ substantively between the capital and remote hinterland regions.

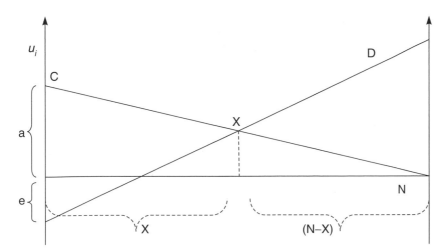

Figure 2.4. Scenario III: Institutional change from below.

The slope coefficient f reflects the marginal increase in individual utility from noncompliance, resulting from a growing number of individuals sharing the same norm. Then the expected reward D from deviation is $e+fX$. The emphasis here is on net utility, defined by gross utilities resulting from sharing a norm minus expected organization costs of overcoming collective action problems. As with e, the slope coefficient f reflects local but not national conditions of trust and cooperation. Different values of f reflect differences in the willingness to cooperate and the associated organization costs, which may well vary between high-trust societies under collectivist cultural beliefs and individualist societies.[57] Similarly, cooperation in homogeneous communities that share the same religion, ethnicity, local tradition, and culture is more likely to benefit from higher trust and lower organization costs (signaled by a steeper slope coefficient f) than in extremely heterogeneous communities.[58]

Both curves will intersect if

(1) $$(a-e) \, / \, (b+f)=X<n$$

Clearly, in any society there will always be some individuals who deviate from formal rules, even though deviation is associated with lower expected rewards (left of the intersection point). In some cases this may reflect random behavioral mutations or certain character traits of the deviators. In other cases deviators may be socially or economically marginalized and denied access to certain social groups or economic activities. Thus the far left position at 0, where all other members of society comply with state-mandated rules, is virtually never realized. Whether this pool of initial deviators will eventually be joined by a substantial group of followers to trigger the rise of a self-reinforcing opposition, however, depends on the net benefit individuals expect from switching from compliance to noncompliance. This is to say, the rewards from rule compliance need to be less than the expected rewards from noncompliance in case one more individual decides to deviate. Hence, self-reinforcing opposition norms emerge only if

(2) $$a-bX<e+f(X+1) \ \text{ or } \ X>(a-e-f) \, / \, (b+f)$$

If we further assume for convenience that the fixed payoff a and marginal decrease b in case of compliance with an established state-mandated rule are given, e and f emerge as crucial determinants to explain whether a decoupling from formal rules gives rise to opposition norms. From equation (2) we infer:

The smaller the fixed costs of noncompliance (e) and the higher the marginal increase of individual utilities (f), the smaller the critical mass ($X+1$) needed for self-reinforcing opposition norms to evolve.

What does this imply? First of all, low fixed costs of noncompliance (e) indicate that the state and its representatives lack either the organizational capacity or the political will to monitor and penalize those who deviate.[59] This may be a central reason why almost all transition economies, which in their early reform period were often politically divided and tied down with administrative restructuring and capacity building, witnessed to a certain extent a decoupling of norms and bottom-up institutional change. Second, values of f increase with smaller coordination costs among those who deviate. This is reflected in the fact that opposition norms often first emerge within locally confined areas or well-defined social groups, where members of society maintain close relations, interact frequently, and maintain high levels of mutual trust.

In light of this graphical and analytical exercise, the idea of the state as a *necessary* arbiter of institutional change evidently builds on a specific set of conditions. Central is the assumption of a relatively disadvantageous reward structure for decoupled norms. Particularly high organization costs to overcome collective action problems (which reduce the slope coefficient f) are widely believed to impede the ability of individual actors to self-organize.[60] However, this may be an overly pessimistic view. There are other robust mechanisms that can promote cooperation within social groups, including frequent interaction in relationships, bilateral monitoring by parties to a contract, and community reputation and sanctioning.[61] The same mechanisms also explain why informal norms can decouple from state-mandated rules at reasonable organization costs and eventually develop into opposition norms as an independent source of institutional change.

Such norm innovations need not remain locally constrained. Depending on the specific network topology, local innovations can quickly gain momentum and trigger contagion effects throughout a regional economy. Network typologies characterized by local clustering of people in small autonomous but interconnected social groups can speed up the diffusion of local innovations substantively, as studies in dynamic game theory show.[62] The recent changes in social norms on smoking in public spaces underscore that new norms can diffuse relatively quickly.

Just as our model predicts a self-reinforcing process toward local institutional change, so it also explains conditions under which a decoupling of norms does not become self-reinforcing. If fixed costs of noncompliance (e) are sufficiently large, and organization costs sufficiently high (reducing f), opposition norms will not reach a tipping point. This scenario reflects the relatively stable political and economic situation before the start of market liberalization in the European and East Asian transition economies. Although individuals may to a certain extent have turned to black-market activities and barter trading, the costs of noncompliance remained sufficiently high to counter a social movement dynamic leading toward capitalist transformation. Due to the effectiveness of mass mobilization campaigns, the power of ideology, and the encompassing interests of an authoritarian leadership, would-be deviators simply faced prohibitive costs in case of noncompliance. Moreover, the lack of markets greatly increased coordination and organization costs, making survival outside the plan virtually impossible.

Capitalism from Below

The emergence of capitalism in China followed the pattern of institutional change endogenous to the transactions of economic actors. The incremental marketization approach taken by reformers in China allowed economic actors to develop, through trial and error, business norms that were quickly adopted by others emulating the success of early business leaders. Many of China's institutional changes were not driven by top-down state-mandated rules. Rather, changes in formal rules legitimating the private enterprise economy tended to follow *ex post* changes in the real economy. Whether in agriculture, industry, or finance, bottom-up endogenous institutional change played a decisive role in shaping China's reform strategy. In Anhui Province, peasant households initiated the decollectivization of people communes in the late 1970s. In an effort to increase agricultural productivity, they repartitioned collective land for individual household production and instituted a community-based land-lease system. A national policy calling for a general decollectivization of all people's communes followed only after other communities had begun to copy the grassroots system, and reports had confirmed the steep productivity increases. Similar processes characterize the financial market. Company managers and owners without ready access to bank loans had already independently developed alternative forms of external finance such as informal trading of company stocks and corporate bonds, when in 1990 the central government finally opened the first national stock markets to regain state control over the uncontrolled growth of the financial market.[63]

After the government's economic reform policies established the legitimacy of market exchange as an alternative allocation mechanism alongside state planning, allocation of factor resources by central planning declined rapidly, from 70 percent in 1980 to 14 percent in 1991. For manufactured goods, the categories of products subject to mandatory distribution through nonmarket channels decreased from 120 in 1980 to 50 in 1988, to make up only 16.2 percent of the total value of industrial output. By 1991, the number of categories dropped to only 21. Parallel to this, the number of commodities distributed by the state supply bureaucracy declined from 256 in 1980 to only 19 by 1989.[64] These massive shifts away from central planning led to significant declines in the redistributive role of the central state. Although the state continued to set the prices for key agricultural and industrial products, by the early 1990s state regulation was no longer the dominant mechanism determining the prices of goods and services. The number of marketplaces more than doubled from 1978 (33,302) to 1991 (74,675). The volume of transactions in these markets increased at an even more rapid rate (over twenty times) from an initial small base in rural free markets.[65] By the 1990s, there was a wide variety of market arrangements, including many types of commodity markets, labor markets, realty markets, financial markets, and lending institutions.

Opportunities for entrepreneurs to profit from market exchange grew concomitant with the expansion of markets. Widespread experimentation with new forms of production and ownership forms followed. Before the start of economic reforms in 1978, China's industrial sector was made up of only two organizational forms: state-owned enterprises and to a lesser extent collective enterprises. Thirty years later, official records of China's National Bureau of Statistics distinguish ten organizational forms in the urban industrial sector. Their increased diversity now spans the continuum from the public corporations listed on China's stock exchanges to modern shareholding corporations *(siying qiye)*, some included on the Forbes list of largest enterprises.

Initially, it was mainly marginal economic actors who responded to the new market opportunities. These individuals had little to lose and much to gain by decoupling from the socialist system of public ownership and central labor allocation. Typically they came from modest backgrounds. Often they were of peasant social origin or were simple factory workers, and many had only

primary education. Their prospects for employment in the state-owned economy were limited, and they did not mind the low status connected with private
commerce. With modest household savings, peasants first opened small family
businesses in agricultural goods, construction material, or farm machinery
repair, or small-scale trading companies. As they began to produce simple consumer goods long neglected by the state's production plans, private firms developed quickly in villages and townships. Machinery was bought secondhand, and
space typically was rented in abandoned factories or buildings. Many started
their first business with the equivalent of just a few hundred U.S. dollars
pooled through savings from family and friends. The entrepreneurs who survived
the early start-up phase could multiply their annual incomes within a short period
of time. These entrepreneurs and their firms became role models, drawing in
large numbers of local imitators, who then also abandoned socialist forms of
production. It was, as Deng Xiaoping noted, "as if a strange army appeared suddenly from nowhere" to found private firms in the countryside.[66]

With growing local density of entrepreneurial efforts, informal business
norms and institutional arrangements evolved to facilitate business operations
within local production networks. As these entrepreneurs were excluded from
access to the state-owned banking system and state-controlled supply and
distribution channels, norms of mutual support developed. Private manufacturing firms co-organized nonstate supply and distribution outlets. Entrepreneurs in Wenzhou Municipality, for instance, set up their own sales agencies
to market local products nationwide. Elsewhere, managers of small-scale operations pooled their individual orders to benefit from cost advantages for
large-scale orders. Mutual short-term lending allowed entrepreneurs to expand and develop their businesses. Frequently private business loans did not
require either contracts or the payment of interest.

Business norms established a solid basis for cooperation. Assistance of
friends and relatives was based on the expectation that mutual favors would
balance out over time. Everybody is aware that without mutual assistance "it
would be very hard to do business" and that "it is impossible to just rely on yourself." A handshake seals the exchange, and gifts (like free products or services)
signal personal appreciation and gratitude. Cooperation in business communities rests on the entrepreneurs' reputation. In such close-knit groups, loans
rarely default. "One default on one loan, this would ruin the entire reputation."
The owner of a factory producing and trading specialized steel stated unequiv-
ocally, "I refuse to do business with someone whom I have heard from three

people bad things about. I will not do business with that person even if they threaten to cut my head off."[67] Through the robustness of relationship-based trading and local business norms, private firms flourished, even while state-guided economic reform emphasized and prioritized public ownership forms.

Over time and with growing density of entrepreneurial efforts, business norms matured within emerging production markets and the payoff for those individuals decoupling from state-mandated rules increased considerably. The pioneering entrepreneurs recall a still-chaotic business atmosphere lacking clear norms and a generally agreed-upon code of conduct, but the followers could rely on a growing group of businesses that could help out with capital, material, technology, and business information, and most importantly, these producers operated within the framework of local business norms. Evidently, the larger the group of entrepreneurs, the greater the expected benefits for those who also planned to found a private business outside of the state-mandated and state-protected property forms. Once a tipping point of local entrepreneurial activity was reached and local business norms were in place (as visualized by point *X* in Figure 2.4), the ripple effect of expanding networks of players further contributed to self-reinforcing institutional change. In many localities, private ownership forms of production simply became dominant among business foundings. Not only could informal arrangements and cooperative norms among entrepreneurs help mitigate uncertainties in the institutional environment, but the rise of local industrial districts of private firms facilitated the acquisition of needed knowledge, as market entrants benefit from mutual observation, signaling, and copying of entrepreneurial behavior.[68] Learning how others detect and realize market opportunities is an essential lesson that is greatly affected by ongoing social interactions of market players. It became commonplace for entrepreneurs to carefully analyze the factors for success and failure for innovative activities by talking about the experience of other market players in their industry. The commonly held belief "If they can do it, I can too" captures well the growing expectations as to individual payoffs, which became a powerful motivating force driving the rise of local industrial clusters. Friends and former employees looked to established entrepreneurs for inspiration and rule-of-thumb guidelines on how to run a successful business. As more new entrepreneurs mimicked the established entrepreneurs, informal business norms and improvised institutional arrangements of the private enterprise economy became more institutionalized and taken for granted.[69] As the expected costs of running a private business declined and the founding rate of private firms accelerated, local entrepreneurial activity spawned a virtual social movement dynamic in the birth of private firms. The owner of a company trading with computer supplies describes the firm of his former employer as a business "virtually spitting out" new companies. Employees at the firm were eager to start up their own businesses as soon as they learned the essential skills and business norms to run a company.[70]

Such expanding circles of founders, however, were not omnipresent in China but rather regionally concentrated. Self-reinforcing processes of entrepreneurial founding developed rapidly where entrepreneurs were not facing heavy penalties and where local administrators—though not necessarily supportive—at least turned a blind eye to the development of entrepreneurship (consistent with small values of e in Figure 2.4). Squeezed by tight public funds and deprived of investment capital for public firm development, local governments of poor regions tended to be more lenient and less discriminatory toward private firms.[71] Private entrepreneurship diffused particularly rapidly in the Yangzi delta region, gradually spilling over to other regions and drawing in individuals from less marginalized occupational backgrounds. Before 1992, 37 percent of founders were either peasants or factory workers; between 1993 and 1996, this number declined to 7 percent. Concomitantly, the average years of education increased rapidly as private enterprise *(siying qiye)* emerged as a legitimate, taken-for-granted organizational form. In 1980, only about 40 percent of firm founders had more than a junior high school–level education, but by 1988, 59 percent did; and by 2002, 88 percent of the entrepreneurs who founded new private firms reported having attained at least a high school–level education or higher.[72]

It is thus through a self-reinforcing process of endogenous institutional change that private enterprise, starting with a small marginalized sector of maverick entrepreneurs who initially decoupled from socialist production to start up illegal to semilegal businesses, eventually developed into an irrepressible economic force. Only after private firms had become a powerful production sector operating on the basis of robust opposition norms, and industry guilds and business associations began formulating the specific interests of entrepreneurs,[73] did the central government eventually complete the legalization process, enacting in 2007 the country's first Property Rights Law, which formally guaranteed protection against expropriation by the state through local cadre corruption and through embezzlement of private assets. By this time, the private economy had already become an important component of the Chinese economy both in terms of tax revenue and as a provider of nonfarm employment. Complementary reforms responded to the improved status of private firms. In 2001, Jiang Zemin lifted the ban on entrepreneurs joining the Chinese Communist Party (CCP), which had since 1989 blocked private businessmen from joining the party. Thus, *ex post,* politicians extended legal rights, and with this, opposition norms that enabled and motivated the rise of the private enterprise economy became legitimated as standard business practices. A 2007 government document even recognizes "private entrepreneurs, small business owners and managerial level staff in private or foreign funded enterprises" as a new social stratum alongside the old classes of farmer, worker, and soldier.[74]

Clearly, the recent formal legalization and legitimacy conferred by the state have led to a further spread of private firms and paved the way to the establishment of a market capitalist economy. However, the growth dynamic of private firms between 1989 and 2007 supports our market-based explanation of the endogenous shift to capitalism, where a decoupling of norms and subsequent rise of opposition norms spurred and shaped institutional change. The greatest growth impetus for private firm registrations was around the early 1990s (see Figure 2.5), following the government's commitment to extend the role of markets but at a time when private property rights were neither formally recognized nor legally protected.

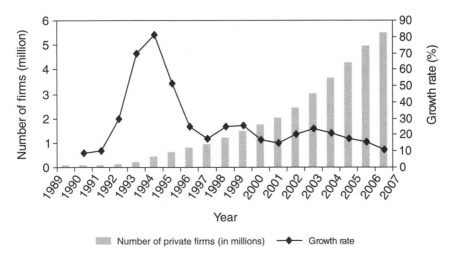

Figure 2.5. Private firm development, 1989–2007. *Source: China Statistical Yearbook,* various years (Beijing: China Statistics Press).

In 1978, private firms contributed 0.02 percent of China's domestic industrial production, but by 2009, the private sector's share was over 40 percent,
clearly exceeding the joint production of traditional state-owned and state-
controlled firms.[75] Already by 2007, the private sector generated a larger export volume than state-owned companies (at $247 billion compared to $225
billion), highlighting the global competitiveness of private firms.[76] Skeptics
may point to the small mean size of private firms compared to the large state-
owned and state-controlled companies. However, China's largest private firms
reported an average return on capital in 2006 of 6.08 percent, compared to 1.4
percent for the largest state-owned and state-controlled companies. Not surprisingly, a growing number of private firms have joined the list of China's
500 largest companies.[77] Private firms in China are not small compared to their
counterparts in advanced industrial economies. For example, in the United States,
78 percent of firms that employ workers have fewer than 10 employees. The share
of companies with 10 to 100 employees is only 8.8 percent, and companies with
more than 500 employees make up only 0.3 percent.[78] In this light, China's
private enterprise economy displays normal structural features compared to
other industrial economies.

Conclusion

China's reforms have sparked interest far beyond pure fascination in the
remarkable transformation of an impoverished state socialist economy into a
dynamic powerhouse of the global economy. From the point of view of economic theory, "the remarkable success of China's economic reforms . . . seems
to defy conventional wisdom,"[79] calling for a reassessment of economic understanding of institutional change. China's experience challenges central lessons
of the economic literature, as for example the proposition that "without the
appropriate institutions no market economy of any significance is possible"[80]
and the assumption that it is the polity that "significantly shape economic
performance because they define and enforce the economic rules."[81]

The rise of private enterprise and capitalism in China was neither envisioned nor anticipated by its political elite. When the elite launched economic
reform in 1978, the aim was to restore vitality to the state-owned industrial
and commercial economy. Instead, the shift to market allocation opened the
door to opportunities for profit making, enough to enable entrepreneurs to
start up private firms. In the first decade of economic reform, private firms, as

a pariah organizational form, confronted formidable barriers to entry enforced by local government and competitive exclusion by state-owned enterprises. Despite formal rules limiting the size of private business to traditional household production, opportunities in decentralized markets fueled the rapid growth of a private enterprise economy. To circumvent barriers to entry and discriminatory legal restrictions on private firms, entrepreneurs registered their firms as "fake" collectives. However, many also stayed the course in the fledgling private enterprise economy. In privately organized markets, entrepreneurs constructed the economic institutions they needed to compete and cooperate in a transition economy dominated by government-owned firms. Through bottom-up entrepreneurial activity, the private enterprise economy grew in scale. With its geographical center concentrated along the coastal provinces, capitalist economic development had by 2000 emerged as the dominant pattern in China's market economy.

The literature on market transition has struggled to reconcile China's reform experience with the state-centered perspective. Some have emphasized beneficial fiscal arrangements instituted by the central government; others have focused on the supportive role of local governments.[82] These studies provide a partial answer to the question why local governments refrained from expropriating private firms. However, they bypass the equally important question of what institutional framework, in the absence of effective rule of law, enabled, motivated, and guided entrepreneurs to develop a thriving private enterprise economy.[83]

Our theory proffers a multilevel causal model of institutional change, where causal forces operate in both directions, from institutional mechanisms embedded in macro structures to micro-level behavior, and from micro motives and behavior to the macro level. We have used a Schelling diagram to model the emergence of opposition norms, and with our multilevel model of institutional change, we sketch the causal chain that led to the emergence of capitalism. The sequence of economic reforms starting in 1978 incrementally legitimized the shift to reliance on market allocation, which in turn fueled a self-reinforcing growth of new profit-making opportunities in decentralized markets, motivating entrepreneurs to decouple from the established economic order to start up private firms. At the micro level, the emergence and diffusion of business norms enable, motivate, and guide entrepreneurs to commit to a private enterprise economy, despite the absence of formal rules safeguarding property rights of the capitalist enterprise. The Schelling diagram

(Figure 2.4) illustrates the dynamic pattern underlying change in individual payoffs as more and more entrepreneurs start up private firms and develop in repeated transactions in close-knit communities and markets the informal economic institutions of capitalism. Norms embedded in networks can provide effective mechanisms to secure economic transactions, and can diffuse relatively quickly given appropriate contextual conditions. Such norms are thus a source of endogenous institutional change.

3

The Epicenter of Bottom-Up Capitalism

If the private enterprise economy in the post-reform period has a geographical center, then it is in Zhejiang Province. This is where entrepreneurs first started private firms and—against then-current law—quickly expanded their businesses. This is where today some of the richest townships concentrate. And this is where domestic and foreign observers first sensed the rise of a distinctive entrepreneurial spirit. The enterprising character of people from Zhejiang, particularly from the city of Wenzhou as the epicenter of private firm development (often labeled the "Wenzhou model"), enjoys admiration nationwide.

Accounts of robust entrepreneurial action and private wealth accumulation are commonplace here and follow a familiar rags-to-riches narrative. Personal memories of the founding years often include stories of poverty and harsh work conditions, where sixteen-hour workdays were not uncommon and the office floor oftentimes had to serve as a place to rest. The owner of a successful furniture factory in Zhejiang recalls that after he graduated from senior middle school in 1988, his parents could not afford to send him to university, though he had passed the entrance examination. Farming in his village provided only a subsistence-level livelihood, and the big-city labor market was still closed to rural migrants. For him, the only viable option to escape rural poverty was to be an itinerant salesman. He was not able to borrow more than ¥1,000 (at that time less than $120) from friends and relatives to buy textiles he carried on his first trading expedition, when he traveled by train to Kunming, the capital of Yunnan Province, about 1,100 miles to the southwest of Zhejiang. Within one year he had earned ¥10,000 in profits from the interprovincial trade route, which provided the capital he needed to rent a small booth in a state-owned department store to sell clothes and textiles. But business there was slow, due in part to the depression following the political turmoil of 1989, and he decided to cut his losses and give up the sales booth. Still confident that he could make it in business, he worked again as a traveling salesman, to generate new start-up capital. This time he decided to trade sneakers, which he bought in Fujian Province and sold again in Yunnan Province. After a year of commuting by train between Fujian and Yunnan, he had earned ¥40,000, enough to establish a textile business in the city of Shaoxing in Zhejiang. The business failed, but by 1994 he borrowed ¥120,000 from a local supplier with whom he had a long-standing personal relationship and founded a textile factory. Bad decisions and low product quality led to financial losses and eventually to the closure of the operation within just two years. The total loss ran up to ¥500,000. After he paid off his debt, he made a third attempt at founding a business, again financed with borrowed capital from friends and relatives. Here his success story began. He partnered with his elder brother to register a furniture company, which started out as a small workshop equipped with used machinery and with only nine workers. This business, which he developed into a well-known furniture factory and interior design firm with more than 5,000 employees, found a niche integrating interior design and remodeling with the sales of new furnishings to newly affluent consumers in the booming economy of Hangzhou.[1]

Some of these rags-to-riches narratives have even received global recognition. For example, Jack Ma, a Hangzhou-born former English teacher from a modest social background, founded in 1999 the business-to-business platform Alibaba.com, which in 2007 became the second-largest Internet IPO after Google. Asked about his success, he described how things were for entrepreneurs when they started up their firms: "We had no money, we had no technology, and we had no plan."[2] The characteristic feature of the entrepreneurial spirit in Zhejiang Province was not to be stopped by this but to devise catch-as-catch-can ways to move ahead.

The personal narratives of entrepreneurs detail the multiple pathways leading to the start-up of first ventures and the serendipitous events that shape entrepreneurial careers. These accounts uniformly underscore the linked motivations to rise out of rural poverty and to secure for oneself profits such as those reputedly made by others who previously started up private businesses and sometimes made a fortune. A first-time visitor cannot help but wonder how much myth-making and hyperbole contribute to the region's seemingly endless supply of self-made entrepreneurs.

The spontaneous rise of a thriving private enterprise economy in Zhejiang Province and its rapid diffusion in the Yangzi delta region could not have been predicted.[3] Although the delta's economy had previously achieved a level of commercialization with handicrafts comparable to that in England before the Industrial Revolution, it was not until the local government–led rural industrialization of the Mao era that the Yangzi delta experienced transformative economic development. As observed in an economic history of the Yangzi delta from 1350 to 1988, this top-down industrial growth stands in contrast to "the bottom-up, from village handicraft industry to small-town handicraft manufacturing" progression of capitalist economic development experienced in England.[4] It seemed likely that China's industrialization and modern urbanization would continue as a top-down process in the post-reform period, dominated by local government–owned township and village enterprises. After all, these government-owned enterprises accounted for 88 percent of the gross income of rural industries in Shanghai Municipality and Jiangsu Province in 1986, while private enterprise was limited to very small businesses that produced a mere fraction of the delta's industrial output. Although in the city of Wenzhou itself entrepreneurs relied on markets to build a freewheeling private enterprise economy, "the potential of the Wenzhou type of development, under present conditions in China, should not be exaggerated. . . . Even within Zhejiang Province itself, Wenzhou is unique." Across the province, collective enterprises were nearly as dominant as in Shanghai and Jiangsu, providing 83.5 percent of gross rural-industry income. "Most of all, we need to keep in mind the singular preponderance of collective organization in the successful rural industrialization experience of areas like the Yangzi delta."[5]

In the 1930s, Zhejiang Province had been the regional center of modern factory production, with up to 57 percent of the national industrial product being manufactured in the Yangzi delta area. The region's living standard was 55 percent higher than the national average, substantially higher than even the Japanese-controlled, industrialized areas of Korea and Manchuria.[6] But during the Mao era (1949–1976), because Zhejiang was viewed as a vulnerable border area facing the Taiwan Strait, the central government largely bypassed the province (apart from its capital city, Hangzhou) for investments in large-scale industrial and infrastructure projects. After those decades of central government neglect, this once-wealthy province, admired ever since the

Song Dynasty (960–1279) for its prosperity, culture, and commercial tradition, was in economic disarray. The standard of living had dropped to levels comparable to the impoverished interior provinces of Gansu, Hubei, Hebei, and Inner Mongolia. Per capita industrial production reached only 10 percent of the national mean.[7] The lack of investment in infrastructure had left many townships and small cities landlocked in mountain valleys without proper access to railroads and modern road systems, making trade with bordering provinces costly. With a majority of the province covered by mountainous terrain, with a historical vulnerability to flooding along the coast, and with a scarcity of natural resources, Zhejiang clearly did not offer ideal starting conditions for export-oriented economic development. Reformers in the central government turned to the southeastern province of Guangdong with its proximity to Hong Kong for leadership in economic reforms.

Despite these improbable initial conditions, today the rapid pace of private enterprise-led economic activity makes an impression on the most casual observer even in the remote areas of this mountainous province. Small villages have been transformed into substantial commercial townships. There are dense clusters of factories near cities of the coastal areas with ready access to harbors and global shipping lanes, and to the new highways and rail lines that integrate the regional economy. Building cranes at construction sites of impressive residential and commercial high-rises dot the landscape, fanning out into periurban farmland producing vegetables and aquatic products for urban markets. More rapidly expanding clusters of new factory buildings in suburban industrial centers underscore the breakneck pace of economic development in Zhejiang. Large proportions of the country's light industrial commodities originate here. These clusters of manufacturing firms using relatively simple production technologies, with modest initial capital requirements, manufacture a huge array of inexpensive household products.

Bottom-up entrepreneurship entails learning by doing and learning by imitation. Often a seed factory trains the first batch of technicians and sales staff and provides the technical groundwork and marketing strategies for a novel product. Through product imitation and modification, clusters of small-scale producers develop rapidly. Competitive advantage is secured through a complex web of industrial clusters of individual household firms that serve as subcontractors and suppliers to the main manufacturing firms. This helps to lower both the technical entry barriers and capital requirements, as complex production processes can be broken down into isolated steps. Local imitation of new products on the market and subtle modification of existing technologies commonly accelerate the buildup of specialty manufacturing, as swarms of new entries compete in a market niche. It is not uncommon for a whole town or village to focus on production of just one consumer item, a phenomenon described as *yizhen yipin* (one town, one product) or *yicun yipin* (one village, one product).

According to incomplete government statistics, Zhejiang Province is home to more than 500 industrial clusters covering 175 different industries, each having a gross output value of more than ¥100 million. In total, more than 240,000 manufacturing companies are organized in clusters, producing more than 50 percent of the provincial output value.[8] This turns industrial clusters into the dominant organizational form of industrial production in Zhejiang. Seventy percent of the international market for lighters is produced in more than 500 firms in Wenzhou Municipality. Qiaotou, a township in this municipality, produces more than 60 percent of the global clothing buttons and more than 80 percent of zippers. Liushi township produces more than 40 percent of the country's low voltage switches, and Datang township in Zhuji Municipality is the largest socks producer in the world, with more than 100,000 knitting machines in over 8,000 companies producing one third of the global supply. Similar clusters of light industrial manufacturing exist in the shoe industry, toy industry, and ball-bearing production. In some locations, a local marketing firm serves as the distributor for a dense network of household firms, enabling these very small businesses to compete as though they were a single manufacturing firm.

In the municipality of Wenzhou, the number of free marketplaces trading local products jumped from 117 in 1979 to 417 in 1985.[9] Today, hundreds of thousands of marketing agents travel throughout China to sell their local products. Wenzhou businessmen even maintain a network of guesthouses throughout the country to offer accommodation for sales agents from the region. The Zhejiang China Commodities City Group Ltd. hosts in Yiwu city the world's largest petty commodity free market, with over 28 million square feet of exhibition space offering factory outlets of light manufactured goods to the global economy. More than 65,000 booths in twenty specialized markets display their products. On a daily basis, 1,100 containers leave the city, accumulating to an annual trade turnover of over ¥40 billion per year. On average, 200,000 traders flock into the city every day. Global distributors from Wal-Mart and Carrefour, representatives of the United Nations, and

purchasing agents from the Middle East and sub-Saharan Africa belong to
the mixed group of domestic and international traders. They fly in on domestic routes from Beijing, Shantou, Weifang, Guangzhou, and Shenzhen or
come in by train from Shanghai to negotiate contracts with domestic manufacturers of this region. With good reason, entrepreneurs boast that they suffer no competitive disadvantage in their hinterland location.

The independent strength of such private-sector entrepreneurship is evident in the southwestern mountainous region of Zhejiang Province, far from
the major urban centers of the Yangzi delta. Despite that distance and despite
the hilly and mountainous terrain, entrepreneurs claim that the dense network
of subcontractors, suppliers, and distributors serving their firms gives them a
competitive advantage over firms located in the big coastal cities. Everything
they need for specialty production is easily available in a third Italy-like sub-
regional manufacturing economy.

Private enterprise soon expanded in the whole Yangzi delta region, gradually crossing the provincial borders of Jiangsu and Shanghai, originally local
strongholds of collective and state-owned production. The low-lying fertile
plains of southern Jiangsu had emerged early in the reform period as a thriving center of rural industry and local government-led economic development.
Stretching east from Anhui Province to the Yellow Sea, this region south of
the lower Yangzi River was historically among the richest commercial regions
of China. Laced with networks of navigable rivers and canals and a well-
developed transportation system of railroad and highways, southern Jiangsu
provided a convenient extension area for the heavy industries of Shanghai and
Nanjing. Gradually, though, this same geography and infrastructure would
come to support private enterprise. Following business trips to neighboring
Zhejiang, Jiangsu entrepreneurs often started their own private firms, mimicking and borrowing from the organizational and institutional innovations
put into practice by Zhejiang entrepreneurs.

Figure 3.1 underscores the Yangzi delta region's unique position amid the
highly uneven interprovincial distribution of private firms in 2004, the year
before we initiated our study. Zhejiang Province, together with the bordering
province of Jiangsu and Shanghai, clearly ranks in the top quintile based on
the concentration of private firms in a population of 10,000 inhabitants. Only
two other regions have reached comparable levels of private-sector development. Both, however, have distinct features that make them less representative of the bottom-up development of capitalism. In the Pearl River delta of

Guangdong Province adjacent to the Special Administrative Regions of Hong Kong and Macau in the southeastern part of the country, the manufacturing sector is dominated by foreign production and overseas-Chinese establishments.[10] In the urban metropolitan area of Beijing and Tianjin in the north, the development of private firms accelerated only relatively recently in the late 1990s and thus does not capture the early rise of private-enterprise capitalism in China.

The Spatial and Economic Geography of the Yangzi Delta

The high density of private firm development in the Yangzi delta makes the region a natural choice for studying the foundations and mechanisms of the endogenous rise of private enterprise capitalism in China. The regional focus,

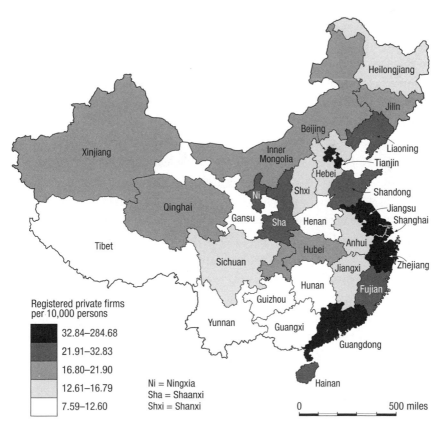

Figure 3.1. Interprovincial distribution of private-sector activities in 2004.
Source: China Statistical Yearbook 2005 (Beijing: China Statistics Press, 2005).

however, does not imply a distinct Yangzi delta culture or homogenous business model. The area is not comparable with regional industrial clusters such as Silicon Valley, a relatively confined geographical area of 620 square miles between San Francisco and San Jose. The Yangzi delta shares neither the industrial homogeneity nor a comparable concentration of specialized technological skills. In contrast to Silicon Valley, the region is characterized by diversity in geographical and ecological conditions. The sixteen municipalities of the Yangzi delta region combined add up to an area of more than 54,000 square miles, slightly larger than Greece. The total population reaches 87 million (15 percent of China's total population), more than the population of Germany. Geographically, the region stretches from alluvial plains to expansive hilly and mountainous terrain. It includes more than 3,000 small islands along the coastline.

The delta ecosystem is shaped by the bowl-like alluvial basin of the Yangzi River, which empties into the Yellow Sea just north of Shanghai, and the Qiantang River, which empties into Hangzhou Bay to the south. Formed over the millennia through silt deposited by the Yangzi River, the lowland of the delta southeast of Lake Tai is at sea level; elsewhere, the lowland rises from ten to sixteen feet above sea level. "Two geographical forces shaped the topography of the delta: the interaction between the Yangzi River and the ocean tides, which built up the basin's ridge-like periphery; and the inundation and sinking of parts of the central land mass sometime in the eighth to twelfth centuries."[11] The delta ecosystem stretches through southern Jiangsu Province and into northern Zhejiang Province. South of the city of Hangzhou, the mountainous peripheral areas of the delta region extend through southern Zhejiang to the borders of Jiangxi and Fujian Provinces.

The Yangzi delta has since the ninth century been the most populous and one of the culturally and economically most advanced regions of China. In the Mao era, however, economic policies introduced great intraregional disparities. Areas with advantageous geographic conditions such as the vast resource-rich plains of Jiangsu Province received massive state investments, which helped to build up a heavy industry base. The less accessible hilly areas in southern Zhejiang Province, in contrast, were notoriously neglected and virtually starved of infrastructural and industrial investment funds. Without sufficient nonagricultural employment, the land-labor ratio decreased, leading to a buildup of high underemployment in agriculture.

These disparate investment strategies had a lasting impact, explaining the different development patterns in the early 1980s.[12] In southern Jiangsu Province, where the industrial base of state-owned and collective enterprise was relatively developed and local revenue streams stable, local governments had both the incentives and financial means to initially foster a collectivist business model, which prioritized township- and village-run enterprises (TVEs). This so-called *Sunan (southern Jiangsu) model,* often described as local state corporatism, followed the aim of the national reform leaders to encourage rural growth and industrialization through the buildup and expansion of local government–owned and state-owned firms.[13] Supported by privileged access to financial capital and international markets, these companies received massive investments from local government revenue and preferential loans provided by rural credit cooperatives.[14] Proximity to coastal ports with convenient transportation, better infrastructure than inland provinces, and ready access to global shipping lanes and international markets spurred rural industrialization and helped to transfer millions of underemployed peasants into nonagricultural employment. Many of Jiangsu's TVEs began their post-reform expansion as subcontractors for state-owned enterprises in Shanghai and Nanjing eager to take advantage of the flexible and lower-cost labor of township and village enterprises. This helped to stabilize their sales development and mitigated intrinsic market risks, and they grew rapidly in the 1980s, many approaching the scale of medium-size state-owned enterprises.

Geographical advantage combined with prerevolutionary cultural and technical legacy and traditions of commerce to provide favorable initial conditions for export-driven development in this part of the Yangzi delta region. In parallel, discriminatory policies against indigenous private firms protected these government-owned companies from private competition. Access to land and business licenses, for instance, remained tightly controlled.[15]

Collective rural enterprises flourished particularly in the first decade of economic reforms, with 90 percent of Jiangsu's rural industrial production originating in collective TVEs by 1987.[16] Notwithstanding, with increasing marketization, these collectively run firms gradually lost their initial competitive advantages of privileged resource access and local government backing. Inefficiencies grew and spontaneous privatization spread. Between 1993 and 2002, the number of collective TVEs fell from 1.69 million to only 0.73 million nationwide. As a result, the total employment in township and village enterprises decreased from close to 58 million to 38 million. Most of the local government-owned TVEs in southern Jiangsu were either privatized or transferred into shareholding companies.[17] This privatization of TVEs aligned local government interests with the performance of private enterprise, which in turn provided greater scope for bottom-up entrepreneurial activity.

In the early years of market reform, community governments in Jiangsu Province had remained heavily involved in business development and took an active role in protecting local collective firms against private competition. In contrast, communities in peripheral mountainous areas and coastal areas of Zhejiang Province that lacked a developed industrial base had no alternative but to rely on the spontaneous development of entrepreneurial activities and local self-help. Here, as one entrepreneur in Wenzhou mentions, "private entrepreneurs never were looked down upon; it was all too clear to the government that private firms would help develop the community."[18] The *Wenzhou model* of individualistic entrepreneurial spirit and acquiescent local government diffused rapidly throughout Zhejiang Province.

Shanghai, with its strong emphasis on state-owned conglomerates and large-scale foreign firms, represents yet another development type. In Shanghai, the inflow of foreign direct investment and concentration of large-scale multinational companies introduced competition and private ownership relatively early, but technical advantages and the pure size of new market entrants, many of them established global players representing major brand names, left only a narrow scope for domestic private start-ups. Thus in Shanghai private firm development expanded even later than in Jiangsu Province. Whereas in the late 1980s already more than 10,000 private firms were officially registered both in Zhejiang and in Jiangsu, only 1,000 entrepreneurs had started a business in Shanghai, where a strong local emphasis on state-owned and joint-venture production effectively discouraged domestic private enterprise. It was not until the early 1990s that private firm development accelerated.

Official registration records from the *Bureau of Industry and Commerce* clearly show the different timing of private-firm development in these three Yangzi delta subregions during the first fourteen years of economic reforms (see Figure 3.2). Zhejiang Province experienced the steepest growth trend and highest density of private firms in the 1980s. At this time, the heavily state-dominated municipality of Shanghai did not provide statistics on company registrations.

The wave of private entrepreneurship swept to Shanghai in the early 1990s. The number of private firm registrations per 10,000 population soon surpassed the numbers in Zhejiang and Jiangsu, and has continued to rise steeply for most of the last two decades (see Figure 3.3). However, private businesses

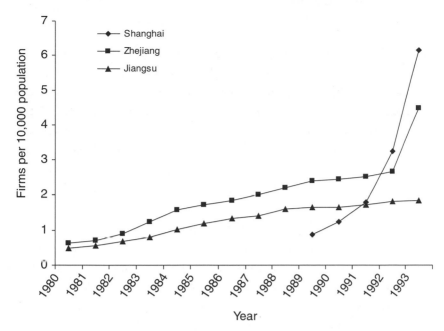

Figure 3.2. Private firm registration in the Yangzi delta, 1980–1993.
Source: Bureau of Industry and Commerce.

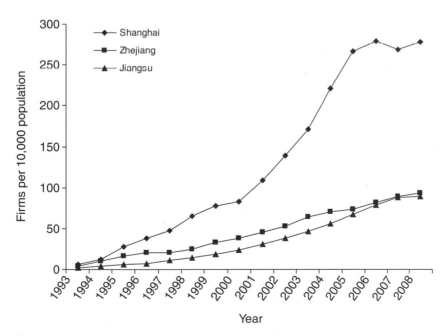

Figure 3.3. Private firm registration in the Yangzi delta, 1993–2008.
Source: Bureau of Industry and Commerce.

in Shanghai have tended to remain particularly small. With only nine employees on average in 2008, most of the establishments are just slightly bigger than household productions. In contrast, private firms in Zhejiang and Jiangsu are somewhat larger, with on average seventeen and sixteen employees, clearly moving away from household production schemes.[19] While underreporting of official employment numbers may lead to a certain downward bias in statistics, average employment figures indicate that private firms still tend to be smaller than, for instance, collective township village enterprises (national average: fifty employees).

Variable local geography and inherited industrial structure reinforce intraregional economic diversity. Today, clusters of high-tech industries are in close proximity to agglomerations of labor-intensive, low-value-added production. Traveling through some of the Yangzi delta's most densely populated and industrialized areas has aspects of travel through the history of industrial development. Clusters of small-scale shoe or button producers operating in nondescript workshops and former storage places locate not far from modern high-technology industrial parks focusing on computer technology representing the local interpretations of Silicon Valley. In parallel, organizational diversity ranges from simple forms of family production to modern corporations modeled on the principles of Western-style corporate governance, staffed with highly skilled graduates from the best national and international universities.

The Yangzi Delta Survey of Entrepreneurs and Firms

Given such diversity, any attempt to systematically study the institutional foundations and mechanisms underlying the Yangzi delta's rise of private enterprise capitalism can neither build on isolated case studies nor focus solely on distinct industrial sectors or specific production clusters. To capture the potential influence of different geographic conditions as well as structural and institutional legacies shaping the region's development, we selected seven of the sixteen municipalities of the Yangzi delta region (see Figure 3.4). These municipalities are all sizeable economic centers of the region and broadly represent the diversity of local development models.

The set of survey cities reflect different historical legacies and varying political and economic starting conditions at the outset of reforms. Included are (1) municipalities with a long-standing private commercial culture, where

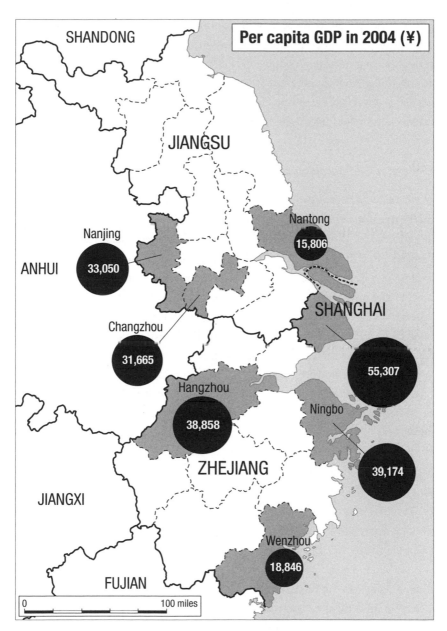

Figure 3.4. The seven survey cities. *Source: China City Statistical Yearbook 2005, China Data Online* (University of Michigan, www.chinadataonline.org).

post-reform private-firm development took off already in the early 1980s (Wenzhou and Ningbo in Zhejiang Province), (2) municipalities with traditionally strong reliance on public ownership (Hangzhou in Zhejiang Province and Nanjing and Changzhou in Jiangsu Province), and (3) municipalities with sizeable state-owned production in combination with massive foreign direct-investment inflows (Nantong in Jiangsu Province and Shanghai).

Cities with a Private Business Culture

Wenzhou is a port city located eighteen miles from the coast of the East China Sea on the river Ou, which gives access to the mountainous interior of southern Zhejiang Province. With a land area of 4,550 square miles, its administrative area includes more than 10 percent of Zhejiang Province. Ninety-six percent of this area is classified as rural, with more than 60 percent of the residents living in villages and townships. Commercial culture in Wenzhou dates back to the Song Dynasty (960–1279), when market production specialized in various crops and handicrafts and merchants were highly skilled in long-distance trading.[20] Foreign trade picked up in 1867 when the city became a treaty port.

The Mao era, however, brought an unexpected economic decline to this once-thriving commercial city. Central government policies systematically neglected Wenzhou. Due to its proximity to Taiwan and its seeming vulnerability to potential invaders, the city was starved of public investment funds. Wenzhou received only 1 percent of Zhejiang Province's fixed investment capital during the Mao era, while it was home to 15 percent of the province's population.[21] In total, between 1949 and 1981 Wenzhou received about ¥655 million of investment capital from public funds. This was less than 25 percent of what the much smaller city of Ningbo received over the same period. Not surprisingly, by the end of the Mao era, Wenzhou's economic development was far below the national average. Per capita income was only ¥55, compared to an already low national average of ¥165.[22]

Geographically isolated, impoverished, and with very limited public funds, the population was forced to rely on local resources and self-help. Even before the official opening of economic reforms in 1978, pre-communist practices had regained prominence, and a parallel economy with individual and private activities, black markets, long-distance trade, and active barter trade had developed. Private farming, household production, and underground factories increasingly replaced collective enterprises for consumer goods production.[23] It has been estimated that 1,844 micro-entrepreneurs were already active in the area by 1979.[24] Under dire fiscal constraints with only ¥23 of per capita fiscal income in 1978, the local government could barely maintain its core functions and had no alternative but to tolerate and openly support private business activities.[25] In particular, local government assisted bottom-up processes of local self-help through the construction of local marketplaces.[26] Local experimentation increased after 1986 when Wenzhou received official status as an experimental zone. A preliminary city-level regulation specified in 1987 local conditions for private-firm activities even before the central Chinese government first legalized such activities in 1988. These temporary regulations acknowledged local business practices that had endogenously developed among private firms. By this time local businesses—amounting to more than 100,000 household businesses *(getihu)* in 1984—had already flourished for years.[27]

Central government support for Wenzhou's development intensified in 1990, when the city opened its first export-processing zone (the Longwan Export Industrial Zone). By 2000, 120,555 out of 122,775 industrial firms were private by nature, with close to every fifth household in Wenzhou holding partial or full ownership in some type of business operation. As noted earlier, much of the manufacturing is organized in highly concentrated industrial clusters, with 20 percent of China's shoe production, 60 percent of its razors, 90 percent of lighters, and 80 percent of sunglasses originating in Wenzhou.[28]

Ningbo, a city of more than 5.5 million residents, is located in the Ningshao alluvial plain along the coast of Zhejiang Province, south of the mouth of the Yangzi River. Thanks to its privileged geographic location, the city has a long history of sea trade dating back to the Qin Dynasty (221–207 BC). By the eleventh century, Ningbo was the most important center of foreign trade on the Chinese coast. Even during the Ming Dynasty (1368–1644) when marine trade was banned, the city maintained its importance as a trading center. During this period, Ningbo served as the only entry port for tributes to the imperial court, which helped sustain the city's foreign relations. By the early Qing Dynasty, with the lifting of the marine ban, Ningbo revitalized and expanded its international trading relations, with shipping lanes stretching from the Southeast Asian region to Japan. During the era of imperialism, the colonial powers used Ningbo as a key entry port. Today's architecture still reflects the commercial activities of the Portuguese, Dutch, and British traders, which helped to transform Ningbo into one of the earliest treaty ports with modern banking facilities and trade services.

In the Mao era, Ningbo lost its role as a trading port. Like Wenzhou to the south, its manufacturing economy remained largely dormant because the state bypassed the city as a site for investment in industrial development.[29] Ningbo's inclusion as one of the coastal cities opened in 1984, however, quickly revitalized the city's commercial and trade tradition. By 2009, Ningbo was home to the second-largest container port in China and the fourth-largest container port in the world, also handling a large portion of Shanghai's foreign trade.[30] Close commercial connections between both cities are likely to further intensify, thanks to the recently opened Hangzhou Bay Bridge, which provides a short and convenient link reducing the distance by seventy-five miles.

Ningbo's industrial structure has naturally adapted to global trade preferences. Private start-ups have focused on manufacturing low-value-added exports, especially textiles, light consumer goods, and home appliances. Many of Ningbo's private firms work as subcontractors for international companies, delivering parts and preliminary products. The casual observer perceives the city as a place of business travelers. What foreign visitors plan to trade and whether help is needed in meeting local producers are not unfamiliar questions when visiting the city. Ningbo's success with exports is indeed impressive. By 2005, 20 of China's 190 most important export brands were located in this municipality.[31]

The local government has sought to support economic development and to promote commercial activity and international trade by minimizing red tape. For example, in 2000, the number of items requiring administrative approval was reduced from 647 to 227. Also the setup of a "Clean Administration Complaint Center" in the same year emphasizes the government's effort to facilitate business through improved administrative services and transparency.[32]

Cities with a Nonprivate Business Culture

Hangzhou, a city of 6.6 million residents, is located about 110 miles west of Shanghai, surrounded by lush hills and situated on the West Lake and the southern end of China's Grand Canal connecting the city with Beijing in the north. It is one of China's oldest settlements, with a history dating back almost 5,000 years, while the city proper was founded about 2,200 years ago in the Qin Dynasty. The population size at the end of the thirteenth century may have been above 1 million, making Hangzhou the largest city in the world at that time.[33]

During the Mao era, Hangzhou, as the provincial capital of Zhejiang, received relatively strong central support. This has led to the buildup of a strong state and collective sector in Hangzhou's economy. After the opening of reforms, the municipal government initially sought to maintain and expand the existing public industrial sector. Thus, private start-up firms developed later than in the cities of Wenzhou and Ningbo and met much stronger political resistance and discrimination. Barriers to entry for private enterprises were erected by the Hangzhou municipal government. Private firms were systematically denied access to land lease and buildings. Higher fees for water and electricity underscored the disadvantaged position of private start-ups. In the mid- to late 1990s, even after privatization of state-owned firms became a high priority of the central government reform agenda, its implementation in Hangzhou proceeded slowly, marked by repeated public disclosure of malfeasance and enrichment by local government officials.[34]

At the end of the 1990s, the city faced strong competition from municipalities in the Yangzi delta region that were more supportive of private enterprise, and it fell behind in economic development. This loss in regional competitiveness eventually forced the local leadership to adopt a more private-business-friendly policy. Since then, the municipality has made substantial efforts to improve the overall business environment and to streamline local administration. Greater transparency of bureaucratic procedures and hotlines for complaints have played prominent roles in modernizing the local business system. Supported by a strong educational base, with thirty-five universities and colleges located in Hangzhou, the new strategy was quickly successful. Already in 2004, the *Forbes* list of the best business environments ranked Hangzhou number one in China, a ranking that was repeated in five consecutive years.[35]

Nanjing is today home to 7.5 million residents. Located on the Yangzi River and surrounded by the Ningzheng Ridge, the city is approximately 180 miles west of Shanghai. Nanjing is one of the great historical sites of China. It was the capital of six dynasties and of the Republic of China. Economically, the city is privileged in its rich natural resource endowments. Among the more than forty different minerals found in or near Nanjing, iron and sulfur have the greatest reserves. During the Ming Dynasty (1368–1644), Nanjing reached an early peak in its economic and political development, becoming a commercial center in East Asia, especially for textiles, printing, and shipbuilding. Around 1400, Nanjing was even among the most prosperous cities in China and globally.

In terms of population size, it overtook Hangzhou, and was supposedly then the largest urban settlement in the world.

After the establishment of the People's Republic of China, Nanjing was chosen as the capital of Jiangsu Province. In the following years, massive investments built up a heavy industry base. The emphasis was on electrical, mechanical, chemical, and steel production, which turned Nanjing into a national center of heavy industry. Today, large-scale state-owned firms such as Panda Electronics, Jincheng Motors, and Nanjing Steel still shape the city's industrial landscape. The government was generally slow to adapt and implement market reforms and has over the years had a reputation of being mired in red tape.[36] While elsewhere in the Yangzi region motorways run along seemingly endless high-tech zones bursting with modern high-rises and glass and steel constructions, Nanjing's outer districts are still dominated by large-scale petrochemical and steel conglomerates, reflecting the city's long-standing emphasis on heavy industry. Although the city government has by now opened four large-scale industrial parks to attract nonstate enterprises, the inflow of private firms cannot yet compete with the neighboring cities of Suzhou and Wuxi, which much earlier invited private development and foreign direct investments. Downsizing of state-owned production and subsequent layoffs have been a further strain for the municipality's socioeconomic development.

Overall, Nanjing still has the feel of a tradition-laden, somewhat mainstream city.[37] Nonetheless, here, as in Jiangsu's other major cities, the wealth of the province is evidenced by the rapid development of residential areas satisfying upscale customer needs. Nanjing, Suzhou, Wuxi, and Changzhou today have among the highest per capita GDP in China. Streets are lined with visually appealing apartment complexes and urban townhouses, often equipped with solar cells and other modern amenities. The modern, partly privately operated freeway system connecting all cities of the province is by now comparable in density and standards with highway systems of industrial economies. Superfast trains between Nanjing and Shanghai allow an easy one-hour commute.

Changzhou is a prefecture-level city of 3.5 million residents in southern Jiangsu Province bordering Nanjing to the east. The city's economic history dates back to AD 609, when the town developed as a transshipment point and commercial center for agricultural trading on the Grand Canal. Main products were rice, fish, tea, and silk. A cotton industry grew in the 1920s, and subsequently the city emerged as a center of textile production. Under Maoist rule, engineering and mechanical industries were added.

Through heavy reliance on the creation of collective township village enterprises in the 1980s and early 1990s, Changzhou was initially extremely successful in limiting rural poverty. Large-scale collective firms run by local government provided the initial growth impetus of the post-reform period. The focus on collective firms left little room for private firm development. Private firms were unwelcome competitors, and administrative discrimination was pervasive. Only when marketization expanded in the 1990s, and collective firms began to gradually lose their relative advantage as organizational hybrids, did market entry of private firms accelerate.

Local industrial policies quickly adjusted and began to focus on foreign and private high-tech firms. A high-tech zone was established in 1992; many of Changzhou's globally competitive private companies are now located there. Contracted per capita foreign direct investment increased rapidly, even surpassing that for the provincial capital Nanjing by the year 2002.[38] Due to its late start in economic reform, the municipal government was able to offer favorable land-lease contracts, at a time when the land markets of earlier developing cities in Jiangsu Province, such as Suzhou, were already tightly constrained. The close proximity to the provincial capital added further advantages. Changzhou is located along the Shanghai-Nanjing railway line, and both cities are in easy reach. In addition, the government plans to soon extend the Suhu expressway to directly connect the city with Shanghai.

Cities under Heavy Foreign Influence

Nantong is a prefecture-level coastal city of more than 7.5 million residents in Jiangsu Province, located on the northern bank of the Yangzi River. Historically (with records dating back to AD 958) the city has played only a minor role in the economic development of the Yangzi delta. Commerce concentrated on salt production on the seacoast, and also rice and cotton. By the early twentieth century, the textile industry was also of some significance.

Nantong was one of the fourteen coastal cities designated by the central government to be opened for international trade and investment in 1984, and thus foreign direct investment played a crucial role throughout the economic reforms. Nantong's proximity to Shanghai and its geographic location on the banks of the Yangzi River with its own seaport contributed to its development into a major industrial hub. In 2008, the opening of the Suzhou-Nantong Yangzi Bridge connected the city with the industrial high-tech clusters of Suzhou and with the national highway network on both banks of the Yangzi River, reducing travel time to Shanghai from four hours to only one hour. Today, Nantong is one of the fastest-growing coastal cities, with large areas of the municipality's 3,000 square miles dominated by new industry construction. Between 2003 and 2006, contracted foreign direct investments tripled, reaching $6.9 billion. In parallel, total industrial investment in fixed assets increased by more than 230 percent.[39] The textile industry's historical strength was maintained, but complemented by factories producing machinery, electronics, and chemicals.

In 2010, the city was continuing a nearly decade-long boom in construction of residential housing and commercial buildings. Entire city blocks were under construction, lined with unvarying high-rise buildings mimicking Shanghai's twenty-first-century urban profile. So extensive were these construction sites that the old city center was difficult to locate, seemingly hidden in the dusty broad streets of the expanded city.

The administrative region of *Shanghai* covers more than 2,430 square miles in the Yangzi delta. Located on the mouth of the Huangpu River, it extends seventy miles from north to south and sixty miles from east to west. The city proper covers only about 12 percent of this; the remainder of the municipality includes periurban townships and vast rural areas in the alluvial plain of the Yangzi River. Today, Shanghai has more than 18.6 million residents, 4.7 million of whom are temporary migrants.

Shanghai's historical records date back to AD 960. During the Ming (1368–1644) and Qing (1644–1912) dynasties, the city developed into a trading port, with transport routes for cotton connecting the Yangzi delta with Beijing and Japan. Shanghai emerged as the region's commercial center when it was opened after the opium wars in 1842 for trade with the European powers. The entry of British, French, American, and Japanese corporations and investors spurred development of manufacturing and trade.

During the Mao era, Shanghai became a base for heavy industry. Large-scale state-owned conglomerates in chemical, petrochemical, and steel production dominated the pre-reform economy. The state-owned sector provided a solid revenue base, which allowed the local government to further invest in state and collective enterprise development during the early economic reforms.[40]

As one of the fourteen coastal cities opened in 1984, Shanghai quickly regained its traditional position as an entry port for foreign investments and trade. Already in the first years of the reform process, through active encouragement, the city successfully attracted large-scale joint-ventures with foreign corporations. Today, the city hosts the third-largest container harbor in the world.

The foreign-investment-driven modernization strategy reached a new stage in 1990, when the local government established a new development zone in Pudong. Since then, Shanghai has attracted the largest expatriate community in China, and is home to thousands of foreign companies. Foreign influence is pervasive. The city is without doubt the country's most westernized, open to foreign culture and business models.

Concomitantly, the local government has never taken an active interest in promoting the development of domestic private start-up firms. Markets expanded more slowly than in other coastal cities in the 1980s, with only relatively few niches opening up for domestic entrepreneurs. The private and individual sector could only attract those who had no hope for public sector employment. Though the number of private businesses began to surge in the early 1990s, most were small, household-scale establishments. Not before the mid-1990s did the private sector slowly lose its extralegal stigma and gain in social prestige.[41] Even so, Shanghai is still characterized as an "anti-entrepreneurial state-guided" city, which has favored the development of both state-owned firms and foreign-invested firms through local regulation, while private firms were subject to systematic discrimination.[42]

The low status of private firms in Shanghai is still tangible. The city center and Pudong development zone across the Huangpu River are dominated by the modern high-rises of multinational companies and domestic state-owned conglomerates.[43] Private firms, in contrast, are barely visible in the central districts of Shanghai. They often lease sections of the remains of shuttered state-owned enterprises in the suburban areas. They occupy areas partitioned from cavernous darkened workshops lined with abandoned machinery of the bankrupt state-owned enterprises.

Along dusty roads of the townships and county towns at the periphery of the municipality, however, it is commonplace to see new factory sites of large private enterprises. Attracted by lower prices for land-lease and labor, most private companies locate in the outer districts of Shanghai bordering the provinces of Jiangsu and Zhejiang. Jiading district, about twelve miles north of the city center,

right on the border of Jiangsu Province, has become a center of automobile supplies. In the westernmost district of Qingpu on the border of Jiangsu and Zhejiang Provinces, private companies contribute more than 50 percent of the district's tax revenue. With more than thirty specialized industrial zones, Qingpu
district is a leader in private-firm development in Shanghai. The growth dynamic is impressive. Companies that at their founding stage did not even have
proper access to public transport or a solid road to the downtown area are now,
within only a few years, at the center of a thriving industrial cluster or rapidly
expanding industrial park reaching deep into the remaining farmland.

Economic Overview

Table 3.1 compares general economic conditions of these seven survey cities
at the time we initiated our first survey wave. They all contributed significantly to their provincial economies, with 28 percent of Jiangsu's gross regional production coming from the three survey cities located there, and close
to 52 percent of Zhejiang's regional production coming from the three survey
cities located there.

Notable are the variations in private-sector development. While domestic
private firms represent in each city a substantial part of the local economy, the
scale of private-firm operations varies greatly. With only nine employees on
average, private firms in Shanghai tend to be particularly small-scale, as
already noted. The coastal city of Nantong in Jiangsu Province registers the
largest average company size, with on average thirty-eight employees.

Industrial Diversity

Today, private enterprises in the Yangzi delta region range from labor-intensive
industries, such as textiles, to capital-intensive industries, such as shipbuilding, to technology and research-intensive industries such as biomedicine.
Local industrial specialization has followed distinct development patterns, in
accordance with local historical traditions, local comparative advantages, and
national and local industrial policies.

For our survey, we selected a stratified random sample of firms reflecting
the heterogeneity of manufacturing technologies in the Yangzi delta region.
To narrow down and control for industrial diversity, we selected five different
manufacturing sectors, by applying the following principles. First, the sectors
should have substantive importance for China's overall industrial development.

Table 3.1. Socioeconomic conditions in the seven survey cities, 2006

	Total population (in millions)	Per capita GDP (¥)	City contribution to gross provincial product (percent)	Number of registered private firms	Persons employed in private enterprise (in millions)	Employees per firm (mean)
Shanghai	18.15	57,695	100	507,500	4.73	9.3
Jiangsu						
Nantong	7.51	22,826	8 12	30,400	1.16	38.16
Changzhou	3.78	44,440	7 25	34,900	0.80	22.92
Nanjing	6.12	46,166	12 81	91,800	0.96	10.46
Zhejiang						
Hangzhou	6.66	51,878	21 86	41,500	0.59	14.22
Wenzhou	7.56	24,390	11 67	47,100	0.80	16.99
Ningbo	5.60	51,460	18 26	46,100	0.69	14.97

Source: Calculated based on data from *Shanghai Statistical Yearbook 2007*; *Jiangsu Statistical Yearbook 2007*; *Zhejiang Statistical Yearbook 2007* (all at China Data Online, http://chinadataonline.org/); China Bureau of Industry and Commerce.

Note: Private enterprises include only domestic firms registered as private firms. Foreign firms are not included.

Second, they should represent different levels of industry concentration, since highly concentrated sectors may involve different market entry and marketing strategies than sectors with rather low concentration ratios. Third, they should reflect the industrial specializations within the Yangzi delta. Lastly, they should cover different production technologies.

The textile and ordinary machinery industries represent labor-intensive production, with national concentration ratios of the top ten producers of 6.5 and 7.8 percent, respectively. Vehicles and auto parts represent capital-intensive industries, with a rather high concentration ratio of around 20 percent. This sector was also a national priority ever since the central government published the first national industrial policy guidelines in 1989. Finally, the pharmaceutical and electronic industries represent technology-intensive production. These industries have concentration ratios of 10 and 20 percent, respectively. In 2006, the accumulated production value of these five sectors reached close to 28 percent of China's total industrial output value. In our survey, the distribution of these five sectors follows roughly the relative importance of these sectors in the region, with textile, automobile, and machinery each accounting for 25 percent of the sample, and pharmaceuticals and electronics for 12 percent and 13 percent respectively.

Table 3.2 indicates the relative share of national gross industrial production in each of these sectors contributed by each of the three provinces. The Yangzi delta region's total contribution to national production ranges from 24.4 percent for medical and pharmaceutical products to close to 50 percent for textile production, which underlines the importance of these Yangzi delta industries.

Table 3.2.   Provincial contribution to national gross industrial output by sector, 2006 (percent)

Sector	Shanghai	Jiangsu	Zhejiang	Total of region
Textile industry	2.34	23.93	22.68	48.95
Medical and pharmaceutical products	4.28	10.45	9.67	24.4
Ordinary machinery	11.14	18.09	14.57	43.8
Vehicle and auto parts	9.30	8.65	8.14	26.09
Communication equipment, computer, other electronic manufacturing	11.85	19.32	4.79	35.96

Source: China Yearly Industrial Data, *China Data Online,* www.chinadataonline.org.

The Sample

Quantitative survey research of private firms poses specific and unexpected challenges. The social science literature reflects this. The majority of such empirical studies focus on stock-listed companies, not only because these are the largest and typically most powerful corporations, but also simply because they are more readily accessible to research, given financial disclosure rules. Even in established market economies, private firm information is often kept secret and financial data is hard to get.

The difficulties of research on private firms are even more pronounced in China. Many were founded when private manufacturing firms were illegal. Marginalized as illegitimate, entrepreneurs often had no alternative but to turn to quasi-legal or partly illegal business practices in the start-up phase, simply to survive. Understandably, entrepreneurs are apprehensive that survey information might end up in the hands of competitors or government authorities.

Our Yangzi delta entrepreneur and firm survey solved these challenges through an innovative use of local networks in approaching entrepreneurs sampled for the study. Given our specific focus on the questions of how China's entrepreneurs become capitalist and where economic institutions of capitalism come from, we did not draw a random sample from the entire population of private businesses. This would have included many short-lived mom-and-pop operations, producing little value added and without any hope to develop into sizeable manufacturing businesses. To more directly target our population of interest, we excluded all companies with fewer than ten employees and all companies in business for less than three years. In line with our interest in understanding the strategic moves of China's "new capitalists," we used a stratified sample that oversamples medium and large-scale companies. Following China's national classification system, we define as small those firms having 10 to 100 employees, as medium those having between 100 and 300 employees, and as large those employing more than 300 workers. The goal was to limit small-scale companies to two-thirds of the sample.

Based on this sampling frame, stratified on location, sector, and size, firms were randomly drawn from local firm registers. In a first step, for each city and industry a sampling pool was established by drawing every *nth* company from complete local firm registers.[44] After confirming the eligibility[45] of the firms, our local partner, the Market Survey Research Institute,[46] approached local entities such as the Bureau of Industry and Commerce, party organizations, and other institutions such as industry guilds for their support and assistance in securing entrepreneurs' participation in our survey. Once local support was secured, the sampled entrepreneurs were invited to participate. Generally, local organizations and authorities gave generous and unconditional support to the research project. Local representatives never interfered or tried to influence the interview process and content, nor did they make any attempt to attend or monitor any of the research visits.

Eligible respondents were the companies' chief executive officers (CEOs). If the CEO could not participate in the interview personally, the interview was rescheduled. This increased comparability of responses across all companies. Moreover, the strategy helped secure more detailed and reliable information on specific processes that fall naturally into the domain of the firm manager. In a majority of cases, the respondent also held ownership shares in the company (83 percent of interviewees) or was even one of the company founders (74 percent of interviewees). This fortunate outcome allows inferences not only on company development in general but also on personal traits and behavioral responses of China's emerging entrepreneurial elite.

Overall, with 711 completed interviews in 2,842 contacted firms, the response rate for our 2006 survey wave was 25 percent.[47] This rate meets standards widely used by the professional survey research industry, which regards overall response rates of firm surveys in the range of 25 percent as satisfactory.[48] Nonresponses often resulted from strict adherence to the rule only to interview the firm's CEO. Extended business trips—partly outside China—or participation in national and international trade fairs made personal visits with CEOs at times simply impossible. If after three contact attempts it was still not possible to line up a personal appointment for a face-to-face interview with the firm manager, we replaced the firm by another randomly sampled participant firm drawn from the sampling pool.

Table 3.3 illustrates the setup of the resulting sample by city, industry, and firm size. The total sample size is 711 in our first survey wave (2006), with between 100 and 103 companies sampled in each of the participating seven municipalities.[49] Overall, 9.8 percent are categorized as large, 23.2 percent as medium size, and 66.9 percent as small. Given that there were 113,866 companies in the five selected sectors in these cities by the end of 2005, the margin of error would be no more than 3.66 at a confidence level of 95 percent (or no more than 4.82 at a confidence level of 99 percent) when making

Table 3.3. Firm sample by city, sector, and firm size, 2006 wave

Industry	Size	Nanjing	Nantong	Changzhou	Wenzhou	Ningbo	Hangzhou	Shanghai	Total
Textile	L	2	5	3	2	0	4	4	20
	M	0	13	5	14	10	11	4	57
	S	10	9	14	10	21	23	11	98
Auto parts	L	1	5	1	1	4	1	5	18
	M	6	3	2	7	5	0	8	31
	S	32	12	12	15	11	7	37	126
Machinery	L	2	5	0	1	0	3	1	12
	M	1	5	1	5	5	8	8	33
	S	24	20	14	27	24	18	3	130
Pharmaceutical	L	0	2	0	1	0	7	1	11
	M	0	5	6	0	0	1	4	16
	S	7	5	18	2	9	9	10	60
Electronics	L	2	2	0	3	0	2	0	9
	M	2	6	7	4	5	3	1	28
	S	13	4	20	9	7	6	3	62
Total		102	101	103	101	101	103	100	711

L = more than 300 workers; M = 101 to 300 workers; S = 10 to 100 workers in 2003.

inferences on this specific population of manufacturing firms in the Yangzi delta region.

The Survey Design

The quantitative survey operationalizes the multilevel causal model of institutional change specified in Figure 2.1, using distinct components of the model to guide the design of the survey instrument. The analytical focus is on the mechanisms structuring the relations between institutions, organizational field, and firm. The questionnaire explores typical entrepreneurial situations and standard operational decisions in key areas of firm activities, including supplier relations, customer relations, firm governance and organization, labor relations, and research and development. It examines company strategies in response to legal constraints, modes of compliance or decoupling, and modes of legitimacy seeking, as well as monitoring and enforcement mechanisms. In parallel, the questionnaire elicits information on the individual founder, the quality of relations with other social groups, and social status assessments. Broadly speaking, the quantitative survey is designed to tease out in different contextual settings the actual micro-level mechanisms enabling and guiding China's transformative institutional change toward a capitalist firm economy.

A separate survey module covers firm size, firm structure, ownership, firm performance, competition, taxation, and finance, for the three years before the survey year.[50] To facilitate the interview process on these rather complex accounting issues and increase the accuracy of the responses, the CEO was invited to ask the chief financial officer (CFO) to complete the second part of the interview or to assist with it.

Before taking our survey to the field, we discussed the questionnaire with focal groups (consisting of both local academics and entrepreneurs) to confirm the appropriateness of the design and framing of questions. We then tested the survey instrument in a small-scale pilot study of seventy firms (ten in each of the survey cities), which were selected based on the same random-sampling strategy used in the main survey. After review, minor adjustments were made.

In order to gain more than just a snapshot of current company performance and strategies, two survey waves were conducted, in the years 2006 and 2009. (For English translations of both questionnaires, see Appendix 1.)

The original motivation was to get more data points, thereby allowing for higher precision in econometric testing, but the unexpected event of the global financial and economic crisis in 2009 also opened up the opportunity to compare firm performance during a period of robust economic expansion in 2006 with performance in a period of rapid slowdown. To increase chances for a higher return rate of interviewees already covered in the first wave, the survey team maintained ties with firm managers over the intervening years through mailing of newsletters and small gifts. The resulting resurvey rate was 75.2 percent. Eleven firms had been sold to other companies, fifteen companies moved to a different location, and ten firms had gone out of business. Another 140 did not wish to participate in the survey again. Among the most common reasons cited were time constraints during the survey period. We replaced 165 firms with a new set of randomly sampled firms in order to retain a sample of comparable size (of 700 firms) and stratification.

Another innovation is the inclusion of a module in experimental economics in the 2009 survey. We asked all interviewees to participate in experiments designed to study behavioral choices in response to risk, uncertainty, and competition. We randomly sampled 200 individuals from three of the survey cities as a comparison group, in order to identify whether entrepreneurial responses are distinctively different from behavioral choices of ordinary people (see Chapter 4).

Both survey waves were carried out in collaboration with Market Survey Research Institute. All interviews were conducted face-to-face by teams of two local interviewers at the factory site, usually in the CEO's office or a conference room, and lasted on average 1.5 hours. Interviewers were able to converse in local dialect if needed. In order to assure standardized implementation of the survey across our seven cities, we worked exclusively with professional interviewers, who held at least a college education and had multiple years of experience as interviewers. Moreover, all participating interviewers took part in special multiday training workshops held by the authors.[51]

We personally conducted from 2005 to 2011 an additional 111 free-ranging face-to-face interviews in the Yangzi delta region. Sixty-seven of these interviews were with entrepreneurs, government bureaucrats, and scholars in the Yangzi delta region not involved in the firm survey, and forty-four were with entrepreneurs randomly selected from those participating in the survey (in total more than 6 percent of the survey respondents). In these interviews we used semistructured questionnaires that focused on one or two themes in order to secure fine-grained subjective accounts of entrepreneurial action not obtainable in the quantitative measures of our survey instruments. The qualitative interviews not only helped to verify information gathered in quantitative research, but even more importantly, they were crucial to understanding micromechanisms, motivation, and the meaning of economic behavior and strategic choices. All of these interviews involved visits to the factory, which helped to contextualize the behavioral data obtained from the quantitative surveys. A number of interviewees agreed to repeat visits, allowing for a dynamic view of how their enterprise developed during the course of the six-year study. Appendix 2 provides a complete list of interviews conducted.

Supplementary Firm Survey

In order to position our findings within the broader context of China's postreform economy, we complement our regional survey material with national studies of firm development. The World Bank's Investment Climate Survey conducted in two waves in 2002 and 2003 allows us not only to examine other regions but also to analyze firm performance across different ownership forms, including state-owned enterprises, collective firms, and sino-foreign joint ventures. Similar to our own study, both survey waves cover company information over a period of three years: initially, from 1998 to 2000; then from 2000 to 2002.[52]

The World Bank survey is based on a random sample of cities and firms, stratified first on subsectors, which were selected to represent the most important (in terms of contribution to national GDP) industries and service sectors, and then on location. The industry mix comprises both labor-intensive and technology-intensive sectors across a broad spectrum of different production technologies and levels of competition. The 2002 survey includes firms located in five middle-size and large cities (N = 1,548), with about 300 firms sampled in each city; the 2003 survey includes firms in eighteen middle-size and large cities (N = 2,400), with 100 to 150 firms per city. Both survey waves combine to a national sample of twenty-three cities located in nineteen of China's thirty-one provinces or independent municipalities.[53] Participating firms were randomly selected in each city, subject to a size constraint of a minimum of twenty (fifteen) employees for firms in the manufacturing (service) sector. The size distribution of private firms covered by the survey is similar to our own study: 65 percent of the firms have up to 100 employees and 12 percent have more than 300 employees. Questionnaires were filled out in face-to-face interviews with senior managers of the respective establishments. Part two of the interviews was conducted with the firm's accountant, who provided quantitative information on costs, expenditures, and asset valuations.[54] Importantly, our own survey instrument incorporated a core set of the questions used in the World Bank firm surveys.

Conclusion

Our survey of emerging capitalism in China focuses on the Yangzi delta region as the most important center of bottom-up entrepreneurship. The characteristic feature of entrepreneurial spirit in the Yangzi delta region was to deal with adverse conditions by devising ways around them. Bottom-up institutional innovations enabled entrepreneurs to cooperate and compete in newly emergent markets. Initially concentrated in Zhejiang Province, private enterprise soon expanded throughout the whole Yangzi delta region, crossing provincial borders and diffusing into original strongholds of collective and state-owned production.

We study this process through a mixed method approach, combining quantitative survey methods with qualitative interviews and field experiments. At the core of our research effort is the survey that operationalizes our multilevel causal model of institutional change. Our objective is to identify the mechanisms underlying and explaining the rise of a private enterprise economy. We focus on seven different cities representing different historical and geographical conditions and on five industries representing different production technologies and concentration ratios, allowing for a relatively comprehensive analysis of the rise of private manufacturing in the Yangzi delta region. Clearly, our study does not aim to represent China as a whole. As in earlier studies of the rise of capitalism in the West, our intention is to study the regional sprouts of capitalist production, which may only gradually spread to other regions to eventually alter the nature of the entire national economy.

4

Entrepreneurs and Institutional Innovation

Entrepreneurial action drives the aggregate dynamics of capitalism, which in turn motivate the entrepreneur. This is the leitmotif in studies of capitalist emergence since the rise of capitalism as a new economic order in the West. In bottom-up accounts, the institutional conditions necessary and sufficient to launch economic growth do not depend *ex ante* on effective formal institutions to secure property rights and protect wealth from arbitrary expropriation by politicians and government. Instead, the focus is on specifying the endogenous rise of new institutional arrangements that enable, motivate, and guide self-reinforcing entrepreneurial action. Thus the entrepreneur is inseparable from explanations of the dynamics of capitalist economic development.

In contrast to bottom-up explanations, the state-centered approach assigns causal priority to the role of political actors and institutions in explaining economic performance. What prevents rulers from using the coercive force of the state to expropriate property and wealth from economic actors? What assures economic actors that the surplus they produce is not at risk of arbitrary confiscation by the state? In top-down accounts of economic development, the entrepreneur is absent, because the explanation turns on what politicians want and the rules they institute.

A study of institutional change following the Glorious Revolution in England in 1688, for example, examines the political factors underpinning the development of financial markets. Prior to the Glorious Revolution, the sovereign was free to reinterpret rules *ex post* and manipulate agreements on interest and terms of repayment of loans to the Crown to its advantage. This historical narrative of the struggle between Parliament and the Crown high-lights the process by which politicians instituted formal rules altering the in-centives for the Crown: "Our thesis is that the credible commitment by the government to honor its financial agreements was part of a larger commitment to secure private property. The latter was clearly a major factor for the institu-tional changes at the time of the Glorious Revolution."[1] As in other top-down accounts, the causes of sustained economic growth are seen to be embedded in the nature and quality of formal institutions. The necessary and sufficient institutional changes that pave the way for entrepreneurial profits and sus-tained economic growth are crafted by politicians and enforced by the state. The focus is on credible commitment by politicians to formal rules that secure property rights in private transactions, guarantee contract enforcement, and eliminate confiscatory behavior by government. Though this case study fo-cuses on preindustrial England, there is a general claim that informal institu-tions resting on repeated exchange and reputation are insufficient to moti-vate economic development. Hence, it is argued, what keeps poor economies locked in economic stagnation is the lack of political institutions that main-tain credible commitment to rules that safeguard property rights of private citizens.

The essential difference between bottom-up and top-down explanations of capitalist emergence and the origins of modern economic growth turns on the question of causal priority. There is broad consensus that modern self-regulating markets require the continuous involvement of the state. But is it correct that norms and networks cannot provide sufficient institutional con-ditions to enable and motivate robust economic activity? Is it necessary for formal rules to be in place *ex ante* to safeguard property rights in order that economic growth and development can be initiated?

Some recent historical studies suggest otherwise. An analysis of land prices and returns in seventeenth-century England, for instance, shows that secure property rights existed at least as early as 1600, and did not substantively in-crease after England's Glorious Revolution. Thus "to read the Glorious Revo-lution as ushering in a stable regime of taxes and property rights that laid the foundation for the Industrial Revolution (beginning in 1760) is to write Whig history of the most egregious sort."[2]

Similarly, it seems implausible that third-party contract enforcement by English courts and law-enforcement agencies in the eighteenth century was what mainly enabled economic growth during the Industrial Revolution. To emphasize only the rule of law, intellectual property rights, and government legislation is to ignore important social factors:

> In this regard, what is significant in the decades before the Industrial Revolution is the growth of a set of social norms that, beyond the formal "rule of law" and explicit penalties for opportunistic behavior, made entrepreneurial activities in Britain more attractive. The Industrial Revolution in the final analysis was propelled by technological progress, but to succeed its propagators (entrepreneurs, engineers, merchants, financiers, and technical consultants) needed contracts, credit, and credible commitments. Given that third-party (state) contract enforcement was rudimentary at best, what was the source of the cement that held British economic society together? The answer is that besides the formal mechanisms of the state, invoked only as a last resort, there was a set of social norms that supported entrepreneurial activity to a point not fully recognized. These norms may be called the culture of the gentleman-entrepreneur. . . . . There were certain things that a gentleman did and others he did not; and while such norms were of course no more perfectly followed than formal laws, breaking the rules of gentlemanly conduct was costly. By the middle of the eighteenth century, before the Industrial Revolution, the idea of a gentleman implies certain behavioral codes that signaled that a person was trustworthy.[3]

As an informal institution, norms of gentlemanly enterprise were a crucial complement to the market in the Industrial Revolution.

Economic development in New England was also historically supported and encouraged by informal norms and practices; in particular, the bottom-up evolution of rural lending networks.[4] In the colonial period, it had been commonplace for farmers in rural Massachusetts, for example, to write promissory notes to secure loans from fellow farmers to meet need for credit stemming from long production periods, seasonal discontinuities, and periodic disasters. A rural credit market evolved from bottom-up processes embedded in self-help norms in New England villages. Such credit relations were already expanding beyond county borders by 1780, about fifty years before the Massachusetts Corporation Law fully established the concept of limited liability. After the Revolution, the rural credit market underwent a rapid transformation, becoming more multilateral, impersonal, and regional. The very wealthy farmers became the largest debtors. Using their land as collateral, they borrowed money from less wealthy farmers to invest in the Boston security market. These informal lending networks in rural Massachusetts were important in mobilizing rural savings to finance the "wheels of industry" at the cutting edge of growth in New England in the early nineteenth century. "The enhanced liquidity of rural portfolios is the capitalist transformation of the rural economy. . . . This phenomenon must henceforth . . . loom large in whatever is meant by the coming of capitalism to the New England village economy."[5] Although New England for over a century had been far poorer than the colonial South, with the lowest per capita wealth of any colonial region, the industrialization of cotton textile and machine tool manufacture fueled a rapid rate of economic growth, and by 1840 per capita wealth in New England was over 30 percent higher than in the South. This industrialization "had its beginnings in the farm economy long before, with the unheralded emergence, proliferation, and articulation of local markets."[6]

To explain the rise of rational capitalism as an economic order in the West, both Joseph Schumpeter and Max Weber employed a bottom-up approach, focusing on entrepreneurial action and resultant institutional innovations, as we discuss in the next section. In parallel manner, to explain the rise of the private enterprise economy and capitalist economic development in China, we then turn our focus to analyzing bottom-up entrepreneurial action and institutional innovation in the Yangzi delta region.

Social Construction of Entrepreneurship

Schumpeter emphatically characterized the entrepreneur as someone who, coming from outside the established order, does not passively accept given economic conditions but is instead an innovator and "agent of economic development, because he causes a change of the economy from within the economy."[7] In essence, "the function of the entrepreneur is to reform or revolutionize the production structure, either through a new invention, or, more generally speaking, through a yet unexploited technical production method of a new good, the production of an old good through a new method, or through exploitation of a new raw material source, or a new market, or through reorganization of the industry."[8] Though Schumpeter recognized that modern capitalism has been shaped by institutional change over time, his analysis of capitalist economic development assumed the modern *Verkehrswirtschaft*, an established economic order with mature markets and efficient allocation of goods and services already in place.[9] This assumption allowed him to abstract from the institutional foundations of the "capitalist process" to focus on the role and requirements of the entrepreneur as the agent of technological change: "What he [the entrepreneur] needs to accomplish his plans are goods of all kinds: Labor, land, tools and raw material and potentially also consumption goods. Once he has these, he can realize his plans."[10] Successful innovation depends on the agent of change, who "takes action" and has the energy and motivation to "confidently navigate outside of the established channel" and overcome societal resistance against innovations.[11]

Schumpeter's focus on remarkable individuals with entrepreneurial talent led to widespread interest in uncovering a set of psychological traits associated with entrepreneurship, as with the idea of "need achievement," a cluster of personality traits of the entrepreneurial type.[12] Extensive empirical effort has not succeeded in demonstrating such distinctive psychological traits, however, and has failed to confirm Schumpeter's view of entrepreneurial talent as an individual-level attribute. Nor has this cumulative research contributed significantly to understanding the unequal distribution of innovative activities between national economies.[13] Empirical studies of entrepreneurship influenced by Schumpeter's theory continued in organizational and evolutionary economics through the 1940s and 1950s, but eventually interest in entrepreneurship research declined.[14] Mainstream economics has sought to resolve the problem by shifting its focus from the entrepreneur to innovative activity: "Can one model major innovations? I wonder. Surely they are not just a matter of serendipity: resources matter, and can be applied more intensively or less; necessity may be the legitimate model of invention."[15]

Though the entrepreneur disappeared from mainstream economics as economists shifted their attention to understanding technological change, Schumpeter's "entrepreneurial function" was replaced by endogenous growth theory, which modeled innovations as induced by economic growth and in turn an endogenous cause of growth.[16] The focus turned to institutional conditions giving rise to routine innovative activities in industries where fierce market competition pressures large corporations to "innovate or die."[17] In sum, the quest to explain the dynamics of capitalist economic development begun by Schumpeter persists today in economics in two core questions: "(1) What macroeconomic circumstances favor major innovations? (2) What macroeconomic circumstances favor rapid exploitation and improvement of major innovations, including the making of the necessary capital investment?"[18] Yet, as with Schumpeter, these questions are examined within the context of already-existing capitalist economies, where efficient market allocation and property rights are firmly in place.

Here, in contrast, we do not assume the existence of the institutional framework, but instead direct attention to institutional innovations that enable, motivate, and guide entrepreneurs in the rise of the private enterprise economy.[19] Key institutional innovations are norms and informal practices that allow producers to shift from small-scale household production to new forms of capitalist enterprise. Broadly speaking, our focus is on norms facilitating long-term planning, providing resource and market access, and allowing contracting and credible commitment to private business agreements.

In *The Protestant Ethic and the Spirit of Capitalism,* Max Weber addressed the question of how capitalism as a new economic order arises from changes in the behavior and attitudes of economic actors. When already established, he observed, capitalism "educates and selects the economic subjects which it needs through a process of economic survival of the fittest."[20] This selection process, he underscores, is guided by social norms and sanctioning of economic actors in competitive markets: "The manufacturer who in the long run acts counter to these norms, will just as inevitably be eliminated from the economic scene as the worker who cannot or will not adapt himself to them will be thrown into the streets without a job."[21] But how did this "system of market relationships"—this seemingly "unalterable order of things"—come about? "In order that a manner of life so well adapted to the peculiarities of capitalism could be selected at all, i.e. should come to dominate others, it had to originate somewhere, and not just in isolated individuals alone, but as a way of life common to whole groups of men."[22] Clearly, for Weber the rise of capitalism is neither the result of an inflow of new capital nor the result of new or specific individual traits embodied in isolated individuals; rather, it is a broad-based diffusion of new attitudes and norms—the rise of a new spirit—which triggers the shift from traditional to capitalist modes of production.

> Now at some time this leisureliness was suddenly destroyed. . . . What happened was . . . often not more than this: that some young man . . . went out into the country, carefully chose weavers for his employ, greatly increased the rigor of his supervision of their work, and thus turned them from peasants into laborers. On the other hand, he would begin to change his marketing methods by so far as possible going directly to the final consumer, would take details into his own hands, would personally solicit customers, visiting them every year, and above all would adapt the quality of the product directly to their needs and wishes. At the same time he began to introduce the principle of low prices and large turnover. There was repeated what everywhere

and always is the result of such a process of rationalization: those who would not follow suit had to go out of business. The idyllic state collapsed under the pressure of a bitter competitive struggle, respectable fortunes were made, and not lent out at interest, but always reinvested in the business. The old leisurely and comfortable attitude toward life gave way to a hard frugality in which some participated and came to the top, because they did not wish to consume but to earn, while others who wished to keep on with the old ways were forced to curtail their consumption.[23]

Transformative change was not without conflict: "Its entry on the scene was not generally peaceful. A flood of mistrust, sometimes of hatred, above all of moral indignation, regularly opposed itself to the first innovator." But competitive pressures encouraged others to behave in accordance with the new norms. Eventually this became a mass phenomenon, gradually building the institutional foundation of the capitalist order.

From Peasant to Entrepreneur

In Weber's account of capitalist development, the entrepreneurs who initially decoupled from the precapitalist production mode did not belong to the established merchant nobility often closely aligned with the polity. In England and Germany in the nineteenth century, it was not "the noble gentlemen from Liverpool and Hamburg with their inherited merchant wealth, but the rising parvenu from Manchester or Rhineland-Westfalia, often stemming from quite simple background."[24] It was traders and artisans, "men who had grown up in the hard school of life, calculating and daring at the same time," who typically did not mind the often strong societal opposition to their entrepreneurial activities. Capital constraints did not deter the innovators. They often started out with only limited amounts of money borrowed from their relatives.

Not unlike the early entrepreneurs in the rise of capitalism in the West, those who started up new firms in the still-stigmatized and semilegal private sector of the Yangzi delta were also typically from simple trader and artisan backgrounds. These rural entrepreneurs, who were traditionally left outside China's central labor allocation system and also the social security system providing housing, health care, and retirement benefits for urban workers, did not mind either the low social status or the widespread risk of discrimination.

Ying Jinhui, for example, was a miner near Yongkang who started a sideline business making grinding stones used to sharpen butcher knives. His son

Weizhong followed his father in both occupations, eventually becoming an itinerant peddler traveling outside Yongkang to distant provinces to sell the knife sharpeners. A customer he met wanted to buy butcher knives from him. So Weizhong bought some in Yongkang, a center of traditional handicraft industry, and sold them in Harbin. He realized when shopping for the butcher knives that it was not difficult to make them. By apprenticing himself without pay to a knife-maker, he learned in two months how to do this. After establishing himself in the domestic market as a manufacturer of butcher knives, he bought more used equipment and began to manufacture for the much larger export market. In reflecting on his experience as a major manufacturer of high-end professional knives, which he currently exports to Germany and Japan, Weizhong attributes his success to a single-minded focus on producing high-quality products competitively. When he was growing up in Yongkang, he and his classmates always knew that in order to survive, they would have to work very hard. "When I started up my business, I didn't really think that much. My brothers lent me money to start up my business, and I just worked hard to be competitive by making high-quality professional knives."[25]

Also of rural origin is Wu Liping, who founded a high-technology design and manufacturing firm specializing in automated packaging equipment. His Joyea Packaging plant has recently begun to manufacture for international corporate clients, who travel to China to order custom-built equipment from him. Born in 1963 in a village and graduating from high school in 1979, the year after the start of China's ambitious economic reforms, Wu found his first job as a worker in a state-owned machinery factory, and earned money after work picking up discarded material and nails from the factory to sell on the recycling market. On a train trip, he helped another passenger with his luggage, and they talked. A few days later that man called and offered him a job at his factory, which manufactured glassware for laboratories. Wu worked there for three years and was promoted to deputy director. But he decided to go into business for himself—even though he was only twenty years old—and in 1983 he started his own factory to manufacture specialty glassware for industrial laboratories. In 1989, however, he closed the factory because it was not profitable. He wanted to move on to something else, but did not yet have a specific project in mind. That he eventually went into packaging was serendipitous. He learned from a friend, an engineer in a state-owned enterprise, about the challenges of packaging technologies. Then a speech by Deng Xiaoping on the importance of science and technology for China's future strengthened his ideas of venturing into high-tech production. In 1992 Wu launched a new business with his friend serving as his chief engineer. His aim was to automate a production process in which workers had been using their hands to package detergent whose enzymes harmed their skin. He licensed his first technology from a local government research institute, but it soon became apparent that the technology was flawed and not appropriate for detergent packaging. After only four years of production, Wu's business went bankrupt. He and his wife and child moved back to his village where they had a small plot of land. There they lived on his remaining savings and farmed the land. At night, Wu studied the old design drawings to improve the technology for a restart. He had learned from experience two crucial requirements in light of the typically low profit margin of detergents: packaging prices had to be low and the measurement precision for the content had to be high. After six years he managed to refine the technology to build his first automated machine fitting the specific needs of packaging detergent. Now his design and manufacturing plant located east of the city of Nanjing wins approval for about twenty patents a year, and has a large domestic market in China for custom-built packaging equipment used in a variety of product lines, such as powdered milk, detergent, sugar, and candy.[26]

Our Yangzi delta survey confirms that those who ventured into the private enterprise sector of the manufacturing economy came from modest to marginalized social backgrounds. The entrepreneurial movement was fueled neither by the technocratic elite of skilled engineers from state-owned companies nor by the country's political and administrative elite. Only 11 percent of the company founders have previously worked in leading positions as managers of state-owned enterprises—and among the older firms established before 1990, only 7 percent. Also there are relatively few former administrative or political cadres among the founders in our sample. Overall, only 5 percent indicate that they had a cadre position in government office before founding their firm, and among the older firms, none of the founders ever held a cadre position.

Although entrepreneurship is no longer exclusively a rural affair, rural founders are still prominent in the overall picture, with 53 percent of our respondents stemming from rural, and often farming, backgrounds. With the increasing legitimacy and social status of private enterprise, however, their relative number is continuously declining. Among the firms in our survey founded since 2003, the share of rural entrepreneurs is already down to 46 percent. The growing participation of urban residents evidenced there is in line with national trends.

Nonetheless, the majority of founders still come from modest backgrounds. In our 2009 survey, a significant number (41 percent) indicate that their parents had either no formal education or only primary education. Only a small minority (10 percent) had at least one parent with some college education. Also the parental profession rarely suggests particular advantages or an entrepreneurial or managerial predisposition. Only 3 percent of the founders have a father who managed a public firm. Only 7 percent indicate that their parents owned a private business. This includes small-scale household production and petty trading. The majority of business founders come from families where the household head was an ordinary worker (35 percent), farmer (23 percent), or technician (16 percent).

In spite of the rather modest parental background, most of the founders have relatively high human capital, significantly exceeding general education levels. Entrepreneurs in our sample have received on average 12.4 years of education, whereas general educational attainment reaches on average only 9.3 years in Shanghai, 7.5 years in Zhejiang, and 7.6 years in Jiangsu.[27] Thirty-five percent have completed vocational schools after graduation from senior high school, 25 percent have a junior college degree, and 15 percent received a full four-year undergraduate education. Only 22 percent have only primary or junior high school education. As would be expected, urban entrepreneurs are slightly better educated (with on average two more years of schooling than rural founders). About a third of the entrepreneurs received some form of specialized professional training either before or during their entrepreneurial activities. Among these, thirty-five entrepreneurs have earned a regular MBA degree; others attended education programs offered by local business schools to earn an executive MBA degree or attended part-time courses in public administration. Overall, the more recently the firm was founded, the higher the average years of education of the CEO. This reflects not only a general increase in average educational attainment but also growing legitimacy of the private enterprise economy, which by now also attracts talented and highly skilled university graduates from urban backgrounds, a group initially interested only in state- and foreign-invested enterprise employment.

Are Entrepreneurs Especially Risk Tolerant?

"Uncertainty must be taken in a sense radically distinct from the familiar notion of risk, from which it has never been properly separated," Frank Knight argued.

"The essential fact is that 'risk' means in some cases a quantity susceptible of measurement, while at other times it is something distinctly not of this character"—that is, it is not calculable.[28] Such are most of the uncertainties that entrepreneurs face. Knight describes, for instance, a type of investment decision that entrepreneurs confront on a regular basis: "A manufacturer is considering the advisability of making a large commitment in increasing the capacity of his works. He 'figures' more or less on the proposition, taking account as well as possible of the various factors more or less susceptible of measurement, but the final result is an 'estimate' of the probable outcome of any proposed course of action."[29] It is this unpredictability of future possibilities and presently unknown outcomes that especially challenges the decision maker. This has led to the common assumption that entrepreneurs may differ from ordinary people in their capacity for risk taking and robust economic action despite the unpredictability.

In China's transition economy, entrepreneurial uncertainties are commonly even larger than usual. Not only are there the standard market unknowns but also uncertainties connected with the state, which has an interest in protecting government-owned firms from the competitive pressures of an expanding market economy. For entrepreneurs, this heightens uncertainty, in part because rules and regulations are unevenly and often arbitrarily enforced by government, thereby increasing the scope of unknown outcomes not subject to calculation of measurable risks.

The experience of Zhu Jinhong vividly exemplifies entrepreneurial action despite Knightian uncertainty in launching a new business. Zhu started a firm in 1995 to produce aluminum coffee makers. He had been selling motorcycles for the supply and marketing cooperative of his village in a remote southwestern mountainous county of Zhejiang Province when he happened to meet an Italian businessman named Rosa at the Guangdong trade fair. Conversation about tea drinking in China led Rosa to talk about coffee drinking in Italy. At the time, it was part of Zhu's job to be on the lookout for new business ventures. He had already considered manufacturing motorcycles, but had decided this was too expensive and complex. However, the village cooperative had a thriving business in recycled scrap aluminum, which Zhu realized is the raw material needed to make stovetop coffee makers. An idea for a new business venture came in a flash when Zhu reasoned that though Chinese typically drink tea, there might be a big market in China for coffee as Chinese consumers become more interested in Western tastes. Experimenting with making molds to see if he could indeed imitate an Italian stovetop model, Zhu realized that it would be relatively easy to manufacture the coffee maker, and with the village's recycled scrap aluminum business he had an ample supply of cheap aluminum. Excitedly, he arranged to meet again with Rosa, along with an interpreter. At this meeting, Rosa placed an impromptu verbal order for 720 coffee makers as a gesture of enthusiasm. Zhu returned to his village to begin production. Though he did not have a written contract, he reasoned that even if Rosa was not serious about his order, he could still try to sell the coffee makers in China for a profit. After this first order, which was successfully completed, Zhu invested his personal savings of ¥1.58 million accumulated over the years from commissions earned selling motorcycles to construct a new plant. Uncertainties pervaded each step of his decision making; notwithstanding, by 2008, Zhu had built his business into the next-largest stovetop coffee maker in the world, second only to an Italian manufacturer. His firm holds eighty-five design patents, four of them in Europe. At the time of the interview, Zhu had entered into a joint venture with an Italian firm to manufacture coffee makers at a new automated plant that would triple his production and allow him to distribute his products under his own brand name in Europe. His Italian joint venture partner had sent a middle-level manager to live in the rural town where Zhu had built his firm to plan the marketing of the new brand.[30]

Clearly, Zhu had good judgment and intuition, which helped him to successfully deal with a highly uncertain situation and even to build up a firm operating globally. Similar accounts are plentiful in the Yangzi delta, where thousands of start-up entrepreneurs have earned a fortune. But to what extent are Zhu and the likes different from ordinary people? Are entrepreneurs indeed a different breed of economic actors with greater uncertainty tolerance, as many scholars following Knight's work hypothesized?[31]

We have approached this question with a standard experimental design capturing the level of uncertainty aversion, following the classical study by Ellsberg.[32] Participants in the experiment were asked to make a choice between two options. Those who choose option A receive a guaranteed amount of money (between ¥360 and ¥90). Option B provides the chance to play a lottery, where the participant receives either a higher payoff (¥580) or a much lower payoff (¥15). The probabilities of receiving a high payoff or a low payoff are unknown and are only *ex post* determined through a random process. Each player makes ten individual choices between A and B, while the amount offered under option A decreases, so that rational players will at some point find the lottery more attractive than the safe payoff. The earlier the player prefers to play the lottery with uncertain probabilities, the higher the revealed uncertainty tolerance. With its maximum payoff of ¥580 ($92), the experiment works with a credible reward. As the experiment can be conducted within twenty minutes, the maximum payoff yields a competitive hourly wage rate even for highly salaried professionals and entrepreneurs.

In the Yangzi delta survey, 523 of the 700 entrepreneurs interviewed were their firm's founders. We compare their choices in the experiment with those of a control group of 200 randomly sampled people from three of the survey cities. If pursuing the entrepreneurial path actually depended on a higher tolerance for uncertainty, there should be a significant difference in choices in this experiment between entrepreneurs and the control group. However, there is no statistically significant difference regarding the switching point from safe payoff to a lottery with uncertain outcomes. The mean value for entrepreneurs is 6.25, and the mean value of the control group is 6.10. The average participant in both groups thus chooses to play a lottery with un-known probabilities of a high payoff of ¥580 and low payoff of ¥15, when the alternative (guaranteed) payment is about ¥210. This similarity sheds doubts on the view that entrepreneurs may simply represent a special breed of people with a higher tolerance of uncertainties than other people in the region, and suggests that it is indeed appropriate to shift focus from individual attributes and behavioral traits to social mechanisms and structures.

Norms of Cooperation

By the end of the Maoist era of state socialism, private firms had become vir-tually extinct, and market exchange survived only in black-market trading and semilegal and illegal household production of agricultural goods and handicrafts for a constricted rural informal economy. In 1980, already several years into China's ambitious economic reform, only 0.02 percent of national industrial output came from individual household firms, whereas 78 percent came from state-owned enterprises.[33] In the manufacturing sector of the na-tional economy, planning authorities administered and controlled supplies of raw materials, intermediary products, capital investment, and labor and passed down production plans reflecting national development goals rather than consumer demands and tastes. This was most clearly evidenced by the strong emphasis on heavy industrial production and the neglect of consumer products and services.[34] In this tightly organized system, the lack of consumer orientation and the lack of market pressure shaped the development of key managerial capabilities. Priority was given to fulfillment of production quotas, management of company relations with responsible planning authorities, and bargaining for centrally allocated resources. In contrast, managerial activities such as the identification of future target markets, product innovation, marketing, and quality control played a negligible role, as production and company sales did not depend on good performance or the threat of economic failure and bankruptcy. Although collectively owned companies enjoyed greater degrees of freedom when it came to the organization and marketing, management of these companies suffered from similar problems. Without the risk of bankruptcy and firm closure, incentives for an efficient use of resources were weak and consumer orientation virtually absent.

With market liberalization and the gradual shift from a producer society to a consumer society, the types of managerial competencies that had suited the state-owned, centrally planned production and distribution system were increasingly devalued. They did not pose advantages for entrepreneurship outside that arena. Skills that had been crucial in a system of central allocation, fixed prices, and economic shortage gradually lost their applicability as price liberalization and free markets forced producers to respond to shifting consumer demands and tastes in a timely manner. Not surprisingly, former managers of state-owned companies or large-scale urban collectives—the old technocratic elite—were not among the early entrepreneurs who started up private manufacturing firms. These pioneers of the private enterprise economy came from outside the socialist production system. Rural areas in particular, neglected over decades by national industrialization and investment policies, saw a rapid revival of market activities, along with decoupling from socialist forms of production. Private commercial activity in villages and townships expanded beyond transactions involving agricultural goods and traditional handicrafts to light manufacture in response to long-neglected consumer needs for goods such as textiles and shoes, or household equipment ranging from simple kitchenware to furnishings.

Historically, a commercial culture had flourished in the Yangzi delta since the fourteenth century. This had been interrupted by the people's commune system for a brief two decades. In the early years of economic reform, market transactions could build on the revival of prerevolutionary commercial practices and institutions, embedded in living memories and local commercial tradition. The cultural factors underlying this tradition derive from

Neo-Confucian ethics, the common cultural basis of East Asian economic development.[35] But a straight-line restoration of traditional commercial practices and institutions did not address adequately the problems faced by private commercial and manufacturing firms.

The most immediate problems centered on property rights in a transition economy that lacked safeguards from predatory expropriation of private assets, not only by politicians but also by neighbors and trading partners. Many private businesses leased productive assets from village and township governments, making them vulnerable to breach of lease agreements and contracts, especially *ex post* demands for additional rents when the business proved to be a profitable venture. Conflicts between economic actors over contracts were frequent, given the absence of established business practices, norms, and reliable legal recourse through litigation. Routine business transactions involving transfer of assets, leases, sales, and compensation for property surrendered to local government were highly problematic for private firms. As an early entrepreneur recalled, "In the very beginning stage of reform and opening up, the economic order was very chaotic, and people were not too trustworthy. Many people used illegal means and outright cheating to make money, rather than hard work and sound business practice. Because many firms at that time did not have much in the way of assets, litigation was useless. Even if there were a legal ruling against the firm, the owner usually ran away with cash in their pockets, and there would be no bank accounts to trace their whereabouts."[36]

When neither a company law nor a contract law was in place to structure and effectively safeguard economic transactions between private actors, it was through a gradual learning process that mutually beneficial business norms developed. Similar trial-and-error processes helped businessmen identify appropriate organizational forms and learn the practical skills necessary to establish and run a private business. These norms and methods then diffused rapidly through mimicking within local and regional business communities. Several mutually reinforcing mechanisms propelled the rapid development of a social movement dynamic in the Yangzi delta region: social learning, on-the-job training, and mutual assistance and cooperation.

Social Learning

Social learning plays an important role when it comes to the spread of local business models and norms. Before founding their first business, most entrepreneurs go through an intensive observation period. Careful study of successful local role models provides important insights on how to set up and run a private business. Asked about the source of inspiration complementing the owner's own ideas on how to run a firm, "mimicking of domestic role models" was most often referred to in our 2006 survey (by 45 percent of respondents). Also business failures and bankruptcies of private firms provide lessons how *not* to behave, how to avoid failure. About 30 percent of the respondents believe that failures of other firms are informative as regards developing a good business model. One businessman operating a small packaging company in Hangzhou explains that he had a particular interest in studying firms that failed because these cases seemed to provide more valuable lessons for his own firm's development.[37] Such success and failure analysis includes a careful review of the specific business transactions that may have invited undue business risks. What contracts are needed to safeguard business transactions? How does one select reliable business partners? How does one develop sustainable mutually beneficial partnerships? And how does one prevent cheating? These are the questions commonly discussed within business communities.

Often friends, former classmates, coworkers, and relatives serve as role models that provide both the initial motivation and information on how to start up a business. Their successful decoupling from established professional routes and career paths motivates followers to take a similar risk and to mimic their strategies. When asked to reflect on their founding decision, most entrepreneurs refer to the successful business start-up of a friend or classmate as a source of inspiration and motivation. "If they can do it, I can do it" is a recurring notion. Entrepreneurs in our survey thought they had similar qualifications and knowledge as others who had already successfully founded their own business. One entrepreneur in Nanjing summarizes how he started an import/export business: "I had that friend, who used to work in that firm. His English was not very good but he had the courage to approach clients and talk to them about goods and prices. Then he suddenly had his own business and was doing pretty well. I thought if he could do it, I could too."[38] In our 2009 survey, 57 percent of the founders indicate that someone else's founding experience directly affected their own decision to also establish a firm, with the highest averages in Zhejiang Province (70 percent in Ningbo) and lowest in Shanghai (37 percent).

Rapid wealth accumulation, most visible in the purchase of new cars, apartments, or houses, provides a strong motivational force to follow other market entrants. Two-thirds of the founders interviewed in our 2009 survey confirm that their founding decision was mainly motivated by their search for higher income and wealth creation. Material incentives play a powerful role, even more so in the early generation of founders, who had experienced long periods of poverty under state socialist rule. The hope for a better life is a strong driver and fuels an endless stream of would-be entrepreneurs. The owner of a Hangzhou-based advertising company recalls that the impressive wealth accumulation of his friend attracted him into business. Increasing success of private entrepreneurs and growing media coverage of these success stories eventually also convinced his parents to support his own business plans.[39]

Naturally this process of social learning and mimicking accelerates as more actors enter the market, providing still more learning opportunities for aspiring entrepreneurs. In turn, with a growing number of private firms entering the previously state-dominated manufacturing sector, survival chances increase, as diffusion of mutually accepted norms helps to reduce risks and costs stemming from missing formal institutions and political discrimination. The ensuing social movement dynamic of business founding then extends beyond bilateral relations between *pioneer* and *follower*. Private business becomes part of the local business culture, increasingly attracting new market entrants. One entrepreneur running a large company producing sewage systems comments on his own decision to migrate to Zhejiang Province: "It struck me that Zhejiang people are shrewd and smart. The private firms were very successful. They are the same people as I, but they did things much better than my hometown's people. People in my hometown would not start their own firms. They would play mahjong after the harvest season, or go out to work in the cities. They never would start their own business. One's surrounding is important. When I came to Zhejiang, I learned from the surrounding. . . . After one year, I started a business with two local partners."[40] In a similar vein, a manufacturer of professional meat grinders in Nantong recalls that a visit to neighboring Zhejiang Province inspired him to get started on his own entrepreneurial venture. "When I worked for a TVE, this firm had business with these Zhejiang firms. On a business trip there, what impressed me . . . was the spirit; they can endure, eat hardship. The good environment was in sharp contrast with my township village enterprise, with its spirit of idleness."[41] Inspired, he returned to his hometown and started his own private firm. Years later, this Jiangsu entrepreneur recalls that "the whole social atmosphere changed" in his province as the entrepreneurial spirit spread there, fueling the wholesale privatization of township and village enterprises and founding of new firms.

Seed Firms and Learning on the Job

The development of key entrepreneurial capabilities and the internalization of local business norms do not rely just on observation. Learning on the job is an important component of the informal economic institutions preparing entrepreneurs for their first business founding. Very few businessmen register their first private firm without any prior experience as wage-workers. Those who start a business right after leaving school typically start with an individual household firm, which helps them to accumulate some business experience and capital. These start-up attempts are rarely successful, however. Those who tried recall serious problems, as they did not sufficiently understand the market, lacked social capital, and eventually suffered repeat losses from trade with unreliable business partners. Many of them give up on the start-up attempt and return to wage labor. One individual who had failed in his initial entrepreneurial activities and then was forced to temporarily return to wage labor recalls: "Within just one year and a half [as an employee], I learned a lot, and my understanding of business totally changed."[42] Most importantly, he learned about the value of human capital, company organization, branding, and quality control. It was this training that eventually helped him to put all his previous experience in perspective and prepare his next founding attempt, which was successful.

The great majority of founders accumulate substantial professional experience as wage earners before starting up their own company. After graduating in 1995 from Fudan University, Yang Xusun found a job in a security firm where he was assigned to do research on local firms preparing for an initial public offering (IPO) in the Shanghai stock exchange. In this job, he closely followed a large portfolio of private firms that rode the long wave of rapid economic growth in the Yangzi delta. He realized that many of the entrepreneurs who founded these firms lacked the capacity for strategic planning to build a management that could sustain their firm's growth rate. Their strength instead was in initially sensing the opportunity for profit (often mimicking others making the start-up move) and enjoying the early phase of rapid growth. With several other partners who like him graduated from universities in the mid-1990s, Yang decided to start a financial service firm specializing in helping promising private firms to make the strategic management changes required for an IPO on the Shanghai stock exchange. Their first IPO, a domestic retail chain, was an enormous success. In 2008, Yang's private equity firm had just moved into an office complex in a newly completed commercial building in Shanghai. Like other young financial service professionals of his generation, Yang Xusun, who was dressed in business casuals at the interview, drives a luxury car and lives in a fashionable residential district of Shanghai.[43]

On-the-job training provides an opportunity to acquire requisite technical knowledge and business experience. Typically, those who start their own firms have accumulated about eight years of professional experience in a couple of positions held prior to the business founding—somewhat less (seven years on average) if this wage employment was in private companies, and somewhat longer (nine years on average) if it was not. As wage labor in private companies used to be less prestigious than employment in the public sector, workers in private companies face lower opportunity costs and may therefore have a greater propensity to become capitalists themselves. Moreover, being socially already integrated into the newly emerging private sector, these entrepreneurs may perceive starting their own business to be less risky and more profitable, as they have already learned and internalized the norms and tools necessary to run a private company.

Prior to their business founding, most entrepreneurs have worked in the same sector, often even in the same product or market niche. In this way, they have not only learned the industry-specific business norms but also developed a valuable network of potential clients and suppliers. They know who is trustworthy and enjoys a good local reputation; they are connected with the informal channels of information; and they are familiar with local government regulations. Li Sui, the entrepreneur of Shanghai Edunburgh Elevator Company, the largest domestic manufacturer of elevators in China, found his first job in an American elevator firm in Shanghai, where he learned about elevator control panels while he was a student in a master's program at Jiaotong University studying textiles. After he completed his degree, he was offered a software job in Japan, but he decided to stay with the elevator firm as vice-director of research and development. Within a year he developed a new automated elevator control panel, but then the firm closed its automation department following an unexpected personnel change. Li then decided to go into business for himself using his elevator control panel design. He borrowed ¥4,000 in 1995 for his initial start-up capital, and together with several retired professors who had taught him at Jiaotong University and no paid employees, he worked on the idea of manufacturing elevators. Two years later he assembled what he needed to start up the firm, and with ¥500,000, he founded Edunburgh Elevator. Li remarked that despite the building boom in Shanghai and elsewhere in China, starting a new elevator company was especially challenging. Why would anyone buy from a small company that had no factory? In his view he had two advantages. He knew the technology well, and he won the confidence of his customers by paying close attention to what they wanted. By 2008, Li's company had developed into a high-technology firm competing effectively in China's booming domestic elevator market, which previously was dominated by multinationals like Otis and Mitsubishi. The firm was preparing for its IPO in the Shanghai stock exchange.[44]

Larger private companies often become the seed firms for local business start-ups in the rapidly growing market for consumer products. One Hangzhou-based entrepreneur trading computers and components reports:

> In our sector it is typical that many firms are spin-offs from a single company. We often joke that the original firm is like a university, chewing out graduates to become bosses. My original mother company has now generated seven or eight spin-off companies like mine. . . . Zhejiang people have a strong desire to become bosses. But just desire is not enough. That is why among our employees there are few Wenzhou people. They would generally set up their own firms a few years after working in the firm. The environment is important, that is an environment that supports learning and getting financing. Zhejiang has a good foundation for this. Many people who want to start up their firms cannot set up their own firms because they do not have money. They have to start by working for other people.[45]

When the manufacturer of professional meat grinders started his company in Nantong, he was the first in his county. But when his success was noticed, others moved quickly into the new niche. Now, there are five other producers in the same district; some are his former workers.[46]

According to a survey of 251 entrepreneurs in Shanghai in the early 1990s, 61 percent had started their companies in sectors where they had some prior professional experience. In contrast, only 19 percent indicated that their founding decision was primarily based on strong market demand.[47] Over time, prior professional experience has remained a decisive factor influencing the industry choice of start-up entrepreneurs. Overall, 66 percent of the firm-founders in our 2006 survey had previously worked in the same sector, more so in Shanghai (78 percent) and less so in Jiangsu Province (43 to 57 percent). The majority of these founders held positions in management (59 percent) or were employed as enterprise director in small businesses (19 percent). Both positions provide crucial insights into internal management and, equally important, experience in the firm's external relations with competitors, suppliers, customers, and local government. Even among those founders who are switching industries, the majority have experience in management (55 percent). This suggests that knowing how to run a company currently seems to be a more important capability than knowing the product. Exceptions are highly innovative companies in mechanical engineering, pharmaceuticals, and electronics. In these sectors, founders with a technical background naturally play a somewhat larger role.

Mutual Assistance and Cooperation

Most entrepreneurs rank the development of networks of mutual assistance and cooperation among the most important factors helping them start up their business. Not only do friends and relatives help with financing, but often friends who have successfully founded their own business play a prominent role in helping the start-up in other ways.

Learning how others detect and realize market opportunities is an essential lesson that relies on ongoing social relationships and information exchange between market players. The owner of a Wenzhou-based electronics company underscores the benefits of consulting with friends in order to assess whether business strategies seem feasible. Friends with prior business experience help with administrative procedures, assist in choosing a suitable factory site, and give advice on a promising product portfolio.[48] A textile producer in Wenzhou recalls that she has helped many of her friends start up firms in her own sector. She provided credit, but also helped set up their commercial operations.[49] Many start-up entrepreneurs also secure their first customers through friends and acquaintances. More than 38 percent of the interviewees in our 2006 survey found their first customers through personal recommendations, three fourths of which were made by a friend.

In established businesses, entrepreneurs have cultivated a reciprocal network in which mutual assistance is an embedded aspect of long-standing business friendships. In China's highly volatile environment, where new local government regulations and policies and the dynamics of markets are hard to predict, informal cooperation and consultation within networks of business friends is a business norm throughout the delta region. As a young start-up entrepreneur in Hangzhou points out: "It is impossible to rely just on yourself. You need to get out and discuss your ideas."[50] When entrepreneurs in our 2009 survey were asked whether they believe that most of their business acquaintances would provide business advice to others, and to indicate on a scale of 1 to 7 how strong this expectation is, the mean value reached 4.8— very slightly higher in Zhejiang Province (4.9) and slightly lower in Jiangsu Province (4.6). The belief that one is oneself expected to provide business advice to others scores comparably (4.8).

Entrepreneurs help each other when it comes to learning about and implementing new production technologies (see Chapter 8). An innovative businessman in Ningbo who constantly works on expanding and improving his product portfolio reports that his business friends allow him to use their technically more advanced equipment for the development of new products.[51] Others confirm that collaboration and help with technical problems are part of a reliable business friendship. On the question of whether most of their business acquaintances would help another out with machinery or technology in case of a major technical problem, particularly in cases where a contract might otherwise be lost, the average score in our 2009 survey was 4.9 on a scale of 1 to 7, with Zhejiang Province (5.0) and Shanghai (5.2) again slightly higher, and Jiangsu Province (4.6) slightly lower. On average, the belief that one is oneself expected to provide such help to a business friend was comparable (4.9).

Introduction to reliable customers and suppliers is also common among business acquaintances. It is part of the general protocol to pass along orders, if temporary capacity problems or particular product specifications do not allow one to fulfill a customer request. Sometimes the referral is financially rewarded; the Wenzhou-based textile producer, for instance, expects her business friends to pay in return a commission of 10 percent of the contract value.[52] Others see this as a mutual favor, where accounts probably balance out over time. In our 2009 survey, the expectation that most business acquaintances pass along orders that they cannot take themselves reached a mean value of 4.8 on a scale of 1 to 7. Again cooperative norms are slightly more pronounced in Shanghai (4.9) and Zhejiang Province (4.9) and slightly less so in Jiangsu Province (4.6). The belief that one is oneself expected to pass along such orders to business acquaintances reaches the same average score of 4.9.

Although cooperative relations among private firms are often complex, and in cases of opportunism expose the individual entrepreneur to the risk of

losing business secrets and market position, they require relatively little formal organization and monitoring. Typically these favors are exchanged within
a circle of friends, often connected through long-term business relations. Receiving help from other entrepreneurs depends on one's reputation, as a machinery producer in Wenzhou emphasizes: "Reputation is like a code of conduct in Wenzhou. Good reputation is needed if you want help from others; if
you have good reputation, people will help you if you have problems."[53] There
is more to maintaining good reputation than just prompt repayment of informal loans, timely delivery of the contracted quality product, and reliable customer service, however. An unwritten rule in business networks is the commitment not to poach on a friend's business and lure away skilled employees
or customers. As a Ningbo-based entrepreneur observed, "There are not many
norms you have to follow, but you should *not compete* with your close business
friends."[54] This explains why entrepreneurs are often willing to help friends
to start up a new firm in their own sector. If the product is not sufficiently
differentiated, it is commonly understood that the protégé will stay clear of
his mentor's business and find a market niche in another locality or serve as a
subcontractor supplying inputs to the mentor's firm. "If someone wants to start
a business, they would do it anyway," he notes. "So it is better to help them, as
a friend will not try to get your customers."

The norm not to compete directly enjoys broad acceptance in the Yangzi
delta. Almost half of the entrepreneurs interviewed in our 2009 survey said
that they would certainly inform others if a business friend began to target
their customers, and two-thirds of them were sure that other members of the
business community would sanction such behavior, indicating a strong sense
of fairness in market competition when it comes to the local economy. Of
course it is generally accepted that customers may switch to other producers.
Almost all entrepreneurs have a strong sense of competition, and generally
regard it as beneficial, a driver of improved company performance. However,
there are moral standards that most entrepreneurs honor. Gossiping or spreading negative rumors or making other negative remarks to lure customers away
from competitors, for instance, is not acceptable. A textile manufacturer in
Nantong illustrates:

> I used to run a store selling interior decoration material. Some competitors
> approached my clients and told them that they bought the product for too
> high a price. I consider this immoral competition because the clients had
> already bought my product. Once a customer has made a purchase you

ought not to go there and try to undo the deal. I went to my competitor's house and explained that he shouldn't have acted this way. My store was the number one home furnishing firm here. After I approached my competitor, this type of unfair competition stopped. So anytime this type of behavior occurs, I just go to the offender, and explain. If they don't do it to us, we won't do it to them.[55]

The "no-competition rule" applied within these personal networks works only because the new capitalists of the Yangzi delta do not have merely a local outlook. Close local collaboration is mutually beneficial because the majority of entrepreneurs target the growing external markets outside the borders of their municipalities. Many are involved in cross-provincial trade and international markets (see Chapter 6). This general business outlook was most clearly expressed by a ball-bearing manufacturer in Ningbo.[56] To him, close cooperation with his competitors, even on technical issues, is a sensible strategy, as nobody in his community is really thinking about the local market. Instead, he interprets competition as a race between the producers in his own township against the "rest of the world." Still, given the intensely competitive nature of the domestic market, there are reasons for entrepreneurs to be wary of cooperation with their local rivals. While this entrepreneur emphasizes the need for cooperation, no doubt others are careful to closely monitor their rivals and to keep their core technology at a safe distance.

The great importance attached to local norms of cooperation and long-standing networks of mutual assistance is reflected by the localism of business founding. In our 2006 survey, about 93 percent of founders indicated that they started up their firm in their home province, 87 percent of them even in their city of birth. Many of these entrepreneurs have actually accumulated some professional experience elsewhere, for instance as traveling salesmen. That they still decide to return to their home community underscores the significance of these local norms and networks necessary to start up businesses in China's bottom-up capitalism. Familiarity with local norms and business communities often trumps other location factors, as interpersonal cooperation cushions the risks associated with decoupling from established forms of production outside the public sector. Even those who have already successfully started a firm are cautious when it comes to the question of relocating their business. Many fear that transferring to a new business environment would be too costly for their company.

Local clustering of firms in the same or a related market niche (see Chapter 6) is one visible consequence of the intense mimicking, self-learning, and mutual cooperation that have enabled and advanced a highly localized social movement dynamic in the Yangzi delta. Often neighborhoods or even townships focus on just a few products such as ball-bearings or electric plugs, dominating the local industrial landscape. Whole streets are lined with companies making similar or even identical items. Concomitantly, mimicking of specialty production has led to the spread of many small and medium-size companies, contributing to artificially low concentration ratios in China's consumer industry. Even at the peak of the global economic crisis, Zhejiang Province witnessed the founding of 45,000 new private firms just within the first half of the year 2009. This equals 252 newly registered private enterprises per day.[57]

Financing the Firm

Difficulty in acquiring start-up capital is a common problem in the founding of private firms. Even in established market economies with highly diversified and market-oriented financial institutions, small-scale start-up companies face severe problems in securing bank loans. In America, most start-up firms in the small business sector are not financed by loans from banks: "Small new enterprises are financed primarily by owners, their relatives and friends, and by suppliers of materials and equipment. Banking institutions extend only slight accommodations to small new businesses."[58] Uncertainty about the business plan, market risks, and the limited business experience of the founder all are contributing factors in the denial of loans from banks.

In China, with the lack of formal banking institutions open to private firm lending, such problems are exacerbated. There is thus an emphatic need for bottom-up solutions and for norms to regulate lending agreements. In the Yangzi delta region, nearly all entrepreneurs start up firms without any funding from banks and instead rely on self-accumulated savings and personal loans from friends and relatives. Mutual lending agreements and informal credit markets persist far beyond the initial founding stage.

Overall, the lending policy and practices of China's formal financial institutions were designed to deter, if not entirely block, the rise of the private enterprise economy. The rules and regulatory structure of China's state-owned banks reflect the government's objectives in initiating economic reforms in

1978, which were to promote the development of state-owned and collec-tive enterprises through increased reliance on market mechanisms. Financial regulations have long reinforced the bias against private firms by state-owned banks.[59] In spite of the market entry of foreign-invested and private domestic banks, the national credit market has remained state-controlled, with more than 60 percent of lending and savings administered by state-owned banks.[60] Moreover, local government plays an important role in lending decisions, channeling capital into favored public enterprises, especially those that fall within the guidelines of the central government's industrial policy.[61]

Although the central government has in the last decade enacted rules favorable to the private sector, such as the 2002 Law on Promotion of Small and Medium-sized Enterprises that explicitly called for the provision of local financial support and service systems, such legislative measures have yet to be credibly enforced.[62] Many entrepreneurs have not even heard about the law, or are unaware of the local government bureau responsible for its implementation. Those who actually seek support are often turned down. Partly due to the lack of national implementation guidelines and partly due to budgetary constraints, local politicians continue to favor large state-owned enterprises and state-controlled corporations. Private firms are still virtually excluded from direct support in the form of preferential access to low-interest loans. Within the state-controlled banking system, it is commonplace for even established medium and large-size private firms to be denied access to credit from commercial banks.

Despite the Yangzi delta region's thriving private enterprise economy, discrimination against private firms by the state-owned credit system remains pronounced. By the year 2000, in Zhejiang and Jiangsu Provinces, the share of loans to nonstate firms was only 5 percent of total loans issued by state-owned banks, of which local government-owned township and village enterprises received the lion's share.[63] Only 20 percent of our 2006 survey respondents had access to some form of commercial bank credit in the previous year. Also, credit allocation under China's huge 2008 stimulus program to fight the global economic recession was biased against private firms, which were unable to secure credit from banks. Instead, the stimulus money was channeled to state-owned enterprises and local government infrastructure projects.[64]

Chen Zengrong, the owner of a textile factory employing fifty workers in Zhejiang Province, was turned down five times before he secured credit from an alternative source through the online private business-to-business site Alibaba.com. Loan officers in the local branches of the China Construction Bank and the Agricultural Bank of China said they turned down the loan application because they didn't think the business had solid enough prospects. They cited a late credit card payment as evidence that Chen lacked "personal integrity."[65]

Not surprisingly, many private businessmen do not even consider applying for bank loans because the probability of getting one is so low. Also, they are apprehensive about the complicated and cumbersome application procedures and stringent collateral requirements, and well aware of corruption in the allocation of bank loans. For obtaining start-up capital, in particular, most do not think of applying for a bank loan as a viable option. With the formal banking sector virtually closed for small-scale loans to private start-up entrepreneurs, those in need of capital typically turn to informal channels.

Most entrepreneurs believe that first investing a small amount of capital accumulated from savings or obtained from informal personal loans is the most reliable strategy to start up a new firm. About two-thirds of the entrepreneurs who founded private businesses in the Yangzi delta relied entirely on savings accumulated through years of wage labor or earned as independent traders, often involving traveling between different provinces or regions to sell petty goods. Many join forces with friends or relatives to pool their savings and jointly found a firm. In total, 65 percent of the entrepreneurs interviewed in our 2006 survey indicate that they had one or two partners when they founded the firm. Upon success, partners often split up after several years, separating the original company into two or even more independent businesses.

Short-term credit from relatives and friends is the most important source of external capital during the founding stage of private firms.[66] Initially, an entrepreneur may borrow modest amounts of money from several such sources to found a small-scale business. Once the business develops and loans are repaid, former lenders may decide to follow the entrepreneurial route. They now turn into borrowers, and the former borrower will feel obliged to return the favor. With a growing number of established local businesses, the number of potential borrowers and lenders connected through close social networks increases, thereby propelling the bottom-up development of informal lending agreements. Most entrepreneurs emphasize that it would be no problem for them to organize small to medium-size loans from their business network within just a few days. Thus, the bottom-up social construction of informal finance develops in a self-reinforcing process of endogenous institutional change.

Those who cannot borrow from their business acquaintances, friends, or relatives may need to turn to rotating credit associations or underground banks to secure some of their start-up capital.[67] Others borrow money from their first clients to purchase production material for their first orders. Generally, access to these private sources of capital determines both the founding size and the technological level and equipment businesses start with. Often this is modest—a small workshop set up in the courtyard of the family home. Most private firms in our survey register a founding capital of less than ¥100,000 (around $15,000) and begin with a workforce of up to twenty employees.

Once the business is established and entrepreneurs have gained experience in managing a firm, they then can invest more in their firm from profits. Expanding the business and upgrading their equipment and plants with better technology are financed primarily through profits and internal savings. Founders of private firms emphasize that they rely on internal savings once their firm is established and profitable. Not only do entrepreneurs believe it is good business practice to avoid debt in this way, but continued reliance on personal loans from friends and relatives to finance company expansion is also viewed as not socially acceptable for firms with the means to accumulate their own investment capital.

In the Yangzi delta regional economy, it is commonplace for entrepreneurs to launch their first enterprise in the competitive low-end sector of manufacturing, and then reinvest accumulated profits to move up the product chain into more profitable lines of manufacture through innovative activity and investments in acquiring up-to-date industrial technology. The strategic goal of many entrepreneurs is to eventually establish a firm higher up in the product chain, and in a niche that offers better potential for growth. About 20 percent of these business founders develop into serial entrepreneurs, who use the first business to acquire initial business experience and to generate additional capital to invest in starting up a new firm. This mode of operation has enabled many entrepreneurs of modest social and economic background to develop sizeable business operations starting out from small business ventures.

A Ningbo entrepreneur, for example, began by manufacturing tools for the textile industry—in particular, equipment to repair imported textile machinery. But reading in *China Textile News* about the difficulties of rising trade frictions and labor costs facing the industry, he decided he needed to open up a second line of manufacturing in mechanical and electrical products. When we visited him in 2008, he had just opened a new factory building, a cavernous modern structure with two large workshops equipped with automated machine tools and lathes, which he was using to produce consumer products subcontracted to him while he was searching for a new product line of his own. He had financed this expansion and diversification through internal savings from his old textile firm.[68] Correspondingly, though in a very different sector, the eight partners of a financial software firm started out with capital from personal savings and borrowed from relatives and friends and with only three paid employees. Through continuing reinvestment of profits and the development of strategic partnerships with private investors, they grew their firm within just ten years to a stock-listed company, housed in a new glass-and-steel office building in Hangzhou's high-technology industrial park, with more than 800 employees and annual sales of more than ¥200 million.[69]

While entrepreneurs typically rely on internal savings to pay for significant improvements in their firms, the institution of informal lending nonetheless continues to play an important role in complementing internal savings in the private enterprise economy. The norm among business friends to provide short-term business loans in times of financial distress enables private firms to overcome temporary liquidity problems. Mutual financial assistance is an important aspect of business friendships in the Yangzi delta, adding value to ongoing social relationships in business circles. Asked to list their five most valuable business ties, 76 percent of the entrepreneurs interviewed in 2009 list their relationships with friends who can be relied on to provide personal loans in case of financial distress. It is in this sense that informal lending represents a crucial bottom-up strategy that helps entrepreneurs to bypass institutionalized barriers to obtaining financial capital from the banking system.

The CEO of a leading information technology (IT) firm in Hangzhou acknowledges:

> I do not think about banks for loans. Even to this day, I do not know how to borrow from banks. I borrow from friends. There are friends who ask to borrow from me. I lend to them. Maybe we are not qualified to borrow from banks. Anyway, we did not think about borrowing money from banks in the first place. In Hangzhou, there are about 2,000 IT firms. My company

ranks among the top ten in terms of sales volume. Of course many of the firms do borrow from banks. I have not looked into the matter. If we were to apply, probably we would get a loan from a bank. But there is no need for that now.[70]

The sheer volume of informal finance prompts the question how entrepreneurs and lenders secure their transactions.[71] The obvious problem is that informal finance is particularly vulnerable to opportunism and malfeasance. The lender, who most likely does not have the technical expertise to properly assess the quality of a business plan or the risk of a specific investment project, completes his side of the transaction in period t, while the debtor meets his obligations in a later period $t + n$. This not only involves the problem of asymmetric information but also gives rise to moral hazard and the potential for *ex post* opportunism. If the enterprise then fails, the lender may face an involuntary default, where part or the total amount of the loan and interest payment may be lost. In addition, lenders face a certain risk of voluntary default. Borrowers may strategically default if they value the current claim of the loan, including the prospect of accessing new loans in the future, lower than the expected benefit from defaulting. This situation typically occurs if borrowers do not intend to continue their business or if they plan to relocate, so that they do not expect to need credit from the same source in the future. In this case, breaking the lending agreement can be a rational choice. Lenders therefore face a critical challenge when they try to assess the underlying motivation of prospective borrowers. Naturally, the risk of strategic defaults is higher if the legal system does not effectively protect the lending agreements. Relatively high conflict resolution costs and weak chances for effective law enforcement can deter lawsuits if the value of the claim is relatively small.

China's businessmen secure informal lending agreements against both involuntary and strategic default through a set of mutually reinforcing mechanisms embedded in close-knit business communities. Broadly, screening of borrowers through social networks, shared interests, and the threat of both bilateral and multilateral sanctions jointly minimize the default risk to levels far below those in the formal banking sector.[72] Alternative formal private sources of credit like Alibaba.com use similar social mechanisms in online bundling arrangements of credit guarantors and public posting of incidents of defaults on loans.[73]

Relationship–Based Lending

Due to high risks inherent in informal lending agreements, informal loans typically build on a high level of trust between prospective lender and borrower. During the founding stage, when investment risks are highest, entrepreneurs seeking capital turn almost exclusively to close relatives and long-term acquaintances like former classmates, often for multiple small-scale loans. Within these close-knit groups, lenders may feel a strong social and moral pressure to meet loan requests.[74] Likewise, the borrower experiences corresponding pressure to meet his obligations. The borrower's subsequent efforts to amortize the loan are high. Often parents or siblings contribute substantial amounts of their lifetime savings, adding further pressure on the entrepreneur to succeed. And if the business venture fails, there is still a moral commitment to repay the loan.

Beyond the initial founding stage, however, many entrepreneurs avoid borrowing from relatives and close friends. This is particularly true when it comes to reinvestments, which, according to the business norm in the Yangzi delta, are expected to be financed through internal savings. The norm is that the owners of an established business ought not turn to relatives to borrow money to increase or secure their own personal wealth. It can only provoke resentment and censure to turn to people who themselves possess fewer assets to ask for a short-term loan. Even in the event of periodic short-term cash-flow problems, entrepreneurs are reluctant to rely on their relatives for additional loans. One businessman notes with some regret: "I went to relatives for money and will never borrow money again from relatives." One problem is that relatives often try to get involved in business and investment decisions. Also, family expectations of financial return often exceed the repayment of the loan, extending to informal property rights in the entrepreneurial project. Such high expectations of wealth creation for family members and fear of failure often exert too much pressure on the entrepreneur. Thus, despite the widespread use of informal lending in the Yangzi delta, most entrepreneurs and operators of private firms say they would actually prefer to borrow from commercial banks.

At this stage, entrepreneurs say that if they cannot generate the money from accumulated savings, they turn to their business relationships for loans to get them through seasonal or cyclical liquidity problems. It is often part of a long-term business relationship to mutually provide short-term credit, if cash-flow problems occur. Typically, borrower and lender are in a supplier or customer relationship and have maintained business over several years. Their interests are often closely aligned through multilateral relationships that extend beyond informal financial assistance. Borrowers and lenders commonly socialize with each other and even cooperate on business-related activities such as sharing strategic business information and the cost of technology development. Through various forms of long-term exchange, not only do the business friends develop a high level of personal trust, but lenders also typically have firsthand understanding of the economic situation and future prospects of the borrower's business. Moreover, through these ongoing multilateral business ties, there is usually much more at stake than the face value of the current loan.

Mutual Dependence between Lender and Borrower

The rapid diffusion and importance of informal lending as a reliable source of capital to finance start-ups underscore the role of bottom-up social construction of economic institutions in enabling the growth of the private enterprise economy. These start up loans are often made without a written contract or collateral. Often the deal is sealed just with a handshake. Even so, entrepreneurs are assiduous in complying with informal lending norms to repay loans on time, as performance on current transactions determines one's reputation and prospects for securing informal assistance in the future. Informal lending also creates expectations regarding reciprocity. Lenders can expect to borrow from their current debtors in the future, so that both sides have an active interest in abiding with the norms of commitment to oral agreements. As one entrepreneur notes, "You can only cheat once; how will you survive next time you need help?"[75] From the borrower's perspective, the cultivation of reliable lending relations is of crucial importance, since only the largest and most successful private firms can expect to have access to formal credit. Informal lending is therefore not a one-shot transaction but is expected to continue to play a role in future periods. This requires the entrepreneur to maintain a clean credit history. Only borrowers who have a reputation of amortizing their loans on time can expect to receive future financial assistance. Even companies that have no expansion plans need access to lending to be able to buffer short-term cash-flow problems in times of financial distress. Borrowers therefore have strong incentives to service their loans according to the loan agreement.

Lenders also benefit from decoupling from the formal banking sector. Depending on the current inflation rate, the fixed interest ceilings on deposits in state-owned banks often do not allow positive returns. With interest payments on informal business loans not below 10 percent, informal lending agreements generally provide an attractive alternative investment for lenders. Beyond the pure material incentive to divert savings from bank deposits into informal lending, lenders may also expect a return favor in the future. It is not only established businessmen who benefit from reliable credit partners for mutual lending. With the Yangzi delta region's atmosphere so strongly influenced by a social movement dynamic of private business founding, friends and relatives too may anticipate a reciprocal favor in the way of future help in starting up their own business.

Sometimes borrowers show their gratitude with small gifts and in-kind payments. When asked about how he and his friends lend money to each other, the owner of an information technology firm responded: "We just write a promissory note; no interest. It is considered a favor between friends. We give gifts as a way to say thank you, for instance a notebook computer or a digital camera. It is a way of expressing *ganqing* between friends. Sometimes there isn't even a note. A friend will just give me the money as a gesture of friendship."[76]

Thus the institutionalized barriers to formal credit from banks have the unintended consequence of locking borrowers *and* lenders into mutually beneficial lending relations, which facilitate economic survival outside the formal financial institutions and in turn attract a growing number of new participants into the informal lending sector.

Reputation as a Screening Device

In spite of the generally close interest alignment between borrower and lender, close monitoring of loan applicants is still crucial. Even if borrower and lender sign simple contracts specifying the total amount of the loan, interest rate, and payment scheme, lenders seldom rely on legal recourse, given the high cost of legal fees, unpredictable outcome, and enforcement costs of lawsuits. *Ex ante* screening of would-be borrowers is important, and information sharing within business communities provides an indispensable screening mechanism to identify reliable borrowers. Local business communities have a vital interest in exposing deviators and contract breach to protect their members against foreseeable losses. Through informal gossiping between business partners and regular social events or meetings of business associations, crucial information on opportunism and malfeasance spreads quickly beyond the immediate networks of an individual entrepreneur. As one respondent notes, "In my industry, there are fewer than 100 players. . . . We get together now and then at business meetings. . . . We all know each other. And hear talk about the other entrepreneurs at these meetings."[77]

Asked whether they believe that most of their business acquaintances would inform others if someone they know commits any form of malfeasance in doing business, survey respondents strongly agreed, with an average of 5.07 on a scale of 1 to 7. In the case of a borrower who defaults on a loan, close to 38 percent of the entrepreneurs interviewed expect that the lender would inform business friends, customers, and suppliers. Given the multiplex networks of the local and regional business community, information spreads quickly through cross-cutting ties that serve as conduits for gossip about malfeasance. The norm of information sharing extends beyond entrepreneurs who participate in informal lending and borrowing: whether or not survey respondents participate in informal credit markets, they expect that accurate negative gossip about opportunism and malfeasance will disseminate through the entire business community. This underscores the robustness of this norm when it comes to the protection of members of the business community against within-group opportunism and malfeasance. The welfare-enhancing effect of such a screening system clearly goes beyond direct borrower-and-lender relations, as major defaults may well have second-order effects on trading partners of the affected lender.

Community Sanctions

With negative gossip thus disseminating through the local business community, voluntary or involuntary default on informal loans has many unfavorable consequences for the borrower. Not only can default lead to the breakup of the bilateral business relationship, but other prospective lenders will base their own lending decisions on prior payment behavior. About 27 percent of survey respondents believe that if someone were to default on a loan, this would also affect the continuation of business relations with other members of the business community, and not only in regard to access to informal credit. The owner of a small-scale mechanical engineering company in Hangzhou, who relies heavily on informal lending and borrowing, observed: "Once you default on *one* loan, this would ruin your entire reputation. . . . But private owners need to run their business normally. So, this is why people repay their loans. . . . To keep their reputation. We actually never had any default."[78] Another interviewee says, "Whoever dares to do something bad, everyone will know about it. Everyone will stop giving credit, and there will be no hope of making it in this business."[79] Such community sanctions provide a highly effective means of norm enforcement in a private enterprise economy virtually excluded from formal sources of credit.

A textile producer in Nantong recalls:

> In some cases, there are people who cannot repay their loan and disappear. Just recently there was such a case. A business man borrowed ¥500,000 from a rural cooperative and ¥1 million from friends and relatives. When the loan was due, he ran away. Company assets were not worth the debts. He had to run away because part of his loans was usurious loan. He would've suffered physical damage if he had stayed. He will not dare to come back unless he can repay the debts. Or after a period of time, three to five years, he returns impoverished. Then people may forgive the debt.[80]

Such stories are most often associated with cases where informal lending within networks has not provided sufficient funds and an entrepreneur has resorted to borrowing from underground banks and loan sharks. In those cases consequences for default are potentially the most severe. In our sample, however, these forms of credit seemingly play only a minor role. Only 1 percent of the respondents indicate that they resort to such loans.

Conclusion

Study of founding processes of private firms in the Yangzi delta region provides first insights into central micro-mechanisms enabling the rise of capitalism. In this analytic narrative, the entrepreneur is the central agent who drives the institutional innovations that give rise to the private enterprise economy. Once established, informal economic institutions structure the framework of entrepreneurial action.

Entrepreneurship in the Yangzi delta region was not fueled by exogenous institutional changes. When entrepreneurs decided to decouple from the traditional socialist production system, the government had neither initiated financial reforms inviting a broader societal participation nor provided property rights protection or transparent rules specifying company registration and liabilities. Instead, it was the development and use of innovative informal arrangements within close-knit groups of like-minded actors that provided the necessary funding and reliable business norms that allowed the first wave of entrepreneurs to survive outside the state-owned manufacturing system.

This bottom-up narrative resembles earlier accounts of the rise of capitalism in the West. As in Weber's description of economic development in nineteenth-century England and Germany, the drivers of institutional change in the Yangzi delta came from outside the established economic order. These entrepreneurs were not part of the political or economic elite, but came from modest social backgrounds. They neither resemble the image of the Schumpeterian pioneer nor embody the Knightian idea of high uncertainty tolerance. As Li Shufu, the founder and CEO of Geely Automobile, notes, his generation of capitalists were "just a bunch of simple farm boys," many coming from impoverished peasant households. The *Wall Street Journal*'s description of Li's socioeconomic origins recapitulates this bottom-up account:

> Behind Geely's transformation is the chairman, Mr. Li, a self-described workaholic who most nights sleeps inside the company's headquarters building in Hangzhou. Born in 1963 to poor farmers in Taizhou, about 250 miles southeast of Shanghai, he came of age during the era of economic reform that began in the late 1970s.
>
> When he finished high school he used his graduation gift of 100 yuan, about $14 today, to buy a used camera. He then opened a photo studio for villagers. With the money he earned, he launched a business stripping gold and other rare metals from discarded appliances and machinery. Later, he opened factories to produce refrigerators and freezers, and then construction materials.
>
> By the early 1990s Mr. Li was thinking about building cars. But at the time, China's central government barred private companies from the auto industry. So Mr. Li began making motorcycles, while still buying cars and stripping them down to learn how they were made. In the late 1990s, as official restrictions began to ease, Mr. Li founded Geely. He came up with the company's first auto prototypes based loosely on competitors' models and began selling cars in 2001.[81]

This is a typical story for the initial entrepreneurs, who simply did not mind the low social status or the stigma of extralegal activities. Like-minded people mimicked each other, which gradually led to the development of norms of mutual help and organization in local business networks. It was through this process of imitation and learning by doing that the once-stigmatized deviators turned into capitalist role models spearheading a social movement dynamic of firm founding. With its own self-help institutions, the private enterprise economy quickly shifted onto a self-reinforcing path of capitalist economic development, the robust nature of which in turn shaped the direction of legal and regulatory change.

5

Legitimacy and Organizational Change

In the past, even with robust markets, traditional handicraft and commercial firms in the Yangzi delta did not give rise to "capitalist shoots" as in England and parts of Europe after the Reformation. Instead, family-owned businesses persisted in their traditional form, reliant on part-time household labor as an extension of the agricultural economy. The Qing government had sought to promote corporate development through the enactment of China's first Company Law in 1904, but the corporate sector remained monopolized by the Western imperial powers and Japan. On the eve of the Communist takeover in 1949, almost 99 percent of the more than 1.1 million industrial and commercial firms in China operated outside the legal framework of the Company Law, and were run as simple proprietorships and business partnerships not registered with the government.[1] A private enterprise economy can thus develop over a long time span without leading to modern capitalism, a core institutional feature of which is the right of economic actors to incorporate as "legal persons" or corporations. Why, then, were these late-century entrepreneurs able to break with traditional family businesses, and to develop capitalist firms?

When entrepreneurs began experimenting with private manufacturing firms in the 1980s, state-owned enterprises dominated the organizational landscape. Western corporate forms—the limited liability company (LLC) and the joint stock company (JSC)—lacked both a historical foundation and political support. Quite naturally, the majority of the early start-up entrepreneurs established single-proprietor companies, which were easiest to form and to operate. Although the government sought to restrict private firms to

production of nonindustrial artisan and craft products, successful private manufacturers quickly outgrew the organizational form of the single-household
firm *(geti hu)*, especially its size limitation to no more than seven employees.
Scant access to capital and scarcity of professional talent forced many founders to explore alternatives. Partnerships and shareholding companies not only
allowed pooling the start-up capital and spreading the risk, but also allowed
the formation of start-up teams with complementary skills, professional experience, and social capital. In these firms, rights and duties of shareholders were
based on mutual agreements between partners, who were often connected
through long-term friendship or family relations. These organizational forms
quickly played far more than a marginal role in the emerging private enterprise economy.

Though entrepreneurs were experimenting with organizational forms enabling them to move beyond household production, the "Provisional Regulations on Private Enterprise" that the national government had put in place in
1988 specified the legal status for private sole-proprietorship firms only.[2]
Reformers in central government did not envision transformative changes of
the underlying economic order dominated by state-owned enterprises. Instead,
they sought to protect the public sector from growing competitive pressures
of a private enterprise economy, in their view an unintended consequence of
economic reform.

During the first decade of economic reform, individual household businesses
were viewed with suspicion and open hostility in communities where, only
recently, Cultural Revolution–era radicalism had directed mass campaigns
against "profiteers" taking the capitalist road. Stigmatized by widespread
negative views of entrepreneurial activity, entrepreneurs early in the reform
period faced the uncertainties of a pariah-like status. "When I applied to open
an individual business, my friends and classmates were amazed," a young man
told a journalist from the southern Chinese newspaper *Guangdong Ribao* in
1983. "They said doing individual business had no political future, no security
of livelihood, no social position, and even finding a girlfriend would be difficult."[3] From late 1988 through 1991, private entrepreneurs faced increasing political attacks as conservatives in the party launched a rectification campaign
to check the spread of bourgeois influence and thought.

Viewed as illegitimate and inferior by local governments, private firms
were vulnerable to special levies and appropriations, regulatory interventions,
and even outright expropriation or firm closure. Many private manufacturing

firms therefore registered as shareholding cooperatives, an organizational type formally regarded as part of the collective economy.[4] Others sought closer ties with local government and negotiated to register formally as collective-owned enterprises, the so-called red hat firms.[5] Under this arrangement they agreed to pay the local government a so-called management fee.

Registration as a collective enterprise formally owned by local government, however, came at high costs. Cooperative firms and red hat firms had to comply with national regulations requiring public firms to meet quotas for reinvestment, to limit dividend payments, and to contribute to the locality's public accumulation fund, set aside for local investment.[6] Although these rules were not consistently enforced in all localities, they implied a substantial dilution of private property rights. Moreover, legal registration as a collective allowed the local government as legal owner to intervene in the firm's operational and strategic decisions. As a result, the boundaries between the firm and the state were often ill defined. In red hat firms, property rights rested on trust that local government was committed to honoring the rights of private owners. Because such trust was embedded in ongoing interpersonal ties between entrepreneur and government officials, normal turnover of government personnel could easily threaten the security of these informal property rights. Such uncertainties increased as successful red hat firms grew in size, especially as the fiscal needs of government grew in the 1990s. When confronted with budgetary shortfalls, local officials often found it irresistible to seek new revenue by forcibly renegotiating the terms of agreement with private owners operating red hat firms.[7] The case of the Pearl River Refrigerator Factory, more widely known as the Kelon Group, founded in 1984 in southern Guangdong Province by the rural entrepreneur Wang Guoduan, highlights the uncertainties involved. Granted a technical assistance loan of ¥90,000 and a credit line of ¥4 million by Rongqi township, the company was formally registered as a collective firm, though all parties involved were aware of its private nature. The entrepreneur quickly repaid the loans, and during the first fifteen years of operation, the township government honored the de facto private nature of the firm. The business flourished and Kelon was able to win substantial market share from the established state-owned refrigerator makers and from the U.S. home appliance company Whirlpool. In December 1998, however, the township government suddenly changed course and replaced the company management after it was rumored to have rejected the township's request to take over a loss-making air-conditioner firm. By 2000, the government had replaced all founding

members, and exercised its de jure control rights as the formal owner of the red
hat company. The township-run, state-owned holding company, which formally exercised control rights, used the opportunity to plunder and expropriate
Kelon's assets.[8]

Clearly, whether for sole proprietorships, cooperatives, or red hat firms, the
lack of legitimacy for private enterprises exacerbated the problem of weak
property rights and increased the risk of loss. Moreover, insecure property
rights effectively barred many private firms from external finance. Pariah status and a need to obtain more financial capital as well as more willing workers
motivated entrepreneurs to seek legitimacy for their private firms in China's
transition economy. Not surprisingly, they sought to distance themselves cog-
nitively from the negative stereotypes of "profiteers" and "speculators" associated since the Cultural Revolution with traditional forms of commerce, the
merchants, vendors and traders. They sought a modern industrial identity that
would allow them to operate private firms outside the collective economy with
external legitimacy and social approval.

It was the early trial experiments by local governments at privatization of
loss-making township and village enterprises and registration of these firms
as shareholding partnerships and limited liability companies that serendipi-
tously opened the way for the sought-after change in identity. Entrepreneurs
followed this lead, adopting the same legal forms as privatized public firms.
Even before the Company Law became effective in 1994, about 17 percent of
private firms followed the new trend and operated as limited liability companies, and 16 percent as shareholding partnerships.[9] In effect, the Company
Law provided the legal foundation of postsocialist corporatization, which
unintentionally accelerated the diffusion of limited liability and shareholding
organizational forms among private firms.

In this chapter, we examine how organizational isomorphism—defined as
a "process that forces one unit in a population to resemble other units that face
the same environmental conditions"[10]—enables private firms to enhance their
success and survival chances. To illustrate this process as an organizational
strategy to gain legitimacy, we highlight key features of the Company Law
of 1994 and detail how capitalist entrepreneurs mimicked the incorporation
of government-owned enterprises.

Despite their compliance with the external forms of the Company Law,
the internal organizational practices and workaday norms of private firms
continued to follow those commonly found in sole proprietor owner-managed

firms.[11] This decoupling between formal organization and workaday practices supports the view that adoption of myths and formal state-sponsored guidelines for a "modern enterprise system" was driven by a search for cognitive and sociopolitical legitimacy. Here *cognitive legitimacy* refers to the acceptance of a venture or organizational form as a taken-for-granted feature of the institutional environment. *Sociopolitical legitimacy* alludes to social approval for this enterprise by government officials, consumers, and the general public.[12]

Isomorphism as Mechanism of Institutional Change

The central dilemma for entrepreneurs of privately owned manufacturing firms was fundamentally rooted in the illegitimate and stigmatized status of private enterprise as an organizational form. They had to either operate below the radar of government regulators or register their firms with local government as "fake" collective enterprises. In effect, insecure property rights biased private investment decisions to favor small-scale, low-technology projects focusing on product lines with little value added. Entrepreneurs sought investments with fast returns and short amortization times, and minimal requirements for fixed assets.[13]

Organization theory has long emphasized that firms need more than resources and technical information to survive and profit in markets; they also need the social acceptability and credibility that come with legitimacy.[14] Without legitimacy, organizational performance is likely to suffer, as actors lack the ability to establish ties with an environment that neither understands nor approves of their existence or purpose. They may not be able to convince others to invest labor, capital, and knowledge in their venture.[15] Significantly, a Shanghai businessman, for instance, transferred his firm to collective ownership in 1988, when he realized that employees he sought to recruit did not want to work for a private enterprise.[16]

Interest in legitimacy motivates organizations to act outwardly in ways that are perceived by the public as desirable, proper, or appropriate, even if this involves disguising their true nature.[17] Thus, for instance, women's groups in the United States at the turn of the nineteenth century increased their political influence by adopting the organizational form of nonpolitical voluntary associations, regarded as culturally legitimate.[18] Similarly, in Toronto, voluntary social service organizations listed in the charitable registry and endorsed by the local chamber of commerce significantly outlasted those not endorsed by institutional authorities.[19] To the extent that the public perceives an organization as a legitimated entity, the organization is buffered from failure due to lack of status and secures better chances for success through increased access to resources and social approval.

A common strategy for new entrants into a market niche is to copy an existing organizational form already perceived as legitimate.[20] Entrepreneurs reproduce and adapt well-defined building blocks of existing organizational forms.[21] Distinct imitated features are typically encountered through observation, local gossiping, and casual business consultations. Once a local niche stabilizes and successful business leaders have emerged, observation and mimetic action accelerate.[22] Geographic proximity—as in the Yangzi delta region—spurs local learning and organizational adaptation.[23] Social networks can also accelerate the diffusion of distinct organizational forms.[24] Typically, business founders build on their prior work experience and mimic the organizational structure implemented by former employers or local competitors in the same niche.

Ironically, it was China's corporatization policy, designed to modernize state-owned companies, that provided private-sector entrepreneurs with an organizational form enabling them to gain the legitimacy they sought. By joining the government-sponsored reform initiative to build a "modern enterprise system," entrepreneurs fell upon a strategy that solved the problem of stigmatized status. Incorporating as a limited liability company *(youxian zeren gongsi)* or as a joint stock company *(gufen youxian gongsi)* not only helped limit risks as regards the firm's registered capital but also provided private firms with a legal structure that made them virtually indistinguishable from incorporated public companies. Private businesses registered as sole proprietorships are easily identifiable by the company's name, but firms registered as an LLC or a JSC could be anything from wholly state-owned to wholly privately owned companies. By adopting these external organizational forms of privatized government-owned firms, private firms claimed legitimacy through the appearance of complying with the government-sponsored reform initiatives for industrial and commercial firms.

Originally, the intent of the Company Law was clearly not to provide a legal framework for the evolving private enterprise economy.[25] Quite to the contrary, China's lawmakers aimed to restructure and shore up the ailing state-owned sector. Taking their cue from local government-led privatization, central government reform leaders sought in the 1990s to turn around loss-making state-owned enterprises through outright and partial privatization. Reformers viewed incorporation of these state-owned firms as an effective strategy to develop a profitable "modern enterprise system" *(xiandai qiye zhidu)*. Through corporatization, the largest of them could also qualify to be listed on the Shanghai and Shenzhen stock exchanges. Their new identity as "public corporations" was appealing to reformers because the new classificatory schema conformed to the myth of becoming modern by adopting the same organizational forms as Western corporations, while these firms still remained predominantly state owned. Driven by heavy state-sponsored propaganda promoting the "modern enterprise system," limited liability and joint stock companies rapidly became synonyms of modernity and economic progress, symbols of legitimacy and prestige in China.

In essence, the Company Law established a hybrid corporate form combining Western standards with the political preferences of the Chinese Communist Party.[26] Still bearing the imprint of the planned economy period, this law provided a legal foundation for continuing state involvement and political control of partially privatized and corporatized public firms.[27] Although Chinese lawmakers borrowed heavily from Western law in bringing organizational standards in line with Western-style corporate governance,[28] the government's antiprivate attitude remained pervasive. Minimum capital requirements set at a high level underscore the law's exclusive focus on established public firms as candidates for corporatization. In a world where state-owned financial institutions do not support private start-ups, the legally required up-front minimum capital of ¥500,000 for LLCs and ¥10 million for JSCs could be expected to be an effective barrier to corporatization for such companies.[29] Even advanced industrial economies such as Germany or Italy have substantially lower minimum capital requirements of only €10,000 for LLCs (less than 20 percent of what is required in China). The United States, France, and the United Kingdom have even recently eliminated capital requirements or reduced them to a purely symbolic amount. In China, the situation was further complicated for private start-up firms because intangible, noncash contributions such as labor input could not replace cash contributions to meet the registered capital requirements of the Company Law.[30]

Even so, enactment of the Company Law in 1994 had the unintended effect of accelerating the adoption of limited liability and shareholding organizational forms among private firms. Entrepreneurs had already experimented with both forms, when first local experiments with (partial) privatization of state-owned enterprises and collective enterprises indicated the new direction of China's corporate development strategy. Attracted by legal status and broad political approval for these corporate forms, private entrepreneurs had strong incentives to escape the uncertain status of sole proprietorships and partnerships by following the example of incorporated state-owned companies.[31]

Incorporation rapidly developed into a mass movement among private entrepreneurs. Many local officials encouraged private firms to register as limited liability companies, not only because such registrations signaled a certain level of modernity within the local industrial landscape and looked good on balance sheets, but also because the new legal status also promised an overall increase in local firm registrations (and local employment and tax revenues), as would-be founders no longer needed to stand in with their private assets. By 1997, just three years after the enactment of the Company Law, 48 percent of private companies across China were formally registered as LLCs, and by 2004 the share had further increased to 65 percent.[32] The situation in our Yangzi delta sample resembles the national pattern, though with an even larger share of firms registered either as LLCs or JSCs, reflecting the pioneering role of the region in terms of private firm development (see Table 5.1). This is true for all seven survey cities, although there is some variation in the choice of corporate forms. The share of LLCs ranges between 56.5 percent (in Wenzhou) and 82 percent (in Shanghai), and the share of JSCs ranges between 11.7 percent (in Changzhou) and 26.7 percent (in Wenzhou and Nantong).

The individual decision to incorporate was seldom based on fine-grained analysis of the Company Law and the rights and duties associated with the legal status of LLCs and JSCs. Most entrepreneurs did not seek legal advice or examine the text detailing the rules and conditions stipulated by the Company Law. Instead, entrepreneurs follow some intuitive rule-of-thumb understanding of the relevant rules and procedures. The owner-manager of an electronic equipment company in Changzhou explains: "I'll tell you why I did not read the law, including the Company Law, before registering my firm. I had some general knowledge about the Company Law, but did not read it. I think the main reason why I did not read the law is that in the current business environment in China, the Company Law is not strictly followed. . . . I am afraid that I'd be constrained if I actually read the law."[33]

When reflecting on their decision to register their firm as an LLC, most entrepreneurs recall that they mimicked successful local competitors in their niche: "At that time, the limited liability company was just the common form," "I just did what was popular in my locality," or "All my friends incorporated as

Table 5.1. Legal form of private companies (in percent)

	Single ownership	Joint ownership	Limited liability	Joint stock	Other	Total
National sample						
1993	63.5	15.8	17.0	—	3.6	100
1997	38.3	13.3	48.4	—	—	100
2000	39.0	7.3	46.4	7.3	—	100
2002	28.7	5.7	57.2	8.4	—	100
2004	20.3	7.6	64.9	7.2	—	100
Yangzi delta						
2006	8.9	6.5	67.0	17.2	0.4	100
Shanghai	4.0	2.0	82.0	12.0	—	100
Nanjing	6.8	16.7	64.7	11.8	—	100
Nantong	—	5.0	66.3	26.7	2.0	100
Changzhou	4.8	7.8	74.8	11.7	0.9	100
Hangzhou	19.8	2.9	62.4	13.9	1	100
Wenzhou	6.9	9.9	56.5	26.7	—	100
Ningbo	19.4	1.0	62.1	17.5	—	100

Sources: Data for national sample from *Report on the Development of Ch na's Private Enterprise 2005* (Beijing: Social Sciences Academic Press, 2005), 246; Yangzi Survey 2006.

LLCs." The owner-manager of a Changzhou chemicals firm notes: "I just felt the limited liability company was the standard form in my region, when I registered. In this industry, this form seemed to have a 90 percent share. I did not really consult with others, but was just following what others were doing. In following the others, I thought that this is probably the appropriate form for a small firm like mine."[34] Other entrepreneurs recall that local authorities advised them to register their start-up firms as LLCs and JSCs to limit their risk in the event of failure. Some entrepreneurs point to potential economic advantages of legitimacy as motivating their decision to incorporate. A widely held belief is that incorporated companies may in the future enjoy advantages in applying for a loan from state-owned banks. Others emphasize that the corporate form simply has a more impressive sound, signaling sizeable and credible firms with a relatively broad business scope. One Ningbo-based owner-manager, for instance, explains, "I registered as a limited liability company because it has simply a better sound *(haoting)* in the market. If I had registered as a simple sole-ownership firm, I could definitely not get this much business. My ideal would be to register even as a business group, because this would surely give me the best business."[35]

Private entrepreneurs were quick to take advantage of the lax monitoring of the Company Law by local officials who had little interest in rigid implementation of the legal requirements. Those entrepreneurs who lacked the minimum capital developed strategies to circumvent this requirement. When registering with the responsible branch of the local Bureau of Industry and Commerce, a common strategy is to use borrowed money paid into a bank account. After registration, the money is immediately withdrawn and returned to the lenders. Many of the entrepreneurs point out that registered capital only "exists on paper and has no actual meaning."[36] Another Changzhou owner-manager estimates that this practice is followed by about 90 percent of the firms in that city.[37]

Also, entrepreneurs often satisfy the Company Law's requirement of multiple shareholders by instituting dummy shareholders. As the electronic-equipment company owner-manager who so forthrightly acknowledged that he "did not read the law" describes, "When we registered, I understood that a limited liability status was reserved for firms with more than one shareholder. So, on paper, my younger brother stepped in and we formally own the firm together. But in truth, I am of course the sole owner. We just registered as a shareholding firm."[38] This pattern is widespread. Oftentimes wife or husband or close relatives are formally listed as shareholders with 1 to 5 percent of the company shares, in order to justify the firm's registration as a legal person. Naturally, the owner-entrepreneur does not regard these formal shareholders as co-owners or involve them in business decisions. They are simply listed to satisfy legal requirements.

Shifting to formal governance structures of a "modern enterprise system" enabled private firms to enter the mainstream of China's industrial economy as legitimate businesses. By adapting the formal structures prescribed by the state and blending into the organizational field of modern corporations, private entrepreneurs benefited from higher social and political approval, which in turn improved their chances of survival. Of the firms founded before 1994 in our Yangzi delta survey, 46 percent were registered as LLCs, and 28 percent as JSCs. This suggests a substantively higher survival rate for companies registered as legal persons than for sole proprietorships and partnership companies. The difference in survival rates persists even if we exclude privatized companies that previously were owned by local government.

Local governments in general are more attentive to the needs and concerns of businesses formally registered as LLCs and JSCs. In our Yangzi delta survey, 64 percent of joint shareholding corporations are occasionally asked by the local government to provide their opinion on the current state of social and economic development in the region. By contrast, only 36 percent of partnership companies are polled for their views. This contrast holds after controlling for company size, location, and industry. Differences in self-perceived social status assessments hint at similar legitimacy effects with respect to public opinion. In our sample, such assessments are typically lowest for single-proprietor firms and highest for LLCs.[39]

Organizational isomorphism with these legal corporate forms embraced by the state-owned economy lowers the individual costs associated with diverging from socialist mainstream and increases the expected net benefits. As portrayed in our theoretical model in Chapter 2, larger expected net benefits associated with private firms in turn reduce the critical mass of followers needed to trigger a self-reinforcing bottom-up process.

Myth and Reality of Organizational Structure

By registering their firms as limited liability and joint stock companies, entrepreneurs sought to gain the legitimacy and political approval they lacked as sole-proprietor firms. However, such outward conformity need not indicate much if any change in the actual operation of these firms. Although entrepreneurs in the Yangzi delta region comply with the external form and rules of the "modern enterprise system," beneath the surface there is a decoupling between external form and actual organizational practices and routines, given the functional operational needs of the owner-managed firm.[40]

The Company Law imposes an elaborate assembly of organizational routines and scripts. Incorporation as LLCs and JSCs legally binds the firms to a hybrid governance structure, reflecting the central government's ambivalence on how much autonomy to allot to industrial and commercial enterprises. Enacted by reformers as a strategy of corporatization for large state-owned enterprises, the law specifies formal rules and structures designed to ensure continuity of Communist Party political controls of the industrial and commercial economy. Article 14 of the Company Law stipulates that LLCs and JSCs must have a Communist Party committee, labor committee, and trade union, jointly regarded as the traditional committees representing political participation. Article 17 specifies that party branches in companies incorporated under the Company Law must abide by the Constitution of the Chinese Communist Party, which grants local party branches the right to get involved in major firm decisions. Compliance with the formal rules and routines of corporate governance thus opens the firm to increased risk of government intervention and political control.[41]

Many of the rules and specifications with regard to decision making and authority sharing between management, board of directors, and shareholders are at odds with the actual operational needs of small and medium-size owner-managed firms. Thus, despite capitalist entrepreneurs' interest in gaining legitimacy through external compliance with the modern corporate forms, entrepreneurs typically engage in ritualistic compliance with the formal routines and organizational structures of the Company Law, while quietly disconnecting the actual operations of their business from these external forms. As noted above, a Changzhou entrepreneur who registered his firm as an LLC said he is afraid that actually reading the law might constrain how he operates his business. "The Company Law," he opined, "just does not fit the requirements of the private firm."[42]

The shift to the legal forms of LLCs or JSCs did not reflect change in the actual organizational form and practices of private firms, but rather a social movement-like process of legitimacy-seeking through convergence in external form with the modern enterprise reforms targeted for government-owned firms, the favored mainstream of the industrial economy. The most obvious example of decoupling between formal guidelines and actual internal routines of the firm is the symbolic listing on organizational charts of formal structures required by the Company Law. According to the original version, both LLCs and JSCs, irrespective of company size and number of shareholders, are legally obliged to convene regular shareholder meetings and to institute a board of directors as the legal representative of the company. However, many private limited liability and joint stock companies do not comply with these requirements. Only 55.2 percent of the LLCs and 72.2 percent of JSCs in our 2006 survey actually convene shareholder meetings (see Table 5.2). And only 35 percent of LLCs and 55 percent of JSCs indicate that they have formally instituted a board of directors. Comparison with official national data suggests that decoupling between legal form and workaday norms is even more pronounced in the Yangzi delta region than in China on average. (One should note, though, that data from the government-approved firm surveys conducted by the National Bureau of Statistics are likely to overstate rule compliance insofar as respondents have an interest in signaling that the firm complies with the Company Law.)

Decoupling from formal rules and specifications is generally based on rational considerations aiming to optimize internal work routines. Companies that

Table 5.2. Implementation of legally required organizational bodies

By legal form	Sample	Percentage of firms that hold shareholder meetings	Percentage of firms that have a board of directors
Single proprietorship	Yangzi	4.7	6.3
	National sample '04	16.6	34.0
Joint ownership	Yangzi	43.4	26.0
	National sample '04	60.5	71.3
Limited liability company	Yangzi	55.2	35.0
	National sample '04	65.1	80.2
Joint stock company	Yangzi	72.2	55.0
	National sample '04	72.5	90.3

Source: Data for national sample from *Report on the Development of China's Private Enterprise 2005*, 248; Yangzi Survey 2006.

do not formally convene shareholder meetings are generally small and owned by a single proprietor and a formal dummy shareholder or a small number of partners. Single-owner LLCs, for example, commonly list the owner's spouse serving as a second shareholder and as the chair of the board of directors. One Changzhou owner explains, "Shareholder meetings and board of directors only exist on paper, since I run this company with my wife. It actually is a fake, just to give information to outsiders. It is actually similar to the registered capital. There is a true amount of capital, and then there is one on paper. Formally we have a board of directors, but of course I make all decisions, and there are no real meetings held."[43] In companies with only two or three shareholders, all of them working in the company, formal shareholder meetings are superfluous for information exchange and decision making. Only 7.69 percent of the LLCs in our sample are managed by minority shareholders who jointly own 50 percent or less of the company's shares (see Table 5.3). On average, LLCs have 2.5 managing shareholders, often including a husband-and-wife team. Thirty-five percent of the firms are run by one single majority owner, 26 percent by two owners, and 22 percent by three owners. Naturally, these owner-managed businesses do not convene shareholder meetings and do not have a board of directors. This underscores the pragmatic approach, driven by the actual operational needs of the firm, when it comes to internal workaday norms.

Even companies that formally convene shareholder meetings and institute a board of directors often do not aim for more than symbolic compliance. But because external compliance with the myths and rituals of corporate governance may have utility for the firm in gaining access to resources and approval from local government, entrepreneurs are attentive to be in conformity with the outward procedural specifications of the Company Law. Applications for new products, for example, require the signature of the chair of the board of directors. Other entrepreneurs utilize the board of directors to involve external members who can serve as consultants on critical decisions and as network ties that may enable the firm to gain access to needed resources.

To assess the actual degree of authority sharing in those companies that do have formal shareholder meetings and a board of directors, we asked survey respondents to indicate who makes key decisions with regard to daily operation, human resources, research and development, investment, opening new subsidiaries, internal organizational reforms, and mergers and acquisitions (see Table 5.4).

Table 5.3. Shareholders in management positions, by corporate form

Legal form	Percentage of ownership held by shareholders involved in firm management (cumulative)							
	≤ 15	≤ 30	≤ 50	≤ 75	≤ 90	≤ 95	≤ 100
Single proprietorship	—	—	—	—	1.69	1.69	100
Joint ownership	—	7.14	21.43	38.10	52.38	57.00	100
Limited liability	0.44	3.08	7.69	24.40	36.92	37.80	100
Joint stock company	0.84	5.88	10.92	22.69	38.66	40.30	100

Source: Yangzi Survey 2006.

Table 5.4. Authority index of shareholder meeting and board of directors, by corporate form

Number of decision types, decisively influenced	Limited liability company		Joint stock company	
	Shareholder meeting total (%)	Board of directors total (%)	Shareholder meeting total (%)	Board of directors total (%)
0	116 (44.11)	80 (47.90)	45 (50.56)	26 (38.81)
1	32 (12.17)	19 (11.38)	11 (12.36	8 (11.94)
2	34 (12.93)	29 (17.37)	10 (11.24)	11 (16.42)
3	32 (12.17)	19 (11.38)	6 (6.74)	13 (19.40)
4	23 (8.75)	12 (7.19)	7 (7.87)	7 (10.45)
5	17 (6.46)	2 (1.20)	4 (4.49)	2 (2.99)
6	6 (2.28)	3 (1.80)	6 (6.67)	—
7	3 (1.14)	3 (1.80)	—	—
Mean value	1.63	1.38	1.49	1.60

Source: Yangzi Survey 2006.

The shareholder meetings and board of directors for many of these companies are clearly symbolic and ceremonial, and decoupled from the actual operations of the firm. Approximately half of these LLCs (44.11 percent) and these JSCs (50.56 percent) indicate that business decisions are not influenced at all by shareholder meetings (de jure the main power organ of the company). Likewise, for a sizeable share of these LLCs (47.9 percent) and these JSCs (38.81 percent), the board of directors is a nominal entity without influence on company decisions. In other cases, however, these formal corporate structures are more than symbolic. Shareholders do have substantial decision-making power with regard to at least three decision types in more than 30 percent of the LLCs and more than 25 percent of the JSCs. And some firms have put in place a board of directors with actual power, responsible for at least three of these decision types in close to 24 percent of these LLCs and close to 33 percent of the JSCs. Company-specific needs are what drive the shift toward greater compliance.

Size and scale of operations play a decisive role in whether a firm actually complies with the formal rules of the Company Law. Motivated to register as LLCs or JSCs principally by legitimacy seeking, most owner-operated firms initially decouple their internal operations from the legal requirements of corporate governance. As a company grows in size, scale, and organizational complexity beyond the efficient control and coordination of the single-owner-managed firm, however, the internal organizational structures and practices appear to gradually comply with more of these external forms and rules. Once a company grows beyond a certain threshold size, reflected in the number of shareholders and volume of assets, the once purely symbolic corporate governance structures are activated, and internal organizational routines and actual authority-sharing practices come to match the external forms of corporate governance specified by the Company Law.

However, among our survey firms, those that convene shareholder meetings actually perform on average weaker than companies without such meetings (see Table 5.5). Similarly, active boards of directors do not contribute to the firm's economic performance, as measured by return on sales (see model 1).

Table 5.5.   Decoupling and company performance

	Return on sales coeff. (std. error)	
	Model 1	Model 2
Percentage of shares held by owners in management positions	0.001*	0.001**
	(0.0003)	(0.0003)
Firm conducts shareholder meetings	−0.048'''	—
	(0.015)	
Number of decisions dominated by shareholder meeting[a]	—	−0.012***
		(0.003)
Firm has a board of directors	0.013	—
	(0.015)	
Number of decisions dominated by board of directors[a]	—	−0.012*
		(0.006)
Legal status	YES	YES
Log of total assets ($t-1$)	−0.007	−0.008
	(0.005)	(0.006)
Firm age	0.0002	−0.0004
	(0.001)	(0.001)
Sector	YES**	YES*
City	YES***	YES***
Observations[b]	546	640
Adj. R^2	0.2975	0.2952

Source: Yangzi Survey 2006.

Note: Coefficients for sector and city dummy variables are not reported.

a. We code companies without a shareholder meeting and without board of directors as having 0 decisions thus enacted.

b. The sample includes those companies that are registered as either limited liability companies or joint stock companies.

* $p<0.10$, ** $p<0.05$ and *** $p<0.01$; robust standard errors.

Instead, firms that report having shareholders and a board of directors with actual decision-making authority obtain weaker economic performance (see model 2). Although the effect is relatively small, these results reveal the advantages of decoupling the firm's operational practice from formal scripts required by the Company Law. By contrast, when shareholders hold positions as owner-managers of the firm, there tends to be a higher net return on sales (see models 1 and 2).

How Internal Structure Adapts to Changing Institutional Environment

Entrepreneurs in our Yangzi delta survey describe firms with well-specified departmental structures that follow standardized conceptions of division of labor and managerial responsibility. Whatever their legal form, most companies organize their activities by functional departments—that is, financing, production, quality control, and sales—reporting directly to the owner-manager. High-technology companies may have an in-house research and development department (see Chapter 7). Internal organizational structure mimics that of national or international firms that these entrepreneurs look to as models.

Conceptions of appropriate organizational structures and practices are often acquired from textbook accounts of Western business models. Many entrepreneurs enroll in popular eMBA programs operated by Chinese and Western business schools, thus bolstering their self-image as entrepreneurs leading modern enterprises. They like to refer to exemplary and notable American entrepreneurs and CEOs as role models to be emulated. Shelves in local bookstores are filled with biographies of corporate leaders such as Andrew Carnegie, Bill Gates, Steve Jobs, or Rupert Murdoch, which entrepreneurs actually buy and read for inspiration and guidance. Wu Liping, the founder of an innovative packaging firm, notes that the study of these famous entrepreneurs has helped him to develop from a mere parvenu into someone who can be respected for his accomplishments. Celebrity domestic CEOs are also popular role models among young start-up entrepreneurs. Jack Ma, the founder of Alibaba.com, for example, is especially admired for his innovative organizational design and bold corporate decisions. As China's economy continues its high-speed growth trajectory, locally successful domestic firms now provide a ready supply of easily accessible models for start-up businesses to mimic. In our 2006 survey, 45 percent of the entrepreneurs who follow a distinct organizational blueprint admit to imitating successful domestic firms.

The owner-manager of a Changzhou chemicals firm, for instance, looks to a local business group in the same industrial park. Not only is he impressed by the visionary approach of the founding entrepreneur and the broad product portfolio of the business group, but he also hopes to copy their organizational structure with well-defined individual responsibilities, their reliance on professional managers, and their successful shareholding concept.[44]

Equipped with readily available building blocks, the new class of domestic capitalist entrepreneurs can rapidly assemble firms that feature the standard institutional elements of the modern capitalist firm. Their commitment to standard organizational practices is signaled by written rules. These internal documents specify the rights and duties of specific departments and chart the internal reporting channels within the company. The internal organizational rules have an important symbolic character in signaling the firm's compliance with socially accepted expectations, scripts, and myths about best practices in modern companies. Thus they form an internal source of legitimacy by establishing standards in dealings with customers, suppliers, employees, and government offices. Nearly all of the manufacturing firms interviewed in our 2006 firm survey have instituted written organizational rules, typically in the second year of the firm's operation.

Many entrepreneurs, however, emphasize a need to maintain an open and flexible organizational structure to accommodate future growth in their businesses as well as unexpected changes in market demand and new developments that impinge on the firm's business model. Their organizational strategy is to establish a core structure that allows for ready adjustments and internal structural change. Often boundaries between different departments can be hard to pin down in firms undergoing continuous rapid growth and accompanying reorganization. A central survival strategy of small and medium-size companies is that staff and management need to be capable and willing to shift flexibly between different tasks, and possess a mix of skills and work experience needed to meet unexpected changes in internal work procedures and in the business environment. Adjustments of internal organization in response to changing operational needs are common, especially as firms successfully outgrow their start-up operation. Overall, 20 percent of the interviewed companies have undergone organizational change and divisional restructuring in recent years.

In companies that have written rules to guide internal work routines and to specify discrete departmental responsibilities, it is not uncommon for actual practice to reflect a paternalistic owner-manager style of leadership that allows for little vertical authority sharing with midlevel managers. A majority of owner-entrepreneurs claim that they approve almost all the decisions taken by their midlevel managers, yet a surprising 83 percent of the firms surveyed report that midlevel managers in their firms in fact have no independent decision-making authority.

In many firms, entrepreneurs remain involved in most company decisions because they cannot afford to hire professional managers. Often they have long-term organizational strategies that envision the need to restructure the firm to bring in professional managers. The owner of a medium-size Changzhou-based machinery company, for example, sets an annual sales volume of ¥80 million as a critical threshold for restructuring. When his company attains this, he plans to hire professional managers, which he feels he will need because he lacks the technical knowledge to manage effectively beyond this threshold of production and sales. Some of his business friends have successfully shifted to reliance on professional managers, and they serve as his role models.

Many of the interviewees signal that they are waiting to see more such successful cases before they would be willing to shift to professional managers. The owner of a small-scale electronics company in Changzhou, for instance, notes that he is aware of advantages of having professional managers but thinks his firm is still too small and there is little experience with professional managers in the local economy. So far, he knows about only one such local competitor, who recruited a Korean manager formerly employed by LG Electronics. Therefore he does not want to rush the decision.[45]

Some owner-managers say that professional managers have not worked out well for private firms because China's current legal system does not provide sufficient protection against manager malfeasance. Others worry that the small supply of professional managers willing to shift from state-owned enterprises to private firms limits the professionalization of management within the private sector.

Still others, however, feel it is time to give it a try. The owner of another electronics company in Changzhou, for instance, considers recruiting a foreign CEO in order to facilitate the shift to adopting international standards of business.[46] An entrepreneur in a Hangzhou-based business group moved his company headquarters from its original base in Wenzhou to that provincial capital in order to find a more suitable environment to professionalize the company's management and corporate approach.[47]

Organizational adjustments (both accomplished and envisioned) generally involve an increase in vertical authority sharing. The introduction of vice-managers allows an additional organizational layer to coordinate activities between midlevel managers and the CEO. This helps to increase functional specialization and frees the top management for strategic tasks.

How private entrepreneurs flexibly develop internal organizational structures and management practices in response to the changing market position of the firm is exemplified by Joyea Packaging Equipment Company, Ltd. It was originally founded in 1998 as a small LLC with only a few departments and little specialization of work routines. The owner-manager, Wu Liping, made all of the company decisions. Ten years later, it has evolved into a high-tech company with an organizational structure and culture that emphasize efficient internal work routines and facilitate innovative activity. It has an active board of directors with seven members, including two independent directors with a legal professional background. The internal organizational structure involves a strict system of vertical authority sharing, with clearly specified responsibilities for each organizational level. Wu designed a bottom-up system for his firm's operational activities, where questions and problems are to be solved at the lowest possible level. Only questions that exceed individual authority and competence of lower-level managers are passed on to the next level. For strategic decisions, the company applies a top-down approach, with Wu, his three vice-presidents, and select researchers forming the firm's intellectual powerhouse. The board of directors focuses on major strategic concerns such as product development and investment. In this way, the company has freed the top management from daily operational routines, and established a clear and transparent separation between strategic and operational decision making.

To secure employee adherence to the company's organizational culture and to the norms guiding its workaday practices and routines, Wu ascribes great importance to recruiting employees who embody the values underlying his vision for the firm. These five core values, spelled out in written guidelines, are not merely symbolic, but actually define a shared identity for workers, staff, and management. In addition, sixteen specific written guidelines formulate work standards and routines, along with operational principles for cooperation in the workplace and for departmental decision making. For instance, to promote the company's reputation as an advanced technology manufacturer offering high-value products with reliable after-sales service, it is a generally agreed-upon standard that the sales staff is not allowed to offer price reductions or to rely on product promotions to sell the firm's packaging machinery. Wu also insists on in-house training of all technical and administrative staff to ensure high-fidelity compliance with the company's management approach, culture, and core organizational practices and routines. If employees are already accustomed to different work practices and product types, Wu believes, high-fidelity compliance is much harder to establish. For technical workers this involves considerable expense, as newly recruited technical personnel require one to two years of in-house training before being able to work independently and effectively.

Joyea's share in China's enormous market for packaging machinery has steadily increased, reflecting the leading position of the firm in its industrial niche. In 2006, Joyea formed a joint venture with Toyota Motors. Its development of an Internet-based problem-diagnosis system and a remote guiding system that monitors machine operations from the firm's headquarters in Changzhou reflects its technical capacity, as do its eighty patents for machinery design. Joyea's rapid development as a leading technology firm and its growing involvement with global firms through joint ventures confirm its successful transition from a small-scale start-up venture to a modern capitalist enterprise. In response to the founding entrepreneur's plans for future growth, the company plans to change its legal form to a JSC. Motivating this change is Wu Liping's commitment to allowing the firm to evolve into an employee-owned company as an organizational strategy to achieve a better interest alignment among employees through equity-based incentives. Managers and researchers who contribute to the firm's development will be rewarded by becoming shareholders. Wu's plan is to gradually reduce his ownership of the firm as the total value of the corporation increases.

Conclusion

Organizational innovators generally face high risks and uncertainties when trying to convince the public of the appropriateness and value of their new venture. This is all the more true in China, where organizational innovation has also involved a decoupling from established "rules of the game" and socialist modes of production. Escaping the stigma of the "capitalist sprout" or "profiteer" in the eyes and minds of consumers, suppliers, workers, and government officials was therefore a central challenge the new population of private entrepreneurs had to overcome.

The dominant strategy throughout the reform period was to mimic already-existing organizational forms generally perceived as legitimate, in order to limit the social and economic costs associated with decoupling from the established social and legal structure. Initially, private entrepreneurs relied on registration as collective firms formally owned by local government (so-called red hat firms). Later, when the government propagated the corporate form as a vehicle to turn the ailing state-owned sector into a "modern enterprise system," entrepreneurs quickly adapted their strategy. Through registration as limited liability companies and joint stock companies, private firms became virtually indistinguishable from incorporated public companies, thereby disguising their true nature.

The lure of increased company legitimacy through the corporate forms, promising improved market access and growth potential, has attracted many entrepreneurs who only formally satisfy the relatively demanding requirements stated by the Company Law. Many private entrepreneurs were quick to take advantage of lax law enforcement and monitoring. Oftentimes, registered capital and shareholders exist just on paper. Beneath the surface façade, there is a decoupling between external forms and actual organizational practices and routines, corresponding to the functional operational needs of the owner-managed firm. Legally prescribed governance bodies such as shareholder meetings and boards of directors remain without substantive functions, unless organizational and operational needs actually call for greater shareholder participation and a formal delegation of power. Briefly, while external compliance increases market access and participation, internal decoupling allows for flexible firm operations, where work procedures and routines respond to substantive needs, rather than legal requirements.

6

Industrial Clusters and Competitive Advantage

As marginalized, semilegal producers located at the low end of the pecking order, private firms should not have emerged as the most dynamic sector of the Chinese industrial economy. Not only were private manufacturers unable to secure financial capital from state-owned banks, but they often experienced long delays and poor quality from government suppliers. It was the rapid entry of new private start-up firms despite these difficulties and the bottom-up formation of integrated industrial clusters *(chanye jiqun)* and production chains *(chanyelian)* of specialty suppliers that allowed private producers to compete in an economy still dominated by state-owned firms.

The defining feature of industrial clusters is the interconnection of firms that cooperate and compete in spatially proximate locations. It is this interconnection that underlies the institutional matrix of competitive advantage.[1] Not only do industrial clusters improve information flows, but social mechanisms embedded in networks also lock in business norms sustaining trust and cooperation. Through cooperation and joint problem solving, producers reduce uncertainty and enhance strategic development of capability in their niche. In the Yangzi delta region, through these bottom-up processes from within discrete industrial clusters, there evolved autonomous networks of producers, suppliers, and distributors decoupled from the state-controlled industrial and commercial economy.

Other private start-up firms mimic the successful early start-up firms in a production niche. As new players enter the market, a critical mass of manufacturers in the same industry attracts suppliers and distributors to serve them and also specialist producers as subcontractors. This allows for the production process to be broken down into discrete steps, thereby lowering capital entry barriers for small manufacturers. Soon the local economy becomes known for its concentration of firms in the same industry, and becomes a magnet for technical workers and other specialty producers. The process then assumes a self-reinforcing growth dynamic of specialization and differentiation. The spatial proximity of hundreds and often even thousands of manufacturers allows for a rapid pace in the production cycle from purchase order to manufactured product. Manufacturers can count on all the needed component parts being readily supplied. Small satellite firms allied to a larger firm as spin-offs provide for a ready ensemble of subcontractors who are connected to that firm through long-standing personal ties and have the requisite human capital acquired from work experience there. As small firms, they are adaptive, flexible, and capable of specialized production on a short time schedule.[2]

A spatial concentration of firms ensures a stable market for skilled workers, continuously drawing in and training specialized human capital. Once an integrated industrial cluster and production chain are established, operational costs decline, as more and more entrepreneurs and vendors in accessory industries are drawn into the cluster by the critical mass of specialized human capital and organizational resources. Spatial concentration, moreover, enables individual manufacturers to economize through subcontracting arrangements with specialized subsidiary firms. The private firms in an industrial cluster and production chain can range in size from household-scale to very substantial enterprises.

In the mountainous southwestern region of Zhejiang Province, for example, when entrepreneurs start up a new business, they are able to draw on an industrial infrastructure of specialized human capital resources, subcontractors, raw material suppliers, and distribution networks. Yongkang is a city of about 530,000 people with over 15,000 registered private firms, about 3,000 of which market their products overseas, while the remaining 12,000 serve as subcontractors, suppliers, and distributors for the export-oriented manufacturing firms. The scale of the manufacturing economy is such that nearly every household has someone involved in manufacturing. By 2006, 83 manufacturers of power tools, 40 companies specializing in metal smelting and rolling, 50 home appliance makers, and 45 stainless steel producers constituted a dense network of upstream and downstream firms organized around kitchenware and home appliance production. With such a dense population of firms in overlapping niches, manufacturers in Yongkang's industrial clusters believe that they cannot find a better location for their purposes. Ying Weizhong, the manufacturer of professional knives, responds confidently to our question probing for the effect of Yongkang's remote location: "It is better to be here than in Shanghai. There's more information, you can find parts, people, and supplies close at hand and at the best price and quality."[3]

Similarly, in rural Datang county south of Hangzhou, about 150,000 people in 120 villages are involved in producing socks and stockings. The main streets of Datang county town and surrounding villages are lined with specialty supplier firms that produce the textiles, yarn, and other inputs for this industry. The county's nearly 8,000 artisan socks and stocking manufacturers are supported by a dense network of specialty supplier and distributor firms, with over 400 firms that trade in material inputs, 1,000 engaged in material processing, over 3,000 suturing shops, 5 print works, about 100 shaping shops, 300 packaging firms, 200 machinery shops, 600 socks and stocking wholesalers and retailers, and 100 shippers transporting socks and stockings to customers. Although no firm can compete alone in the global marketplace for socks and stockings, the spatial concentration of small manufacturers and the diversified network of specialty suppliers and distributors in this industrial cluster enable artisans and very small firms in Datang to achieve economies of scale.[4]

Why have industrial clusters spread across the Yangzi delta region? The advantages are clear, as a manufacturer of food processing machinery in Nantong summarizes: "First, there is a marketing benefit, because everybody knows what we are producing in this area; then it is easier to get matching parts. . . . For instance, if clients want something simpler than our product, we can go to other producers and let them produce for us. We then apply our brand name. . . . And finally, we work faster because of the competition and the higher pressure."[5]

The competitive advantage of the manufacturing economy in the Yangzi delta region is rooted in multiple overlapping industrial clusters. No other region in China has a comparable density of them. About 85 percent of private production in Zhejiang Province is concentrated in industrial clusters.[6] Most municipalities here are home to several, which evolve naturally or are located in local government-sponsored industrial parks or districts.

The spatial concentration of newly founded private firms has contributed to the development of a regional economy sharply different from the overall structure of the national economy. Whereas state-owned production dominated in most of China's northeastern and inland provincial economies well into the late 1990s, in the Yangzi delta region industrial districts created expanding "islands" of private production early in the economic reform. This enabled and motivated individual manufacturers to rapidly decouple from state-managed supply and distribution channels to establish independent networks of suppliers and distributors. Indeed, in the Yangzi delta region, private firms have almost entirely decoupled from the state-owned and state-controlled sectors of the industrial economy. These firms transact predominantly with other private firms, both as suppliers and as customers. Subcontracting relations with state owned and collectively owned companies, in contrast, are rare, underscoring the economic independence of the private sector in the Yangzi delta.

In this chapter, we analyze the social structure within the industrial clusters of the Yangzi delta region. In particular, we highlight personalized exchange and multiplex relationships, where actors deal with one another across a number of different activities, as key features of stable business networks. Through information sharing, joint market development, and various tools of short-term financing, economic actors reinforce reciprocity and trust in business relations in the industrial cluster. Reciprocity and trust add value beyond the pure economic transaction to ongoing business relationships, providing the "social glue" that stabilizes business networks. We highlight how these mechanisms facilitate market participation and render malfeasance and interruption of business relations costly, thereby promoting norm compliance, a key prerequisite to the rise and survival of private firms outside the mainstream economy.

Social Structure of Industrial Clusters

That industrial clusters offer productivity advantages through agglomeration effects is hardly disputed. Whether in the textile clusters around Prato and Veneto in northern Italy or the information and communication technology (ICT) clusters across the globe from Silicon Valley to Bangalore, such concentration seems to offer substantial benefits, independent of sector and firm size. Geographically concentrated industrial clusters save transportation costs by proximity to suppliers and distributors, and allow the development of common labor markets for specialized human capital. Moreover, collocation facilitates informational spillovers. In view of these advantages, Paul Krugman argues that geographically concentrated production should represent the rule rather than the exception in modern manufacturing.[7] In his formal model, geographic concentration results from a unique interaction of economies of scale (reached within manufacturing regions) and transportation costs to consumer markets.[8]

To more fully understand the advantages of industrial clusters, one needs to incorporate a broader focus on the local institutional structures of markets and networks, for the "simple fact of spatial proximity evidently reveals little about the ability of firms to respond to the fast-changing markets and technologies," as a comparative analysis of the regional economies of Silicon Valley and Route 128 observes.[9] What matters even more are the ongoing social interactions through crosscutting networks of entrepreneurs, engineers, researchers, and venture capitalists that bring together new combinations leading to start-up ventures.[10] Spatial proximity fosters networks that facilitate innovative activity. Agglomeration induces endogenous growth, in that "if one man starts a new idea, it is taken up by others and combined with suggestions of their own; and thus it becomes the source of further new ideas."[11] It is also through face-to-face interaction that economic actors in geographically concentrated manufacturing districts carry out detailed processes of signaling and screening. Without these, reputation building, cooperation, and deal making would be virtually impossible. Indeed, the economic analysis of the industrial cluster advantages outlined above "is likely to be incomplete unless grounded in the most fundamental aspect of proximity: face-to-face contact."[12] In a similar vein, it has been argued that "the flow of ideas and values that occurs through face-to-face interaction may be the most important feature of cities."[13]

Ongoing connections promote trust and cooperative behavior. As an ethnography of high-end Italian, Jewish, and Chinese garment manufacturers in New York City details, "embedded ties entail joint problem-solving arrangements that enable actors to coordinate functions and work out problems 'on the fly.' These arrangements provide more rapid and explicit feedback than do market-based mechanisms such as 'exit' . . . they enable firms to work through problems and to accelerate learning and problem correction."[14]

Personalized Exchange

Choosing reliable and trustworthy business associates is a critical factor shaping the firm's economic performance. For key inputs, the assurance of an agreed-upon standard of quality at a specified price and their timely delivery are crucial in the production process. For sales of products, timely payment upon delivery is a precondition to manage a firm's cash flow in a predictable and sustainable way. With intense competitive pressure, with dynamic shifts in supply and demand along with corresponding price effects, and with market uncertainties, entrepreneurs can never be entirely sure whether business associates intend to deliver on their promises or will choose to behave opportunistically. For instance, how can producers be sure that technological upgrading, training, and investments in response to customer requests will amortize in the long run if customers can easily end the business relation? How can they be sure that business secrets or technological innovations are not passed on to competitors? Such concerns become even more critical when legal recourse is expensive and enforcement of court rulings uncertain. Under such conditions, personalized exchange is a standard strategy to cultivate a network of reliable suppliers and customers. Personal interaction reduces information asymmetries between business associates, lessens the likelihood of opportunism, and thereby nourishes mutual trust and cooperative behavior.

In competitive markets generally, uncertainty poses a dilemma for firms, in that economic actors must make investment and production decisions that shape long-term business strategy and performance despite not being able to assess downstream risks. Despite all of the uncertainty, producers must commit themselves and their facilities to a certain level of production over a certain time period: "What counts is that there be commitments visible as signals to induce and support market interfaces shaped by both upstream and downstream context."[15] These commitments directly affect others, both suppliers and distributors as well as competitors, and these others adapt their own choices accordingly. In the industrial clusters of the Yangzi delta, such commitments are especially likely to be concretely made through personal interaction.

Through personalized exchange, producers receive timely market information, secure quality deliveries and timely payments, and maintain a cooperative atmosphere for joint problem solving. This allows quick responses to new market developments and order adjustments in line with sudden shifts in supply and demand. In Wenzhou, a strong emphasis on price and quality in personal dealings with suppliers enables firms to gain market share in competitive domestic and global markets.

It is essential that the contracting parties regard each other as partners in a mutually beneficial situation. This involves respectful exchange between them, as a Nanjing-based machinery manufacturer reports: "Before we have a supplier working with us, we have a series of meetings where we build a common understanding. We emphasize we want to make money *together*. We share technology, design, and even share management skills. We want them to understand that we have to make profit together. If one step in this chain is problematic, we won't be able to make a profit. . . . For this reason, we do not squeeze them to push for the lowest price and establish a fair price system in the very beginning of the business relation. We only push for constant quality improvements."[16] Close and personal ties facilitate mutual understanding and respectful behavior. Many entrepreneurs confirm that they have intense contacts with their suppliers, often involving company visits, training, and joint technology development. Many producers attend business associations, professional meetings, and trade fairs to maintain ties with current and potential suppliers. Others get together with informal circles of friends and long-term business partners to exchange information, discuss market developments, and cooperate on specific problems.

Entrepreneurs and CEOs in all the cities surveyed confirm the important role of relational ties when asked to assess their individual use of personalized exchange on a Likert scale ranging from 1 (low) to 7 (high). For supplier relations, the average score was 5.0, with about 35 percent of respondents indicating a score of 6 or 7. In contrast to the extensive reliance on business friendships, family members play only a minor role in supplier networks. Only 5 percent of respondents receive input supplies from other family-owned companies.

Producers in the Yangzi delta region also emphasize personal contact in their customer networks. Particularly in the early start-up phase, many entrepreneurs rely on personal introductions to find potential clients. Personal introductions help build trust when a track record of business conduct is as yet unavailable, the product quality unknown, and reliability of deliveries untested. This form of relational customer recruitment often begins well in advance of the actual founding and formal company registration. As previously noted (see Chapter 4), 38 percent of respondents found their first customer through personal ties, overwhelmingly through personal introduction by a friend.

After this initial start-up phase, customer acquisition is predominantly impersonal, but even so, most entrepreneurs try to cultivate personal ties with new customers. Producers we interviewed in our 2006 survey estimate that they know about 60 percent of their current customer base well enough "so that they would recognize them on the street and stop for a chat." It is commonplace for smaller producers who mainly serve local markets to socialize with their customers, extend dinner invitations, and send small gifts to secure contracts. Even large-scale manufacturers seek to cultivate ongoing personalized exchange in their main product line. Such investments are mainly for symbolic value since most entrepreneurs allocate only a modest budget for social events and gift giving. In extreme cases, however, these expenses can reach up to 20 percent of the expected contract value. Substantial investments in customer acquisition through social events are common in Shanghai and the provincial capitals Hangzhou and Nanjing, where private firms struggle to secure market share from large state-owned enterprises and multinational firms. Entrepreneurs make a point of socializing at trade fairs and exhibitions. It is common for entrepreneurs to visit each other's firms to learn more about specific customer needs and technical product requirements. Producers in Wenzhou exemplify this form of customer acquisition and customer care. With the majority of their customers located outside Zhejiang Province, Wenzhou entrepreneurs set aside only modest budgets for local social events but maintain frequent and intense business relations with out-of-province customers. According to the self-assessment of participating managers regarding personalized exchange with their customers, Wenzhou entrepreneurs score the highest on the Likert scale (5.8, whereas the mean value of the sample is 5.0).

Modern communication devices such as telephone, fax, e-mail, and the Internet allow producers to cultivate and maintain personal ties that reach out tentacle-like across the regional and national economy far beyond local business networks. Widely used business-to-business websites like Alibaba.com provide open access to new business contacts. This underscores the fact that the crosscutting business networks in the Yangzi delta region are generally not prone to closure but allow for dynamic adjustments and extensions linking entrepreneurs to new business opportunities.

Multiplex Business Relations

Personal interaction among business partners facilitates the development of strategic alliances and informal business networks for joint problem solving. With many official government policies such as credit programs and technology support still discriminating against private firms, particularly medium- and small-scale firms, producers are eager to cultivate ties with other like-minded entrepreneurs. The common notion that "you cannot survive just by yourself" spurs an active search to assemble a group of strategically positioned business contacts ready to collaborate in some of the most critical fields of company development. The pooling of individual knowledge and resources in business networks generally follows the principle of reciprocity and mutual benefit. Most interfirm alliances and informal types of cooperation focus on otherwise hard-to-secure resources, such as finance, market knowledge, and technology. In this way, multiplex business relations assist with advancing technological capability, defining product specialization, and strategically positioning the firm, and thereby facilitate survival outside the public-owned economy. Clearly, collaborative initiatives between contract partners increase the value of bilateral trading relations beyond the discounted value of expected sales contracts. Breach of contract or noncompliance with local business norms not only would jeopardize the continuation of a trading relation but also would have a profound effect on daily business operations and overall strategic planning.

Within a network of the five most important business contacts, a hypothetical producer representing the statistical mean in the Yangzi delta region is likely to engage in collaborative activities with two key suppliers and two major distributors. Further, the producer would have in his core network another manufacturer, not always from the same industry. Within this network, the producer would find one person to jointly purchase material inputs, another person for reciprocal lending, one or two persons for joint technology development, two persons to cooperate with in sales and marketing, two or three persons to discuss new market trends and pricing, one or two persons to assess new government regulations, and two or three persons to serve as brokers and reliably introduce new customers. Some producers report up to five different joint activities with a single key supplier or customer. The multiplex exchange relationships underscore the operational and strategic importance of a producer's core network.

Yet personalized exchange has not led to network closure. Other contacts are regularly introduced, and this mixture of strong and weak ties provides social capital enabling robust entrepreneurial action. In sum, the joint activities reported by entrepreneurs and managers of firms indicate that multiplex social relationships within industrial clusters serve as conduits for information sharing and interfirm cooperation, while maintaining open boundaries that readily admit new business contacts and new business opportunities.

Market Development

Being small and financially weak in comparison with the resource-rich state-owned and collective enterprises, private producers in the early years of market reform simply lacked the bargaining power to secure low-priced supplies. Moreover, access to the predominantly state-owned wholesale market was often closed. The owner of a machinery engineering company in Hangzhou recalls that it was impossible for private firms to secure competitive steel prices from the still heavily state-controlled steel market. No private firm could have established a competitive production based on the prices asked by local steel producers. However, he quickly learned to adjust. The way out was to organize joint orders. He collected small-scale orders from various private firms and combined them until there was enough volume to secure discount prices from the local steel factory. While this entrepreneur has turned his idea into a trading company for raw materials, many other entrepreneurs in the Yangzi delta region relied on the same strategy and jointly organized their supplies, often in loosely organized buyer collectives.[17]

More than 70 percent of the 2009 survey respondents had collaborated on material purchase with at least one of their five closest business contacts. More than 20 percent belong to informal buyer collectives specializing in different key input materials. Typically, these buyer collectives are formed by a group of entrepreneurs operating in the same industry, but not competing directly with each other in the same product niche.

Interfirm connections also facilitate the development of joint distribution channels and marketing strategies. About 76 percent of the respondents report collaboration in sales and marketing. Such joint organization, usually with other businesses in their niche, is cost efficient, and it helps Yangzi delta manufacturers to penetrate distant interregional markets. Cooperative marketing strategies often involve the development of independent distribution channels shared by the participating firms. For example, in Wenzhou, entrepreneurs jointly invest in maintaining a network of sales representatives who travel widely to promote local products in domestic and international markets.[18]

Information Exchange

Beyond these relatively stable, often contract-based cooperative arrangements, entrepreneurs in the Yangzi delta maintain an active information exchange with their key business relations. In business networks, multiplex ties serve as conduits for the flow of information critical to timely initiatives in entrepreneurial deal making, effective coordination between producers and their suppliers, and flexible adaptation to production cycles.[19] Suppliers and customers are often well positioned to provide information crucial for a firm's market development. Such information exchange can have tangible short-term effects, as with reciprocal recommendations of new customers that greatly help expand the client base and often lead to major sales contracts, thanks to the personal introduction. A great majority of entrepreneurs (more than 86 percent) utilize the key circle of business contacts—mostly suppliers and loyal customers—to exchange customer recommendations. Only a small minority do not rely on business friends in their immediate network to learn about potential customers.

A strategic form of information exchange among business friends and acquaintances concerns new market trends, pricing, and shifts in supply and demand. In this way, entrepreneurs position themselves in their specialized niche and receive market signals early enough to allow for timely and flexible adjustments of product portfolio and pricing. Distributors are the first to sense changes in demand, and are well informed about the product pricing of main competitors operating in the same product niche. Often suppliers are the first to identify general shifts in consumer taste. For instance, textile producers learn from their suppliers about changing taste and fashion in terms of color schemes and quality of fabric.

More than 90 percent of the surveyed entrepreneurs emphasized the importance of these diverse forms of information exchange with their key business contacts. It is not unusual for information exchange on new market trends and technologies to lead to collaboration between business friends in joint innovation projects (see Chapter 8). Direct communication with competitors, however, is less frequent. Most entrepreneurs maintain arm's-length relations with their competitors and watch their strategic moves from a distance. Only about 15 percent of the respondents exchange market information with their competitors.

A majority (close to 70 percent) of entrepreneurs share information with their closest business relations about government policy and regulations. Entrepreneurs are concerned about sudden and unpredictable policy changes. Moreover, regulatory changes are seldom transparent and information is often not widely available. The general manager of a textile company in Hangzhou, for example, recalls when his firm was eligible to receive a VAT exemption for purchases of domestic equipment. The local government, however, informed only a small number of large firms about the new policy. It was through his business network that he learned about his rights and eventually received preferential tax treatment.[20]

Short-Term Finance

In the Yangzi delta, information exchange within close-knit business communities facilitates the extension of mutual short-term loans and trade credit. This enables firms to develop their businesses without having access to formal bank lending. Assume a small-scale producer B needs supplies worth ¥10,000 from producer A in order to deliver on a sales contract worth ¥100,000 with customer C. Without retained earnings or access to bank loans, B could not sign a sales contract with C. But if A offers B a trade credit with a generous payment scheme, firm B can accept the order and sell to C, and use part of the sales profit to pay for supplies received from A. In this illustration, producer and supplier realize a combined sales value of ¥110,000 due to the extension of trade credit, which they otherwise would have missed.[21] A Nanjing-based machinery producer recalls the early days of his business: "I started from zero, so I had to know a few tricks to start my business. There are cases where I paid nothing to my suppliers, to produce for my own buyers. This system works well, if everybody in the chain is of high reputation. Only if there is a buyer who cheats, the chain breaks and I would need to borrow from friends to deliver the payment to my supplier."[22] Others occasionally benefit from up-front payments. "My clients even paid before the delivery of goods. So we were benefiting from having liquidity to support our operation. Of course these customers were my friends. They did this, because we know each other well. I first sold to friends in Shanghai, and they introduced their friends in the cities of Wuxi, Nanjing and in Anhui Province to me."[23]

Trade credit helps firms to flexibly deal with short-term financial constraints in all market economies. It is the most important source of short-term external finance for firms in the United States.[24] The reported trade credit is about 18 percent of sales in the United States and in China, for a national panel of private and state-owned firms,[25] but in our Yangzi delta sample, 25 percent of the total sales volume is sold on credit and 62 percent of entrepreneurs extend credit to their customers. Trade credit plays an even larger role in the upstream market. Overall, 70 percent of the respondents rely to some extent on trade credit for purchasing supplies. On average, manufacturers buy 45 percent of their supplies on trade credit. Generous payment schemes allow producers to stretch payment over the entire production process and to finance their supplies through sales. In our survey, the average key supplier of the main input, for instance, offers trade credit for about two months, with 25 percent of the respondents reporting even longer credit periods.[26]

In addition, entrepreneurs typically maintain mutual lending agreements with at least one business associate. Among our respondents, about three-quarters do so. This form of informal lending helps to bridge short-term liquidity problems or to finance short-term investment opportunities. Even owners of medium- or large-scale companies, who might also turn to bank lending, appreciate the flexibility and short-term availability of informal lending. Loan approval procedures can be time consuming and cumbersome, and the investment opportunity may have long passed by the time the loan is approved or denied.

To sum up, ongoing business relations in the Yangzi delta region rarely remain simply a single-purpose market connection. Nonmarket interactions embedded in the social structure of industrial clusters add value to bilateral business relations, and help entrepreneurs mitigate individual business risks stemming from institutional uncertainties and market risks. Through various forms of cooperative activity and joint problem solving, bilateral interfirm relations go far beyond the face value of ongoing sales contracts. Producers are tied to their most important business relations through a diversified and stable multiplex network. These cooperative arrangements enable private firms to develop robust informal solutions wherever formal institutions discriminate against private entrepreneurs or provide insufficient services.

Norm Compliance and Conflict Resolution

Despite the nearly universal use of formal contractual agreements in large companies in America, in fact "contract and contract law are often thought unnecessary because there are many effective non-legal sanctions. Two norms are widely accepted. (1) Commitments are to be honored in almost all situations; one does not welsh on a deal. (2) One ought to produce a good product and stand behind it."[27] The informal norms of business are enforced through an extensive web of interpersonal relations between firms, involving not only agents directly engaged in buying and selling but also the firms' executives. The personal connections across firms linking manufacturers with suppliers and distributors cumulatively exert pressure to conform to expectations. It is commonplace for agents to gossip about competitors, shortages, price increases, and incidents of breach of contract. Further, executives of firms involved in business transactions know each other and maintain formal and informal social ties. Within this context of ongoing multiplex relationships between manufacturers and their suppliers and distributors, all parties to the exchange have an interest in avoiding conduct that jeopardizes repeated transactions. Mutual obligations, expectations, trust, and reputation serve as mechanisms ensuring the stability of the business relations. Because both buyer and seller have a mutual interest in repeated exchange, they are subject to "counterbalancing sanctions," and the implicit threat of these informal sanctions functions to check opportunism and malfeasance. The manufacturer can turn to another supplier, shifting business away from a firm that does not conform to expectations. On the other hand, the present supplier may have specialized skills and an exclusive process that the manufacturer needs. Switching to a new supplier entails transaction costs. Suppliers can prioritize which buyer gets early delivery of inputs and most favored treatment when there are shortages. Thus it is in the manufacturer's interest to invest in good will with the most important suppliers. Informal and formal blacklisting of firms serves as a formidable mechanism enforcing conformity to business norms. In sum, noncontractual relations are the more salient in durable interfirm arrangements because both the threat and actual use of litigation as a means to resolve disagreements and disputes are costly, and the gains from repeated exchange benefit both buyer and seller.[28]

Entrepreneurs in the Yangzi delta emphasize these same business norms of contract compliance and quality guarantee. Professional reputation is built on the promise to deliver quality at a determined price, and to stand by the business agreement, no matter whether this is an oral agreement or a written contract. Personal interaction and specialized interpersonal arrangements involving joint problem solving provide an institutional matrix that fosters information exchange, norm compliance, and contract enforcement within business communities and industrial niches. While business disputes with suppliers and customers are not particularly uncommon, contracting parties are generally able to internally work out solutions acceptable to both parties. If the contracting parties are unable to reach an agreement, entrepreneurs typically bring in business friends or associates willing to act as mediators. External solutions involving arbitrators from outside the immediate business network, such as involvement of local government authorities or courts, are extremely uncommon.

The threat of legal litigation is not a strong driver of norm compliance. One reason for this is that in spite of massive efforts to promote the implementation of China's first unified national Contract Law (1999), not all transactions are based on written contracts. In general, contract reliance with regard to suppliers is lowest in cluster locations such as Wenzhou (61 percent) and highest in Shanghai (86 percent) and Nanjing (90 percent), where private firms still form a minority in an economy otherwise dominated by publicly owned and foreign companies. On average, according to our survey, 75 percent of supplies are based on written agreements between transacting parties. For sales, contract reliance is slightly higher, with on average 83 percent of the annual sales volume based on written contracts. Then too, execution of the Contract Law frequently collides with the traditional interpretation of contracts. Whereas contracting parties in the West can expect a contract to be executed as formulated, "the saying goes, that in China, signing a contract signifies the *beginning* of negotiations" and rarely more than the parties' agreement to desirable contract goals.[29] Finally, contractual enforcement is questionable as long as law continues to be a tool for the state. Intervention by the state in the firm's business can never be ruled out, as contracts may be deemed illegal if they "disrupt social and economic order or harm the public interest"—clearly a clause providing much room for interpretation.[30] Under the guise of "consumer rights protection," local governments have begun to actively monitor contracts and interfere with the right of "freedom of contracts."

Most producers indeed have no experience with litigation, and rarely rely on local courts to protect their interests. In contrast, social mechanisms embedded in close-knit producer communities drive and enhance the spread of generally accepted and mutually beneficial business norms. Social relations help to build trust and spread information necessary to create a collaborative business atmosphere that allows for joint problem solving. Even in relatively clear-cut business disputes, entrepreneurs in our survey mostly did not pursue legal recourse as a viable strategy. The general manager of a business service company recalls the situation when one of his business partners made unauthorized use of his brand name. He turned to the government to seek advice and to learn about his chances to protect his rights by filing a lawsuit. To his surprise, the government official did not recommend seeking legal recourse. The official warned that an expensive lawsuit might eventually produce a favorable ruling but that this would most likely not be enforced by the legal system.[31] Other entrepreneurs described financial difficulties encountered in the early years of economic reform when buyers refused to pay their bills and receivables accumulated. But when the value of a claim is modest and costs of litigation high, neither lawyers nor courts are interested in dealing with such business disputes.

Among the entrepreneurs in our survey who encountered some form of business dispute with at least one of their suppliers between 2004 and 2006, the great majority (84 percent, or 101 out of 120 firms reporting disputes) worked out an acceptable solution through bilateral negotiations. Ten percent (twelve firms) utilized personal ties to resolve their disputes. Only 3 percent turned to local government for mediation, and another 3 percent of the firms resorted to litigation. The picture is similar for business disputes with customers. In total, almost 20 percent of our survey firms experienced business disputes with one or more customers between 2004 and 2006. These cases are also typically solved through bilateral negotiations (120 out of 139, or 86 percent). Four percent of these firms (five firms) utilized personal connections, 2 percent (three firms) sought government intermediation, and 7 percent (ten firms) saw no alternative but to file a lawsuit.[32]

Clearly, the threat of legal recourse plays only a minor role in shaping business norms and disciplining business partners. This is in line with the fact that written contracts do not yet seem to play a decisive role in mitigating business risks. In terms of contract reliance, there is no statistical difference between the group of companies that experience business disputes with suppliers or customers and those companies that do not encounter any disputes.

Instead, the robustness of supplier and customer relations, broad norm compliance, and the ability to solve problems through private means rests on fluid information exchange within the business community and the strong role of reputation effects. "Good relations are based on trustworthiness, which involves not treating others as fools," an entrepreneur explains. "As time passes, others will find out about everything."[33] If both trading partners are unable to work out a satisfying solution in case of conflict, word will quickly be out, warning others about deviators and potential norm-breakers. The threat of such negative reputation effects provides a strong motivational force to work out mutually acceptable bilateral agreements. Moreover, deviators have to calculate with ensuing community sanctions, which can substantively increase the expected costs of contract breach. Naturally, spatial proximity in cluster locations can be helpful in avoiding business conflicts through improved *ex ante* screening of business partners and monitoring of business transactions, although information exchange often extends outward and does not necessarily depend on spatial proximity. In our survey, we find that stronger reliance on local suppliers and customers reduces the probability of encountering business disputes. In contrast, dependence on international suppliers and customers is associated with a higher probability of disputes.

To underscore the effectiveness of the underlying social mechanisms in the Yangzi delta region, we return to the two key business norms identified above.

1. *Commitments are to be honored in almost all situations; one does not welsh on a deal.* Intracommunity information exchange provides an effective mechanism to enforce oral or written agreements and to sort potential deviators from honest businessmen. Almost 50 percent of respondents in both our 2006 and 2009 surveys believe that they would find out if one of their suppliers cheated on another client. This is true for young and old firms, for small-scale and large-scale producers, and independent of the industrial sector. Information exchange usually develops spontaneously as a mutually beneficial and self-reinforcing strategy within informal business networks and is typically not tied to membership in formal organizations. Entrepreneurs without organizational affiliation enjoy as much access to information on supplier malfeasance as members of industrial associations (or guilds) or local branches of the Association of Private Entrepreneurs.

Joint interests and interpersonal relations through joint problem-solving strategies in particular industrial niches define the boundaries of these informal information networks. Spatial proximity is not necessarily a critical determinant. Thanks to the strong reliance on personalized exchange, information on supplier malfeasance seems to be equally available to producers with supply channels across province lines as to those relying on local suppliers. Furthermore, this type of community information exchange is prevalent in all survey cities independently of the local spread and density of cluster production or local commercial traditions. In Shanghai, where private producers typically rely on supplier networks located in adjacent provinces, 60 percent of the respondents believe they would learn about supplier malfeasance; whereas in Wenzhou, a city with strong reliance on cluster production of small- and medium-scale producers, only 46 percent of entrepreneurs expressed similar confidence.

With regard to standard cases of contract breach—late deliveries of supplies and delayed payments—somewhat less than half (about 42 percent) of respondents indicate that they would bring the former to the attention of other business contacts such as customers and suppliers, and almost half (47 percent) would discuss the latter. Clearly, in both cases, mutual information sharing can help to identify potentially unreliable or untrustworthy business partners, and thereby may prevent other members from future economic losses.[34] In parallel, community sanctions increase the expected costs for deviators in such cases of contract breach and thereby help to reduce business risks. On average, approximately a quarter (26 percent) of respondents expect community sanctions if word gets out that a supplier does not honor the contractually agreed-upon delivery time. Somewhat more (31 percent) expect community sanctions if financial commitments are not promptly honored.

These mechanisms appear to be a powerful deterrent against uncooperative behavior. Payment issues are typically settled internally. Entrepreneurs are usually willing to deal with delays in payment or bad-quality deliveries. A common notion is that sanctions should always depend on the way the delinquent contracting party handles these issues. Hard-and-fast rules often seem counterproductive and not able to capture the specific circumstances. A Nanjing-based machinery producer summarizes, "Of course problems with payments do exist, but we will always talk with the firm. The good ones will tell us when they can eventually pay. The bad ones will just delay us longer and longer. . . . I then decide on a case-by-case basis whether I will continue to deal with them. For me it is important to know whether they really were in a financially difficult situation and could not make their payment on time."[35] Others confirm the importance of transparency and communication. A Nantong-based textile producer, for instance, says, "Normally clients will alert us, if there is a liquidity problem and they will try to give us a later payment date. This is then OK for us."[36]

2. *One ought to produce a good product and stand behind it.* Reliance on social mechanisms for norm enforcement is most pronounced when it comes to product quality. More than half of the respondents would discuss quality issues with others, if the producer is not willing to correct subquality deliveries in line with the business agreement. A significant number (33 percent) expect that such information would affect other business deals as well, and induce other firms to cut business ties or reduce contract volume with the respective producer. Noncooperative behavior on quality issues is therefore clearly a self-defeating strategy, as quality-reducing cost savings are likely to be outweighed by loss of other business. Whereas information exchange is almost ubiquitous, such community sanctions depend to a greater extent on spatial

proximity and close-knit cluster structures. This form of third-party enforcement is therefore less common in Shanghai, where private-firm communities have not yet reached a density comparable to that in the provinces of Zhejiang and Jiangsu.

Most entrepreneurs report that quality issues can always be settled through joint negotiations. Many private companies have internal guidelines to respond to quality issues within a certain period of time. Major quality issues are solved by replacements; minor issues are usually settled through price deductions.

However, entrepreneurs need to make sure that there is no abuse of the reputation mechanism. They communicate within their network if clients make unjustified complaints trying to reduce the price for deliveries. A ball-bearing manufacturer in Nantong describes the case of one of his business associates who has an output value of ¥10 million a year but has faced requests of ¥1.5 million for refunds. These refund cases, however, are anything but clear. "Bearings are usually made of alloy and axles are of metal. . . . Alloy is soft and metal is stiff and therefore there are many reasons for damage, such as low-quality gasoline or impurities on the parts. But the engine producer always blames us for low-quality bearings." Clearly, he and his friends exchange views in such cases and seek to avoid clients who are known to make unjustified complaints. "We collect concerns from our peers and report them to the Chinese National Internal Combustion Engine Association, which is in charge of bearing and engine associations. But this is of no use. When dealing with this type of firm, our strategy is that they have to pay up front; only after that will we do business. It's impossible to have an industry-wide approach."[37]

Clearly, industrial clusters in the Yangzi delta have distinct social and institutional functions going well beyond effects of local industrial specialization on the work process, including fostering norm compliance in an environment devoid of effective law enforcement. Through fluid intracommunity information exchange, norm breakers are likely to be identified and exposed to the broader community. The risk of community sanctions increases the expected cost of noncompliance and may deter and limit malfeasance.

Autonomy of the Private Enterprise Economy

Many entrepreneurs point to great difficulties in doing business with state-owned companies. They often do not have sufficient knowledge of internal procedures there and lack the social capital to deal with those companies when business conflicts arise. In contrast, entrepreneurs appreciate the more cooperative atmosphere in dealing with private businesses. Because they share similar conditions, they can understand and respect each other's constraints and problems, and this contributes to the rise of mutually beneficial and generally accepted business norms.

Interviewees emphasize that business transactions with private firms are generally more efficient, given management style and responsiveness to requests. Higher competitive pressure within the private sector coupled with hard budget constraints has led to greater flexibility and adaptability, which in turn have fostered the development of internal procedures that guarantee a quick turnover. This applies at each stage, from successful negotiation of a supply or sales contract to shipment of product, receiving payment, and provision of after-sales service. The new owner of a food processing company formerly owned by local government observed, "When we became a private firm, things somehow became simpler. As long as you have integrity, admit the problems you have, and are willing to improve, you can maintain your business. As a township village enterprise, we spent a lot of time on questions like who to contact and how much kick-back to provide. Now our focus is on improving quality and improving reputation." He added, "Of course, one may encounter quality problems with products from private companies, but private firms will always try to adjust. Township and village enterprises, in contrast, would not pay attention to our complaints."[38]

Supplier Networks

In manufacturing, timely delivery of inputs by suppliers is critical for execution of the production schedule. Also, the quality of these inputs obviously affects the quality of the product and ultimately the firm's market performance. Thus reliable and sustainable supplier relations are crucial. In the Yangzi delta region, manufacturers rely on multilateral and multiplex networks of private firms serving as suppliers. When assessing the source of their competitive advantage, entrepreneurs often praise their private suppliers for being more flexible and cooperative than state-owned companies. They point out that private suppliers share a similar mindset with them, and are more likely to respond to their specific needs and problems.

Zhu Jinhong, the second-largest manufacturer of stovetop coffee makers in the world, relies on an entirely local network of highly specialized small firms in

Yongkang which supply him with needed inputs. Many involve former employees, and with them he has verbal agreements. With others, Zhu has written contracts for key specialty inputs. They are bound by these contractual agreements to produce these key inputs exclusively for him, as a measure to safeguard patented components from his competitors. Still other suppliers provide general inputs such as boxes to package Zhu's coffee makers. Although written contracts are routine in his business dealings with these suppliers, he does not regard them as legal documents since he rarely litigates disagreements with them. To illustrate, he described the production of industrial molds, among his most important inputs since they involve patented designs. With the supplier that makes the mold, he has a contractual agreement to share 50 percent of the cost of production, which secures him property rights over the mold. In this arrangement, the written contract is less important than the alignment of shared interests between supplier and the manufacturing firm. In Zhu's assessment, close proximity and durable relations with his supplier networks provide an indispensable competitive advantage, enabling him to gain market share in the global economy for aluminum stovetop coffee makers.

Almost three-quarters (74 percent) of the CEOs interviewed in our 2006 survey indicate that their most important supplier is another private firm. In contrast, only 10 percent rely on a state-owned firm as their main supplier (see Figure 6.1). Some others receive their inputs from collectives, foreign firms, or joint ventures. The strong emphasis on private suppliers is evident even in a subsample of fifty-eight privatized state- or collective-owned companies. Only 25 percent of these formerly publicly owned firms received their main inputs from a state-owned company. And it is evident even in Nanjing and Shanghai, the regional manufacturing centers of collective and state-owned firms in the pre-reform period, where a solid majority of private manufacturers (65 percent in Nanjing and 69 percent in Shanghai) indicate that their most important supplier is a private firm. Moreover, this reliance on private suppliers is true for all industries covered by our survey. Only firms in the pharmaceutical and medical industry are somewhat more likely to utilize state-owned suppliers, with 15 percent having state-owned suppliers as their primary source. This is consistent with the higher level of regulation of the medical health industry, which only recently became open to private enterprise participation.

Many of the suppliers are located in the same city as the firms, or in close proximity in the same region. Spatial proximity not only reduces transportation costs, but corresponds with a strong reliance on local business norms in industrial clusters in the Yangzi delta region. It also enhances cooperation and joint problem solving between firms. Wu Liping, the founder of the automated packaging equipment company in Danyang, emphasizes his principle to work only with suppliers located within twenty to thirty miles from his company. This reduces training costs at the start of a cooperation and allows flexible and timely troubleshooting should problems arise. Overall, according to our 2006 survey, producers located in the same city deliver on average 35 percent of a firm's key supplies. About another 30 percent come from suppliers located in the same region, and only 30 percent come from suppliers located in a different province. (The residual comes from imports.)

However, spatial concentration in supply networks varies across the Yangzi delta region, reflecting the different timing of private development and the uneven distribution of industrial clusters (see Figure 6.2). Reliance on same-city suppliers is strongest in Zhejiang Province (38 to 60 percent), home to the largest agglomeration of industrial clusters, and slightly less pronounced in Jiangsu Province (24 to 45 percent), where private firm development took off later than in Zhejiang Province. It is uncommon in Shanghai (4 percent), where private firms lack access to government-designed technology zones, populated by large-scale state owned and foreign-owned corporations. In Shanghai, private firms concentrate in the suburban districts of the municipality,

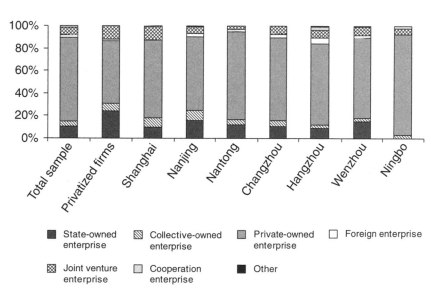

Figure 6.1. Ownership type of largest input supplier. *Source:* Yangzi Survey 2006.

where they engage in cross-border trading with private firms located in Jiang-su and Zhejiang Provinces.

Reliance on local supply networks is not simply a convenient initial strat-egy for small start-up firms. On the contrary, it appears to strengthen over time, with older firms relying more on local suppliers. Moreover, it is inde-pendent of firm size, as large firms also establish and cultivate local supply networks.[39]

These networks tend to be stable and durable. Most manufacturers in our 2006 survey had been dealing with their main input supplier for more than six years. The common pattern is for firms to establish stable business relations with their key supplier within the first two years of business operation. The connection is strengthened as the firm gains confidence in the reliability of the supplier. Durable business ties with local suppliers do not imply the absence of competition, however. Firms typically rely on several sources for their key sup-plies. This mitigates the risk of delivery delays, and assures the flow and quality of inputs needed to meet the firm's production schedule. Individual suppliers have an incentive to remain competitive in the supplier network because manu-facturers could always withdraw orders and transfer them to another. The num-ber of supply sources increases with a firm's age, as does the duration of business relations with the suppliers for the firm's main inputs. Manufacturers have an implicit business strategy to encourage competition among their suppliers as bilateral business relationships mature. Private firms in the 2006 sample re-ported an average of six different suppliers for their most important input; only 5 percent of the survey firms relied on a single source. This contrasts with 15

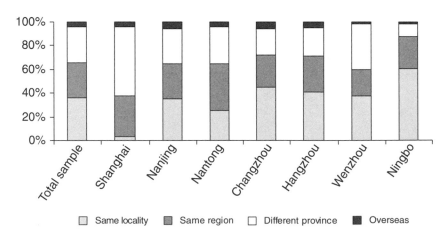

Figure 6.2. Spatial distribution of suppliers. *Source:* Yangzi Survey 2006.

percent of a national sample of firms, according to the World Bank Investment Climate Survey (2003). Supplier diversification thus appears more pronounced among private firms in the Yangzi delta region.

Customer Networks

As with the reliance on private supplier networks, manufacturers distribute their products mainly through nonstate marketing networks, underscoring the autonomy of the private enterprise economy in the Yangzi delta region. Here too, shared circumstances and mutually accepted norms ease business relations.

In particular, timely payment by customers is much more important for private firms than it is for state-owned companies, because their need for short-term finance is not met by loans from state-owned banks. A machinery producer based in Nanjing recalls earlier experiences with late payments for purchases by state-owned companies: "To deal with them you need the right relationships. If you lack this you have no way, even if you make gifts to them. Sometimes we have waited for two years for a one-month payment. Private firms, however, are most concerned with the financing chain. Once the chain is broken, the firm goes bankrupt. There is no use to go to court. All we can do is to avoid these state enterprises. The only firms I want to deal with are foreign firms and private firms with a good reputation."[40] Similar problems are reported with respect to collective firms. Another entrepreneur notes, "Township village enterprises do not pay cash, they only pay on a monthly basis, and their personnel asks for kick-backs. . . . I'd rather have private firms as clients because it is simpler to deal with them and get payment; it was just too difficult to deal with township village enterprises in general; there were many problems with respect to payments."[41]

Sales to government units and state-owned businesses are very limited in scope. Among survey firms, 54 percent do not report any sales to state-owned enterprises, and 86 percent do not report any sales to government units. Even those that do report some such sales sell only a small proportion (on average 19 percent) of their total production there. In the provincial capital cities—Shanghai, Nanjing, and Hangzhou—more private manufacturers (25 percent) report sales to government (see Figure 6.3). Firms in Nanjing and Hangzhou also rely more on sales in local and provincial markets (see Figure 6.4), which suggests that reliance on sales to government-owned units reflects weaker market orientation and competitiveness. Private firms in Nanjing are more engaged in subcontracting relations with local state-owned enterprises. By contrast, most private firms in Zhejiang Province, where private firm development is most advanced, report no sales to government units. Only some of the privatized companies rely heavily on business with state-owned or collective firms. A Ningbo-based entrepreneur operating a small-scale company producing plastic material, for instance, proudly reports that his key customers are some of China's largest state-owned steel companies—customers that his company already maintained ties with when his firm was still run as a small workshop belonging to a collectively run township village enterprise. After privatization, it seemed a natural strategy to maintain these ties and to use the existing network with state-owned companies to further expand the customer base.[42]

Longtime party members and former managers of state-owned enterprises are still prone to sell their products to government entities. This is in part a reflection of *ex ante* business relations at the time of privatization, and signals that information flow in these firms continues to be channeled through political connections (see Chapter 9). Overall, however, higher consistency of business norms and management style leads to an extensive reliance on privately organized distribution networks in industrial clusters. The overall pattern of very limited sales to state-owned enterprises is consistent with the private enterprise economy's independence from the state-owned and state-controlled sectors of the transition economy.

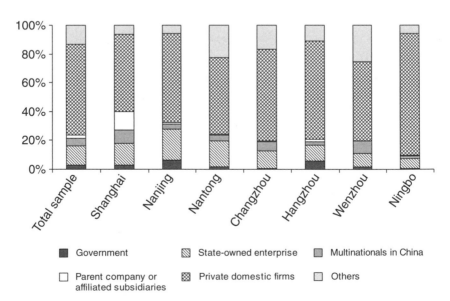

Figure 6.3. Ownership structure of customers. *Source:* Yangzi Survey 2006.

Competitive Advantage on a Wider Stage

Following the principle to cooperate locally in order to be more competitive outside the local economy, most private manufacturers (60 percent) aim to market their products both domestically and internationally. The far-ranging array of customer networks stands in sharp contrast to the spatial concentration of supply networks in the Yangzi delta region.[43]

To gain market share in a highly competitive environment, with large numbers of small- and medium-scale competitors crowded in product niches, producers need to accurately assess their price-quality ranking in the domestic and international markets. Attentive to market signals from other firms in their niche, they adapt their products accordingly, differentiating and specializing with respect to price and quality, and thus self-organizing in a hierarchy.[44] "It is all about finding the right balance of quality and price," notes a manufacturer of medical equipment based in Nanjing.

> Over time there is a development process of price and quality. . . . We would like to have a higher quality, but you also need a competitive price. . . . My own firm is currently at a middle stage. In my industry the highest standard is produced by Hitachi and Olympus, and their price is about eight times that of my product, but the quality is only about 15 percent above my product. Once we overcome the 15 percent gap, we will double our own price and we will still be four times lower than Japanese brands. Now some Japanese companies buy our products. In this industry the mid-range products from Italy, Spain, and France have a higher price, but the quality is comparable. Only three years ago, these mid-level companies still had 50 percent of the market, but now they are almost gone.[45]

After-sales service and having a well-known brand also play an important role in price-setting strategies. Careful analysis of his own quality ranking allowed a Nanjing machinery manufacturer to gain market share in North America. With only a 2.4 percent return rate for his steel welding machines, customers are willing to pay a price 15 percent above that for competing products.[46]

Another Nanjing machinery manufacturer is well established in the domestic market, where he maintains a market share of 40 to 45 percent, and thus is already able to ask a price 15 percent higher than that asked by his domestic competitors. Now he is observing the strategic moves of his two main competitors, from Korea and Taiwan, both producing comparable quality at an even higher price. Through the Internet and his client network, he follows changes in their product line and pricing policy to position his own firm. Only recently he learned from his customers that both companies are rethinking their strategy and are considering leaving the Chinese market—an opportunity he does not want to miss.[47]

Producers in the Yangzi delta region keep close tabs on their competition by regularly attending trade fairs both in China and abroad. Even though they may lack English-language competence, many routinely travel to the United States and Europe to observe and learn about their competitors' products and to show their own. Via the Internet, entrepreneurs also examine products displayed by their competitors on websites. Technical specifications and drawings there can be detailed enough for another firm's designers to use them as the basis for up-grading its own product lines. Moreover, international purchasing agents routinely bring with them samples of products for Chinese manufacturers to mimic.

Alliances with foreign firms, whether as clients or as partners, typically involve a different institutional logic than do domestic relationships. Entre-preneurs view entering into business relations with foreign clients as a strategic move that contributes to their firm's development. Foreign firms force private companies to adapt international standards and to improve product qualities. Through original design manufacturing (ODM) agreements, firms get access to technological specifications and quality control programs. These are "stretch relationships," where cooperation with sophisticated international clients helps entrepreneurs to "pull their companies out of second-rate practices and drag their companies to world-class practices and performance levels."[48] Clearly, these business relations with foreign firms also send positive signals to domestic clients, helping to increase domestic market share. "This is because of the Chinese way of thinking," the ball-bearing producer in Nantong explains. "If foreign firms like our quality, it must be good for domestic clients as well. We actually use foreign firms to attract domestic clients. . . . Of course, I do not try to get the best foreign firm right away. First we do business with number two or three, and then try to move up the ladder. . . . And eventually we have both domestic and international clients."[49] Most companies prefer to trade with a small and select circle of foreign firms in order to avoid develop-ing a dependent relationship with any one of them.

The wide-ranging spatial spread of customer networks confirms the suc-cessful quality-and-pricing strategies of the majority of producers located in the Yangzi delta region. Most entrepreneurs in our survey have shifted out of the local market and produce for the domestic national and international markets. Only 18 percent of the survey firms focus on provincial markets, and only 8 percent view their locality as the main target market. The ranking in relative importance of different target markets is consistent across all municipalities, though the percentages vary (see Figure 6.4). Wenzhou, the city with the highest density of industrial production clusters, has the greatest share of out-of-province trade, which underscores the effectiveness of local industrial clusters in manufacturing nationally and internationally competitive products.

Despite their far-flung nature, customer networks show a stability similar to that of supplier networks. A majority of sales are based on repeat exchange, with on average 68 percent going to return customers. Repeat exchange appears to be slightly higher for Zhejiang-based companies than for those in Jiangsu, with both substantively higher than for those in Shanghai (at 54 percent).

In highly competitive industries with small product differentiation, some new market entrants try to attack the client relations of established producers by undercutting their market price. However, a textile producer in Nantong points to the limited growth prospects of these predators: "In my market, the pricing is relatively clear-cut. Cloth usually sells at ¥21,000 a ton, but some sell for 19,000 a ton, not making any profit. In my industry the price of raw material is transparent; even management costs are comparable, so if the price is too low, there cannot be any profit. . . . It is usually well known in the industry who these predators are. But we do not talk about it. There is just no point to quarrel, as the market will solve the problem."[50] A commonly held

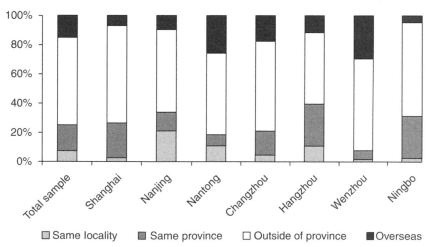

Figure 6.4. Spatial distribution of sales structure. *Source:* Yangzi Survey 2006.

belief among established players is that customers will not walk away, as long as producers offer a good price-quality mix.

Conclusion

That industrial clusters provide competitive advantage through agglomeration is hardly disputed. In geographically concentrated clusters, producers economize on transportation costs by proximity to upstream and downstream markets, find a large pool of specialized human capital, and benefit from informational spillovers. While these factors are important, they do not entirely capture the full potential of industrial clusters. What is missing in this account is the role of personalized exchange in the competitive advantage of industrial clusters. The spatial proximity in cluster locations provides fertile ground for the social processes necessary for the bottom-up development of business norms sustaining trust and cooperation. It is within these close-knit business communities that entrepreneurs have the necessary information and monitoring tools to facilitate cooperation and timely deal making. Personalized exchange and multiplex business relations provide the social glue, strengthening norm compliance and promoting cooperative forms of conflict resolution within robust networks.

In the Yangzi delta region, industrial cluster location helped like-minded actors to develop mutually agreed-upon norms and behavioral codes that were decisive in facilitating the private sector's decoupling from standard rules and norms guiding socialist production in the mainstream economy. Spatial proximity of trading partners as well as competitors has thus helped to limit the costs of decoupling and institution building. Without close-knit and highly specialized business communities, it is doubtful whether entrepreneurs in the Yangzi delta would have been able to rapidly develop independent supplier and distribution networks outside the state's marketing channels. Contracts and deal making would have simply been too risky without the provision of private safeguard mechanisms embedded in the social structure of industrial clusters.

It is important to note, however, that reliance on personalized exchange has not limited the geographic expansion of markets and sales. Customer networks are far less localized than supplier networks, with widespread reliance on cross-provincial trade and worldwide export. Clearly, private entrepreneurs have by now developed into fully integrated market players, who appear not to be confined by local network boundaries.

7

The Development of Labor Markets

An abundant, nearly limitless supply of young, healthy, and literate workers ready to shift out of agricultural production was a key factor fueling the rapid growth and competitive advantage of the private enterprise economy. In the early 1980s, in response to robust grassroots action to return to household farming by peasants in Anhui Province, one of the poorest and most populated provinces, reform leaders crafted the first major reform policy to dismantle the institutions of collectivized agriculture. In its place, the central government promoted nationwide the household responsibility system, which assigned to every rural household on a per capita basis arable land formerly farmed by the production team and brigade. The initial contract duration of one or two years was soon extended to fifteen years and in later revisions up to fifty years. In this new arrangement, each household signed a contract with local government to produce a specified quota of agricultural goods to be sold to the state, with above-quota production available to the peasant household either for consumption or for sale in rural free markets. The new system provided effective incentives at the margin, and stimulated a swift increase in individual labor productivity and growth in rural income.[1] Whereas annual per capita production of grain was about 661 pounds in 1978, it had increased to more than 881 pounds by 1984. Overall, the nominal production value in farming increased in that period by more than 100 percent.[2] Eighty percent of the productivity increase has been attributed to the replacement of collective farming by a household-based production system.[3]

With the substantial increase in labor productivity, the shift to the household system also unveiled the massive extent of underemployment in agriculture.

After decades of strict migration controls between rural and urban areas inhibiting structural employment changes, the surplus labor in the agricultural sector was estimated to range between 100 million and 156 million, or between 35 and 55 percent.[4] This large pool of workers was ready to shift out of agriculture. Furthermore, the small average size of allotted plots of only 0.5 hectares per household (about two thirds of a football field) meant that reliance on farming alone mainly met only the peasant family's subsistence needs. In the densely populated Yangzi delta, the average land holdings declined to 0.04 ha per person in Zhejiang, 0.07 ha in Jiangsu, and 0.02 ha in periurban farms near Shanghai.[5] The household responsibility system thus gave rise to structural incentives for peasant households to diversify their income streams through starting up small businesses and seeking off-farm employment. In sum, in the early 1980s, a large pool of workers ready to shift out of agriculture opened the way for bottom-up institutional innovations that cumulatively created intra- and interprovincial labor markets supplying workers for private firms.

Many households maintained the farm as a quasi–social security arrangement to satisfy subsistence needs, while members also sought nonagricultural work in nearby rural townships or in the thriving coastal cities. Land-lease contracts provide migrant workers with long-term security and a subsistence guarantee, as is evident in these interviews with young female laborers in Shenzhen:

> My parents keep my land certificate, and I do not know much about what's written there. The village committee divides up the land and the production team does the practical work of assigning specific plots of land. I am not worried that I will lose my land right because I work in Shenzhen and have other people farm my land. As long as I live the land is always mine, whether I make money or not, rich or poor. I am not a city resident. As long as I am a peasant, I should have my plot of land. My son can inherit and use the land, especially if he turns out to be mediocre in other lines of work. At least he has this last resort of returning to the land.

> All of us who come to the city to *dagong* [find work] have a psychological goal. For myself, I need to make at least two thousand yuan net per year, or about six hundred yuan per month. Otherwise it is not worth leaving home. Shenzhen's 574 yuan minimum wage is barely enough. The situation turned from bad to worse when our factory stopped paying us for three months when there was no order. Not even livelihood allowances. How can we survive? In my home village, growing rice and corn alone does not make any money. But peasants can earn about two thousand yuan by selling vegetables,

grain, or fruit. I am thinking of going home for good. Some of my coworkers from Sichuan have gone home. It's not worth it, working in the city.[6]

In the early 1990s, almost all rural households (97 percent) worked the land, even though about 43 percent of them already earned some form of local nonagricultural income, according to a survey conducted in 1994 by the Ministry of Labor. In the more developed coastal provinces of the Yangzi delta, many families also leased part of their land to other households, freeing the whole family to seek off-farm employment.

An unintended consequence of this subsistence guarantee from farming was to provide rural migrants with a reservation wage and bargaining position in their search for off-farm employment. Its effect on the terms of labor relations in the private enterprise economy was to set the minimum nonfarm wage at a level higher than what a peasant laborer could earn from farming the land and selling surplus produce on the market. At the same time, the household responsibility system kept the cost of off-farm labor relatively low because the basic subsistence needs of the peasant family were assured through long-term land leases. This in turn facilitated the endogenous rise of flexible, extensive, and diversified labor markets supplying firms with both skilled and unskilled workers willing to accept short-term and part-time employment. Thus the emergence of labor markets was inexorably tied to welfare assurances provided by the reforms in agriculture. Maoist-era investments extending primary and junior middle school education and basic health services to peasants also contributed to the readiness of a willing and able workforce.

The only employment channel readily available for off-farm job seekers was the newly rising nonstate sector operating outside the central labor allocation system. Formal employment in state-owned firms and urban collectives remained essentially closed for rural job seekers. The government maintained its strict household registration system (implemented in 1958) classifying residents into rural and urban households, and placing permanent rural-urban migration under a tight system of state control and approval. While millions of rural-urban migrants bypassed formal migration rules to live temporarily (and often illegally) outside their legal place of residence, the system continued to effectively control access to urban public-sector labor markets. Urban residents had exclusive access to the central labor allocation system (in place until 1994) and social welfare benefits such as lifelong employment, subsidized housing, health care, child care, and pensions. This effectively shut rural migrants out from qualified and well-paid work in the public sector. Furthermore, with about 20 to 30 percent of underemployed workers, public-owned industrial enterprises in urban China recorded levels of labor surplus similar to that in the agricultural sector.[7] Scope for new recruitments was therefore limited to temporary work and tasks that urban workers were unwilling to fulfill. Meanwhile, labor relations in the emerging private economy were not subject to government regulation and monitoring in terms of conditions of employment and wage policies, but instead followed principles of free-market exchange and industry-specific norms. It was not until the first Labor Law (effective in 1995) that the state even attempted to provide a general legal framework applicable to all types of employment relations. The national Labor Contract Law did not become effective until 2008.

In this chapter we examine the emergence of labor markets as a core economic institution enabling the rapid development of the private enterprise economy. We highlight how entrepreneurs developed both personal and impersonal recruitment channels to flexibly respond to different labor market conditions for skilled and unskilled workers in their localities. We then compare employment relations across ownership forms, confirming an ongoing process of institutional isomorphism that legal enforcement cannot fully account for. The chapter concludes with a discussion of how mimetic and normative pressures fostered the development of human resource policies, gradually enabling private firms to compete with public and foreign firms for skilled and experienced professional staff.

The Emergence of Labor Markets

An unintended consequence of the decollectivization of agriculture was the hidden subsidy provided by the arable land assigned to rural households, which assured that the basic subsistence needs of peasant families were met and thus enabled private firms to benefit competitively from a much lower wage structure. Although entrepreneurs were denied access to formal loans from state-owned banks, the surplus agricultural labor in their locality was a form of capital readily accessible to them. It was not uncommon for the start-up phase of private firms to depend on unpaid family labor and temporary or part-time nonfamily workers. Oftentimes the initial workforce was made up of the entrepreneur's relatives, friends, and immediate neighbors. As the firm grew in size, these employees provided the personal referrals used to recruit new workers.

How can an informal system of personal referrals initially relying on relatives, friends, and acquaintances give rise to extensive and differentiated labor markets? Although entrepreneurs starting up small firms may rely on personal referrals of available workers in the immediate vicinity, as the firms' labor demands grow and subsequent referrals (some coming from the workers themselves) multiply, recruitment chains lengthen and referrals can quickly spill outside the local context. The mix of recruits—some brought in through weak ties—eventually becomes independent of the characteristics of the local network or set of personal relationships from which recruitment began. Mixing and random interaction in job referrals renders the process ergodic, or one that "forgets" its initial state—in other words, a memoryless Markov process.[8] With growing numbers of small start-up firms, labor recruitment by network referrals evolves into a dynamical system, becoming increasingly impersonal.

In this way, from local networks that recruited off-farm workers through relatives, friends, and acquaintances, a diversified interprovincial labor market gradually developed to meet the growing labor demands of the Yangzi delta's thriving regional economy. Many workers came from the bordering highly populated agrarian provinces of Anhui and Jiangxi. These and other inland provinces with high population density, small plots of land, and lagging nonagricultural development became net exporters of labor, increasingly replenishing the thriving labor markets in the coastal areas.

In labor migration from impoverished inland regions, the social mechanisms are essentially the same as in international migration from Mexico to the United States.[9] The first migrants leave villages, rural towns, and smaller cities in poorer and less developed regions in search of work in the thriving economies of the coastal provinces, often drawn by hearsay regarding lucrative opportunities in higher-paying manufacturing and service jobs. Many of the rural migrant workers learn about and secure off-farm employment through their personal network before they leave their village.[10] They are typically the young, healthy, and better educated (most have junior middle school education), generally without prior experience in off-farm work. After migrants secure jobs, they send remittances back to their families, providing supplementary cash income that affords the family a higher standard of living than that of other families without migrant workers with off-farm jobs. During holidays like the Spring Festival, migrant workers return to their homes to visit and rest, often laden with gifts, and spread the word about job opportunities in the local economy where they work. Other rural youths sub-sequently decide to pursue these opportunities themselves, and soon a chain migration is launched, with the earlier migrants providing information and direct assistance to the new off-farm job seekers in securing jobs and resi-dence. As in international migration, the costs and risks of migration are re-duced as more and more young workers from a locality find employment and settle in migrant neighborhoods and communities in industrializing town-ships and cities.[11] The labor migration continues until essentially all who seek off-farm employment have left villages, rural towns, and smaller cities to find manufacturing jobs.

Rural workers provide a continuous supply of low-skilled but literate labor for factories in the Yangzi delta region, most often employed in those indus-tries that heavily depend on manual work and simple production techniques. Often work routines in factories can be learned within hours or a few days, without professional training or prior work experience in manufacturing. Of salience to employers is the willingness of rural migrants to take entry-level, low-status manufacturing and service jobs that urban workers do not want.[12] Despite often hazardous conditions of work, especially in "dirty" in-dustries such as chemicals and plastics, the pay attracts a continuous flow of young rural migrants seeking cash income to supplement family subsistence farming.

Entrepreneurs in the Yangzi delta region underscore the advantages of market-based employment relations for private firms. First, unlike state-owned enterprises, private firms benefit from flexibility in such relations and are not encumbered by guarantees of lifelong employment. Workers in the private sector are prepared to accept short-term and part-time employment and re-spond flexibly to the specific needs of the factory. Second, the wage system rewards individual productivity, and is more effective in motivating workers than the egalitarian compensation of state-owned enterprises. Entrepreneurs emphasize that the more competitive mindset of their employees, compared to that of workers in state-owned firms, is an important source of their suc-cess. Finally, private firms do not have the burden of providing generous welfare benefits as state-owned enterprises do.

Nationally, by the year 1994, more than one-third of rural households had at least one member who migrated to seek off-farm employment.[13] Census data indicated that rural migrants represented a majority of about 60 percent in an estimated national migrant population of about 131 million. More recent estimates of the National Bureau of Statistics suggest an ongoing increase of rural labor migration, with about 140 million rural migrants in 2008, although migrant streams no longer favor exclusively the coastal areas.[14] By 2006, the year of our first survey wave, about 31 percent of newly created urban jobs in Jiangsu Province were filled with rural workers; and in Zhejiang Province, 54 percent.[15]

Matching Workers to Jobs

In established industrial clusters in the Yangzi delta region, many entrepreneurs do not actively search for unskilled migrant laborers. Instead they rely on a constant self-sustaining flow of rural migrants who travel from inland provinces in search of factory jobs. The general manager of a textile company in Hangzhou recalls, "When we founded the firm, there was just no shortage of workers at that time. They applied themselves. They came from Anhui, Jiangxi, and Henan Provinces. We did not need to advertise because our plant is located in a well-known industrial park, and migrant laborers just came to us to apply for work."[16]

When more such workers are needed, entrepreneurs presently rely mainly on impersonal means, such as listings at local employment agencies, which describe on bulletin boards the nature of the work, qualifications required, and compensation. The standardized nature of job descriptions for entry-level shop floor jobs and the sheer volume of rural migrants contributed to this shift to reliance on impersonal recruitment channels.

Whereas there has generally been an abundance of unskilled labor, finding the necessary skilled labor can be more problematic. In contrast to the common stereotype of the Chinese family firm, entrepreneurs in the Yangzi delta region have realized that family labor usually does not satisfy their growing demands for skilled labor. The owner of a Nanjing-based company that manufactures biochemical appliances takes a typical position: "My rule is to employ relatives for their merit, and not to use them for the core structure of the company. The main idea is that we search for talents and skills and very few relatives would satisfy both conditions. In most cases we would rather not employ relatives."[17] Similarly, a textile producer in Nantong emphasizes, "Nobody works in a specific position just because they are my relatives. We go by capabilities; some are on halftime positions, some are responsible for production, and some are common workers. We do not make a distinction; we focus on performance rather than the individual."[18]

As private firms were positioned outside the formal state-run labor allocation system, the development of autonomous labor recruitment channels was
a crucial institutional innovation allowing survival outside the mainstream
economy. Most importantly, private entrepreneurs needed mechanisms that
not only provided access to the large pool of unskilled rural workers but also
allowed them to recruit skilled and experienced professional staff. Clearly,
this posed a critical challenge during the early reform phase, when the central
labor allocation system still siphoned off the most qualified urban workers for
employment in state-owned and collective-owned enterprises, handling more
than 90 percent of recruitment in these public firms.[19] After the abolishment
of the central labor allocation system, many workers continued to seek public-
sector employment for its higher status and better wages and benefits. To re-
serve the best urban jobs for local job seekers, municipal governments maintained strict migration policies.[20] Shanghai and Nanjing, for example, restricted
nonresident university graduates from changing their household registration.[21]

Private employers responded to these constraints by developing a diversified system of formal and personalized recruitment channels, the former predominantly used for unskilled labor as well as technical workers and the latter
used especially for managers and professionals (see Table 7.1). This is broadly
similar to the use of recruitment channels in the U.S. labor market.[22] Having
moved well beyond the limitations of family-run businesses, private companies in the Yangzi delta region are thus utilizing a standard mix of different
search channels also characteristic in Western market economies.

According to our 2009 survey, employers in the Yangzi delta region recruited
three-quarters of their technical workforce through formal recruitment channels, especially direct applications by jobseekers and human resource fairs, where
employers meet potential applicants. Entrepreneurs who seek high-powered
management staff also rely to a growing extent on formal recruitment channels.
In our 2006 survey, entrepreneurs who regard skills as "important" in the selection of managerial staff found on average 38 percent of their managers through
market search. Those entrepreneurs who regard skills as "very important" recruited a substantively higher share of 53 percent of managers through the
market.

"Competition is all about human capital," a machinery builder in Nantong
observes. "Once we have human capital, we can achieve just about everything.
We advertise, and offer high salaries to attract experienced engineers, but it
is not easy to compete with the big cities."[23] High-technology firms often

Table 7.1.   Recruitment channels, 2009 (in percent)

	Management	Technical staff	Unskilled labor
Formal channels			
Direct application by job seekers	25.4	29.1	22.8
Shanghai	*48.4*	*41.2*	*18.1*
Nanjing	*32.6*	*41.8*	*41.4*
Nantong	*23.2*	*26.9*	*23.0*
Changzhou	*22.0*	*27.3*	*29.2*
Hangzhou	*16.3*	*21.95*	*9.6*
Wenzhou	*22.9*	*26.4*	*27.0*
Ningbo	*12.4*	*18.2*	*11.3*
Human resource fair	23.7	34.4	9.5
Shanghai	*23.2*	*25.1*	*5.2*
Nanjing	*19.5*	*26.4*	*16.3*
Nantong	*25.5*	*34.0*	*12.3*
Changzhou	*24.4*	*34.5*	*20.34*
Hangzhou	*19.3*	*37.6*	*3.5*
Wenzhou	*22.3*	*30.5*	*5.2*
Ningbo	*31.7*	*53.1*	*3.9*
Employment agency	1.8	10.2	27.6
Shanghai	*5.0*	*13.7*	*45.6*
Nanjing	*1.5*	*8.1*	*14.3*
Nantong	*1.5*	*9.7*	*26.1*
Changzhou	*1.4*	*9.05*	*21.0*
Hangzhou	*0.9*	*9.95*	*27.1*
Wenzhou	*2.6*	*12.3*	*27.7*
Ningbo	*0*	*8.7*	*29.6*
Posted advertisement	1.1	1.7	10.0
Shanghai	*1.6*	*2.0*	*2.0*
Nanjing	*1.3*	*1.1*	*1.6*
Nantong	*1.1*	*1.5*	*1.4*
Changzhou	*1.5*	*2.9*	*0.9*
Hangzhou	*0*	*1.4*	*2.0*
Wenzhou	*2.4*	*2.1*	*3.5*
Ningbo	*0*	*0.8*	*0.7*
Labor dispatch	0.1	0.2	1.7
Shanghai	*0*	*0.1*	*2.0*
Nanjing	*0.2*	*0.6*	*1.6*
Nantong	*0*	*0*	*1.4*
Changzhou	*0.5*	*1.0*	*0.9*

(continued)

Table 7.1 (continued)

	Management	Technical staff	Unskilled labor
Hangzhou	*0*	*0*	*2.0*
Wenzhou	*0.1*	*0*	*3.5*
Ningbo	*0*	*0*	*0.7*
Subtotal	**52.1**	**75.6**	**71.6**

Informal channels

	Management	Technical staff	Unskilled labor
Through family or relatives	8.7	2.0	1.3
Shanghai	*1.2*	*0.6*	*0.6*
Nanjing	*8.7*	*1.3*	*1.8*
Nantong	*9.9*	*1.3*	*1.7*
Changzhou	*11.2*	*1.6*	*2.3*
Hangzhou	*10.7*	*3.1*	*0.3*
Wenzhou	*9.0*	*4.6*	*5.1*
Ningbo	*10.2*	*1.8*	*1.9*
Through friends	13.9	5.9	2.1
Shanghai	*4.8*	*3.7*	*0.8*
Nanjing	*15.8*	*3.8*	*2.9*
Nantong	*12.2*	*3.8*	*2.8*
Changzhou	*17.5*	*7.9*	*4.9*
Hangzhou	*24.0*	*9.9*	*0.5*
Wenzhou	*11.3*	*6.2*	*1.7*
Ningbo	*11.6*	*6.0*	*1.5*
Through acquaintances	11.0	7.0	4.0
Shanghai	*5.1*	*3.4*	*5.0*
Nanjing	*13.1*	*8.3*	*5.6*
Nantong	*7.1*	*6.0*	*2.5*
Changzhou	*10.7*	*10.1*	*6.1*
Hangzhou	*17.2*	*8.4*	*3.6*
Wenzhou	*13.8*	*6.3*	*2.8*
Ningbo	*10.4*	*6.9*	*2.4*
From previous enterprise	6.5	6.8	3.3
Shanghai	*8.1*	*7.3*	*4.8*
Nanjing	*4.1*	*3.1*	*1.6*
Nantong	*16.1*	*15.0*	*7.5*
Changzhou	*3.7*	*3.6*	*2.4*
Hangzhou	*3.8*	*6.3*	*4.1*
Wenzhou	*8.3*	*8.7*	*2.4*
Ningbo	*1.5*	*3.4*	*1.5*

Table 7.1 (continued)

	Management	Technical staff	Unskilled labor
Chain recruitment through workers	0.7	1.7	17.0
Shanghai	*0.7*	*2.0*	*12.3*
Nanjing	*1.8*	*4.4*	*8.7*
Nantong	*0.3*	*0.7*	*12.8*
Changzhou	*0.5*	*1.2*	*5.7*
Hangzhou	*0*	*2.3*	*27.8*
Wenzhou	*1.6*	*0.9*	*17.45*
Ningbo	*0*	*0*	*32.4*
Other	7.1	1.0	0.7
Subtotal	**47.9**	**24.4**	**28.4**

Source: Yangzi Survey 2009.

experience particular difficulties in recruiting for skilled technical and managerial positions due to the limited supply of top-flight local professionals. One of the founders of a software-developing company based in Hangzhou explains:

> There is just not enough qualified talent in the market. This is a big challenge and problem for Hangzhou, and maybe for China. Hangzhou has also problems to compete with locations such as Shanghai, Beijing, Shenzhen . . . this is the biggest problem. . . . Three years ago our firm was competitive in the market for top talent. Now competition is much stronger in attracting top talents. Global firms have business units and conduct research and development in China. They are very strong; they have a brand name and management culture, salary, and clear career path. . . . Now we are in a lower tier in the job market. So, this is a big challenge for us. We have to face this and solve this difficulty if we want to continue to grow.

This company is addressing this challenge by searching more widely:

> Now we are recruiting on the national labor market. Fifty percent of our new employees come from outside Hangzhou, from cities like Wuhan, Nanjing, Chengdu, Dongbei, Dalian, and Shenyang.[24]

Rapid technological upgrading by firms in the Yangzi delta region is fueling a growing tendency for many to recruit skilled labor through a similarly far-ranging market search.

Similar recruitment problems exist in other highly specialized product niches. One entrepreneur worries about the lack of college graduates qualified to work in his particular niche of specialty machinery building. Although he follows the market of new college graduates carefully, it is very difficult for him to recruit the human capital he needs. He found a technical college in Chengdu that provides the appropriate type of technical training, but out of a class of thirty-eight graduates, only two students decided to work in his product niche. Competition for these graduates was intensely fierce.[25]

Generally, management and technical staff are much easier to recruit in the manufacturing center of Shanghai than in the relatively remote cities of Zhejiang Province. Whereas employers in Shanghai can fill on average 48.4 percent of their management positions with applicants who apply directly to the firm, employers in Ningbo fill only 12.4 percent of their management positions in this way. In total, companies in Shanghai fill on average 78.2 percent of their management positions through various formal recruitment channels, 26 percentage points more than the regional average (see Table 7.1). The pattern is similar though far less pronounced for skilled technical staff.

Clearly, a firm's choice of recruitment channels is strongly influenced by local labor market conditions. The manager of a company producing water-cleaning systems confirms a close link between his firm's recruitment policy and the company's location: "In our old rural location, most of our recruits were junior high and senior high school graduates. They all had a flavor of peasants. . . . Since the company restructured, and moved to the city, we now only recruit in Hangzhou. Now we do our job searches through TV ads and newspapers. . . . We do not go back to our former location to recruit anymore. Now we are relying on the local talent markets. Here in Hangzhou most applicants are college educated. They are of a higher level."[26]

Formal recruitment channels are not infrequently complemented with personal referrals, especially for entrepreneurs who do not have access to rich local talent markets or who operate in highly specialized niche markets. Whereas entrepreneurs in Shanghai, for instance, recruit on average only 11.1 percent of their managerial staff through referrals from family, friends, and business associates, the corresponding proportion is 51.9 percent in Hangzhou, 39.4 percent in Changzhou, and 37.6 percent in Nanjing.

In the recruitment of key personnel, where tacit knowledge of the industry is important to the success of the firm, personal referrals can play a critical role. Small-scale and new firms can particularly benefit from personal referrals, as they still lack the reputation to attract well-qualified applicants through formal recruitment channels such as job postings or ads. Personal contacts can bring young, private companies located away from the rich talent markets of the coastal cities to the attention of potential job applicants who would possibly not respond to a formal search. Personal contacts can also provide important previews of the company, expected professional tasks, and working conditions.[27]

Referrals from individuals who know potential job candidates personally, having originally become acquainted in some context unrelated to this job search, also provide employers with better *ex ante* information as to qualifications of these candidates.[28] The use of personal relationships helps the employer to gain requisite information about capabilities not revealed in formal job applications.[29] The fine-grained information passed through social networks enables employers to assess personal traits such as trustworthiness, social skills, and technical competences. Employers often expect to find a better fit between the applicants' skills and ambitions and the firm's needs through personal referrals.

Useful recommendations tend to come from friends and acquaintances, including industry associates, more often than from family and relatives (see Table 7.1). "Sixty percent of the managers in my firm were recommended by my equipment suppliers, and then hired away from other firms," the general manager of a company producing chemical fiber acknowledged. "Equipment is always leading in our sector. Equipment providers have a longer history than we have. They have special expertise, so they know who is good in what area."[30] The general manager of a high-technology firm in Hangzhou observed: "I have never hired anyone through the talent market or by advertising the job. All the employees that I have now are those who worked for other companies I was familiar with."[31]

As for referrals by fellow workers, employers in the Yangzi delta region seem generally wary with regard to management and technical staff but much more open to them for unskilled labor. In the city of Ningbo, employers fill on average 32.4 percent of such positions through chain recruitment; the regional average still reaches 17 percent. These referrals mainly provide a cost-efficient solution to fill shop-floor positions, which do not require specific qualifications. Also, employees like to join other fellow workers they already know from their hometown or previous job, as they appreciate a social network in a workplace far from home. More than a few workers apply in teams, and do not wish to separate from each other for a new job.

Generally, personal referrals do not replace but rather complement standardized recruitment and selection strategies. At later stages in the employment process, impersonal evaluations also come into play. Wu Liping, the automated packaging equipment entrepreneur, for instance, emphasizes that technical pen-and-paper exams are still important to assess the applicant's ability and personal attitudes, although many of his job interviews are initiated by recommendations from employees or from teachers at local colleges.

Referrals tend to bring in well-qualified applicants, as referring parties put their own reputation at stake. Reliance on personalized recruitment of managers also helps to limit employee turnover, as employees may sense a higher level of obligation, given that friends, acquaintances, or family have extended their social capital to secure the position. This can be particularly important in locations away from the more attractive big cities of the Yangzi delta region. Studies of the U.S. labor market, correspondingly, find generally lower turnover rates for employees hired through referrals than for those hired through formal search channels.[32] Economic advantages can be substantial. Firms with

Table 7.2.   Formal recruitment and labor turnover, 2003–2005

	Turnover of managers coeff. (std. error)	Turnover of technical staff coeff. (std. error)	Turnover of unskilled workers coeff. (std. error)
Formal recruitment	0.066***	0.024**	0.001
(in percent)	(0.01)	(0.01)	(0.04)
Total assets (log)	−0.056	0.083	−1.049
	(0.50)	(0.52)	(2.09)
Number of employees	3.619***	3.392***	20.844***
(log)	(1.16)	(0.796)	(4.099)
Employment growth,	0.146	0.906*	6.962**
2003–2005	(0.576)	(0.53)	(2.343)
Share of job category	0.156	0.229***	0.107
	(0.09)	(0.07)	(0.07)
Sector	YES	YES	YES*
City	YES***	YES***	YES**
Constant	−21.477***	−16.155***	−68.214***
	(6.579)	(3.49)	(16.13)
Pseudo R^2	0.056	0.055	0.028
N	626	626	626

Source: Yangzi Survey 2006.
Note: Coefficients for sector and city dummies are not reported.
* $p < 0.10$, ** $p < 0.05$, *** $p < 0.01$; Tobit analysis, estimated with robust standard errors.

continuity in core managerial and professional staff have a comparative governance advantage. Employees in positions with high human-capital specificity are costly to replace because a new recruit will lack job-specific knowledge that can only be accumulated over time. For managers, this often includes long-standing personal contacts with suppliers, customers, and regulatory authorities and familiarity with the firm-specific development strategies. For technical workers, this includes familiarity with the firm's production process and technology.

Analysis of our survey data (see Table 7.2) suggests that formal impersonal recruitment of managers in the Yangzi delta region is associated with a higher turnover of managerial staff, which is consistent with the claim that the use of personal referrals increases continuity in employment of managers. For technical staff, there is also a positive association between formal recruitment and turnover. In contrast, the use of formal labor market recruitment channels has no impact on turnover rates of unskilled workers. The estimated coefficient even has a negative sign.[33]

Convergence of Employment Conditions

As might be expected, thin profit margins and a volatile market can result in less-than-optimal treatment of employees, such as over-long workdays and irregular or late payment of wages. A recent survey in Zhejiang Province finds that the working hours of 40 percent of private firms exceed the legal working time by 30 to 50 hours per month, that is, by 1.2 to 2 hours per workday.[34] Likewise, the economizing necessitated in undercapitalized start-up firms often contributes to a harsh work environment. Although "satanic mill" abuse of workers is on the decline, labor conditions for unskilled migrant workers frequently fall short of rules specified by the Labor Law.

Despite persistent reports of Labor Law violations and poor working conditions, however, a majority of migrant laborers appear to be fairly satisfied with their migration experience.[35] This suggests that the majority of companies are at least in nominal compliance with most of the basic requirements. And indeed, abusive and exploitative treatment of workers is not a viable long-term strategy for business success.[36] Firms with a reputation for unfair and abusive work conditions experience difficulty in recruiting skilled workers. And rural migrants often are quick to leave jobs where they are dissatisfied with working conditions, for they can easily find new jobs in the local economy.[37]

The rapid pace of economic growth in the coastal provinces continuously opens up opportunities for job mobility through a constant stream of new jobs listed by start-up firms and by expanding manufacturing plants. A common pattern in Dongguan, a large industrial city in Guangdong Province, for instance, where 70 percent of the factory workers are young female migrant workers from less developed inland provinces, is for a newly arrived migrant to secure the first available job upon arriving, responding to job listings posted by the factory or acquired through personal contact.[38] Subsequently, there is often a rapid series of job changes, as the migrant gains work experience and learns about new job openings. The same pattern is seen in U.S. immigrant labor markets, as migrants search for a better fit between their expectations, their abilities, and opportunity.[39] In the Dongguan labor market and elsewhere in the region, factory workers readily leave their jobs if they don't like their bosses or become dissatisfied with their pay and work conditions. It is not uncommon for factory girls to spend their spare time studying in local correspondence schools or acquiring new skills as they position themselves to move up the job ladder in the thriving manufacturing economy.

Although harsh and abusive work conditions continue to characterize some labor-intensive industries, "satanic mills" are becoming a phenomenon of the early reform period, as many private firms in the coastal economies move up the product chain and develop technology-driven manufacturing. Take the example of the manufacturer of aluminum stovetop coffeemakers, Zhu Jinhong. His factory's basic manufacturing process involves channeling molten aluminum into molds to produce the coffeemakers. His first workshop was equipped with used equipment and outdated technology, while a newer second workshop relied on semiautomated equipment. Recently, the firm moved to a new fully automated plant, which quadrupled its production capacity. The sequence of development from the start-up phase of "satanic mill" nineteenth-century technology involving pouring molten aluminum by hand into industrial molds in darkly lit workshops filled with fumes to the new automated twenty-first-century plant occurred within a ten-year period. Brute labor jobs have been eliminated; now, in this much-expanded enterprise, employment involves controlling advanced machinery or engaging in administrative tasks or marketing.[40]

Although the supply of unskilled migrant labor has been abundant, it is not endless, and employers are mindful of the need to keep employees content. Such awareness was already evident in the mid-1990s:

Knowledge of higher compensation rates or better treatment at other firms gives an incentive to leave for better paid work elsewhere. Urban employers are aware of these incentives, and often make efforts to keep up with wage rates in other, similar firms. One informant (G2), an employer of unskilled factory labor in Guangzhou, believes that there is a limited supply of rural migrants who are willing to perform this kind of work. His firm raises its starting wages accordingly, in order to remain competitive with other employers. For him, migrant workers are not desperate people, willing to work for any wage. "If migrant workers don't make enough money to live on and to send money home to their families, then they just aren't willing to work." Incentives to leave the work place are especially strong when the employment relationship is unsatisfactory in other respects. This knowledge inspires other employers to develop warmer, more friendly employment relationships, for fear that an oppressive work environment will send employees running for jobs with slightly better wage packages. I once asked another employer of unskilled labor how he punishes employees who do not work hard. He was at a loss for how to respond to my question, indicating that harsh punishments cannot have a place in firms where employees can easily take their labor elsewhere. "It used to be that bosses were like emperors to their workers, but you can't act this way anymore. Your workers won't stand for it and will refuse to work for you. Now a boss has to be more like a cooperator."[41]

Among employers generally, there appears to be widespread agreement with these attitudes. A majority of the respondents participating in our 2006 survey indicate that their employment model probably best reflects the aim "to maintain a long-term friendly relationship through a two-way commitment with their employees."[42] Employers of skilled labor have especial cause for concern; they risk the defection of experienced workers with valuable production skills and technical knowledge acquired on the job to competitors' firms if they provoke worker dissatisfaction.

While the production structure in the Yangzi delta region remains labor intensive with an emphasis on unskilled labor (in our survey, on average 67 percent of the workforce is in this category), tight labor markets in which firms must compete to recruit and especially to retain their employees have led to a rapid improvement of employment conditions. The owner of a small-scale company producing office equipment expresses concerns: "Labor shortage is now a serious problem. There used to be a lot of workers coming to us from the provinces of Jiangxi and Anhui. But now their provinces are developing, and they are no longer willing to work away from home. Right now, I simply do not have the number of workers I would like to hire. My old workers now have their own houses, and do not want to work for me anymore."[43] Similarly, the owner of a Ningbo-based specialty machinery company summarizes: "Firms are growing and need more workers. But there is a shortage of workers now even in the countryside."[44]

Not only do employers need to compete with other firms for a limited pool of labor, but workers are increasingly aware of their improved bargaining position. The production manager of another Ningbo-based company notes: "Compared to the year 2002, when I started to work for this firm, there is a big change. In 2002 and 2003, workers would never complain about overtime work, as long as there was work to do. At most we had two Sundays off each month. Now they take Sundays off. And the maximum overtime work is three hours per day. Now our workdays end at 4:30 PM. And if we need overtime work from our employees, it has to be done no later than between 6 and 9 PM. And of course we will compensate them."[45]

Just as ongoing personal connections and social norms constitute the sinews of personalized exchange between firms in the Yangzi delta region, so is the employment relationship regulated by norms of reciprocity and appropriate behavior. Although a 2002 survey indicated that 98 percent of private entrepreneurs feel essentially free to both hire and fire their employees, and 94 percent feel free to both increase and decrease employee incomes,[46] entrepreneurs are careful to follow local norms and standards. They are mindful not only of their reputation in the business community but also of appropriate terms in the relationship between employer and employee. Bottom-up informal institutions of labor relations diffused rapidly and spontaneously outside the state-controlled labor system. By the time the 1995 Labor Law was enacted, providing the first general guidelines on labor recruitment, work hours, minimum wages, and dispute settlements, private firms already employed more than 55 million workers. Competitive pressures and legitimacy-seeking behavior in a diversified industrial landscape in which private firms still suffer the stigma of the once-marginalized underdog have jointly led to a pattern of isomorphic convergence with general standards of labor compensation, social insurance packages, and also workplace safety offered by competing firms in the private and public sectors.

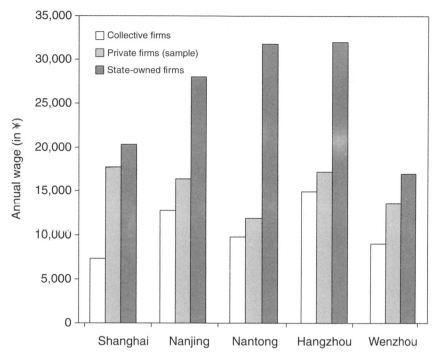

Figure 7.1. Average annual wages in manufacturing sector by ownership and city, 2005. *Sources:* Data for collective and state-owned firms is from *Shanghai Statistical Yearbook, Nanjing Statistical Yearbook, Nantong Statistical Yearbook,* and *Wenzhou Statistical Yearbook,* at *China Data Online,* University of Michigan, www.chinadataonline.org. The cities of Changzhou and Ningbo do not provide wage data disaggregated by ownership form. Data for private firms are from the Yangzi Survey 2006.

Labor Compensation

Private firms have not been able to keep wage levels artificially low. Instead, tightening labor markets have forced entrepreneurs to offer competitive wage packages. "As long as the salary and benefits are all right," one producer reasons, "workers will certainly not run away." Whereas he pays a piece-rate, he makes sure that the expected monthly pay is between ¥2,500 and ¥3,000, a rate that is comparable with salaries paid by the bigger firms in his locality. "This is the reason why my workers are willing to work for me," he concludes.[47] Another manager notes, "The only way to limit the turnover rate is to increase salaries. Once the skillful workers leave, it is hard to train new workers. Right now is really a good time for the workers. They can make up to ¥40,000 a year. If there is a market salary, I just have to follow it. If other firms pay 40,000 per

Table 7.3.   Average annual wage, 2005

	Average annual wage (in ¥10,000) coeff. (std. error)
Return on assets	0.249***
	(0.07)
Value of total assets (log)	0.280***
	(0.06)
Total number of employees (log)	−0.274***
	(0.05)
Firm age	−0.000
	(0.01)
Percentage of managers in workforce	0.007
	(0.01)
Percentage of technical staff in workforce	0.005**
	(0.00)
Sector	YES
	(0.11)
City	YES**
	(0.11)
Constant	0.899***
	(0.30)
Adj. R^2	0.194
N	674

Source: Yangzi Survey 2006.
Note: Coefficients for sector and city dummies are not reported.
* $p < 0.10$, ** $p < 0.05$, *** $p < 0.01$; robust standard errors. Variance inflation factors do not indicate any multicollinearity issues.

year, I have to follow suit. If there are skilled workers I need, I simply have to pay the higher salary."[48] A ball-bearing producer in Ningbo similarly describes wage policies within his local industrial niche: "One simply has to pay a reasonable salary and benefits. We know of course the market salary, and then we tend to pay a little more. It varies of course for different firms, but we know more or less what the other firms offer for the various positions."[49]

Some entrepreneurs even make specific efforts to increase the transparency of their wage policy and to introduce bilateral negotiations with their employees. The owner of a specialty machinery factory in Ningbo, for instance, reports, "I like to keep old workers because we have an emotional tie. I raise their wages twice a year, because they have skills and experience. At the end of every year, every department head asks workers to propose how much they think they should earn. If I can meet the demand, I'll give this amount. If not, I negotiate with workers on their pay raise. The department head will tell me how much they think the employee should make. Employees actually won't give unreasonable estimates. If we can't arrive at a negotiated agreement, then I have no choice but to let the person go."[50]

Overall, entrepreneurs in the Yangzi delta region appear to structure compensation in private firms substantively higher than wages in local government-owned collective firms, even though they cannot keep up with the relatively generous wages and benefit packages offered by state-owned enterprises (see Figure 7.1). National statistics indicate that employees in private firms received an average annual wage of ¥15,331 in 2005.[51]

Work compensation and firm success are closely linked. Controlling for other factors (firm size, firm age, employment structure, location, and industry), there is a substantive and significant positive association between the average wage rate and a firm's return on assets (see Table 7.3). In other words, the more profitable the firm, the higher the labor compensation and thus the better a firm's chances to recruit and retain skilled workers, which is the opposite of the Marxist view that profitability is secured through intensification of exploitation.[52]

Social Insurance

Historically, nonwage benefits—unemployment, health care, and pension funds—were a privilege of employment in government jobs or in state-owned and collective enterprises. Until a Social Insurance Law became effective in July 2011, there was no mandatory and nationally unified social insurance system requiring firms to provide health care and retirement insurance for all workers. The social insurance system remained fragmented, governed by different policy directives at both the central and provincial levels. Prior to the enactment of this Social Insurance Law, only preliminary regulations issued by the State Council in 1999 offered guidelines to urban firms on the provision of employee insurance benefits.[53] Rural migrants as well as all of rural China were excluded from this regulatory measure.[54] Without effective enforcement of the State Council regulatory guidelines, compliance even by the public sector was irregular. For example, in state-owned enterprises in Shanghai, only 63 percent of workers were covered by unemployment insurance.[55] It was not until the enactment of the Labor Contract Law in 2008 that all employers were legally required to contribute to the national social insurance system.

Nonetheless, in their competition for skilled labor and in an effort to limit turnover rates, many private firms have offered social insurance to their employees despite weak enforcement of State Council rules, and before the implementation of the Labor Contract Law. In our 2006 survey, 68.5 percent of the companies were contributing funds to some social insurance, for health care, retirement, or unemployment. Out of these, 37 percent were contributing to a general employee insurance package combining these. The highest rate of provision was in Shanghai, where nearly 95 percent of private firms contributed to some employee social insurance, and the lowest was in Zhejiang Province, where only 50 to 65 percent of companies did so.

The owner of the Ningbo-based office equipment company notes that it is particularly important to provide insurance for migrants, who are normally not covered by general insurance programs. His company calculates ¥3,000 to ¥4,000 for insurance costs per worker.[56] Overall, the mean contribution to employee insurances in our 2006 survey was ¥2,666 per worker per annum. On average, the highest contributions were paid in Shanghai and Jiangsu Province, the stronghold region of state-owned enterprises and international firms benchmarking which employment conditions are to be considered just and fair. The lowest contributions were in Ningbo and Wenzhou, cities where the state had not heavily invested in establishing a local state-owned industrial economy.

Isomorphic pressure to achieve legitimacy only partly accounts for why so many private firms contribute to employee nonwage benefits; competitive pressure from tight labor markets is also a significant factor. In the Yangzi delta region, as with the pattern of adaptive changes in human resource management discussed below, there is a close association between a firm's technological aspirations and its decision to provide employee social insurance. Firms holding patents and conducting research and development are more likely to provide their employees with pension funds, health care, and unemployment insurance. In our seven-city survey, 80 percent of the firms holding patents provide their employees with these nonwage benefits, while only 64 percent of firms without patents do so. Controlling for firm size, firm age, employment structure, location, and industry, we still observe that technically more

Table 7.4.   Decision to offer employee insurance, 2005

	Company offers employee insurance coeff. (std. error)
Total assets (log)	0.190***
	(0.06)
Total number of employees	0.147*
	(0.08)
Firm age	0.020
	(0.01)
Percentage of managers in firm employment	0.012
	(0.01)
Percentage of technical staff in firm employment	−0.008
	(0.00)
Firm holds a patent	0.301**
	(0.15)
Sector	YES**
City	YES***
Constant	−0.429
	(0.40)
Pseudo R^2	0.201
N	683

Source: Yangzi Survey 2006.
Note: Dummy variable equals one, if firm participates in pension insurance, unemployment insurance, health insurance or "general employee insurance" (an insurance package combining pension, health, and unemployment). Coefficients for sector and city dummies are not reported.
* $p < 0.10$, ** $p < 0.05$, *** $p < 0.01$; probit estimation using robust standard errors.

advanced firms holding patents are more likely to offer employee insurances than technically less sophisticated companies (see Table 7.4). Competitive pressure from labor markets motivates these private firms to offer their employees terms of employment and work conditions comparable with (or better than) those available in the public sector or elsewhere.

Workplace Safety, Legal Rights, and Litigation

Increased monitoring by local labor bureaus may have contributed to increased workplace safety and legal protection. More than 50 percent of the private firms we interviewed in 2006 had experienced at least one labor and social security inspection in 2005. Only one firm was issued a fine, though, which is consistent with a World Bank survey report that fines were imposed on only 1 percent of all firms nationwide.[57] Most entrepreneurs observe that local authorities do not strictly enforce labor regulations. The owner of a small-scale start-up company in Ningbo summarizes, "We all know about the Labor Law and its revisions, but nobody is really practicing it. There is really not much impact of the Labor Law on firms like mine. I started this firm during the time when the Law was being implemented. I checked the contracts and found out even big firms didn't implement the Law. How could I implement it then?"[58] Indeed, the office-equipment company owner in Ningbo notes, "Now there is no government monitoring. Before the year 2000, there was some monitoring. But now, they do not come themselves. We just turn to the government, when we have problems."[59] In any case, official statistics documenting work-related accidents in China support the view that work safety in private firms does not differ much from conditions in state-owned and collective-owned companies.

In spite of weak government enforcement, the enactment of the Labor Law has substantively strengthened the position of workers vis-à-vis employers. As the Ningbo-based office-equipment company owner explains, "Although I never read the Law myself, I do pay attention to worker rights. If I would not pay attention, the workers would simply revolt. Workers are naturally

Table 7.5. Labor disputes, 1996–2007

Year	Number of workers involved in lawsuits (includes collective labor disputes)	Cases won by workers	Cases won by work unit	Cases partly won by both
1996	189,120	23,696	9,452	13,395
1997	221,115	40,063	11,488	19,241
1998	358,531	48,650	11,937	27,365
1999	473,957	63,030	15,674	37,459
2000	422,617	70,544	13,699	37,247
2001	467,150	71,739	31,544	46,996
2002	608,396	84,432	27,017	67,295
2003	801,042	109,556	34,272	79,475
2004	764,981	123,268	35,679	94,041
2005	744,195	145,352	39,401	121,274
2006	679,312	146,028	39,251	125,501
2007	653,472	156,955	49,211	133,864

Source: *China Labour Statistical Yearbook 2008* (Beijing: China Statistics Press, 2008), 495–496.

concerned about regulations on insurance, salary, days off, and it is the workers who pay close attention."[60] Not only has the number of workers' lawsuits increased nationally more than sevenfold over the last decade, but workers generally won the majority of their lawsuits in labor disputes with employers (Table 7.5).

The highest frequency of labor disputes involved employers in collective enterprises owned by local government and companies run as joint ownership and limited liability corporations (see Figure 7.2). In these companies, on average 3 to 4 employees out of 1,000 sought recourse either by mediation or by arbitration lawsuit against their employers in labor disputes in a sample year (2003), with the majority of cases settled through arbitration. Though the frequency of labor disputes in both "state-owned" and "private" enterprises appears to be much lower, these figures are misleading. A majority of private firms now register as limited liability companies (see Chapter 5), while the majority of joint ownership companies are partially privatized state-owned companies incorporated as joint stock companies. Thus, the distribution of labor disputes reported in Figure 7.2 very likely indicates simply that large corporations are more likely to be involved in labor disputes than the smaller,

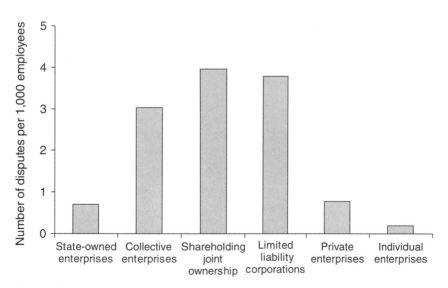

Figure 7.2. Frequency of labor disputes, 2003. *Source:* Data from *China Labour Statistical Yearbook 2004* (Beijing: China Statistics Press, 2004), 513. Data for 2003 are used, since later statistical reports no longer provide a breakdown of disputes by ownership form of employer.

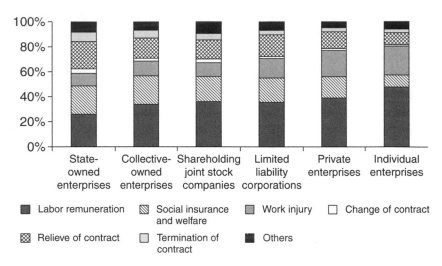

Figure 7.3. Cause of labor disputes, 2003. *Source:* Data from *China Labour Statistical Yearbook 2004*, 514.

noncorporatized companies, without evidence of a substantive difference between public and private companies.

Disaggregation of lawsuits by cause of labor dispute further shows that, across all corporate forms, the majority of cases involved disputes over labor remuneration, often connected with bankruptcies and firm closures (see Figure 7.3). Among the most common issues in such disputes are delayed payments, arbitrary wage cuts to punish weak performance, and refusal of contractually agreed-upon bonus payments. Disputes over insurance coverage and compensation payments in cases involving workplace injuries are the next most frequent cause of lawsuits.

Most notably, by the year 2003, official records no longer support any substantive structural differences in employment conditions and labor disputes between ownership forms. Instead, official statistics suggest a high level of convergence.

Human Resource Policies

In the thriving manufacturing economy of the Yangzi delta region, as private firms develop and grow in size, their increased complexity motivates the development of internal governance mechanisms shaping and guiding employment relations. Competition for human capital, moreover, focuses attention on organizational strategies that enable the firm to recruit and to retain employees, especially in view of the tight labor markets for high-value managerial, professional, and technical workers. Also motivating entrepreneurs to incorporate institutional arrangements commonly found in state-owned enterprises is legitimacy seeking in response to public perception of private firms in the earlier reform period as a pariah organizational form (see Chapter 5).

For institutional models, entrepreneurs in private firms look to state-owned enterprises, public corporations, and foreign firms. Not surprisingly, they mimic core elements of the employment practices of these mainstream firms to conform to the expectations of the workers they recruit, whether experienced personnel (sometimes from such firms) or new graduates of technical schools and colleges. As more and more of the most successful private firms institute formal human resource policies, competitors mimic these internal arrangements in order to achieve greater legitimacy themselves and to attract these well-trained workers. The implementation of these policies signals to prospective job applicants the firm's legitimacy and modernity, and thereby enhances its competitiveness in the recruitment and retention of high-value personnel required for the firm's survival. Development of appropriate employment models in private firms has thus involved isomorphic organizational change driven by mimetic and normative mechanisms.[61] It broadly resembles the development of human capital management practices observable all over the world, as individual firms in every country pursue specific economic or strategic interests and conform through mimetic and normative pressures to expectations of the institutional setting.[62]

In the Yangzi delta region, where decades-long high-speed economic growth has generated intense interfirm competition for high-value human capital, effective human resource policies reduce the risk that skilled and experienced technical workers and professionals will be easily lured away by competitors offering higher salaries or better bonus packages. Such turnover threats become particularly costly where technical requirements and skill specificity in employment are high.

High-technology firms are particularly eager to develop human resource strategies to reduce employee turnovers. An entrepreneur in a software development firm observes, "It is a challenge to keep good people. Our turnover

rate is less than 10 percent, which is lower than the average of about 15 percent. But we are facing a growing challenge in the effort to keep our top
employees. We offer a career path, salary and bonus, a nice working environment. We train our top managers to be attentive to creating a positive work
environment; you see, all this needs to be executed by managers. Then there is
the office space, housing and so forth. All this needs to be taken care of so we
can hold on to our top personnel."[63]

Long-term labor contracts, specifying rights and duties between employer
and employee, are one common safeguard mechanism against rapid turnover
of talent. They also are an important instrument to signal employment security and labor standards comparable to the public sector's.[64] Contract duration
tends to be closely associated with human capital requirements such as firm-
specific skills and technical knowledge. Among our 2006 survey firms, more
than 50 percent of management contracts exceed two years of duration, compared to 38 percent for technical staff and only 23 percent for unskilled workers (see Table 7.6).

Although existing competitors or new market entrants can certainly still
make better offers to lure away experienced staff, anecdotal evidence suggests
that long-term contracts provide some protection. On the one hand, employees perceive their position and employment conditions as more secure, which
increases organizational involvement and job commitment. On the other
hand, competitors tend to respect existing commitments, particularly in the
local production market. The chairman of a textile association in Nantong, for
example, himself a leading textile producer in his county, observes that entrepreneurs rarely try to lure away key personnel from direct competitors in their
niche. "Such behavior would simply not work out, since you know all the
other producers personally."[65]

Table 7.6.   Contract type and job category (in percent)

	Management	Technical staff	Unskilled labor
1 year or less	35	43	68
2 years	12	18	9
3 years	16	17	4
5 years	9	7	3
Other	28	14	16

Source: Yangzi Survey 2006.

The more advanced the technological underpinnings of a company, the more likely the firm is to rely on long-term contracts. Firms that conduct regular research and development activities recruit more than 30 percent of their managerial staff with contracts that have a minimum length of three years, whereas firms without such activities do so only for 20 percent. The difference is even larger for firms with a proven track record in technology development. Firms holding patents recruit about 40 percent of their managers with at least three-year contracts, while firms without any patents use such long-term contracts for fewer than 20 percent of their managerial and technical employees.

Written job descriptions also reflect the ongoing institutionalization of human resource strategies. Seventy-nine percent of private firms in our survey use written job descriptions to increase legitimacy and transparency by clearly specifying on-the-job obligations. Formal job descriptions protect employees against undue ad hoc requests to perform additional tasks. At the same time, such descriptions facilitate layoffs if employees do not comply with the specified job requirements. Moreover, the existence of written job descriptions follows role models of large corporations, thereby signaling conformity with industry standards. Again there is a link between formalization and technological needs, reflecting the intensity of competition for professional and technical workers. In our survey, 88 percent of firms with research and development (R&D) departments use formal job descriptions, whereas 72 percent of those firms without R&D units do so.

The development of competitive pay scales (as in 68 percent of interviewed firms) usually complements standardized job descriptions. Most entrepreneurs in our 2006 survey regard attractive pay and bonus packages as key for attracting managerial and technical talents.[66] Most of these employers also include some form of incentive payment linking work and firm performance. An extreme case reported elsewhere is the company Haier, which has made wages 100 percent performance variable and has linked individual salaries to monthly market targets.[67] Other firms rely on the distribution of employee shares to increase interest alignment and organizational commitment of key managerial and technical staff. Wu Liping, the owner of the automated packaging equipment firm, for instance, introduced an employee stock ownership plan that ties the distribution of new shares to the annual increase in the firm's value. Thirteen members of his key managerial and technical staff participate in the program. The distribution of individual shares is based on a complex ranking system, assessing individual performance along sixteen distinct criteria. In this way, Wu reasons, "employees can be sure that participation in the stock distribution reflects the individual contribution to the company value."

Finally, private firms in the Yangzi delta region develop internal labor markets to enhance the predictability of career paths and to allow for job mobility of high-value professional and skilled employees. This is a natural way to respond to intense competition for skilled labor in the Yangzi delta region. Internal training and promotions are key mechanisms private firms rely on to recruit medium- and top-level managers, positions private firms often cannot fill with qualified external applicants. The career path of the production manager of an automotive company located in Ningbo is illustrative. He was recruited directly from college in 2002 to oversee the factory's supply room. Finding this in bad shape, he took the initiative to reorganize the area by introducing a new control system, which quickly led to a reduction in defective components and parts. Management noticed his initiative and organizational skills, and quickly promoted him to purchasing-department head, a position he filled temporarily because he was soon promoted to assistant to the general manager in charge of accounting and cost calculations. By the end of his fourth year with the company, he was promoted to production manager—a position he was now highly qualified for, thanks to his broad in-house experience with supplies, quality standards, and cost accounting.[68] While his career path is impressive, it reflects a general promotion strategy of private companies. "We generally fill higher positions through promotions from our own workers," emphasizes a vice-CEO running a ball-bearing company in Ningbo. "We just know them better and can better assess their skills."[69]

Among the most common instruments in internal labor markets are written performance reviews (66 percent) and clearly specified promotion procedures (45 percent). These are even more frequent in high-technology firms that have proven R&D capabilities. Transparent promotion procedures increase the predictability of internal careers and can thereby lower the employees' incentive to leave for external offers. At the same time, close monitoring and individual performance assessments reduce information asymmetries between employer and employee and improve organizational efficiency and job involvement. These procedures are not always institutionalized as standard organizational practice, however. A female entrepreneur emphasizes:

> I promote whoever I value. I look at the person's sense of responsibility, his capacity, and let him try managing. I am managing at the same time. And

then gradually we try it out. As a private firm we all know about the talents in the firm. We don't use a standardized procedure. If someone is capable, we'll promote him. Employees of this type might not be all-around people; for example, they might not have high levels of education. We make mistakes too in selecting. But since I myself am involved in managing, I can always replace the unsuitable ones. We hire people into the company as we grow. Our middle-level managers are all involved in the production process.[70]

The private company Haier, today the number one producer of household appliances, has emerged as one of the role models of internal training and employee motivation. Haier began to assess production workers on a daily basis against their quantity and quality objectives. In the past, those who underperformed "were forced to stand on a set of yellow footprints at the end of the working day and confess to their assembled coworkers that they had failed to meet their goals."[71] When Haier tried to export this practice to its U.S. subsidiaries, threats of lawsuits against this humiliation forced the company to change from the practice of public blaming to a practice of public reward. Thanks to unexpectedly good experience with this, Haier reimported the new system back to the Chinese workshops, where now the positive role models are presented to share their success stories. Many of the private firms we visited practice similar reward systems. Announcements of model workers who have shown exceptional performance or provided innovative ideas are fairly common. Company blackboards filled with pictures and names of the top performers create incentives to emulate and to catch up with these leaders.

The diffusion of human resource policies in recent years underscores the intense competitive pressures on firms to upgrade work conditions as a means to recruit and retain first-class managerial, professional, and technical employees. Clearly, competitive labor markets and legitimacy-seeking behavior by private firms have jointly led to a pattern of isomorphic convergence with working conditions in state-owned firms. That the emergence and diffusion of human resource policies in private firms followed an endogenous process of institutionalization, and were not imposed exogenously by government labor bureaus enforcing the Labor Law and related labor regulations after 1995, can be seen in the timing of a firm's development of formal rules and procedures governing the employment relationship (see Table 7.7). The majority of firms that were older than nine years (i.e., registered before 1995) already had

Table 7.7.   Timing of standardization of employment relations

		Average number of years of firm operation before instituting formal rules			
	Total sample	If firm age less than 5 years	If firm age 5 to 9 years	If firm age 10 to 15 years	If firm age more than 15 years
Formal written job descriptions	1.3	0	0.7	2.9	5.2
Formal written performance assessments	1.3	0.1	0.8	2.7	5.1
Formal written pay scale	1.4	0	1.0	2.8	4.8
Formal written promotion procedure	1.6	0	0.8	3.3	5.5

Source: Yangzi Survey 2006.

institutionalized the use of formal job descriptions, performance assessments, and pay scales by the time the Labor Law was enacted. Firms older than fifteen years (founded in 1990 or earlier) took on average four years more to institutionalize human resource policies than the sample mean, but this does not mean that external regulations played a decisive role in the institutionalization process. These firms were established when the institutional environment imposed less competitive and technology-driven pressures on firms in recruitment and retention of high-value employees.

These human resource strategies do appear to have a stabilizing effect, albeit modest, on continuity of employment (see Table 7.8). Long-term employment contracts are associated with a lower turnover of technical and unskilled workers, though against expectations they do not actually appear to reduce management turnover among our survey firms. All else being equal, only written performance assessments seem to be effective in limiting management turnover. For companies regularly conducting such assessments, turnover rates of both managers and technical workers are reduced. Most likely, this is achieved by signaling prospects for internal promotion and greater predictability of future career paths within the firm.

Conclusion

The emergence of self-enforcing labor market institutions enabled firms to quickly distance themselves from reliance on family labor as in the traditional

Table 7.8. Market recruitment, governance, and turnover

	Turnover of managers coeff. (std. error)	Turnover of technical staff coeff. (std. error)	Turnover of unskilled work coeff. (std. error)
Market recruitment (in percent)	0.022**	0.008*	−0.027
	(0.01)	*(0.01)*	*(0.04)*
Percent contracts >3 years' duration	−0.007	−0.012*	−0.124**
	(0.01)	*(0.01)*	*(0.06)*
Written job description	0.631	−0.660	−5.982
	(0.68)	*(0.88)*	*(6.45)*
Written performance assessments	−1.425**	−1.729**	2.975
	(0.64)	*(0.77)*	*(5.65)*
Written pay scale	0.413	0.931	−1.318
	(0.44)	*(0.67)*	*(4.38)*
Written promotion procedures	0.279	0.364	0.728
	(0.68)	*(0.74)*	*(3.62)*
Value of total assets (log)	−0.356	−0.025	−0.938
	(0.30)	*(0.36)*	*(1.94)*
Number of employees (log)	2.363***	2.609***	19.749***
	(0.65)	*(0.58)*	*(3.86)*
Employment growth	1.798	2.510***	12.261**
	(1.51)	*(0.93)*	*(6.19)*
Share of job category	0.045	0.152***	0.041
	(0.04)	*(0.05)*	*(0.06)*
Sector	YES	YES**	YES
City	YES***	YES***	YES**
Cons	−9.624***	−10.402***	−67.528***
	(2.96)	*(2.58)*	*(15.91)*
Adj. R^2	0.167	0.258	0.246
N	704	704	704

Source: Yangzi Survey 2006.
Note: Coefficients for sector and city dummies are not reported.
* $p < 0.10$, ** $p < 0.05$, *** $p < 0.01$; robust standard errors. Variance inflation factors do not indicate any multicollinearity issues.

Chinese household business. Through a mix of personal and impersonal recruitment channels, entrepreneurs flexibly responded to different regional labor market conditions for skilled and unskilled workers. Network recruiting at the local level gave rise to the self-reinforcing development of differentiated and extensive labor markets drawing from inland provinces unskilled workers shifting out of subsistence farming. In the recruitment of managerial and technical employees, private-sector firms were compelled to compete with higher-status public-sector firms. Here, in response to the public's perception of private firms as an upstart illegitimate sector of the manufacturing economy, entrepreneurs sought legitimacy by incorporating formal institutional arrangements commonly found in state-owned enterprises. Competitive pressures, in parallel, have not only supported the adaptation of formal symbols of modern employment systems, but jointly spurred a rapid upgrading of employment conditions.

Comparative analysis of employment relations across ownership forms confirms an ongoing process of institutional isomorphism, as evidenced by declining structural differences in employment conditions. Certainly the relatively recent enactment of various labor rights and the lackadaisical enforcement of the Labor Law cannot fully account for this development. Instead, the changing norms shaping and guiding employment relations were driven by the specific economic and strategic interests of private entrepreneurs, responding to normative pressures as well as tightening labor market conditions.

Driven by labor market competition and increasing technical and organizational complexity, many private firms in our sample have sought to conform to the expectations of high-value managerial, professional, and technical workers recruited from state-owned enterprises, foreign firms, professional and engineering schools, and government agencies. As more and more of the most successful private firms began to institute human resource policies, competitors have copied these internal arrangements in order to achieve greater legitimacy themselves and to attract these well-trained workers.

8

Institutions of Innovation

A distinctive trait of capitalism is that manufacturers need to innovate not only to profit but also to stay in place and to survive. Without the ability to innovate, they would lose market share to a continuous entry of new start-up companies. Large numbers of new market entrants contribute to cycles of boom and bust characterized by quickly eroding profit margins and low survival rates. Absent the leading edge of innovation, such cycles will not give rise to sustained economic development. If the business cycle reflects only the effects of intense, predatory competition without the gains from innovation that are the hallmark of modern capitalism, the erosion of profit margins drives out both new and old firms.[1] In Joseph Schumpeter's theory, entrepreneurs—distinct from capitalists and businessmen—are the purveyors of innovation. Their robust entrepreneurial action generates the "new combinations" that "incessantly revolutionize the economic structure from within, incessantly destroying the old one, incessantly creating a new one."[2] The innovative process is the recognition of opportunities for profitable change and the pursuit of those opportunities all the way through until they are realized as new products or new business practices. Under pressure of competitive markets in capitalism, this becomes a mandatory, life-and-death matter for the firm. In other types of economies innovation is fortuitous and optional.[3]

Over the course of three decades of economic reform, China has developed into a highly competitive market economy, characterized by low market concentration ratios in most industrial sectors. Whereas in the United States the five largest machinery manufacturers, for instance, have a combined market share of 69 percent, and in Japan the top five hold 42 percent, the top five in China have only 20 percent of the market.[4] Competition drives innovative activity not just for large-scale firms but also for smaller businesses.[5] As the owner of a textile company with only 40 employees in Zhejiang Province emphasized, "We strive to be unique for a short period of time. We need to be different. Only by differentiating our products from competitors do we get the volume of sales we must have to be profitable."[6] And the owner of a start-up packaging company in Hangzhou adds, "Innovation is a necessity. There is a saying among private manufacturers: Think about dangers while you are still safely profitable. You have to know what you do in three years. Others see the niche you have, so you need to have new products to survive the competition."[7] Those who do not respond to the extreme market pressure are quickly pushed out, and may at best hope to sell simple contract work. The process of decline is rapid, as the owner of a small workshop in Ningbo reports. Without any innovative products and thus without a sufficiently appealing product portfolio, he lost contracts, and had to lay off most of his workers. Now he can only hope for small contracts to produce simple tools and instruments for other local companies. "Clearly, I am no longer an entrepreneur," he notes. "I just think of myself similar to other professionals; I am just working for a wage *(dagong)*."[8]

Without much if any funding for research and development (R&D), innovation is not easy for these smaller companies. An entrepreneur in a high-technology start-up firm summarizes the dilemma he shares with many private businesses: "Of course we have to innovate to survive, but as we are operating only a small firm, I have to drive innovation myself and come up with new ideas." He adds optimistically, "In the future, I hope, I may be able to recruit my own staff for R&D."[9]

Following the folk wisdom of entrepreneurs in the region that even "small innovations can make a difference," it has become commonplace for firms to introduce changes in their products, their technology, and their organizational practices to improve their profit margin. Changes can range from minor shifts in product design or adjustments to a warehouse management system, for instance, to the introduction of entirely new production technologies involving automation of previously manually performed work processes.

While most manufacturers make only marginal improvements and modifications of existing products and product lines, some continuously expand or modify their main line of business, and some develop entirely new product lines as a strategy to move into less crowded niches offering higher profit margins.

These firms make bold technological shifts that can require substantial investments in research and development. For instance, an entrepreneur who pioneered the production of standard household scissors in Wenzhou shifted his main line of production to x-ray bulbs when the market for scissors became crowded with imitators. By 2008, he was preparing to shift to x-ray machines because he detected signs of crowding in the market for x-ray bulbs.[10] Others reported similarly bold moves, shifting from textile to electronic production, or motorcycle to automobile production. A Ningbo-based entrepreneur who only three years ago still had to supplement his production of textile machinery tools by making simple low-value-added items, such as plastic mousetraps, is rapidly moving up the technology ladder in an effort to escape the tight competition in the saturated textile market. Most recently, he launched the production of an energy-efficient motor, which reduces energy consumption by about 50 percent. He plans to introduce this motor in various new product lines ranging from air conditioners and refrigerators for use in luxury cars to electric lawn mowers, which he plans to sell on the North American market.[11]

Such a sequence of bold leaps up the technological ladder has evolved as a recognizable mobility strategy for entrepreneurs in the Yangzi delta region. Often the entrepreneur starts up an initial business in a niche with a low entry barrier and low capital requirements. Success in the entry-level venture enables the entrepreneur to accumulate financial and human capital while in search of new products that usually require higher capital and technological inputs. Entrepreneurs believe that this type of strategic action will allow them to secure higher profit margins as they distance themselves, at least initially, from the intense competition in crowded niches lower in the value chain. At each step, they are driven by competitive markets to innovate. In ascending the technological ladder, they rely on business savvy gained through previous ventures, intuitive judgment of opportunity, and an entrepreneurial spirit of innovativeness.

In the case of Shanghai Maple, a leading private automobile manufacturer, the founding entrepreneur used the profits from a first venture in manufacturing plastic bottles to shift up the production chain into making water pumps used in irrigation, followed by a brief venture into manufacturing motorcycles. After discovering that the domestic motorcycle market was saturated and profit margins had become razor thin, the entrepreneur precipitously decided to build a new plant to manufacture automobiles, without a business model or prior experience. His boldness was rewarded with success. From the start-up firm producing plastic bottles in a rural township near Shanghai to a private automobile firm with a national dealers' network in China and a rapidly growing export business, the firm has traversed the entire span of industrial development in the Yangzi delta.[12]

Although patentable innovations are rare among the firms in our survey, more than 50 percent of them introduced new products, and almost as many upgraded existing product lines (see Table 8.1). More than 60 percent of these firms introduced new production processes, new management techniques, or new quality controls. On average, these firms implemented three different types of innovation. Fifty-five percent of them implemented more than three.

State-sponsored programs designed to spur innovation in industry mainly focus on promoting linkages between national institutes of science and technology and large state-owned and state-controlled enterprises. Since the passage in 1985 of the "Resolution of the Central Committee of the Communist Party of China on the Structural Reform of the Science and Technology System," the central government has made massive national investments in science and technology. But only 5.8 percent of government funds earmarked for innovative activity went to private firms in 2007 (for example), with 82 percent being awarded to state-owned enterprises and public corporations where government units owned the majority shares.[13] Very few private manufacturers benefit from government-sponsored R&D programs aimed at promoting national brand-name firms in the high-technology sector. Those receiving support typically are already successful leaders in their industrial niche, and generally represent industries of national strategic importance.[14]

Table 8.1. Firm innovation from 2002 to 2009 (in percent)

Type of innovation	2002–2005	2006–2009
New patent approved	n.a	5
Introduce new product	58	52
Upgrade existing product line	50	41
Discontinue at least one product line	22	15
Process innovation	62	66
New management technique	65	64
New quality control	61	41
New joint venture with foreign partner	20	7
New licensing agreement	20	4
Outsource major production activity	24	5

Source: Yangzi Survey 2006 and 2009.

Despite this huge inequality favoring state-owned enterprises in the allocation of government funding for research and development, the gap in terms of innovative activity and output is no longer that large. In China overall, state-owned and state-controlled manufacturing firms accounted for only 29.3 percent of R&D departments in 2007, while 19 percent of R&D departments were located in private firms.[15] In 2008, 31 percent of patent applications submitted by large and medium-size enterprises were from state-owned and state-controlled enterprises, but 18 percent were from private firms.[16] In our survey, only the larger private firms with an average of 180 employees have the means to operate their own in-house R&D department. Yet even so, among companies without a formal R&D unit, 36 percent introduced at least one new product between 2006 and 2009 (in comparison to 69 percent of the firms with R&D units) and 58 percent introduced new production processes (compared to 74 percent of the firms with R&D units). Clearly, even without government funding for research and development, private firms are prioritizing innovation and successfully carrying it out.

The Social Structure of Innovation

Competitive pressures motivate the entrepreneur to innovate, but do not provide the ability to do so successfully. What allows private firms to innovate to such a significant extent without government funding to support R&D and without loans from state-owned banks to fund innovation projects? How are small firms without formal R&D units able to engage in innovative activity on a regular basis?

It is, we argue, the bottom-up construction of economic institutions embedded in networks that has enabled private firms to move up the technological ladder and to break into markets previously monopolized by state-sponsored public enterprises. For innovation is a social process involving cooperation and competition. Incentives to innovate and the means to do so successfully are matters not only of micro-level motives and decisions but also of social structures. Far from the image of the atomistic market of neoclassical economic models, in actual markets networks provide the conduits and pipelines through which timely information and resources flow. Silicon Valley's culture of innovation— to point to a familiar example—is embedded in the extensive web of workaday relationships spanning established and start-up high-technology firms. A detailed account of the bottom-up economic institutions key to Silicon Valley's success highlights how the "entrepreneurial process was nourished by the region's networks of social relations and technical infrastructure."[17] Silicon Valley's regional advantage as an industrial district evolved from the rapid diffusion of innovations across interfirm networks. In such geographically concentrated industrial districts, tacit knowledge crucial to cooperation in innovative activity is embedded in networks that channel the flow of fine-grained information between firms.[18] As the philosopher Michael Polanyi argued, "We know more than we can tell."[19] Formal contracts provide the closed conduits that enable transfer of technical information and intellectual property between specified parties. But beneath the surface of formal ties, personal relationships are leaky channels, "more like sprinklers, irrigating the broader community," as has been observed in a study of the Boston-area biotechnology industry.[20] Innovative activity is not tightly bound within individual firms, but resides thus in fluid and evolving networks, informal and formal, that connect firms, universities, research laboratories, suppliers, and customers.

As with mutual lending agreements (see Chapter 4) and bottom-up construction of supply and distribution channels (see Chapter 6), entrepreneurs rely on their interfirm networks to overcome institutional barriers impeding R&D activities of private firms. In response to internal and external resources available to the firm, entrepreneurs develop a portfolio of different research collaborations, including both informal cooperation based on the reciprocity principle *do ut des*—"I give so that you might give"—and formal contractual agreements that clearly specify the rights and duties of parties engaged in a joint research project. When arranging formal contractual agreements, entrepreneurs often build on preexisting personal relationships. However, with the emergence of markets for innovation, entrepreneurs increasingly also use impersonal search mechanisms provided by business-to-business Internet platforms, for the best match in technology exchange. Overall, given the complexity of the fields involved, interest in minimizing and sharing the uncertainties inherent in R&D motivates interfirm cooperation.[21] As in advanced industrial economies, firms "turn to collaboration to acquire resources and skills they cannot produce internally, when the hazards of cooperation can be held to a tolerable level."[22]

Social Sources of Ideas

Without access to state-sponsored funding for high-technology research, innovative activities of private entrepreneurs have developed a strong market orientation, focusing on applied solutions serving the specific needs and wishes of their customers. Wu Liping, the entrepreneur in automated packaging equipment, remarks, "Of course, innovation comes from the market; we are just chased by our customers. . . . Every little innovation actually makes a difference in the profit margin."[23] In elaborating on his innovation strategy, he emphasizes that his customers constantly request improvements and cost reductions in the packaging equipment they order from him, as their businesses expand. In his company, the technical and design departments work hand in hand with core customers. Every new product his clients want to bring to the market will most certainly require technical modifications of the packaging machinery, as contents, package, and packaging material require tailor-made solutions. For instance, depending on the substance to be packaged, different hygienic standards and precision levels in measurement are required. During our visit, the company was just optimizing the measurement function of packaging machines designed for a European milk powder producer. The development of new packaging machines often also requires adjustments and modifications of the production process and improvements in quality management to guarantee certain product standards.

Another private firm, Haier Electronics, China's largest producer of electrical household appliances, learned that rural customers were dissatisfied with the reliability of the company's washing machines. Looking into the cause of frequent breakdowns, their customer service staff discovered that in villages farmers were using the appliances for washing vegetables. Haier responded by developing a new model for rural customers, which allowed switching between two modes, one for clothes and one for vegetables.[24] Other models in their product line also stemmed from responding to customer feedback: for instance, a mini washing machine designed for small urban apartments (the model "little magic kid") and an energy-saving air-conditioning system (the model "little superman").[25]

A strong customer orientation is also found in the market for industrial goods, parts, and components, where producers meet with their key customers to discuss future projects and explore ways to modify existing products to match their new requirements. The owner of a Nantong-based welding machinery firm describes his innovation strategy: "We first analyze our client network and forecast what kinds of products they are going to use in the future. Then we develop new products. . . . For example, a ship-building firm nearby is the most sophisticated in the world; it's a joint venture with a Japanese firm. We follow closely their demands, and develop products according to their technical needs. We are taking advantage of them. They are only a ten-minute walk from our firm. We have regular meetings with them to learn about their needs, and we know what they are buying."[26] His company's recent development of more sophisticated welding machines reflects an adjustment to his client's expansion in the market for bulk carriers and container carriers, which require highly efficient and automated welding machines for the production of shipbuilding steel.

Of course, customer requests for product modification do not always involve much innovation, and may not go beyond simple imitation. Customers sometimes ask for copies of products they have seen. A producer of special machinery in Wenzhou, for example, reported with professional pride how he and his staff, through reverse engineering, successfully copied a machine now displayed in his workshop.[27] Nonetheless, satisfying a particular customer's request often does involve significant innovative activity. In our 2009 survey, 82 percent of the entrepreneurs regard their customers as among the three most important sources of new ideas (see Table 8.2).

Entrepreneurs in the Yangzi delta also develop new ideas by examining competitors' products in their market niche. Generally speaking, as entrepreneurs in a niche jockey for competitive advantage, they take "cues and clues" from each other. Innovative (as well as imitative) activity emerges from the

Table 8.2.   Top sources of new ideas

Listed among the top three sources of ideas for innovation	Percentage of firms that list sources among top three
Customers	82
Other businesses in own industry	50
Own employees, R&D-unit	39
Technical or industry standards	31
Suppliers	30
Conferences or trade fairs	29
Businesses in other industries	8
Books and scientific journals	8
Universities, research institutes, research services	8
Industry association	7
Overseas / international companies	5
Government assistance	3

Source: Yangzi Survey 2009.

ongoing interactions of firms responding to signals revealing how competitors are positioning their products by price and quality in the market's pecking order.[28] In our 2009 survey, 50 percent of private-firm entrepreneurs list other companies in their own industry among the top three sources of ideas for innovations. Additionally, given the dense network of competitors and suppliers in the marketplace, many entrepreneurs (30 percent) indicate that their suppliers serve as one of the most important sources for ideas.

The owner of a small-scale packaging company in Hangzhou, for instance, frequents local shops and supermarkets to look for ways to improve on the existing packaging technology displayed on the shelves. The strategy of the owner of a small firm manufacturing traffic equipment is also illustrative: "We study our competitors closely and try to maintain advantage over them . . . for instance to provide better after-sales service etc . . . We send people to study competitors to find out what they are doing . . . and learn from their clients. Sometimes we use our relatives and our competitors' relatives to get information. We use the Internet to get information on competitors. We even chat with security guards from competitors. . . . Then we assess the information right away. If they have new products, we will copy them."[29]

Indeed, those who mainly look to their competitors for ideas frequently do imitate their products. The owner of a textile company producing for export markets proudly showed off the company's research department where employees downloaded from the Internet patterns and designs of luxury clothing, to produce cheap knock-offs.[30] However, copying products and technology from other firms is not the dominant strategy for developing new products. Competitive pressures impel entrepreneurs to do more than imitate if they wish to rise above the crowd.

Conferences and trade fairs, showcasing new domestic and global developments in specific industries and niche markets, facilitate interfirm comparisons and help identify future market trends. Trade fairs also provide a platform to test ideas and receive immediate customer responses. In our overall sample, 29 percent of the respondents indicate that conferences and trade fairs are among the three main sources of ideas for innovation. Careful observation when traveling abroad is another essential tool to better understand different preferences of international customer groups. The textile producer cited above emphasizes, "You really need to know the wishes of your prospective customers. We apply a very simple way of information gathering. We just go there, visit different countries, and study the local standards in terms of size, colors, and patterns. . . . All that you need is an analytic eye for consumer taste and trends."[31]

New technical and industry standards provide additional incentives and ideas. Many entrepreneurs, for instance, report that industry standards such as ISO 9001, an international standard for quality management systems, led to various innovations necessary to satisfy the detailed specifications. New environmental regulations issued by the central government also play a role. One entrepreneur reports that his move into the production of environmentally friendly tires was motivated by a general shift toward green technologies in China.[32] Others feel inspired by the government's guidelines on energy saving and have moved into the development of energy-efficient technologies. In total, 31 percent of all interviewees regard technical and industry standards as one of the three most important sources for new ideas.

Other sources include businesses in other industries, books, scientific journals, research institutes, and industry associations. Overseas companies and government sources are also cited.

The different sources of ideas—requests from customers, imitation of competitors, or observing market trends—tend to be associated statistically with different types of innovation (see Table 8.3). Customers tend to be associated with process, management, and quality control innovations. Product innovation, in contrast, seems to be linked more to formal market institutions such as trade fairs, industry standards and regulations, institutions of higher education, and even government assistance services. Notably, firms that mainly rely on competitors and suppliers in their own industry are distinctly less innovative.

Informal Networks of Learning

The innovations driving China's private enterprise capitalism are not breakthrough inventions of global novelty. On the contrary, they mostly entail routine and piecemeal innovations embedded in learning by doing and learning by imitation. Much of this learning takes place through multiplex relational ties between entrepreneurs in the region.

As Schumpeter emphasized, "the innovations which it is the function of entrepreneurs to carry out need not necessarily be any invention at all."[33] An idea may be old hat for one individual or group, but when brought to another, it is innovative and valued. Though in the strict sense of intellectual property law it would be regarded as an imitation, an idea that is new to the people

Table 8.3. Sample mean comparison tests for top sources of innovation ideas and different types of innovation, 2009

Among top three sources of new ideas	Group	Introduces a new product	Upgraded a product	New production process	New management techniques	New quality control in production
Customers	Yes	0.49	0.41	0.67**	0.67***	0.42*
	No	0.62	0.39	0.59**	0.54***	0.36*
Firms in same industry	Yes	0.49	0.34	0.62	0.58	0.34
	No	0.54	0.47	0.69	0.70	0.47
Own employees/R&D dept.	Yes	0.51	0.47***	0.62	0.67*	0.46**
	No	0.52	0.37***	0.68	0.62*	0.38**
Technical standard	Yes	0.56*	0.33	0.72**	0.66	0.32
	No	0.50*	0.44	0.63**	0.64	0.45
Suppliers	Yes	0.45	0.34	0.69	0.57	0.36
	No	0.55	0.44	0.65	0.67	0.43
Conferences/trade fairs	Yes	0.58**	0.45	0.62	0.68*	0.48***
	No	0.49**	0.40	0.67	0.63*	0.38***
Firms in other industry	Yes	0.59	0.52**	0.70	0.52	0.39
	No	0.51	0.40**	0.66	0.65	0.41
Books/journals	Yes	0.42	0.36	0.44	0.6	0.33
	No	0.52	0.41	0.68	0.65	0.41
University, research institute	Yes	0.71***	0.33	0.72**	0.66	0.64***
	No	0.50***	0.44	0.63**	0.64	0.39***
Industry association	Yes	0.52	0.44	0.72	0.76**	0.58***
	No	0.52	0.41	0.65	0.63**	0.40***
Foreign business	Yes	0.57	0.49	0.77*	0.65	0.51*
	No	0.51	0.41	0.65*	0.64	0.40*
Government assistance	Yes	0.68*	0.68*	0.63	0.58	0.31
	No	0.51*	0.40*	0.66	0.64	0.41

Source: Yangzi Survey 2009.
Ha: mean (0) − mean (1) < 0; * $p < 0.10$, ** $p < 0.05$, *** $p < 0.01$.

involved is in practice an innovation.[34] In this respect, "creativity is a diffusion process of repeated discovery," in which a good idea is carried through networks to be "discovered in one cluster of people, rediscovered in another, then rediscovered in still others—and each discovery is no less an experience of creativity for people encountering the good idea."[35]

In the Yangzi delta region, informal types of technology collaboration are ubiquitous. Many entrepreneurs view the mutual exchange of ideas, the joint search for technical solutions, and the joint use of equipment as the natural outgrowths of long-standing business relationships. The expectation of mutual help and support in close-knit networks of entrepreneurs contributes to information exchange about new technologies during casual business talks. The informal exchange of ideas in networks often is the starting point for discussion about the joint development or acquisition of the new technologies.[36]

It is common for members of business networks to share resources and skills to jointly develop and improve their firms' technical capabilities, as a means to avoid the substantial costs of stand-alone R&D departments. The owner of an auto parts company located in Changzhou underscores this motivation for interfirm cooperation in technology: "As a mid-level player, we are afraid of the costs of innovation. We simply don't have the status and ability to do the whole thing by ourselves. We can only do point-to-point innovation, which is important to keep customers. But to be able to realize bigger innovation projects, we have to build up a network of people that we can collaborate with in the future."[37]

As the majority of private firms in the Yangzi delta lack government funding for R&D, the decision to start major innovation projects involves new challenges. Research departments involve substantial start-up and operating costs, which exceed the financial means of most small and medium-size businesses. Moreover, smaller firms have difficulties in recruiting technically qualified R&D employees. Given the growing demand and the limited supply of experienced engineers and technical workers, many private firms cannot compete with the compensation packages and career plans offered by multinational companies and state-sponsored firms. The increased complexity of technologies means that nearly all private firms lack core competencies required to engage in state-of-the-art R&D.[38]

The owner of a Ningbo-based machinery-building company lacked the facility to develop a novel energy-saving technology he learned about from a friend who works in a Shanghai research institute. He turned to a business friend who owned a larger factory for help to develop and test the new product, emphasizing the huge domestic market for just this type of energy-saving technology. His friend allowed him to use his spare capacity for trial productions during the development stage.[39]

More than 65 percent of entrepreneurs surveyed in 2009 reported ongoing informal technical collaborations with at least one member firm in their immediate network (that is, among their five most important business ties). Forty percent collaborated with more than one. When asked about the beneficial effects of various forms of informal learning from networks, 27 percent of the entrepreneurs value highest those business contacts with whom they collaborate on technical problems.

This type of informal and personalized interfirm cooperation is closely associated with a firm's overall innovativeness (see Table 8.4) Firms with informal technical collaborations tend to introduce more changes than firms without such collaborations (3.2 innovations, on average, compared to 2.7). Sources of advantage lie in the areas of product upgrades, decisions to discontinue certain products, and the introduction of new quality control instruments.

In interfirm networks, cooperation helps lower costs of innovation, facilitates learning, and alleviates resource constraints. Cooperation in R&D, however, involves specific risks, as partners may have an interest in securing key technologies without contributing equal efforts or sharing the gains from commercialization. These risks are significantly more severe in China than in countries with well-protected property rights, where contract law, corporate law, and arbitration institutions guide and safeguard economic transactions. As one entrepreneur notes, "If we were in the USA, we would not need to work so hard to protect ourselves, because you can rely on intellectual property rights. Here, if you have a very good idea, before you start business, you must worry about someone copying from you. The legal system is just not good enough to protect intellectual property rights."[40]

In this environment, the bottom-up rise of R&D cooperation—dependent as it is on social interaction and geographic proximity—has itself provided crucial problem-solving mechanisms. It is commonplace for entrepreneurs in the Yangzi delta to carefully analyze the factors for success and failure in innovative activities by talking about the experience of other market players in their industry. Through observation and consultation with others, they learn how to create ideas and, similarly, how to protect their ideas from imitation. Not only do economic actors learn whom to trust and how best to cooperate, but

Table 8.4. Sample mean comparison tests for informal collaboration and different types of innovation, 2009

Innovation types	Firm maintains informal technical exchange with at least one of five most important business contacts	Statistical mean
Introduce new product	No	0.56
	Yes	0.49
Upgrade existing product line	No	0.28***
	Yes	0.48***
Discontinue at least one product line	No	0.10***
	Yes	0.18***
New joint venture with foreign partner	No	0.06
	Yes	0.08
New licensing agreement	No	0.03
	Yes	0.05
Outsource major production activity	No	0.04
	Yes	0.05
New production process	No	0.68
	Yes	0.65
New management technique	No	0.62
	Yes	0.65
New quality control	No	0.29***
	Yes	0.47***
New patent approved	No	0.05
	Yes	0.05
Total of innovation activities (0–10)	No	2.70***
	Yes	3.17***

Source: Yangzi Survey 2009.
Ha: mean (0) − mean (1) < 0; * $p < 0.10$, ** $p < 0.05$, *** $p < 0.01$.

they also learn which measures are effective in safeguarding core technologies. They develop and share specific means to protect against loss of intellectual property rights. This includes special regulations for workers involving security standards at the workplace, as well as screening methods to check the market for potential copyright infringement.[41] Entrepreneurs also learn from each other how to resolve disputes over intellectual property.

Very few companies ever file formal charges against imitators. The owner of a Nanjing-based machinery company said he often learns from clients about rivals who imitate his products, but he feels it is a waste of time to seek legal recourse because they are short-lived small companies: "Imitators deliver lower quality. They are essentially competing with each other and not with me, so they don't threaten my business."[42] When a manufacturer of medical equipment in Nanjing learned from a customer that another firm was trying to sell him an imitation, he handled the matter himself:

> We didn't file a formal complaint to the authorities, but took care of the problem our own way. . . . The point is we control the core technological components of our products. They can imitate but cannot penetrate. I actually went to the company and talked with the boss. He was embarrassed and nervous. He showed me the production line where they were doing the imitation. . . . It was obvious he was having technological problems imitating our product, so I proposed a subcontracting arrangement. You see, there are no enemies forever; there is only interest forever. There are no competitors forever; it's just a difference in interests. This applies to both individuals and firms.[43]

Formal Contractual Agreements for R&D Collaboration

Nonetheless, informal technical cooperation has its limits and downsides. Given that collaborators do not want to lose their competitive advantage or key capabilities, an obvious limitation is that informal technical exchange does not provide sufficient safeguard mechanisms for joint development of new products or patents. This is why entrepreneurs seeking to develop patentable innovations typically rely on formal technology agreements, where contracts specify *ex ante* the respective duties and rights of the collaborating parties and the distribution of future profits. It is common practice for firms to enter into formal cooperative contracts for R&D to share research capabilities and knowledge among themselves, taking advantage of economies of scale, while excluding rival firms not in the research network. Firms also participate in such strategic alliances in order to gain access to the other firms' technologies, to reduce the time span required for innovations, and to open new market niches through joint product development.[44]

Close to a third of the patents reported by private firms in our survey involved formal technology cooperation, with contracts providing the closed conduits that channel technology development between specified parties (see Table 8.5). However, not all of these patents lead to the introduction of new products. Some are only utility or design patents, and others might not be taken to the market given their limited economic value. Furthermore, not all companies even try to patent new inventions, given the weak legal protection

Table 8.5.   Formal research agreements of innovating firms in 2009 (in percent)

	Firms[a] with formal R&D cooperation[b]	With other firms	With research institutes	With universities
New patent approved	32.4	14.0	19.0	3.0
New joint venture with foreign partner	19.6	19.6	0	0
Outsourcing of major production activity	18.2	12.0	3.0	3.0
New product	17.4	12.0	5.0	1.6
New licensing agreement	17.2	7.0	7.0	7.0
New production process	8.9	7.0	2.0	0
Upgrade of existing product line	8.0	4.2	3.0	1.4
New quality control	7.0	4.9	1.7	0.3
Discontinued at least one product line	4.6	2.7	1.8	0
New management technique	4.2	2.0	1.7	0.4

Source: Yangzi Survey 2009.
a. Out of firms that innovate.
b. Sum of disaggregate values may exceed total due to existence of multiple collaborative agreements.

provided. In assessing the real-world effects of such technology collaborations, it is therefore useful to focus instead on new products. In our 2009 survey, 17.4 percent of the entrepreneurs who have brought new products to the market have relied on formal technology agreements.

As with informal technical cooperation between firms, formal contractual agreements often build on long-standing personal relationships between contracting parties, where each knows about the other's business reputation and technical capabilities. In the Yangzi delta, legal contracts typically reinforce trust and cooperative arrangements already in place, and are often the outgrowth of ongoing business ties between entrepreneurs. A Changzhou entrepreneur, for instance, points out that his technical cooperation with a firm based in Fujian Province was successful mainly because both parties knew each other fairly well. Over the years, they had built up close business relations, becoming familiar with each firm's product quality, technical standards, and customer expectations. A good fit of company cultures facilitated communication and collaborative efforts between the firms' technical departments, which then led to a formal agreement to jointly develop new technology, cementing R&D cooperation that had begun informally.[45] This pattern is not uncommon. Given weak legal protection for intellectual property, many entrepreneurs prefer to choose collaborators for R&D cooperation from within their business networks.

Introductions of new contract partners by close business associates are also common. Through personal introduction and fine-grained information passed through social networks, the "broker" typically signals trustworthiness and reputation of the prospective business partners. Moreover, it is in the broker's interest to make good recommendations, as most business partners will tend to reward their networking contacts in one way or another. Such introductions can span the social gaps or "structural holes" between groups.[46] The owner of a Ningbo-based automotive company, for example, found her new business partner through a close friend working in the local highway construction business. The friend introduced her to a firm in Beijing that was looking for a reliable production partner in the Ningbo area. She plans to pay her friend a reward of 1 to 2 percent of the contract value, a benchmark number that is discussed in her locality as appropriate for this kind of favor.[47]

Although long-standing business relations help to reduce information costs and uncertainties in finding partners for formal technology agreements, they do not always provide the best match in terms of technical capabilities and competence. Thus larger firms especially have gradually extended their search for technical and research partnerships beyond their local business networks. As an additional safeguard mechanism to protect firms against loss of technology, entrepreneurs form strategic alliances where both partners have strong intrinsic interest in contract compliance. There are a variety of such strategic alliances. Some emphasize asset-specific investment in technology and capabilities that lock both partners into a collaboration that would be a poor fit for other partners. Others seek partners whose firm is small enough to depend on contract fulfillment, with production capacity too small to transfer the jointly developed technology to parallel lines of production, which could then be sold on the partner's individual account. And finally, some make it a general rule to enter into technology collaborations only if the expected time to copy the entire technology would be long enough to allow the innovators to still capture substantive profits.[48]

In the emerging markets for innovation, entrepreneurs routinely use Internet-based business-to-business services such as Alibaba.com as a convenient information pool to screen and select potential partners for technical collaboration. Alibaba is the largest online market for China's small and medium-size enterprises, with more than 34.8 million registered users in virtually all major consumer categories. The ready access to business-to-business platforms like Alibaba has dramatically reduced search costs for interfirm technical cooperation. For an annual fee of $400–$3,000, private businesses can list their product line and information about their factories and receive links to potential partners.

When a Changzhou-based entrepreneur came up with the idea to upgrade his line of electric bicycles by switching from traditional mechanical locks to fingerprint locks, his company lacked the technical capability. He did not want to invest heavily in acquiring the technology for this product upgrade, and decided instead to search for a potential technology partner. He was looking for a company well established in the production of fingerprint door openers, producing in the medium quality and medium price range and willing to adjust this technology to outdoor conditions to make the lock waterproof and ready to use for bicycles. Through Alibaba.com he found a production market for fingerprint locks, and he selected potential partners based on location, company size, quality, and product price. Within weeks, he settled upon a partner, and both parties signed an agreement launching the collaboration to develop a fingerprint lock suitable to his line of middle-of-the-range bicycles.[49]

Similarly, a ball-bearing manufacturer in Ningbo was contacted by a company located in Nantong that had used Alibaba to find a potential partner to develop a new water-saving mechanism. The crucial component that was needed for underwater use was a bearing without any metal parts, a specialty that only a few bearing or plastics manufacturers could deliver. Since the company in Ningbo had a reputation for high-quality bearing parts made of plastic or glass, it appeared to be an ideal partner for the project.[50]

In finding partners to develop specific technical components, entrepreneurs typically emphasize product quality and technical fit as decisive. Often the search for a potential partner is a highly competitive process. A specialty machinery manufacturer based in Nantong reports that in his search for a firm able to design a specific engine type, "there were eight companies that collaborated with us on the motor. We eliminated seven firms that could not produce the right motor. The last company produced the right motor. . . . We informed them about the market prospect of our product to motivate them. They were enthusiastic collaborators. We spent a year to work together to develop the motor. Finally we got the right product and we signed a contract."[51]

Others follow the example of China's global brands, such as Lenovo, Haier, or Alibaba, which have benefited from international collaboration in innovation projects and joint research laboratories. Even small and medium-size private companies in the Yangzi delta express growing interest in establishing international technology agreements. The packaging entrepreneur Wu Liping recently formed a joint venture with a Japanese partner to develop technology his firm needed to close the technology gap with international competitors in specific product lines. Similarly, the owner of a Hangzhou-based software developing company feels that joint agreements with international partners helped his company attract global customers.[52] In observing the leading players in their own product niche, many entrepreneurs identify international collaborations as an important advantage of those market leaders. Those actively involved in such collaborations realize crucial advantages in speeding up the innovation process involving their key technologies. International alliances also have a strong reputation effect, signaling the firm's compliance with international quality and technology standards, which helps to attract new domestic and global customers.

Finally, companies with specific needs in certain areas of basic research sometimes collaborate with technical schools or research institutes. Often these are local university institutes, with existing personal relations between former students and teachers. Additional contacts between companies and research institutes are facilitated through government-sponsored road shows where representatives from a number of these institutes present themselves as potential partners in technology collaboration. These recent initiatives typically address larger, already-established local firms with good prospects for future development. Entrepreneurs participating in our survey emphasize that these tours mainly serve as communication platforms, where potential contractors can meet researchers and learn about the specific research fields and capabilities of participating research institutes. Although by absolute numbers such collaborations still play a minor role, they contribute significantly to patentable innovations. In our 2009 survey, 19 percent of firms indicate that their patent applications involved a research institute as a technology partner.

Effects of technology collaborations can go beyond the contracted project and yield unexpected innovation outcomes. The specialty machinery manufacturer based in Nantong developed his main product—a high-pressure seal machine—as an unforeseen side-effect of a technology collaboration:

> It was an accidental opportunity that I developed this product. It was [through] a friend's introduction that I got the idea to develop the product.

I have a former colleague who works as president's office director at a university. . . . At the beginning we didn't know about the market potential and we didn't know much about the product. It was not clear to us. We didn't know whether the seal machine needed an automatic machine with a central processing unit (CPU). We were uncertain whether there is a market for this product. So we did some market research. The key breakthrough was when we learned from the Chinese national patent bureau that there were more than 30 patent applications for an automatic seal machine waiting for approval. I decided there must be a market, given so many applications. Our market research showed that there was no product that was ready to be brought to market. We did research to find out what the problem was. . . . We realized that our firm has, in-house, all of the technological requirements needed to manufacture the machine. So we began the design of the machine. The first requirement for the seal machine is that it can apply different pressure to various weights of paper. Even the same weight of paper can in different locations and at different times of the day require a different level of pressure because of variations in temperature and humidity. The American company WIDMER sells a mechanical machine for ¥55,000 in China, but with a CPU inside we can get better results adjusted to different conditions. If it is only a mechanical machine, it does not have this flexibility. Ours is a 'smart' seal machine. It is our innovation. We applied for it and received a Chinese patent.[53]

Depending on the technical capabilities and financial resources of the contracting parties, the majority of entrepreneurs choose between one of several standard contract types:

1. Entrepreneurs without tight financial constraints but with weak technical capabilities favor the purchase of R&D services for specific innovation projects. In this contractual model, an entrepreneur agrees to pay a certain amount for the development of a clearly specified technology design. Profit and also risk are with the entrepreneur. The tire producer in Changzhou, for example, paid ¥1 million up front for new environmentally friendly synthetic rubber technology. His contract specifies ten years of exclusive use and full right to profits.[54]

Sometimes the technology already exists. Large manufacturing firms with strong R&D departments typically develop a certain number of product innovations that they do not bring to the market, either because expected sales are likely to be too small in volume or because the innovation is not yet technically suited to mass production. Entrepreneurs in smaller firms learn about these innovations through personal ties with management in the larger firm, and buy the technology and design to produce for the market.

2. Manufacturers often turn to suppliers for technical innovations they need in components used in their main product line. The manufacturer guarantees to purchase a minimum volume from the supplier, who in turn guarantees not to sell this specialized component to a third party. This type of technology contract has developed into a popular business model where suppliers offer technical designs pro bono to producers. A successful example is the Shenzhen-based Comtech Group, a distributor of standard electronic modules for large semiconductor companies like Broadcom, SanDisk, Matsushita, and others. Comtech's business model focuses on working with its customers to learn what they are looking for in their new products and also on offering custom-designed modules integrating chips from more than one source. In this way, the many small and medium-size firms manufacturing electronic products from cell phones to telecommunication and consumer electronics can outsource their R&D and benefit from economies of scale.

3. Entrepreneurs willing to get involved in a long-term agreement to share financial costs for technical development and future profits choose to establish a technology joint venture. Private firms with in-house R&D units often enter into strategic alliances that share financial costs and future profits with a domestic or international company to gain access to state-of-the-art technologies or manufacturing capabilities. Typically, the quid pro quo in such long-term formal agreements is expectation of market access in product niches difficult to penetrate. For example, in May 2010 the leading Chinese auto battery producer BYD signed an agreement with the German carmaker Daimler to establish a ¥600 million R&D joint venture to develop electric automobiles. The plan is to capitalize on Daimler's know-how in electric vehicle architecture and BYD's strength in battery technology and e-drive systems to market the vehicle jointly under a new brand name in the domestic Chinese market.[55]

Numerous small and medium-size private companies mimic the successful technology joint ventures of the firms like BYD with global brand names and search for domestic or international partners to establish technology-based strategic alliances.[56] The Ningbo-based machinery tool producer, for instance, describes his new company producing brushless direct-current electric motors as an ideal way to pool the different resources he and his partner have. After he had searched for years for a new product he could bring to the market, he finally joined forces with a local engineer who had previously worked for another company. The engineer brought in the idea for the new energy-saving motor that can be used in air-conditioners and other appliances. As the engineer himself lacked the financial means to develop his idea to patentable stage and bring the product to the market, they set up a new limited liability company, in which both partners hold shares.[57]

The bottom-up development of this broad range of formal technology agreements allows even firms that do not have an in-house R&D department to pursue significant technological advances. Among such firms in the 2009 survey, 11 percent maintained formal technology agreements, compared with 22 percent of the firms that do have in-house R&D. Such joint research activities are effective, particularly as regards new product developments (see Table 8.6). Whereas 80 percent of the firms involved in formal technology collaborations

Table 8.6.   Sample mean comparison tests for formal collaboration and different types of innovation, 2009

Innovation types	Firm maintains any type of formal technical collaboration (with firms or research institutes)	Statistical mean
Introduce new product	No	0.46***
	Yes	0.80***
Upgrade existing product line	No	0.40*
	Yes	0.47*
Discontinue at least one product line	No	0.15
	Yes	0.15
New joint venture with foreign partner	No	0.04***
	Yes	0.23***
New licensing agreement	No	0.03***
	Yes	0.11***
Outsource major production activity	No	0.03***
	Yes	0.12***
New production process	No	0.62***
	Yes	0.83***
New management technique	No	0.63
	Yes	0.68
New quality control	No	0.39**
	Yes	0.51**
New patent approved	No	0.04***
	Yes	0.13***
Total of innovation activities (0–10)	No	2.8***
	Yes	4.0***

Source: Yangzi Survey 2009.
Ha: mean (0) − mean (1) < 0; * $p < 0.10$, ** $p < 0.05$, *** $p < 0.01$.

introduced new products, only 46 percent of other firms did so. With regard to most other types of innovation, differences between both groups are significant as well, though less substantive.

Beyond the relatively densely populated industrial clusters of the Yangzi delta region, aggregate provincial-level data comparing the number of technology agreements and patenting activities (normalized by provincial population) show the widespread effectiveness of interfirm networks and technology collaborations. Provinces with relatively active markets for formal technology agreements have a leading position in total patent counts; those provinces that register only relatively small numbers of technology agreements tend to have modest patenting activities (see Figure 8.1).

Indeed, there is a significant and substantive influence of both informal and formal types of technology exchange on firm innovativeness, as evidenced by new patents, the introduction of new products, sales share of new products, product upgrades, new production processes, and new quality control measures (see Table 8.7). While informal cooperation between firms in R&D is more likely to increase substantively the probability of product upgrades (by 25

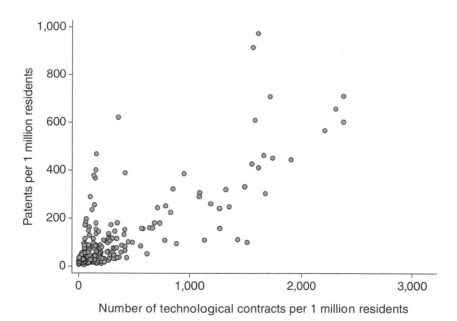

Figure 8.1. Provincial markets for technology and patenting, 1995–2006. *Sources:* Patent data from *China Statistical Yearbook,* vol. 1996 to 2007 (Beijing: China Statistics Press); technology contract data from *China Statistical Yearbook on Science and Technology,* 1996 to 2007 (Beijing: China Statistics Press).

Table 8.7. Technical cooperation and innovativeness

	New product coeff. (std. error)	Share of new products coeff. (std. error)	Product upgrade coeff. (std. error)	Process innovation coeff. (std. error)	New quality control coeff. (std. error)	New patent coeff. (std. error)
Informal cooperation	−0.070	1.090	0.710***	−0.026	0.557***	0.140
	(0.111)	(2.049)	(0.115)	(0.110)	(0.114)	(0.206)
Formal cooperation	0.829***	16.461***	0.082	0.522***	0.283**	0.511**
	(0.164)	(2.469)	(0.141)	(0.152)	(0.141)	(0.200)
Own R&D unit	0.646***	10.369***	0.281**	0.249**	0.135	1.001***
	(0.112)	(2.143)	(0.111)	(0.112)	(0.113)	(0.242)
Log of firm age	0.083	−1.721	−0.153	−0.179	−0.233*	−0.130
	(0.125)	(2.993)	(0.123)	(0.125)	(0.124)	(0.224)
Log of total assets	0.103**	2.989***	0.170***	0.094**	0.069	0.140**
	(0.05)	(0.821)	(0.044)	(0.046)	(0.046)	(0.071)
Sector	YES**	YES***	YES**	YES*	YES*	YES
City	YES***	YES***	YES***	YES***	YES***	YES
Constant	−1.545***	−29.444***	−1.914***	−0.274	−0.542***	−3.498***
	(0.394)	(7.253)	(0.396)	(0.402)	(0.398)	(0.627)
Model	Probit	Tobit	Probit	Probit	Probit	Probit
Wald chi-square	150.57		100.92	82.38	120.52	61.07
R² / Pseudo R²	0.181	0.052	0.128	0.091	0.144	0.195
N	700	700	700	700	700	700

Source: Yangzi Survey 2009.

Note: To reduce the risk of confounding effects, each model also controls for firm size (total assets), in-house R&D, and firm age as well as a set of dummy variables for firm location and industrial sector. Coefficients for sector and city dummies are not reported.

* p<0.10, ** p<0.05, *** p<0.01; robust standard errors. Results are not driven by multicollinearity.

percent) and implementation of new quality controls (by 20 percent), formal interfirm collaboration is more likely to increase the probability of new product development, production process improvements, and success in registering a new patent. Formal contractual agreement can be marginally even more effective than having an in-house R&D department in promoting a firm's innovativeness. Among our survey firms, the probability of new products increases by 30 percent, for instance, as compared with 25 percent for in-house R&D, and the probability of process innovation by 16 percent as compared with 8 percent. Further, entrepreneurs with formal technology collaborations are much more successful at marketing their new products, reporting a higher share of new products in total sales.

In general, those entrepreneurs fare best who rely on a balanced mix, combining informal technology exchange, within their closest business network, with contract-based formal technology advancing specific innovation projects. Figure 8.2 illustrates the different levels of average firm innovativeness associated with different combinations of cooperation strategies. Informal collaborations are less effective than formal technology agreements, but companies with formal agreements can still further increase their firm innovativeness if they also continue to maintain informal types of technology exchange.

Ongoing exchange of knowledge through interfirm networks develops and strengthens the R&D competence of the firm. "Over time, firms develop

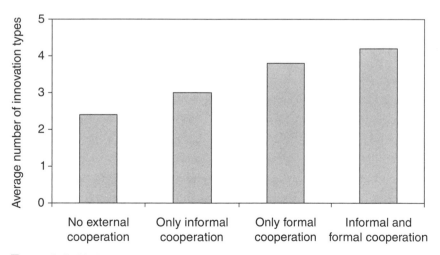

Figure 8.2. Technology cooperation and firm innovativeness.
Note: The index ranges from 0 to 10, and includes all innovation types covered in Table 8.1. *Source:* Yangzi Survey 2009.

capabilities for interacting with other firms. . . . Firms with access to a more diverse set of activities and those with more experience at collaborating are better able to locate themselves in information-rich positions. . . . Put colloquially, a firm grows by being a player; it does not become a player by growing."[58] Hence, beneath most formal contracts "lies a sea of informal relations" that accumulate over time, and these informal network connections offer a continuing source of benefits beyond any particular exchange.

Thus technology collaborations provide effective tools to mitigate internal resource constraints. Depending on capability and need, entrepreneurs can advance innovation projects through informal cooperation and/or through formal contractual agreements. Both frequently evolve from ongoing personal relationships. Contacts for formal technology exchange are also frequently made through business-to-business Internet platforms. These diversified institutional arrangements available to entrepreneurs seeking interfirm collaboration in technology development clearly play crucial roles in the culture of innovation.

How Do Private Firms Compare with the Mainstream Economy?

Whether innovation strategies relying on informal and formal interfirm ties will enable private firms to survive in China's highly competitive marketplace is a question of relative performance. Only if private firms are at least as innovative as their nonprivate competitors can they develop into an independent and sustainable economic force, sufficiently powerful to influence and shape institutional and economic development. If, to the contrary, private firms are not able to close the innovation gap with the mainstream economy, marginalization of the private sector is likely to persist. In particular, a shift to high value-added production with greater profit margins would be very unlikely. For a tentative assessment of the sector's relative innovation performance, we therefore broaden our empirical basis, and shift focus to a private versus public comparison.

Descriptive statistics have long supported an ongoing closure of the innovation gap between private and public firms. Already in the mid-1990s, firm-level surveys suggested that private companies invested more resources in innovation projects than state-owned enterprises. Whereas in 1996 state-owned companies invested on average 2.87 percent of their sales revenue in R&D, private firms invested 7.43 percent.[59] The higher relative investment in innovative activities by private firms proved to be highly effective. About 44 percent of private companies ascribed the introduction of new production technologies to their own research activities, whereas only 28 percent of state-owned firms indicated that such technologies were developed or modified in-house.[60] More recent national firm surveys indicate that private companies have over the years also placed a stronger emphasis on new product development. In 2006, for instance, 54 percent of private companies reported an increasing share of new products in their total sales over time, whereas 39 percent of state-owned firms reported this.[61]

To systematically assess the relative performance in innovation of private and public firms, we use national data sets from the World Bank Investment Climate Surveys conducted in 2002 and 2003. These surveys provide a broad canvas selection of the very different institutional environments and market structures found in China's transition economy. These range from the poor hinterland provinces to the rust-belt heavy industrial northeastern provinces, and to the mixed economies of the inland provinces adjacent to the affluent market economies of the Yangzi delta and Pearl River delta regions. The 2002 survey includes 1,548 firms located in five middle-size and large cities; the 2003 survey includes 2,400 firms in eighteen such cities. These twenty-three cities are located in twenty different provinces, from the southwestern province of Guizhou, with only 1 percent private employment and practically no private enterprise economy, to Shanghai, with more than 41 percent of employees in the private sector.[62] Participating firms were randomly selected in each city. The industry mix comprises both labor-intensive and technology-intensive sectors across a broad spectrum of different production technologies and levels of competition. Both surveys share a set of in-depth questions covering innovative activities and related firm-level strategic decisions. Importantly, the data set allows us to replicate the testing strategy and set of dependent variables measuring different types of innovative activities reported in Table 8.7.

With regard to innovativeness, we compare private firms with state-owned enterprises, collectively owned firms, and partially privatized shareholding companies. The state continues to own the majority share in all of these, and they all continue to enjoy substantial advantages over private firms in access to state-controlled financial markets and government funds earmarked to support innovativeness through R&D.[63]

As a proxy for density of informal technology exchange, a measure not covered by the World Bank surveys, we use the regional proportion of private-firm activities in a particular industrial niche. The assumption is that the share of private-firm activities is closely associated with the intensity and frequency of interfirm activities such as learning from networks, mimicking, and informal technical cooperation.[64] The share of private-firm activity within each industry varies considerably across provinces.[65] For "traffic, transport and storage services," for example, it ranges from 1.16 percent in Jiangxi Province to 34.37 percent in Zhejiang Province; for "electrical appliance for daily use," the most privatized sector, it ranges from 69.02 percent in Beijing to 100 percent in Chongqing, Guizhou, Heilongjiang, and Shaanxi Provinces. Within each province, the extent of private-firm activity varies greatly across the different industrial sectors. It is typically lowest in the state-dominated and highly regulated service sectors, and most pronounced in light industrial manufacturing, where new market entrants found open and quickly expanding opportunity structures. Overall, the scope of private-firm participation in markets in our sample has a mean value of 45 percent.

For formal technology collaborations, the World Bank data set provides distinct measures for alliances between the firm and (1) other firms, (2) universities, and (3) research institutes. Combining these, we use binary variables to capture the existence of contractual agreements and strategic alliances for cooperative research and development (R&D) for each of the three years preceding the survey.

Our results (see Table 8.8) suggest that predominantly state-owned public corporations no longer enjoy systematic advantages when it comes to innovativeness. Both state-owned companies and collective firms perform weaker than private firms. Even partially privatized shareholding companies seem no longer to secure significant advantages over private companies. This indicates that private firms have apparently succeeded in growing out of their pariah-like status of marginalized low-tech producers to compete with the traditional mainstream economy in terms of innovativeness.[66]

Innovation strategies employed by private firms have become universal tools, advancing innovativeness across a broad spectrum. Formal contractual agreements in technology exchange are effective drivers of all types of innovation under review. Moreover, the extent of private-firm activity in distinct market niches—our measure of informal collaborations—has a positive effect on innovativeness. Opportunities for tacit learning and informal exchange embedded in the social structure of private markets contribute to a higher level of innovativeness of even state-owned enterprises.

Table 8.8. Ownership, technology exchange, and innovation

	% new products in total sale coeff. (std. error)	Product innovation coeff. (std error)	Process innovation coeff. (std. error)	Quality control innovation coeff. (std. error)	Patent coeff. (std. error)
Marketization					
Proportion of private economy	13.515***	0.486***	0.894***	0.369***	0.294*
	(3.334)	(0.101)	(0.097)	(0.104)	(0.175)
Research cooperation					
R&D cooperation with firms	11.541***	0.458***	0.354***	0.274***	0.216
	(2.236)	(0.070)	(0.091)	(0.077)	(0.155)
R&D cooperation with universities	8.232***	0.250***	0.143	0.173***	0.22
	(2.216)	(0.076)	(0.095)	(0.064)	(0.145)
R&D cooperation with research institutes	5.737**	0.343***	0.415***	0.400***	0.116
	(2.565)	(0.086)	(0.087)	(0.093)	(0.170)
Competition					
Market share > 10%	7.028***	0.219***	0.264***	0.201**	0.099
	(1.932)	(0.081)	(0.076)	(0.082)	(0.102)
Number of competitors in main business	6.043*	0.349**	0.318***	0.167**	0.103
	(3.139)	(0.165)	(0.108)	(0.084)	(0.132)
Number of competitors[2]	-1.326***	-0.067**	-0.054***	-0.030**	-0.033
	(0.497)	(0.026)	(0.018)	(0.013)	(0.021)
Firm exports	3.944**	0.107*	0.159*	0.176**	-0.017
	(1.917)	(0.055)	(0.051)	(0.069)	(0.117)

(continued)

Table 8.8 (continued)

	% new products in total sale coeff. (std. error)	Product innovation coeff. (std. error)	Process innovation coeff. (std. error)	Quality control innovation coeff. (std. error)	Patent coeff. (std. error)
Ownership[a]					
State-owned firm	-4.379*	-0.036	-0.121*	-0.233***	-0.460***
	(2.306)	(0.070)	(0.067)	(0.071)	(0.154)
Collectively owned firm	-6.434**	-0.106*	-0.072	-0.035	-0.383***
	(2.586)	(0.064)	(0.074)	(0.083)	(0.138)
Partial state ownership in limited liability or joint stock company	-0.578	0.042	0.13	-0.053	-0.218
	(4.311)	(0.158)	(0.123)	(0.133)	(0.208)
Firm controls[b]					
Firm is founded after 1978	-0.41	-0.038	0.015	0.284***	0.078
	(2.399)	(0.059)	(0.069)	(0.086)	(0.125)
Log of average firm assets	1.03	0.036	0.022	0.041*	0.028
	(0.659)	(0.026)	(0.026)	(0.021)	(0.040)
Constant	-68.616***	-2.673***	-2.320***	-2.186***	-2.938***
	(9.068)	(0.308)	(0.271)	(0.297)	(0.395)
Method	Tobit	Probit	Probit	Probit	Probit
R^2 / Pseudo R^2	0.052	0.207	0.186	0.143	0.415
N	2859	2937	2934	2930	2128

Source: World Bank Investment Climate Survey 2002 and 2003.

a. Reference: private.

b. Other control variables not reported here include a broad set of variables such as the stock of patents, the existence of in-house R&D, the average R&D-to-sales ratio, location in industrial park, membership in business associations, financial leverage, number of employees, education of manager, and survey year. As our measure of marketization is based on city and sector, we do not include additional control variables for city and sector.

Note: In parentheses are robust standard errors; * $p < 0.10$, ** $p < 0.05$, *** $p < 0.01$. Results are not driven by multicollinearity.

Conclusion

The ability to innovate is a prerequisite to survive market competition. As such, firm innovativeness may possibly serve as the most informative litmus test to explore the causal priority of the role of formal institutions in the rise of a market economy.

As a social process involving both cooperation and competition, innovation is usually assumed to require a certain set of formal institutions to be in place, in order to regulate economic transactions between collaborators and to safeguard innovators against imitators by protecting intellectual property rights. But many economic transactions in fact are guided informally by mechanisms regulated by ongoing social relationships. In particular, the self-enforcing social structure of markets enables private firms to develop endogenously the norms and conventions of cooperation and exchange needed to compete in innovative activity.

This chapter has illustrated the rise of an innovation culture in an environment not conducive to intellectual property rights protection. In spite of weak formal institutions, entrepreneurs in the Yangzi delta region have from the bottom up constructed the necessary norms and institutional arrangements to initiate and protect technology collaboration. The common assertion that innovation and collaborative efforts flourish only where formal institutions provide the scope and legal protection to do so is thereby controverted.

As our case studies show, the rise of innovative activities is deeply embedded in social network structures, which facilitate marginal innovations and diffusion of technology through informal collaboration. Competitive pressure also leads to the increasing use of formal technology agreements to advance product development and patenting activities. In this way, China's once-marginalized private entrepreneurs have developed into an independent economic force, gradually closing the innovation gap with public firms. Significantly, of the four Chinese companies appearing on a 2010 list of the fifty most innovative firms in the world, three are private (BYD, Lenovo, and Haier), and only one is state controlled (China Mobile).[67]

In sum, our evidence strongly supports our hypothesis that the effectiveness of social norms, beyond the shadow of the law, is not limited to close-knit communities of economic actors such as tribal and peasant societies. In fact, social norms can provide robust mechanisms explaining cooperation within large social groups, thereby enabling dynamic economic development.

9

Political Economy of Capitalism

The bottom-up evolution of economic institutions made possible the diffusion of private enterprise as an organizational form. In the 1980s, private firms not registered as fake collectives operated in a gray zone as formally illegal businesses, significantly disadvantaged; yet private manufacturing grew in size and scope. Entrepreneurs started up small manufacturing firms with capital borrowed from friends and relatives and recruited unskilled and skilled employees in informal labor markets. In close-knit communities and social networks, enforceable trust and bounded solidarity motivated credible commitment to emergent business norms and economic institutions. Expectation of trustworthy behavior cemented confidence in contracts between principals and agents, even in the context of weak property rights and other uncertainties that characterized the transition economy. Cooperation norms fostered mutual assistance and strategic alliances between firms. In specialty industrial clusters, private firms built autonomous supply and distribution networks and cooperated to secure economies of scale and competitive advantage. These strategic alliances and networks served as conduits for the flow of information across market interfaces, providing entrepreneurs with access to novel ideas and technical innovations from the global economy. Such bottom-up institutions provided the private enterprise economy with sufficient autonomous resources to fuel capitalist economic development in the Yangzi delta region and other coastal provinces.

Our focus on micro-level mechanisms residing in these strategic alliances and networks does not deny the significant role of interaction between economic actors and the state. Not only are political actors continually responding to changing market conditions by incrementally adjusting and adapting to demands imposed on the ground by the pace of economic development, but economic actors—either formally in local people's congresses and business associations or informally through political connections—lobby for change of formal rules or for favorable interpretation of existing rules to better match their interests.

As with the rise of modern capitalism several centuries earlier in England, informal economic practices embedded in social norms and networks provided the institutional foundations that enabled and motivated the growth and diffusion of private enterprise.[1] But as in the West, for capitalist economic development to be sustainable, it also is necessary for the state to change the ground rules to secure the formal rights and legitimacy of the private enterprise and free-market system. In the course of the Industrial Revolution in England, the rise of modern capitalism required continuous interventions by the state to enact rules establishing the legal and regulatory framework of a national market economy. As Karl Polanyi observed, economic liberalism and "the introduction of free markets, far from doing away with the need for control, regulation, and intervention, enormously increased their range."[2] Similarly, in China over the past several decades, "the progression of market reforms created both the demand for new institutions to sustain the emerging markets and the conditions to restructure and rebuild institutions." Indeed, "progression of market competition ushered in such transformations in economic conditions that the strong bonds between state institutions and enterprises began to weaken, making it easier for political entrepreneurs to reshape the state-business relationship, get state institutions out of the business of doing business and restructure government institutions."[3]

A recent study of the role of law in China's economic development concludes that "it is impossible to make the case that formal legal institutions have contributed in any important way to China's remarkable economic success. If anything, economic development has fostered the development of law, rather than the reverse."[4] Although we emphasize the causal priority of endogenous institutional change in the rise and diffusion of the private enterprise economy, transformative change giving rise to modern capitalist institutions relies not only on evolutionary bottom-up processes but also on state actors enacting and enforcing new formal rules in response to changing parameters in the real economy. While formal laws had little or nothing to do with the emergence of the private enterprise economy, accommodative changes in formal laws are essential if economic growth is to be sustained.

The Accommodating State

The rise of entrepreneurship and modern capitalism in China was an unintended outcome of the economic reforms initiated by the Communist Party. As swarms of private entrepreneurs entered new industrial sectors, they competed for market share as they challenged the hegemony of government-owned firms in the manufacturing economy. By the time conservatives in the political elite turned their attention to the challenge posed by private firms, entrepreneurship had become a broadly based social movement. Entrepreneurial profits from private businesses were too large and widely distributed for the state to even attempt to put a stranglehold over development of the private sector. Further, unrelenting competitive pressure from private manufacturing firms led to a relative decline in market share of state-owned enterprises. As growing numbers of bankruptcies and privatization of state-owned firms reduced the size of the state-owned economy, politicians increasingly came to view the private enterprise economy as an important source of taxable revenue and as indispensable to economic development. Additionally, the private sector had emerged as the largest source of jobs, employing millions of migrant laborers shifting out of subsistence agriculture.

Reformers in central government responded by shifting to policies of accommodation, supportive of the rapidly growing private enterprise economy. Through deregulation and enactment of laws providing formal legal status to private enterprise as an organizational form, the state gradually conferred legitimacy to capitalist economic development, bringing formal laws closer to the economic realities. Such adaptations are most evident in the measured and repeated amendments to China's constitution finally establishing—at least de jure—a level playing field between state-owned firms and the private enterprise economy. The 2006 revision of the Company Law, which not only greatly reduced minimum capital requirements but also introduced single-person limited liability companies, was a clear response to the widespread use of "dummy shareholders" and the frequent undermining of the formal requirements specified by the original Company Law in 1994.

That the state would incrementally respond through accommodative legal and regulatory changes to a rapidly expanding private enterprise economy was not a given. Political actors could have sought in earnest to enforce legal and regulatory rules limiting the size and scope of private businesses, and could occasionally have punished deviators harshly. In the Maoist era, private entrepreneurship would not have reached a critical threshold level triggering a self-reinforcing growth of private firms, even with the support of some local governments. Moreover, even if political actors responded in a lenient way to deviators, allowing opposition norms to arise at the margins of society, the state could still have continued to deny adjustments of formal rules, prolonging the marginalization of private entrepreneurial activities.

Whether or not political actors accommodate endogenous institutional change is determined by the nature and direction of changing incentives. China's policy of fiscal decentralization played a key role in explaining their responsiveness to entrepreneurial activity.[5] That policy required lower-level governments to submit a fixed proportion of fiscal revenues to their superior government unit, but they could retain the residual for their own budget. The aim was to make local levels of government rely increasingly on self-financing to meet growing responsibility for funding local public goods. Further, merit-based standards used to evaluate the performance of local officials "focused overwhelmingly on rapid industrial expansion but also included targets for provision of public goods, such as education, infrastructure, and public order."[6] Remuneration, tenure of office, and chances for promotion were thereby linked to success in local economic development. With revenue maximization positively linked to economic performance, fiscal decentralization greatly strengthened incentives for local government officials to do what they could to assure that local firms prospered.[7] Though originally designed to spur the modernization of the public economy and rationalize public spending, China's quasi-federalism thus concomitantly also created incentives for local and provincial government to accommodate entrepreneurial endeavors, particularly if state-owned sources of income were insufficient to support local government activities.

Therefore an unintended consequence of fiscal decentralization was to compel poor localities to be first to support the rise of private enterprise. Our model (Chapter 2) predicts that in poor localities unwilling to crack down on entrepreneurs, the private enterprise economy will achieve a tipping point earlier. It is hardly surprising that in the Yangzi delta region the city of Wenzhou, with a registered per capita public revenue of only ¥23 in 1978 (a third of the average per capita revenue in Zhejiang Province and 14 percent of

the national provincial average), took the lead in developing a private enterprise economy. In contrast, Shanghai, the municipality with the largest state-
owned industrial base (and per capita government revenue seventy-five times
larger than that of Wenzhou), was the last of our sample cities to witness notable private firm activities (see Figure 9.1).

With the rise of a national market economy in the 1990s, increasing financial responsibilities and hardening budget constraints imposed additional
pressure on local governments to privatize their local economies. While the
state succeeded in maintaining the size of the public sector until the mid-
1990s, this sector continuously lost market share in the competition with the
private sector. Company profits of state-owned firms dropped by 50 percent
between 1994 and 1996 alone, in spite of a still-increasing production value.[8]
In 1996, loss-making state-owned enterprises generated a total loss of ¥79 billion, and income tax collected from the sector did not reach 12 percent of total
tax revenue.[9] Under the pressure of growing expenditures spent on open and
hidden subsidies and accumulating bad loans granted to state-owned firms, a

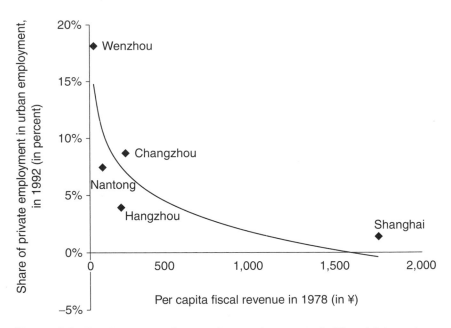

Figure 9.1. Fiscal revenue and private firm employment in the Yangzi delta region.
Comparable data for Ningbo and Nanjing are not available. *Source:* Data retrieved
through *China Data Online, City Statistical Yearbook*s.

change in central government policy on privatization in the mid-1990s eventually opened the floodgate to a national wave of privatization. Following the national policy of *"zhuada, fangxiao"* (grasp the big ones and let the small ones free), local governments divested or sold their small and medium-size state-owned firms, usually in manager or employee buyouts. The central government's aim was to consolidate the state-owned economy around the largest public firms, which also were partially privatized as public corporations listed on one of China's two stock exchanges. The number of state-owned enterprises declined by more than 70 percent between 1996 and 2004, from 113,000 to 31,000, and total national employment in them plunged from 110 million to 64 million, while their total production value stabilized at around 35 percent of gross industrial output.[10] Analysis of provincial data for the reform period from 1978 to 2009 confirms the close negative relation between reliance on state-owned production and per capita tax income, and the steep increase in tax revenue after the central government launched its privatization policies in the late 1990s (see Figure 9.2). This explains why governments at all levels responded readily to the change in national policy by accelerating privatization and divestiture of loss-making government-owned firms under their administration. They realized not only that loss-making state-owned firms were a drain on government coffers, but also that dependence on those firms corresponded with a slower pace of local economic development, as resources were tied up in unproductive use. Between 1996 and 1999, the total amount of subsidies equaled 44 percent of income tax collected from the sector.[11] Capitalist economic development gained stronger traction and support the more government officials came to understand the relationship between growth of private economic activity and an expanding base of taxable income.

Prospects for State Capitalism

When departing from state socialism through market reform, the state must simultaneously dismantle the institutions of central planning and put in place the requisite rules of competition and cooperation of a capitalist economy. However, political actors are rarely willing to institute a new economic system that completely deprives them of direct control rights at the firm level. And economic actors, in turn, seek political connections to gain access to resources and to try to assure some protection in a highly insecure and rapidly

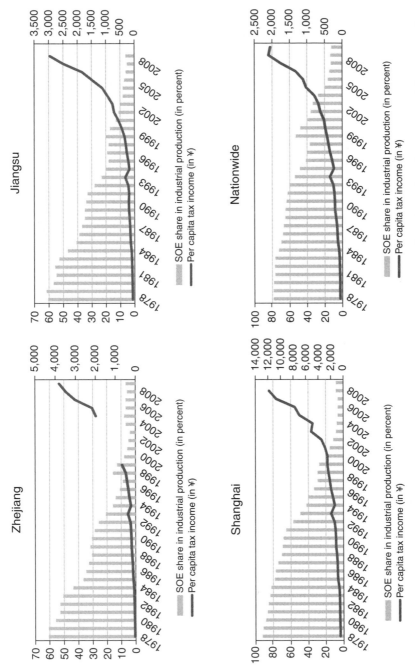

Figure 9.2. State-owned enterprise production and tax income, 1978–2009. *Source:* Calculation based on provincial data retrieved from China Data Online. For the years 2000–2002 and 2004, Zhejiang's *Statistical Yearbooks* do not provide data on tax income.

changing business environment. As a result, "there is still a much different atmosphere of interaction between government and individual economic agents in ex-socialist countries than in countries with a long tradition of free markets."[12]

While it is indisputable that markets have emerged as the main coordinating mechanism of the Chinese economy, the political hegemony of the Communist Party remains intact. Thus these questions arise: Despite economic reform and the accompanying legal and regulatory changes to accommodate the needs of capitalist economic development, does the underlying nature of top-down political governance of economic life persist essentially unchanged? What is the role that political connections play in the success of entrepreneurial action and the performance of firms?

In the early years of reform, private entrepreneurs not infrequently relied on political connections and diverse forms of favor seeking to bend the regulatory bars and gain access to scarce resources or ad hoc most favorable treatment from local government (i.e., acceptance of private firms as fake collectives, lowering of security and environmental standards, or tolerance of poor labor conditions).[13] To what extent do state-firm relations in the emergent market economy still depend on bending existing rules through political connections to acquire economic advantage over unconnected competitors?

Answers to these questions have broader implications, as they indicate whether China's market economy is a distinctive form of state capitalism, where political capital is still the primary asset that companies need for their individual survival and success. Alternatively, if China's current form of capitalism is en route to a full-blown market economy, we should observe constraints on the politicized nature of economic decisions as the role of the state shifts to greater emphasis on building formal market institutions, including property rights and an effective legal system.

That political connections grease the wheels in all economic orders is a nearly universal supposition. Economic actors in all economies invest in some form of political capital to secure positional advantages. In market economies too, political actors impose restrictions on economic activities, giving rise to rents that agents compete for. Whether to control entry of new competitors or to promote strategic interests, desire to capture or channel the coercive power of the state motivates the demand for regulation favorable to an industry or firm.[14] In nonmarket economies, production and distribution turn on the power of principals at the center of a hierarchy. Political actors directly set the prices; hence, agents seeking comparative advantage compete for positional power in the hierarchy, and cultivate political connections.[15]

As to the overall economic value of political capital in China given the seemingly incorrigible nature of Communist Party rule, there is no simple answer. Some evidence indicates that state-owned firms with connections to the old political elite perform worse than private firms.[16] Firms with partial state ownership are typically forced to maintain higher employment levels and often serve as tools for private enrichment of politicians.[17] Several studies observe a declining reliance on personal connections *(guanxi)* in transactions with government.[18] There is also some indication, however, that political capital has a positive impact on the firm's equity value and performance. This suggests that politically connected firms can secure positional advantages, even if overall firm productivity might be lower. Such advantages may be most pronounced under conditions of tight resource constraints.[19]

One needs to ask not simply whether political capital is valuable for firms, but more specifically, to what extent do entrepreneurs still benefit from political capital and in what institutional domains are political connections helpful to the firm's chances for survival and profitability? Is political capital a prerequisite for survival and economic success in the private enterprise economy? Is it a necessary form of insurance to secure political protection and legitimacy? Or do we see evidence of constraints on the fungibility of political capital, as economic actors successfully lobby for formal legal reforms, forging an increasingly rule-based market environment?

Political Capital in Institutional Contexts

Political capital shares with other forms of capital (physical, human, social) the capacity to make possible, under certain conditions, the realization of interests that otherwise would not be achieved. Like social capital, which "inheres in the structure of relations between actors and among actors,"[20] political capital accumulates in relational ties. However, political capital has the additional feature of being linked to the positional power of the politician, and thus it is rooted in institutional structures, both formal and informal, of the political order.

For the economic actor, political capital accrues through personal connections with politicians and with the party in power. Political connections serve as conduits of information between economic and political actors, with information flow favoring those with an inside track to the politician. The institution of lobbying turns on the fungibility and productiveness of political connections as the basis of mutual expectations, obligations, trust, and timely information. Importantly, because political capital inheres in relationships, both economic and political actors can secure gains cumulatively in maintaining them. Expectations, obligations, and trust stem from social exchange in which a politician does something for a constituent, with some idea that the favor will be reciprocated in some degree sometime in the future. If a politician accumulates a large volume of credit through favors conferred by virtue of positional power, then the analogy to economic capital is clear.

Because political capital is embedded not only in social relationships but also in political institutions, analysis of its effects must incorporate a focus on the institutional context in which transactions are conducted. To specify the productivity and fungibility of political capital, we need to examine transactions between economic and political actors in concrete institutional domains.

In command economies, the state assumed monopoly power over the allocation of all resources. Productive assets from farmland to factories were owned and managed by the state, which set prices by administrative fiat. Clearly, under the central plan, government bureaucrats and party officials maintained an overwhelming advantage in power over economic actors. A firm's access to resources and its bargaining over production quotas mainly depended on positional advantage stemming from political connections with the planning authorities.

The gradual replacement of state planning by market allocation and the resulting empowerment of the consumer leads to a shift in the balance of power from the established political actors toward economic actors. Moreover, the shift to market allocation causes changes in relative rewards that reduce the payoffs of network advantages based on political position and offer incentives and opportunities for economic actors to engage in productivity-enhancing entrepreneurial activity. This endogenously motivates strategic adjustments by firms to the emergent market economy, which in turn undermine the previous institutional foundations of firm survival. Whether firms choose to rely on organizational improvements (see Chapter 5), on better access to suppliers and distributors (see Chapter 6) or skilled labor (see Chapter 7), or on higher innovativeness (see Chapter 8), markets shift the focus to the importance of capabilities, as opposed to investing in positional advantage through political capital.

With the continuing expansion of markets, the economic success of firms becomes increasingly independent of the direct involvement of politicians. Vertical ties linking economic actors in firms with the state decline in significance as horizontal ties—interfirm networks and network ties between buyers and sellers based on repeat exchange—gain in importance. In other words, markets cumulatively shift the interest of economic actors away from self-enforcing reliance on vertical political connections characteristic of state socialism to self-reinforcing investment in horizontal network ties that sociologists emphasize as the basis of social capital in market economies.

Naturally, this does not imply that political capital has lost its utility for economic actors. But political capital has greatest valuation in those institutional domains where government restricts economic activity. The stronger the government's commitment to competitive markets in an industrial and commercial sector, the more the value of political capital will decline in that sector.

The complexity and challenges of entrepreneurial action give rise to various context-specific reasons for entrepreneurs to cultivate "good" ties with local officials. Some entrepreneurs simply seek to establish good relations with local government as "insurance" to reduce the risk of unfavorable treatment by politicians and regulatory agents. Political connections also provide a conduit for timely and critical information from politicians, which limit the uncertainties of a highly dynamic and volatile political environment. Overall, good relations with local government—fostered, for instance, by participation in industry-wide associations sponsored by local government or by membership in the Communist Party—confer legitimacy to the firm.

In actuality, most entrepreneurs in the Yangzi delta region expect little tangible advantage from political networking. The general manager of a computer company in Zhejiang Province summarizes: "Politics is just another game. Since I chose to play the game of business, I do not want to play another game. Among my circle of friends, those who do business, they are not very interested in that. There is a feeling that companies that want to have a close relationship with the government must have something to hide. Besides, in my sector, the government cannot give me much, not many tax breaks, and not much government contracts."[21] Benefits from political connections are generally not anticipated. "Just because I become a party member, my business will not be running any better" is an assessment with which most entrepreneurs would agree. Close to 80 percent of private entrepreneurs do not believe their success mainly depends on having good connections with party and government officials.[22] For a small elite, however, political capital does produce decisive advantages. Many on China's growing list of parvenus are politically connected, and a third of China's richest 800 entrepreneurs are party members, indicating that the "right connections" can still help to secure super profits.[23] Understandably, the demonstration effect of a small elite gaining from political connections is incentive for many entrepreneurs to secure political capital in some form.

The most readily available source of political capital is membership in the Communist Party. For entrepreneurs stigmatized by the low status of private enterprise in the pecking order of the industrial economy, party membership signals to government officials and bureaucrats commitment to the established political order. Especially for entrepreneurs experimenting with new forms of production or risky business ventures, the signal of political approval conferred by party membership can be critical for survival. Also, as party members, entrepreneurs can gain access to privileged and timely information on changes in the regulatory environment. Not surprisingly, by the late 1980s up to 15 percent of owners of private manufacturing firms were party members.[24] Our random sample confirms that Communist Party membership is commonplace for CEOs of private firms. Although entrepreneurs do not expect to exercise decisive influence on public policy through party membership, they still sense that the local government pays more attention to the opinions of party members than to those outside the political establishment.

Not only has the Communist Party sought to recruit successful entrepreneurs, but between 1997 and 2002 more than 9,000 entrepreneurs were selected to be delegates to People's Congresses at and above the county level.[25] In our 2006 survey, 2.6 percent of the entrepreneurs were members of the People's Congress, though the majority of them served only at the township and county levels.

However, we find no evidence to support the view that party membership was a crucial factor in the rise of the private enterprise economy in the Yangzi delta region. In fact, the share of entrepreneurs in our survey who had joined the party before founding their businesses is substantively lower in older firms than in younger firms (see Figure 9.3). There are two different possible reasons for this pattern: (1) party membership among entrepreneurs may have been more frequent in earlier years than appears here, but the survival rate of those firms was lower; or (2) party membership among entrepreneurs has increased more recently, as private sector has gained more legitimacy and attracted individuals who previously worked in the public sector. In either case, party membership was obviously not determinative for entrepreneurial success in the early reform years.

Today virtually all firms routinely interact with government units, whether in dealing with the tax bureau, local offices when applying for business licenses, or government inspectors visiting the firm. It has become commonplace for entrepreneurs and managers to have personal ties with government officials. In our 2009 survey, most reported that they personally know at least one high-ranking party official in the county government. Those who do not have a direct political connection with government and party officials say they can easily establish a personal contact with the help of a relative or acquaintance. The owner of a textile company in Hangzhou observes, "I know a few officials in police, business administration, and taxation departments. These officials all are pertinent to our business. It is easier for us to consult with them. It makes getting communication and policy information faster. Procedure-wise, I might need some red tape dealt with today, but because I know these people, I could make up for it the next day rather than having to do it today. Otherwise there are no benefits. Sometimes, the officials would tell you some information within the boundaries of policies. What projects the government will support and which not."[26] The great majority of entrepreneurs in our 2006

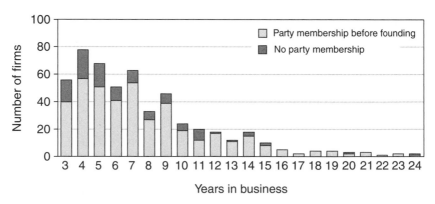

Figure 9.3. Party membership of founders. *Source:* Yangzi Survey 2006.

survey likewise confirm strong reliance on personal connections in their dealings with government authorities, with an average of 4.7 on a Likert scale (1–7).

It is not unusual for government authorities to take the initiative to strengthen and intensify contacts with select members of the local business community. A successful start-up entrepreneur running a software company in Zhejiang recalls how government relations suddenly changed once his business success was apparent. "It was not us who approached the government. We were already the number one company in our sector, so the government was proud of us and wanted to meet us. Then you just manage your relationship with government as you do with customer relations."[27] Politicians especially seek out the views of local business leaders as to how to improve the business environment. Such overtures from the local government signal legitimacy and approval of the economic success of private firms. In turn, regular consultation with government officials offers entrepreneurs a routine mechanism to strengthen their political connections.

Financial contribution to party activities is one of the most direct ways to invest in political connections and to "make up for political deficits."[28] Eighteen percent of the entrepreneurs interviewed in our 2006 survey and 16 percent in our 2009 survey regularly make donations to finance activities of the local party branches. As one entrepreneur explained, "In the future, when we want to expand our business, we have to rely on a good relationship with the government. When you are not famous, and your firm is not big, the authorities will not come to knock on your door. But once you are big, then you must have good relationships with the government." After a pause he added, "If the party wants you to die, you have no way to live."[29] There is in fact a close association between the size of a firm and financial contributions it makes to the Communist Party. Entrepreneurs in our 2009 survey who make regular donations to the party operate firms that are on average five times larger than those who do not donate money. While financial donations to the local party branch may buy a good relationship with government, it is also in the interest of politicians to be supportive of the larger firms that contribute more to local economic growth, nonfarm employment, and tax revenues. The owner of a textile company remarked, "It is like a car moving on a highway. Once the car is on the highway, government will let you move along, rather than slow you down."[30]

To assess the varying extent to which political connections matter in a firm's chances for survival and profitability, we examine their impact in different institutional domains characterized by high, moderate, and low levels of marketization. We contrast the product market's liberal market environment with four partially liberalized market sectors displaying increasing degrees of state control in resource allocation: the credit market, the market for government contracts, the market for land use rights, and the privatization of public company assets.[31] One should note that whereas the product market involves everyday transactions, the credit and government contract markets represent transactions that occur only sporadically; and the other two markets involve transactions that are relatively rare, which most private firms do not experience more than once (if at all) during their operation.

Product Market

The product market is the most competitive in China's transition economy. Market liberalization started early, allowing for a rapid commercialization of most product lines. By 1991, 86 percent of GDP was produced and sold outside of central allocation plans. Product differentiation is high, and producers compete fiercely for customers and market share. Only a few sectors are still dominated by state-owned monopolies, as evidenced by the low industrial concentration ratios. The largest ten domestic manufacturers in each of the five industrial sectors included in our Yangzi delta survey account for at most 20 percent of the market share in their niche.

Our 2006 survey in the Yangzi delta region supports our prediction that such competitive markets do not reward firms holding political capital (see Table 9.1). Controlling for a standard set of management and company qualities, we found that smaller firms, firms with younger managers, and firms with managers who were recruited from different locations experience faster sales growth than other firms. There is no indication that political capital provides tangible advantages. Instead, firms making regular financial donations to the party experience slower growth rates than do other firms.

We can only speculate on the potential reasons for this last finding. It is plausible that economically weak firms with small sales growth are all the more interested in "buying" political support in anticipation of future problems and favors they hope to receive in the future (for instance, loan guarantees or tax breaks). Or the "habit to make regular party donations" may simply reflect a different management behavior or ideological outlook of the manager, which could also be correlated with a less aggressive sales strategy.

Credit Market

Liberalization of commercial banking started relatively late and proceeded slowly. As one of the less liberalized markets, the credit market provides excellent conditions for the political elite to secure preferential treatment.[32] In spite of the market entry of foreign-invested banks and private domestic banks, the credit market is still heavily state controlled, allowing local authorities to influence decisions of local loan officers, oftentimes with reference to industrial policy priorities and local economic development needs. By 2008, China's four state-owned commercial banks still held 57 percent of bank assets, allowing for substantial control over domestic capital allocation.[33] It has been argued that lending decisions by state-owned banks are increasingly based on economic fundamentals; however, marketization remains weak, with only 1 percent of their loans allocated to private firms.[34]

Our analysis confirms the continuing influence of political capital in loan decisions (see Table 9.1).[35] Those entrepreneurs who were long-standing party members enjoy some advantages. Thirty-two percent of private firms founded by party and government officials got their start-up capital as loans from state-owned banks. By contrast, only 14 percent of the entrepreneurs without cadre background succeeded in securing such start-up loans. Credit access also varies between long-standing party members and nonmembers. Whereas 26 percent of the founders with party membership secured bank loans, only 12 percent of nonmembers received a loan. In addition, party members secured larger loans, providing a bigger share of their external capital.

Government Contracts

In the market for government contracts, political connections easily undermine competitive bidding guidelines. Despite the enactment of a law (effective in 2003) to ensure fairness and impartiality in government procurement, the actual bidding process lacks transparency. As one respondent remarked, "Competitive bidding is just a form. It does not involve the entire process in terms of results. The country is making progress in making the bidding process rule-governed. But process and results are different matters. Political connections

Table 9.1. Political capital, networking, and success in regulated markets

	Sales growth in 2005 coeff. (std. error)	Bank loan at founding stage coeff. (std. error)	Percent of government contracts in sales coeff. (std. error)	Government support to get land use rights coeff. (std. error)	Asset privatization coeff. (std. error)
Firm characteristics					
Log of registered founding capital	0.004 (0.009)	0.237*** (0.072)		0.025 (0.083)	0.109** (0.053)
Log of total sales (in 2005)			-2.744 (1.931)		
Log of total sales (lagged $t=2$)	-0.041** (0.013)				
Firm age	0.000 (0.005)	0.010 (0.012)	1.151*** (0.257)	0.002 (0.018)	-0.026 (0.024)
Human capital					
Years of schooling (founder)	-0.011 (0.012)	0.011 (0.021)	1.542 (1.384)	0.000 (0.021)	0.013 (0.038)
Male (founder)	0.030 (0.041)	-0.021 (0.121)	0.962 (6.118)	0.277** (0.126)	0.289 (0.288)
Age (founder)	-0.004* (0.002)	-0.006 (0.011)	-0.049 (0.203)	0.004 (0.007)	0.011 (0.013)
Born in same city (founder)	-0.067 (0.019)	-0.273*** (0.086)	-6.512*** (1.688)	-0.109 (0.167)	0.303 (0.275)

Political capital

	OLS	Probit	Tobit	Probit	Probit
Party membership before firm founding	0.063	0.262**	−9.240**	0.136	0.371***
	(0.055)	(0.122)	(4.508)	(0.117)	(0.131)
Former cadre position	0.025	0.099	23.230***	−0.367	0.791***
	(0.042)	(0.217)	(8.522)	(0.436)	(0.204)
Current cadre position of relative	0.004	−0.020	7.120***	0.275**	0.125
	(0.025)	(0.189)	(2.104)	(0.137)	(0.154)
Regular party donations	−0.055*		15.584**	0.484**	
	(0.025)		(6.508)	(0.212)	
Networking intensity with political government	0.006		5.199	−0.011	
	(0.007)		(3.430)	(0.072)	
Networking intensity with administration	0.003		0.563	0.234***	
	(0.011)		(2.364)	(0.064)	
Constant	0.606***	−2.063***	−70.493*	−1.807***	−2.740**
	(0.044)	(0.691)	(40.208)	(0.658)	(1.243)
Method	OLS	Probit	Tobit	Probit	Probit
N	619	523+	710	581[a]	523[b]
Adj. R² / Pseudo R²	0.143	0.225	0.084	0.110	0.199

Source: Yangzi Survey 2006.
Estimated coefficient values for sector and city dummies are not reported

a. The sample covers only de novo start-up firms.

b. Since the outcome variable refers to the founding stage, the total sample includes only firms that are currently run by one of their founders. Robust standard errors clustered on city.

* p<0.10, ** p<0.05, *** p<0.01. Results are not driven by multicollinearity.

are still as important as before. Of course, if some senior government official gives a signal we will get the project. Sometimes we lose bids because someone else gets the nod from a senior official."[36] Also, bribe taking is an acute concern. An entrepreneur who was formerly a party secretary worries, "There is now a lot of corruption in government; officials require kick-backs, which a small firm like ours cannot pay. For instance, treating officials to dinner in Beijing costs easily more than ¥20,000; this is hard to pay for small-scale companies. But securing these government contracts is important. With these deals, big firms can still make a profit margin of more than 100 percent. Their costs might be just ¥600 per piece, but they can sell for 1,500 to 2,000 to government. Without such deals, my own profit margin is down to 12 to 14 percent."[37]

Thus the market for government contracts can be readily used to redistribute rents to bidders with political connections. Many bureaucrats actually leave office for a business career with the idea of becoming a government supplier. As former cadres, their extensive ties with government provide effective conduits of information and personal contacts that are invaluable in securing lucrative government contracts.

Our analysis confirms that cadre entrepreneurs and entrepreneurs with relatives in cadre positions rely to a greater extent on sales to government (see Table 9.1). Financial contributions to the local party branch offices are also positively associated with the likelihood of signing deals with the government. However, intense cultivation of personal ties with government officials and administrators is not associated with a higher ratio of government contracts in a firm's sales structure. Moreover, party membership even appears to have a negative impact on getting government contracts. A possible reason for this surprising finding is that membership in the party comes with closer public scrutiny, and this may actually impede rent-seeking activities of ordinary party members.

Market for Land-Use Rights

As with government contracts, the market for land-use rights provides local government authorities with a ready means for distributing rents to political supporters and protégés. Government bureaus act as monopolists and enjoy undivided control rights over land resources. Administrative interference and influence often go well beyond the legally specified regulations for land distribution. A 2004 study revealed that about 80 percent of illegal land-use cases could be attributed to local government malfeasance.[38]

Land-use rights are the most valuable assets local governments control and distribute. That land distribution does not necessarily follow market-based allocation is evident to the most casual observer traveling in the Yangzi delta region. Government-owned public companies usually settle in central urban locations and possess vast factory grounds, while the majority of private firms start up in remote suburban locations. The availability of prime commercial property with easy access to infrastructure affects a firm's potential to survive and grow. Many of our respondents recall that in their early founding days public transport and road systems were still under development near their sites. Often no other bidder was interested in the piece of land approved for start-up firms, and prime locations were neither available nor affordable. Politically connected entrepreneurs, however, can hope for priority treatment when it comes to newly opened industrial or technology park developments. Moreover, prize location can yield significant profits from sales on the market for land use titles. A politically favored private firm in our sample was offered a state-owned enterprise, a well-managed electrometer company with a national reputation, as part of the privatization initiative directed by the central government. The new owners encountered persistent opposition from the firm's management and workers during the privatization process, however, and were not successful in restructuring the firm. Nonetheless, the takeover turned out to be enormously profitable for them thanks to the transfer of land: "We have a factory site with 70 mu (11.5 acres) and the local university will pay ¥150 million for this site to purchase it. The government will then give us a new site to move to, where we only pay ¥260,000 for one mu. As new owners, we are making a windfall profit just from the real estate appreciation of land. The employees get a golden parachute. And we are making a fortune."[39]

Our survey confirms a close association between political capital and government support in the allocation of land use rights (see Table 9.1). Entrepreneurs who invest in political connections are more likely to be granted land-use rights from local government. Further, regular financial contributions to the party improve the chances of securing prime real estate.[40] Clearly, these results are well in line with the common notion that local governments use land markets as a ready mechanism to distribute rents to politically favored clients.

Asset Privatization

That long-standing political connections are a determinative factor in the transfer of state assets to former cadres is a truism. In almost all transition economies, well-informed insiders were successful in appropriating often the best and most prestigious assets offered for privatization.[41] China is no exception. Political capital played a decisive role in the privatization processes of the Yangzi delta region. In the bidding process for collective township village enterprises or state-owned companies, members of the local political elite enjoyed advantages, especially in southern Jiangsu Province, where such enterprises flourished until the late 1990s. Reflecting the rich opportunities there for rent seeking in privatizing state assets, a majority (66 percent) of the private firms in our random sample that were previously government owned are located in that province. In total, 81 of the 130 privatized companies in our sample were taken over by new owners who had been long-standing party members, had held government positions, or had relatives who were government officials. Long-standing party members and cadres are significantly more likely to acquire assets scheduled for privatization than nonparty bidders who lack strategic personal connections with politicians (see Table 9.1).

Oftentimes, government handpicked political allies and clients to transfer ownership to, as a reward for past loyalty. With regard to the above-mentioned electrometer company, the manager recalls:

> The government just approached the new owner, who was already a well-known reputable private entrepreneur. He was also a member of the People's Congress. He had very close personal relations with government officials and was always socializing with them. The government approached him: "Because you are so outstanding and you have the means and the reputation we would like to sell the company to you." The privatization process followed the formal government regulations drafted by the central government policy. But there was no price asked for the assets, the buildings, the equipment, and the land. The new owner just had to take over the debt of the state-owned company.[42]

Preferential access to public assets for the politically well connected is a structural feature of privatization. Although the national government instituted formal rules of public bidding on state assets to increase procedural transparency and fairness, the actual bidding procedures favor the old political elite, principally the former factory directors, who are mostly long-standing Communist Party members. Such favoritism often is concealed in the detailed specifications of rules on the bidding process for state-owned assets. It is common practice for local governments to require bidders not only to propose a business plan but also to prove capability to manage the company, and to possess prior management experience in the product niche of the firm to be privatized. Obviously, such rules offer the standing company manager a decisive competitive advantage in a bidding process decided by a closed committee of local government officials. Sometimes local governments explicitly prioritize former employees over external bidders for state assets. Also, outsiders are naturally disadvantaged because they lack crucial information needed to prepare a compelling business plan. Through a host of restrictive requirements specifying appropriate bidders, government limits the number of bids, and usually enables insiders to secure public assets below market price. In many cases, there is only one bidder—the factory director—submitting a proposal in the privatization of government-owned firms. Further, it is not uncommon for local government to provide politically favored bidders with a start-up loan from a state-owned bank to purchase the firm.

This gives cadre entrepreneurs and party members substantial advantages, as they can secure the largest and most valuable public assets available through privatization. Whereas start-up entrepreneurs in our 2006 sample realize on average a relatively modest sales volume of ¥2.7 million in the first year of operation, privatized companies promise much larger first-year sales. Cadre entrepreneurs who secure privatized assets realize a sales volume eleven times larger, on average, and long-standing party members a sales volume ten times larger. By contrast, new owners of privatized firms without political connections secure much smaller firms that generate on average an annual sales volume of ¥8.3 million in the first year.

In sum, political capital does confer ongoing advantages in these highly regulated markets, but not in competitive markets. These findings are consistent with earlier studies of the U.S. economy. For example, there is a close positive correlation between the presence of Washington lawyers, regulators, or politicians on corporate boards and the extent of regulation in the industry.[43] Notwithstanding the ready fungibility of political capital in the privatization of state assets, growing reliance of local government on tax revenues from private firms reinforces incentives to make resource allocation decisions based on assessment of financial performance (and its impact on the career mobility of government bureaucrats, whose own status depends in part on success in promoting economic growth). In other words, political connections do not override local government's interest in securing a growing base of tax revenues, along with increased opportunities for nonfarm employment for the local population.

Does Political Capital Explain Economic Success?

Where government controls use rights over key resources, political capital provides for entrepreneurs a decisive advantage. However, success in rent seeking, defined as any activity whose objective is receiving most-favored treatment from politicians, does not assure long-term competitive advantages for economic actors.[44] Successful rent seekers can simply decide to directly transfer any resulting profits into their private pockets instead of investing in the firm's development. Also, gains secured through political connections can be lost due to weak management or strategic mistakes.

To address the question of whether entrepreneurs who have invested in political capital enjoy long-term competitive advantages, we rely on quantitative assessments of the overall economic value of political capital. We evaluate this along with the other possible determinants of a firm's size as measured by total sales in 2008 (see Table 9.2) and a firm's return on assets (see Table 9.3). We limit our analysis to the firms that participated in both survey waves, which allows us to examine the effect of prior investments in political capital, as recorded in the 2006 survey, with economic outcomes collected in the 2009 survey. To assure the accuracy of data assessing the quality of political capital at the start-up stage, we further limit our sample to the firms where a researcher interviewed the founding entrepreneur. Our goal is to uncover whether investments in political networks in prior years have a causal effect on a firm's prospects for future growth. We also want to rule out that firms just perceive their relationships with local government as based on close (or weak) ties *because* they are currently economically successful (or not).

Initially, we include only the personal characteristics and political capital of the firm's founder (model 1). We find that positional power stemming from party membership or cadre status is not associated with larger firm size (as measured by sales volume) or with a higher return on assets.[45] Only political capital stemming from financial contributions and personal ties with government authorities is positively associated with the firm's economic development (model 1). But when we add to our analysis the firm's size at founding, the political connections fall out as a determinant of sales volume (model 2). Further, when we control for the firm's current assets, financial contributions to the party also fall out as a statistically significant determinant of economic performance (models 3 and 4).

We then examine whether cadre entrepreneurs who secured physical capital through privatization—who thus received most-favored treatment from politicians—are able to maintain their initial political-capital advantage (model 5). The interaction effect does not confirm that such initial advantages have long-term benefits in economic performance. By 2008, cadre entrepreneurs operating privatized businesses have lost all their initial advantages in terms of sales volume. In fact, all else being equal, cadre entrepreneurs appear to realize lower sales volumes (about 1/2 standard deviation smaller) than others. This is consistent with the finding that insiders who secure physical capital through political connections often lack the managerial ability and authority to make the necessary strategic and operational changes. An external investor in a privatized firm describes the dilemma of the former factory director as the new owner of the firm: "Employees were not willing to work hard. And the new owner could not deal with this issue because he lacked authority in the eyes of the workers. Eventually he asked me to step in as the majority shareholder. In return I let him run the business without interventions from my side. But whenever he encounters problems to enforce changes—for example, if employees are not willing to work hard—I will step forward to intervene. Because I don't have prior ties with these people, I can even fire them."[46]

Our analyses of determinants of company profitability confirm the limited effect of political capital on economic success. None of the above measures of political capital—neither party memberships nor cadre status nor financial contributions to the party nor personal ties with government authorities—is statistically associated with superior firm performance.

In sum, our results do not indicate that political connections increase chances for a company to thrive in China's market economy. While political connections are fungible in regulatory markets, entrepreneurs with political capital do not differ from others with respect to entrepreneurial success. Empirically, there is no evidence suggesting that the movement of bottom-up entrepreneurs in the Yangzi delta region depends on positional advantages and social privileges held by company founders.

Table 9.2. Political capital and firm size

	Log of total sales in 2008 coeff. (std. error)				
	Model 1	Model 2	Model 3	Model 4	Model 5
Founder characteristics					
Age (founder)	0.003	−0.011	−0.002	−0.005	−0.006
	(0.009)	(0.008)	(0.005)	(0.005)	(0.005)
Founder born in same city	−0.331	−0.320*	−0.187	−0.193	−0.175
	(0.243)	(0.132)	(0.180)	(0.154)	(0.145)
Male (founder)	0.287	0.117	0.156***	0.129***	0.134***
	(0.215)	(0.069)	(0.034)	(0.031)	(0.031)
Years of education (founder)	0.0378	0.002	−0.011	−0.017	−0.016
	(0.024)	(0.010)	(0.012)	(0.011)	(0.012)
Firm characteristics					
Log of assets (in 2008)			0.902***	0.795***	0.800***
			(0.038)	(0.059)	(0.056)
Log of sales (founding year)		0.481***		0.146***	0.144***
		(0.041)		(0.026)	(0.024)
Previously public firm		−0.011	0.008	−0.052	0.000
		(0.122)	(0.141)	(0.119)	(0.113)
Firm age		0.071***	−0.001	0.015**	0.015**
		(0.008)	(0.006)	(0.005)	(0.005)
Political capital					
Regular party donations[a]	0.956***	0.561***	0.076	0.098	0.114
	(0.238)	(0.127)	(0.080)	(0.069)	(0.078)

	(1)	(2)	(3)	(4)	(5)
Networking with political government (1–7)	0.008	0.014	−0.027	−0.022	−0.024
	(0.030)	(0.030)	(0.036)	(0.033)	(0.034)
Networking with government authorities (1–7)	0.085**	0.070	0.016	0.018	0.018
	(0.033)	(0.054)	(0.033)	(0.033)	(0.034)
Founder was party member before founding	0.108	0.037	0.015	0.005	−0.005
	(0.154)	(0.114)	(0.137)	(0.118)	(0.126)
Founder is former cadre	0.422	0.093	0.169	0.128	0.501
	(0.233)	(0.210)	(0.289)	(0.264)	(0.365)
Former cadre*previously public firm					−0.559*
					(0.271)
Founder has relatives with cadre rank	−0.068	−0.071	0.048	0.022	0.026
	(0.143)	(0.181)	(0.064)	(0.072)	(0.065)
Controls					
Sector	YES	YES	YES**	YES***	YES***
City	YES***	YES***	YES***	YES***	YES***
Constant	5.896***	4.195***	1.066**	1.165***	1.125***
	(0.528)	(0.463)	(0.343)	(0.224)	(0.205)
N	406	401	406	401	401
Adj. R^2	0.236	0.530	0.819	0.838	0.841

Source: Yangzi Survey 2006 and 2009.

Robust standard errors clustered on city.

Coefficients for sector and city dummies are not reported.

a. As reported by 2006 survey.

* $p < 0.10$, ** $p < 0.05$, *** $p < 0.01$. Variance inflation factors do not suggest multicollinearity concerns

Table 9.3. Political capital and profitability

	Return on assets 2008 coeff. (std. error)				
	Model 1	Model 2	Model 3	Model 4	Model 5
Founder characteristics					
Age (founder)	0.001	0.001	0.002	0.001	0.000
	(0.003)	(0.003)	(0.004)	(0.004)	(0.003)
Founder born in same city	−0.089	−0.072	−0.087	−0.088	−0.077
	(0.116)	(0.109)	(0.115)	(0.108)	(0.094)
Male (founder)	0.048*	0.050*	0.059*	0.048*	0.051*
	(0.021)	(0.018)	(0.026)	(0.022)	(0.022)
Years of education (founder)	0.006	0.006	0.010**	0.008**	0.009*
	(0.004)	(0.004)	(0.004)	(0.003)	(0.004)
Firm characteristics					
Log of assets (in 2008)			−0.063**	−0.100**	−0.097**
			(0.022)	(0.038)	(0.035)
Log of sales (founding year)		0.009		0.051*	0.050*
		(0.009)		(0.024)	(0.022)
Previously public firm		−0.036	−0.011	−0.031	0.002
		(0.059)	(0.058)	(0.056)	(0.027)
Firm age		−0.003	−0.002	0.004	0.004
		(0.003)	(0.003)	(0.003)	(0.003)
Political capital					
Regular party donations[a]	−0.055	−0.043	0.011	0.016	0.026
	(0.053)	(0.042)	(0.039)	(0.038)	(0.041)

	(1)	(2)	(3)	(4)	(5)
Networking with political government (1–7)	−0.007	−0.007	−0.004	−0.002	−0.004
	(0.014)	(0.016)	(0.014)	(0.014)	(0.017)
Networking with government authorities (1–7)	0.005	0.004	0.009	0.010	0.010
	(0.012)	(0.013)	(0.015)	(0.014)	(0.017)
Founder was party member before founding	0.005	0.001	0.010	0.005	−0.002
	(0.069)	(0.068)	(0.071)	(0.064)	(0.067)
Founder is former cadre	0.134	0.144	0.153	0.140	0.312
	(0.187)	(0.195)	(0.199)	(0.186)	(0.321)
Former cadre*previously public firm					−0.352
					(0.301)
Founder has relatives with cadre rank	0.048	0.044	0.040	0.032	0.035
	(0.042)	(0.046)	(0.043)	(0.048)	(0.046)
Controls					
Sector	YES*	YES*	YES*	YES	YES
City	YES*	YES**	YES***	YES***	YES***
Constant	0.077	0.223	0.574***	0.606	0.581***
		(0.122)	(0.092)	(0.088)	(0.079)
N	406	401	406	401	401
Adj. R^2	0.077	0.080	0.122	0.154	0.170

Source: Yangzi Survey 2006 and 2009.

Coefficients for sector and city dummies are not reported.

Robust standard errors clustered on city. Variance inflation factors do not suggest multicollinearity concerns.

a. As reported by 2006 survey.

* p < 0.10, ** p < 0.05, *** p < 0.01.

A National Perspective

Skeptics may claim that the limited fungibility of political capital merely reflects the unique institutional context of the Yangzi delta region, which may not represent the general conditions of emerging capitalism in China. To evaluate this, we extend our analysis to incorporate a national perspective, covering all regions.

As in Chapter 8, we use data from the 2003 World Bank Investment Climate Survey, which provides an in-depth account of 2,400 firms of different legal status—state owned, collective, private, and foreign. We exclude those firms still registered as traditional state-owned enterprises, as they have developed distinct state-firm networks. We thus focus on the 1,764 nonstate firms in the sample. In line with our analysis in the Yangzi delta region, we first examine the value of political capital in different market environments and then the influence of political capital on firm profitability. The firm's sales growth in 2002 reflects performance on the liberalized product market; for regulated markets with rich rent-seeking opportunities, we include the market for formal bank loans and the market for government contracts. To measure firm performance we replicate our regression on return on assets. We are not able to evaluate firm development through total sales growth, since the World Bank survey lacks information on the founding size of the firm.

We selected four variables measuring different dimensions of a firm's political capital, which combined represent the best match with our survey design for the Yangzi delta region. First, as a standard measure of political capital, we include whether the firm manager also holds a position as party secretary or deputy party secretary. We use party position instead of party membership, since party membership (at 67 percent, more than ten times higher than in society at large) is overrepresented in the World Bank survey. Second, we note whether the firm manager has previously held a government position. Third, we include as political capital whether the government was directly involved in the recruitment of the firm's top management. Lastly, we constructed an index of government assistance as a signal of general political support of the firm. This variable is most similar to our measure of reliance on government connections in the Yangzi delta region.[47] Measures of party donations or philanthropy are not available.[48]

Consistent with results in the Yangzi delta region, political capital provides no advantages on the product market (see Table 9.4). Quite to the contrary, if local government was involved in management recruitment decisions, companies tend to realize smaller sales growth.

As in our Yangzi survey, political capital retains a significant impact on economic transactions in the state-controlled credit market. Government support is positively associated with success in securing formal bank loans. As expected, political connections—specifically, a good standing with local government, as indicated by the government support index—also provide significant advantages in securing government contracts. These results closely replicate those presented in Table 9.2. If anything, they suggest slightly weaker advantages for firms run by politically connected managers. This, however, may well be associated with the less rigorous measurement of political capital available in the World Bank survey and the serious overrepresentation of politically connected managers.

Analysis of company profitability further confirms our findings for the Yangzi delta region. There is no indication that political capital has a significant impact on a company's return on assets. Other empirical studies similarly have failed to uncover positive performance effects (based on return on assets, return on equity, or stock returns) for politically connected firms.[49] And comparative studies of local and returnee entrepreneurs show that neither the strength of government ties nor the strategy employed to deal with government authorities influences revenue or firm performance.[50]

It is possible to argue that political connections came to full play at earlier stages of market transition and have helped to build up specific company characteristics that now—at an advanced stage of transition—independently yield positive effects on transaction outcomes. Company size, for instance, might theoretically be the result of earlier asset appropriations in the course of privatization policies. While the World Bank data do not provide the necessary information to control for such effects (as in Table 9.2), some observations contradict this idea. First, company size and our measures of political capital are only moderately correlated, with a negative correlation for former government officials. Second, even the exclusion of company size as a control variable would not substantially affect our results for political capital. Hence, the national sample seems to replicate our findings from the Yangzi survey data, suggesting no permanent economic advantages due to potential asset accumulation of politically connected firms in prior periods.[51]

Table 9.4. Political capital, rent seeking, and company performance in China, 2002

	Sales growth coeff. (std. error)	Credit access coeff. (std. error)	Sales to government / total sales coeff. (std. error)	Return on assets coeff. (std. error)
Management characteristics				
CEO holds university degree	59.149	−0.195	10.244***	0.835
	(43.882)	(0.112)	(3.883)	(0.634)
Log of CEO tenure	−45.580*	0.102*	−0.785	−0.161
	(25.891)	(0.056)	(1.692)	(0.191)
CEO has incentive contract	−21.080	0.167*	6.499**	−0.420
	(39.747)	(0.094)	(2.635)	(0.400)
Firm characteristics				
Log firm age	12.002	−0.092*	−3.362	−0.080
	(9.594)	(0.052)	(2.156)	(0.318)
Log sales (lagged)	−76.851			
	(37.380)			
Log assets (lagged)		0.184***	−0.108	−0.210
		(0.025)	(0.679)	(0.307)
Debt-to-equity ratio (lagged)	0.411	−0.002	−0.017	0.006**
	(0.454)	(0.001)	(0.065)	(0.0020)
Capital-to-labor ratio	0.570***	−0.0001*	−0.015	0.000
	(0.168)	(0.000)	(0.009)	(0.000)
Located in industrial park	107.38	0.070	−4.418	0.263
	(93.882)	(0.049)	(2.943)	(0.182)
Listed company	−32.269	0.475**	14.600**	0.544
	(59.549)	(0.201)	(6.385)	(0.729)
Government ownership shares	0.851*	−0.000	0.107*	−0.010***
	(0.428)	(0.002)	(0.056)	(0.003)
Sector (14 industries)	YES**	YES***	YES***	YES*
Political capital				
CEO holds a party position	26.597	0.147	1.401	−0.111
	(23.668)	(0.103)	(2.782)	(0.176)
CEO previously held government position	79.312	−0.029	7.747	5.915
	(98.600)	(0.170)	(5.160)	(5.628)
Government involvement in CEO appointment	−59.756**	−0.129	4.367	−0.045
	(24.983)	(0.132)	(3.597)	(0.061)
Government support index	−11.517	0.088***	3.729***	−0.045
	(9.577)	(0.032)	(0.950)	(0.061)
Constant	−312.829	−1.502	−4.135	8.584
	(463.898)	(−1.237)	(27.864)	(6.504)
Method	OLS	Probit	Tobit	OLS
Adj. R^2 / pseudo R^2	0.181	0.160	0.049	0.029
N	1503	1447	1418	1484

Source: World Bank Investment Climate Survey 2003.

Coefficients of sector dummies and regional control variables are not reported.

Robust standard errors clustered on city, * $p < 0.10$, ** $p < 0.05$, *** $p < 0.01$. Results are not driven by multicollinearity.

Conclusion

Particularly in Western accounts, the image of the "red capitalist" enjoys broad acceptance as a common stereotype of entrepreneurship in China. Our empirical account reveals a more complex story. Clearly, political rent seeking seems to be alive, as it is in most regulated domains of any Western market economy. Consistent with our analysis, anecdotal evidence suggests that positional advantages are usually pervasive in highly regulated sectors, such as the real estate sector, the construction industry, banking, or foreign trade, where the "right connections" can help to secure super profits. Not surprisingly, China's first U.S. dollar billionaire, former China vice-president Rong Yiren, made his wealth as the leader of the state-controlled China International Trust and Investment Corporation (CITIC).[52] Such often-cited examples, however, are hardly exceptional in the business world. Nor are they indicative of a specific form of "red capitalism."[53]

China's experience as a young market capitalist economy is not dissimilar from the experience of the U.S. economy in the nineteenth and early twentieth centuries, where for instance Leland Stanford as governor of California obtained a government-backed monopoly and massive state financial subsidies and land grants to build the Central Pacific Railroad, and the creation of corporations such as Union Pacific and Northern Pacific was facilitated by political connections. Not only historical examples come to mind. In highly regulated institutional domains, rent-seeking activities tend to persist. Take the recent case of Senator Tom Daschle, whose windfall profit of $5.2 million after leaving the Senate became a source of growing controversy in the confirmation hearings for his nomination to head the Department of Health and Human Services: "The real story is the massive transfer of power and wealth now underway from the private sector to the political class. Mr. Daschle could make so much money and achieve such prominence because he was expected to be a central broker in that wealth transfer. . . . Had Mr. Daschle been confirmed, he would have been the most important man in a health-care industry expected to be $2.5 trillion in 2009, which is larger than the economy of France."[54]

Whether in China or in the United States, political connections are valued by firms in transactions that are directed toward securing competitive advantage to acquire resources controlled by the state. Crucially, however, we cannot identify systematic advantages of politically connected firms in terms of company growth and economic performance. The so-called red capitalists and rent seekers do not tend to dominate the pecking order in their industries. This suggests that firms that rely solely on their political capital to engage in unproductive rent seeking are unlikely to emerge as winners in China's intense market competition over the long run. First, transactions in state-controlled institutional domains often do not constitute the critical component for survival and profits when viewed from the perspective of the overall range of a firm's business operations in competitive markets. Second, even if politically connected firms rely heavily on repeat transactions in state-controlled institutional domains, the firm's capability development, combined with management's ability to detect and react to market opportunities, is likely to constitute a more decisive prerequisite to pass the market test.

These findings confirm earlier predictions on the declining value of political capital as a consequence of the emergence of a market society, which incrementally results in transformative change in the direction of more relative autonomy between the political and economic spheres, not dissimilar from established market economies.[55] In sum, in departures from state socialism, the predicted change in relative power between political and economic actors explains not only bottom-up entrepreneurial activity but also the emergence of a market economy. Markets not only create incentives for profit making; they also provide the opportunities to decouple from the political sphere as producers shift from unproductive rent seeking to productive entrepreneurship.

10

Conclusion

What broader lessons do we draw from our study of the rise of capitalism in China? Our theory-driven narrative of the endogenous rise of economic institutions in the Yangzi delta region turns on mechanisms that are general. A duality of agency and social structure organizes this narrative: Entrepreneurs are the central agents who drive institutional innovations enabling capitalist economic development; once established, these emergent economic institutions facilitate additional bursts of entrepreneurial action that lead to tipping points in the expansion of the private enterprise economy. Within business communities, multiplex relationships provide the sinews of enforceable trust and the conduits of information flow enabling robust entrepreneurial action. Emergent social norms are effectively enforced through mechanisms as common and universal as social approval (reputation, status) and punishment (bilateral sanctions, accurate negative gossip). Thus, over a surprisingly short time span, a dynamical process starting with small numbers of marginal economic actors in peripheral locations gives rise to a social movement–like growth and diffusion of entrepreneurship across the regional economy.

In the private enterprise economy, from the start-up on through the development phases of a firm, all of the key factors required for successful entrepreneurship could be found and secured through network ties and bottom-up institutional arrangements. Producers huddle in industrial clusters, where they benefit from a stable chain of suppliers offering the mix of technical support and material inputs needed for flexible and adaptive production. Producers also benefit from close access to downstream distribution networks linked to domestic and global markets. While most firms are small or medium-sized and lack established brand names, common identity and norms of cooperation within distinct industrial clusters provide an aggregate competitive advantage. Though most firms lack in-house research and development departments, the multiplex links and interfirm networks within industrial clusters, along with the ease of access to critical inputs, facilitate innovative activity. Local knowledge gained through a cumulative wealth of manufacturing experience, in combination with regional markets for new technology, contributes to rapid cycles of innovation. Business-to-business online exchange further augments local resources. Thus, though entrepreneurs deal with the pressures of intensely competitive domestic and international markets, the private orders of industrial clusters provide them with institutional sources of competitive advantage.

With networks connecting producers with upstream and downstream markets, advantages of industrial clusters go well beyond specialization effects of the work process. Equally importantly, the spatial proximity in cluster locations provides fertile grounds for social interactions required to develop enforceable trust and ongoing interfirm cooperation and to engage in deal making. As we have detailed, mechanisms such as personalized exchange, mutual dependence in multiplex business relations, and community sanctions provide the social glue that binds principals and agents to implicit contracts and fosters cooperative forms of conflict resolution. Without close-knit and highly specialized business communities, it is doubtful whether entrepreneurs could have developed so effectively the norms required to survive and thrive outside the state's production system. In other words, industrial cluster location helped like-minded actors to overcome collective action problems and jointly develop cooperation norms decisive in facilitating the private sector's autonomous growth decoupled from the mainstream state-controlled economy.

How could the private enterprise economy and its regional advantage emerge in the Yangzi delta region so rapidly? How could capitalist sprouts of small start-up entrepreneurial firms spread so quickly to drive the transformative institutional change giving rise to a capitalist economic order characterized by self-reinforcing economic growth and private wealth accumulation? What happened was often just this: Drawn by new opportunities for profit making following the decollectivization of agriculture, some individuals started their own household firms in rural communities, hoping to escape poverty and gain self-employment. In towns and cities, unemployed youths, demobilized soldiers, and other marginal actors also started small private businesses, likewise decoupling from the state-owned sectors. Many of these pioneering entrepreneurs made a number of unsuccessful attempts, and lost their start-up capital repeatedly, due not just to poor business ideas and product quality but also to a lack of business experience and supporting institutions. Through trial and error, these entrepreneurs learned to improvise routines and eventually devised local institutional arrangements needed to support private enterprise development. They learned how to bypass the state-controlled banking system and accumulate the start-up capital they needed, and how to set up supplier and customer networks in an economic environment still dominated by state-controlled supply and distribution channels. They learned how to recruit, train, and retain workers to compete with the socialist mainstream economy; they learned how to quickly respond to shifting market conditions by developing and adapting new products and production processes; and they learned how to secure their transactions against business risks and uncertainties. Most importantly, they realized that their reputation was their most important asset. Fair treatment of others would be reciprocated by others, whereas unfair treatment, contract breach, or strategic default would not only risk ongoing business relations with current contract partners but would potentially invite fierce sanctions from others in their local business network. "Because you can only cheat once," economic survival would ultimately be impossible if one acted against the norms of local business conduct.

Attracted by the apparent economic success of the pioneering entrepreneurs, followers—at first, neighbors and friends, and later employees and distant observers—entered the market at an accelerating pace. Rudimentary business norms evolved and diffused across the region. With a steadily growing pool of entrepreneurs following the same norms, a self-reinforcing process of market entry of private firms developed, drawing in an expanding circle of new entrepreneurs from increasingly mainstream social backgrounds. As private enterprise gained in legitimacy and uncertainties declined, technical and managerial staff were increasingly willing to leave their jobs in state-owned enterprises and government for new job opportunities in the private sector.

As we have shown throughout this book, it was only after the private enterprise economy was an emergent social and economic force in China that political elites, in central and local government, began to put in place the legal and regulatory structures to legitimize private enterprise as an organizational form and model of economic development. Only many years later was legislation such as China's first "Property Rights Law" enacted, and an ensemble of other legal rules and institutions extended legitimacy to private enterprise as an organizational form. This sequence—bottom-up institutional change reflected in the rise of informal norms of business practices, followed by changes in the formal rules to secure and consolidate the gains in economic performance already in place—turns the predictions of state-centered theory on their head. Contrary to the view that politicians are the central arbiters of institutional change, while informal norms operate merely as cultural filters, explaining survival of old behavioral patterns and thus the slow progress of state-crafted institutional change, our analytic narrative underscores the dynamical nature of institutional change as a bottom-up process of emergence and diffusion. In this narrative, in contrast to state-centered theory, political actors maintained a wait-and-see position, moving only when economic powers had already shifted so pronouncedly that institutional adaptations could no longer be postponed.

In sum, in the years after the state's market reforms, bottom-up institutional innovations in the private sector initially enabled the development of a dynamic capitalist economy, and then the political elite followed up with institutional change legitimizing what already had taken place on the ground to enable the gains in productivity to be channeled into taxable revenue. Despite the rapid emergence of a dynamic private enterprise economy in coastal provinces, it took more than two decades for the state to respond to the growing need for business regulation and property protection by enacting laws and regulations designed to secure the political and social legitimacy and legal rights of private businesses.

As standards of behavior based on widely shared beliefs about expected behavior in a given situation, norms account for why humans are capable of large-scale cooperation. Widespread compliance with laws depends on them: "Legal enforcement mechanisms cannot function unless they are based on a broad consensus about the normative legitimacy of the rules—in other words, unless the rules are backed by social norms."[1] General mechanisms such as information sharing, mutual monitoring, and community sanctions can account for the effectiveness of social norms in principal–agent relations. What has not been well understood, however, is how social norms enable and guide business conduct in an institutional environment where legal and regulatory structures discriminate against private firms.

Our analysis of the Yangzi delta region suggests that the collective action problem in institutional change may have been overstated. The rise of entrepreneurship and corresponding business norms in the Yangzi delta region confirms that a shift in social norms and in preferences may indeed become an independent source of institutional change. Not much is needed, in fact. As long as expected state sanctions in scenarios of decoupling from established formal norms are limited and expected benefits sufficiently large, as modeled in Chapter 2, social problem solving and cooperation can travel a long way. Clearly, the rise of social norms as drivers of change can no longer be relegated to tribal and peasant societies, or highly specialized market niches with only a limited number of market players. Bottom-up institutional innovations followed by top-down accommodative change of formal rules by the state is a more common pattern than has been acknowledged in causal narratives.

In the Yangzi delta region, the reliance on social norms has not limited the geographic expansion of markets and sales. Consumer markets are far less localized than supplier networks, as widespread reliance on cross-provincial trade and development of export markets document. Private entrepreneurs and firms have emerged as fully integrated market players in the Chinese economy, accounting for 70 percent of the gross domestic product. They are no longer confined within peripheral enclaves by local network boundaries, but are now the main drivers of economic growth. This actuality calls for the explicit recognition of emergent and recombinant social norms and networks as a source of endogenous institutional change.

Firm Surveys

(English translation from Chinese original)

Questionnaire ID: _____

Firm name: _____

Respondent name: _____

Date of interview: _____ Year _____ Month _____ Day

Industry classification: _____

Firm address: _____

City: _____

E-mail contact of respondent: _____

Located in industrial development park/district?   1) Yes ____   2) No ____

Interviewer name:

  1) Main interviewer _____

  2) Secondary interviewer _____

Interview length: _____ minutes

Interviewee agrees to be recorded?   1) Yes _____   2) No _____

Personal Background

A1. Gender   1) Male _____   2) Female _____

A2. When were you born?   Year _____

A3. What is your birthplace?

  _____ province _____ /city/county   zip code _____

A4. Under which *hukou* were you born?   1) Rural ____   2) Urban ____

A5. Did your parents ever own or operate a private business?

  1) Yes_____   2) No _____

A6. What is the highest education level you reached?
  (Please show card A 6. Single choice.)

  1) Doctoral degree abroad
  2) Doctoral degree at home
  3) Master's degree abroad
  4) Master's degree at home
  5) Undergraduate education abroad
  6) Undergraduate education at home
  7) Junior college
  8) Vocational school / high school

9) Junior high school
10) Primary school
11) No formal education

A6.1. How many years of formal schooling have you received? ＿＿

A7. Have you received any specialized professional training? *(If no, go to A 8.)*

1) Yes ＿＿＿＿＿＿ 2) No ＿＿＿＿＿

A7.1. Which training did you receive? *(Multiple possible.)*

1) MBA
2) eMBA
3) Public administration
4) Other—please specify the most important

＿＿＿＿＿＿＿＿＿＿＿＿＿＿＿＿＿＿＿＿＿＿＿＿＿＿＿

A8. In which year did you take up the position of general manager / CEO in this firm? ＿＿＿＿＿

A 8.1. How many years have you served in the position of a general manager / CEO (including time served as CEO in other firms)? ＿＿＿＿＿

A 9. Are you one of the owners of this firm? *(If no, go to A 9.5.)*

1) Yes ＿＿＿＿＿＿ 2) No ＿＿＿＿＿＿

A 9.1. Are you the biggest shareholder of the firm?

1) Yes＿＿＿＿＿ 2) No ＿＿＿＿＿＿

A 9.2. Are you a founder of the firm? *(If no, go to A 10.)*

1) Yes ＿＿＿＿＿＿ 2) No ＿＿＿＿＿＿

A 9.3 Is this the first firm you have founded? *(If yes, go to A 10.)*

1) Yes ＿＿＿＿＿＿ 2) No ＿＿＿＿＿＿

A 9.4. How many firms did you start before? _____
(Go to A 10 after respondent answers.)

A 9.5. Were you hired by the owners?

1) Yes _____   2) No _____

A 9.6. When was the first CEO recruited, to the best of your knowledge?

Year _____

A 10. Does your contract include performance incentives?

1) Yes _____   2) No _____

A 11. Where did you work right before serving as CEO of this firm?
(Interviewer show card A 11. Single choice.)

1) State-owned enterprise, same industry
2) State-owned enterprise, different industry
3) Nonstate firm, same industry
4) Nonstate firm, different industry
5) Research institution
6) Higher education institution
7) Government office
8) Other (please specify) _____

A 11.1. Have you ever worked as the manager of a state-owned enterprise?

1) Yes _____   2) No _____

A 12. Did you yourself ever have a cadre position in government office?
(If no, go to A 13.)

1) Yes _____   2) No _____

A 12.1. Please indicate at which government level you have worked.
(Single choice.)

1) Provincial/ministerial
2) Bureau/municipal

3) County/division

4) Township/department

A 13. Do any of your relatives have a cadre position in government office? *(If no, go to A 14.)*

1) Yes _____   2) No _____

A 13.1. Please indicate the highest cadre rank of your relatives. *(Single choice.)*

1) Provincial/ministerial

2) Bureau

3) Division

4) Departments

A 13.2. At which administrative level does that relative hold a cadre position?

1) Provincial/ministerial

2) Bureau/municipal

3) County/division

4) Township/department

A 14. In a typical week, how much time do you spend on the following activities?

1) Reading a domestic newspaper	____ hours	____ minutes
2) Reading an international newspaper	____ hours	____ minutes
3) Reading Chinese business books	____ hours	____ minutes
4) Reading foreign business books	____ hours	____ minutes
5) On the Internet	____ hours	____ minutes
6) Watching the business news on the TV	____ hours	____ minutes

A 15. In a typical month, how much time (in hours) do you spend on events, conferences, etc. organized by professional/occupational groups or other business associations where you meet other entrepreneurs and managers?

_____ hours

A 16. Are you a Chinese Communist Party member? *(If no, go to A 17.)*

1) Yes _____   2) No _____

A 16.1. In which year did you join the party? _____

A 16.2. What is your current position in the party? *(Interviewer:*
   Don't read the choices. Circle the corresponding answer directly after the inquiry.)

   1) Party Committee Secretary
   2) Party Committee Deputy Secretary
   3) Party Committee Member
   4) General Party Branch Secretary
   5) General Party Branch Deputy Secretary
   6) General Party Branch Committee Member
   7) Party Branch Secretary
   8) Party Branch Deputy Secretary
   9) Party Branch Committee Member
   10) Regular Party Member

A 16.3. Have you previously held a position in the party? *(Interviewer:*
   Don't read the choices. Circle the corresponding answer directly after the inquiry.)

   1) Party Committee Secretary
   2) Party Committee Deputy Secretary
   3) Party Committee Member
   4) General Party Branch Secretary
   5) General Party Branch Deputy Secretary
   6) General Party Branch Committee Member
   7) Party Branch Secretary
   8) Party Branch Deputy Secretary
   9) Party Branch Committee Member
   10) Regular Party Member

A 17. Now I want to ask you how much you trust different types of people. On a scale of 1 to 5, where 1 means very distrustful and 5 means very trustful, how much do you trust the people in these categories?

(Show card A 17.)

Shopkeeper	
Teachers	
Local government officials	
Banking staff	
Central government officials	
Strangers	
Your own suppliers	
Police	
Your own customers	
Judges and staff of courts	
Entrepreneurs/businessmen	

B 1. In which year was the firm registered as a private firm? _____

B 2. Did the firm exist before it registered as a private firm?
(If no, go to B3.)

1) Yes _____   2) No _____

B 2.1. In which ownership form did the firm exist before?
(Interviewer, show card B 2.1. Single choice.)

1) State-owned enterprise
2) Urban collective-owned enterprise
3) Rural collective-owned enterprise
4) Private firm
5) Other (please specify) _____

B 3. In the year the firm was registered as a private enterprise, how many investors were there? _____ persons

B 4. What was the total number of full-time paid employees when the firm started? _____ persons

B 5. What were the annual sales in the year the firm started?

_____ 10,000 Yuan

B 6. Under which legal status was the private firm founded?
(Interviewer, show card B 6. Single choice.)

1) Sole ownership enterprise
2) Joint ownership enterprise
3) Limited liability corporation
4) Shareholding corporation Ltd.
5) Subsidiary/division of a domestic enterprise
6) Other (please specify) _____

B 7. Has there been a change in legal status since founding of the private firm?

(If no, go to B 8.)

1) Yes _____   2) No _____

B 7.1. How many legal changes did the firm have since the founding as a private firm? _____ times

B 7.2. In which year did the last legal change take place? _____

B 7.3. Which legal status does the firm currently have?
(Interviewer, show card B 7.3. Single choice.)

1) Sole-ownership enterprise
2) Joint-ownership enterprise
3) Limited liability corporation
4) Shareholding corporation Ltd.
5) Subsidiary/division of a domestic enterprise
6) Other (please specify) _____

B 8. Is your firm listed on a stock market (domestic or international)?

1) Yes _____   2) No _____

Governance

C 1. Do any of the shareholders of the firm also hold management positions in the firm? *(If no, go to C 2.)*

1) Yes _____   2) No _____

C 1.1. How many shareholders hold such positions? _____

C 1.2. What percentage of shares are held by those shareholders in the management positions? _____ %

C 2. Do you have shareholder meetings in your firm? *(If no, go to C 3.)*

    1) Yes _____   2) No _____

C 2.1. How many shareholder meetings are held per year? _____

C 3. Do you have a board of directors in your firm? *(If no, go to C 4.)*

    1) Yes _____   2) No _____

C 3.1. How many members does the board of directors have? _____

C 3.2. Does the board of directors have independent members?
    (If no, go to C 3.4.)

    1) Yes _____   2) No _____

C 3.3. How many independent directors does the board have? _____

C 3.4. Are there retired executives on the board?   1) Yes _____   2) No _____

C 3.5. How often does the board of directors meet every year? _____ times

C 3.6. Are you also the chairman of the board?   1) Yes _____   2) No _____

C 3.7. How many directors also hold ownership shares in other firms you are doing business with? _____ persons

C 3.8. How many directors hold parallel official positions (board members, board of trustees, management positions, etc.) in other firms you are doing business with? _____ persons

C 4. Do you have a board of trustees in your firm?

    1) Yes _____   2) No _____

C 5. Since the founding of the firm as a private firm, has there been any change in the position of the CEO? *(If no, go to C 6.)*

    1) Yes _____   2) No _____

C 5.1. How many CEOs have served this firm (including the current CEO)? _____

C 6. Who exerts the major decision-making power in the following decision types?

(Interviewer, show card C6. Single choice. If the specific activity has not occurred in the firm, write NA.)

Decision Types	CEO	Largest shareholder	Shareholder meeting	Board of directors	Division manager	Other (please specify)
Labor issues (hiring/firing)						
Investment						
R&D development						
New subsidiaries						
Internal organizational reforms/restructuring						
Daily operational decisions (price, sales, supply)						
Merger/acquisition						

Supplier Relations

D 1. In 2005, what percent of material inputs and supplies for your firm (including all subsidiaries) were

Purchased from domestic sources	
Purchased through imports	
Total	100%

D 2. What is the ownership type of your largest supplier?

1) State-owned enterprise

2) Collective-owned enterprise

3) Private-owned firm

4) Foreign (wholly owned) enterprise

5) Joint venture enterprise

6) Cooperation enterprise

7) Other (specify)

D 3. Please provide information on your most important input:

Name of the input	Total number of suppliers you use for this input

D 4. Thinking about your main supplier for your main input (listed above), may we ask some questions concerning this relationship?

Was the supplier introduced to you through family, relatives, friends, or acquaintances? *(If yes, write "1"; if no, write "2")*	How long (number of years) has your relationship with the supplier existed?	Do you buy on credit? *(If yes, write "1"; if no, write "2")*	If you buy on credit, number of days before supplier will urge you to pay

D 5. On a 7-point scale (from very little to very much), please circle the number best describing the extent to which your firm has utilized guanxi connections with suppliers.

1—2—3—4—5—6—7

D 6. Where are your company's important suppliers located? Please give the percentage for the following locations:

   1) Within the same locality as your company   ____ %
   2) Within the same region as your company   ____ %
   3) Within China but not within the same province   ____ %
   4) Overseas (including Hong Kong, Macau, and Taiwan)   ____ %

D 7. Do relatives of the owners of your company own any of the suppliers of your company's production materials?

   1) Yes _____   2) No _____

D 8. Have you had disputes with suppliers, such as a delay, suspension of payment, return shipment, or cancellation of future shipments over the last two years?
   (If no, go to D 9.)

   1) Yes _____   2) No _____

D 8.1. If yes, how many disputes?   _____

D 8.2. How does your firm generally handle disputes with your suppliers?
   (Show card D 8.2. Single choice.)

   1) Ignore
   2) Try your best to negotiate, and work it out between you two
   3) Bring the matter to local government or administrative
      authorities
   4) Go to court / file a lawsuit
   5) Utilize personal connections to resolve
   6) Other means (please specify) _____

D 8.3. How many disputes did you resolve through court over the last two years?

   _____

D 9. If one of your suppliers deceives another firm, would you find out?

    1) Yes _____   2) No _____

D 10. What percentage of your total supply volume (value) is based on written contracts with your suppliers?   _____ %

D 11. What would you base your decision on, before choosing a new supplier of a crucial input material?
(Interviewer, show card D 11. Single choice.)

    1) Just rely on my own experience
    2) Good reputation according to long-term business partner
    3) Good reputation according to information from business
       administration
    4) Good reputation according to information from friends and family
    5) The quality, price, and the supply time of the product.
    6) Other (please specify) _____

Customer Relations

E 1. What is the major market for your main product?

    1) Your city
    2) Your province
    3) China
    4) Overseas (export)

E 2. Approximately what percentage of your firm's domestic sales in 2005 were to each of the following?

    1) The government   ____ %
    2) State-owned enterprise   ____ %
    3) Multinationals located in China   ____ %
    4) Your parent company or affiliated subsidiaries   ____ %
    5) Large domestic private firms (those with 300+ workers)   ____ %
    6) Small private firms or individuals   ____ %
    7) Other (please specify)   ____ %

E 3. Do you socialize with customers in order to secure a major contract?
(If no, go to E 4.)

1) Yes _____   2) No _____

E 3.1. What percentage of the contract value would you usually spend on banquets, gifts, travel costs, etc.?   _____ %

E 4. What percentage of your sales volume is from return customers?

_____ %

E 5. How many of your customers do you know in person (such that you would recognize them on the street and stop for a chat)? (Give proportion.)

_____ %

E 6. On a 7-point scale (from very little to very much), please give us the number best describing the extent to which your firm has utilized guanxi connections with buyers.

1—2—3—4—5—6—7

E 7. On average, how long has your firm done business with customers in your main business line?

1) Less than 1 year
2) 1 year or more, but less than 2 years
3) 2 years or more, but less than 3 years
4) 3 years or more, but less than 4 years
5) 4 or more years

E 8. Measured by sales, where are the purchasers of the products in your main business line located? (Give proportion)

1) Within the same locality as your company   ____ %
2) Within the same province or municipality as your company ____ %
3) Within China but not within the same province   ____ %
4) Overseas (including Hong Kong, Macau, and Taiwan)   ____ %

E 9. Did you have business disputes with customers over the last two years?
(*If no, go to E 10.*)

1) Yes _____   2) No _____

E 9.1. If yes, how many disputes?   _____

E 9.2. How does your firm generally handle disputes with your customers?
(*Show card D 8.2. Single choice.*)

1) Ignore
2) Try your best to negotiate, and work it out between you two
3) Bring the matter to local government or administrative authorities
4) Go to court / file a lawsuit
5) Utilize personal connections to resolve
6) Other means (please specify) _____

E 9.3. How many disputes did you resolve through court over the last two years?

_____

E 10. What percentage of your total sales volume (value) is based on written contracts with your customers?   _____ %

E 11. Did your firm find the first customer through social contacts?
(*If no, go to E 12.*)

1) Yes _____   2) No _____

E 11.1. If your firm found the first customer through networks, please specify the nature of the connection.
(*Multiple possible.*)

1) Family and relatives
2) Friend
3) Acquaintance

E 12. Did the firm find its currently most important (largest sales) customer through social networks?
(*If no, go to E 13.*)

1) Yes _____   2) No _____

E 12.1. If so, please specify the nature of the connection. *(Multiple possible.)*

1) Family and relatives
2) Friend
3) Acquaintance

E 13. Now I want to ask you some questions on strategic orientation. On a scale of 1 to 7 (where 1 = strongly disagree and 7 = strongly agree), how would you rank your firm?

In making strategic decisions, we constantly seek to introduce new brands or new products in the market.	1—2—3—4—5—6—7
In making strategic decisions, we quickly respond to signals of market opportunities.	1—2—3—4—5—6—7
We search for big market opportunities and favor large bold decisions despite the uncertainty of their outcome.	1—2—3—4—5—6—7

E 14. Rank the following aspects of sales strategy according to importance for your firm (1 = least important, 7 = most important). *(Interviewer, show card E14. First read all options, and then let the respondent answer. Note: Except for the value 0, the same rank for more than one item is not allowed, and every item has to be ranked.)*

	Ranking 0, 1–7
Low price	
High product quality	
Fast delivery	
Providing seller's credit	
Sales location	
Reputation	
After-sales support	

E 15. Organizational performance

    1) Sales growth rate in 2005: _____

        1) $<5\%$
        2) $5<10\%$
        3) $10<15\%$
        4) $15<20\%$
        5) $20<30\%$
        6) $30<50\%$
        7) $>50\%$

    2) Net profit growth rate in 2005: _____

        1) $<5\%$
        2) $5<10\%$
        3) $10<15\%$
        4) $15<20\%$
        5) $20<30\%$
        6) $30<50\%$
        7) $>50\%$

E 16. Thinking back to the founding stage of your firm, rank the following aspects of sales strategy according to importance for your firm (1 = least important, 7 = most important). *(Interviewer, show card E14. First read all options, and then let the respondent answer. Note: Except for the value 0, the same rank for more than one item is not allowed, and every item has to be ranked.)*

	Ranking 0, 1–7
Low price	
High product quality	
Fast delivery	
Providing seller's credit	
Sales location	
Reputation	
After-sales support	

Labor

F 1. What proportion of your total staff is in each of these categories?

Management staff	Technical staff	Unskilled labor	Other	Total
				100%

F 2. Which channels do you use on average to hire labor in these categories? (Give percentage of total within the last three years.)

	Management staff	Technical staff	Unskilled labor
Market			
Through family or relatives			
Through friends			
Through acquaintances			
From previous enterprise before transformation of ownership			
Other (please specify)			
Total	100%	100%	100%

F 3. Provide information on the contract types you use. (Give percentage of total.)

	Management staff	Technical staff	Unskilled labor
1-year contract			
2-year contract			
3-year contract			
5-year contract			
Other (please specify)			
Total	100%	100%	100%

F 4. What was your average labor turnover per annum over the last three years (number of employees who left + number of newly hired employees)?

Management staff	
Technical staff	
Unskilled labor	

Innovation

G 1. Has your firm (including all subsidiaries) undertaken the following initiatives in the last two years?

	Undertaken?	
	Yes	No
Introduced a new product		
Upgraded an existing product line		
Discontinued at least one product (not production) line		
Agreed to a new joint venture with a foreign partner		
Obtained a new licensing agreement		
Outsourced a major production activity		
New production process improvements		
New management techniques		
New quality controls in production		

G 2. Does your firm conduct its own R&D activities / have an R&D department?

(If no, go to G 3.)

1) Yes _____   2) No _____

G 2.1. What is your firm's annual budget for R&D activities?

_____ ¥10,000

G 3. Does your firm hold any patents (for products or technology)?

1) Yes _____   2) No _____

G 4. Please evaluate your firm's technological and managerial strengths, using a 5-point scale, from lowest 20% to top 20% in the industry:

To the best of your knowledge, how does your firm compare to close (direct) competitors in your industry with respect to technological skills and abilities?

_____

To the best of your knowledge, how does your firm compare to close (direct) competitors in your industry with respect to managerial and organizational skills?

_____

H 1. Has your firm received any of the following forms of formal or informal assistance *(Check ✓ yes or no)* from a national, regional, or local government agency or government official who assisted you to?

	Yes	No
Obtain bank loans		
Identify foreign investors		
Locate foreign technology to license		
Identify potential foreign clients		
Identify potential foreign customers		
Identify domestic clients		
Get land use rights		
Obtain discounts for renting buildings, machinery, etc.		
Other (please specify) _____		

H 2. Do or did you have a government position?
　　(If no, go to H 3.)

　　1) Yes _____　　　2) No _____

H 2.1. What level of government position do or did you hold?
　　(Check ✓ the corresponding answer.)

Rank	Now	Earlier
Provincial/ministerial level or higher		
Bureau level		
Division level		
Department level or lower		

H 3. Are you currently a member of the following organizations? At which level? *(Please check ✓ the corresponding level and then provide details.)*

	Yes	No	Level					State exact position
			Town and village	County	Municipal	Provincial	Central	
People's Congress								
CPPCC								
All-Commerce Association								
Association of private entrepreneurs								
Other (please specify)								

H 4. Were you previously a member of the following organizations? At which level? *(Please check ✓ the corresponding level and then provide details.)*

	Yes	No	Level					State exact position
			Town and village	County	Municipal	Provincial	Central	
People's Congress								
CPPCC								
All-Commerce Association								
Association of private entrepreneurs								
Other (please specify)								

H 5. Do or did any shareholders other than yourself (if you hold any shares) have a government position?

(If no, go to H 6.)

1) Yes _____   2) No _____

H 5.1. If yes, indicate the highest cadre rank.

(Check ✓ the corresponding answer. Single choice for each column.)

Rank	Now	Earlier
Provincial/ministerial level or higher		
Bureau level		
Division level		
Department level or lower		

H 6. Is there a CCP organization within your firm?

(If no, go to H 7.)

1) Yes _____   2) No _____

H 6.1. Assess the influence of the party committee on the following decisions.

(Check ✓ the corresponding answer. Single choice for each row.)

	No influence	Moderate influence	Strong influence
Labor issues			
Investment			
Production			

H 7. Do you regularly fund the party's activities?

(If no, go to H 8.)

1) Yes _____   2) No _____

H 7.1. What is the annual sum you expect to set aside for such funding?

_____ ¥10,000

H 8. Does the firm have a labor union?

(If no, go to H 9.)

1) Yes _____   2) No _____

H 8.1. Assess the influence of the union on the following decisions.
(Check ✓ the corresponding answer. Single choice for each row.)

	No influence	Moderate influence	Strong influence
Labor issues			
Investment			
Production			

H 9. Does your firm have any consulting contracts with external experts, who advise the management and board on important firm decisions?
(If no, go to H 10.)

1) Yes _____   2) No _____

H 9.1. Indicate the professional background of the contract holders.
(Multiple possible.)

1) Research institutes / institutions of higher education
2) Government decision makers and administration office
3) Business sector
4) Other (please specify)

H 10. Is your firm occasionally asked by government agencies and local administration to provide information on economic and social development?

1) Yes _____   2) No _____

H 11. Does your firm organize social events (e.g., banquets, festivals, or short holidays) to celebrate company anniversaries or major Chinese holidays, such as spring festival?
(If no, go to H 12.)

1) Yes _____   2) No _____

H 11.1. Please indicate what guests typically attend these events.
(Multiple possible.)

1) Employees
2) Clients

3) Suppliers

4) Shareholders

5) Local officials

6) Local bureaucrats

7) Others (specify)

H 12. On a 7-point scale, where 1 = very little and 7 = very much, please circle the number best describing the extent to which you and your firm have utilized guanxi connections with different government authorities.

With various levels of political government	1—2—3—4—5—6—7
With industrial authorities	1—2—3—4—5—6—7
With other government authorities, such as taxation bureaus, banks, industrial and commercial administrative bureaus, and the like	1—2—3—4—5—6—7

Bureaucracy

I 1. How many times in the last year was your firm inspected or were you (or your staff) required to have mandatory meetings with officials of each of the following agencies in the context of regulation of your business? What fines were imposed on your firm or what was the value of goods that were sealed up (in ¥10,000)?

	Number of inspections	Number of meetings	Fines imposed
Tax inspection			
Labor and social security			
Fire and building safety			
Environmental protection			
Other (please specify)			
Total			

I 2. Do government agencies or officials become involved in the following types of decisions by your firm?

	Yes	No
Investment decisions		
Employment/layoff decisions		
Sales		
Pricing		
Merger and acquisition		
Dividends		
Location of a subsidiary		
Wages		
Other (please specify)		

Organization

J 1. Does your firm development follow any organizational blueprint?
(If no, go to J 2.)

1) Yes _____   2) No _____

J 1.1. Where do you look to develop the organizational blueprint?
(Interviewer, show card J 1.1. Multiple choices possible.)

1) Owners'/founders' ideas
2) Professional management staff
3) Firm management educational and training programs
4) Self-study/books
5) Mimicking successful national firms
6) Mimicking successful international firms
7) Learning from own failures
8) Learning from failures of other firms
9) Professional consultants
10) Others

J 2. Please tell us about the formalization degree of your company organization.

	Regulations within the firm *Check ✓ if yes*	Decision maker(s) *Please write down their positions*	Year of implementation or institutionalization
Formal, written organizational rules			
Formal, written job descriptions			
Formal, written performance assessments			
Formal, written pay scale			
Formal, written promotion procedures			
External financial auditing of books			
International certification (including ISO 9000, 9001, 9002, 9003, or 9004)			

J 3. Please tell us about your firm's major internal organizational changes during the last 5 years.

Type of change	*Check* ✓ *if yes*	Year of the change
Change in business mission		
Division/department restructuring		
Implementation of new technology		
Mergers		
Major collaborations		
Adjustments in firm scale		
Outsourcing		
New management programs such as total quality management, re-engineering		
Other (please specify)		

J 4. In general, for how many years do you try to plan in advance in terms of strategic/organizational development of your firm?
(Single choice.)

1) No development plan
2) 1-month to 4-month plan
3) 4-month to 1-year plan
4) 1-year to 3-year plan
5) 5-year or longer

J 5. What was the initial business strategy when your firm was founded?
(Single choice.)

1) Creating new products for new potential markets
2) Improving upon products to sustain current market shares
3) Marketing and distribution of products
4) Combining innovation and enhancement in market competitiveness
5) Lowering production costs

J 6. Does your firm have the same business strategy today?
   (If yes, go to J 7.)

   1) Yes _____   2) No _____

J 6.1. When was the initial strategy changed?   Year _____

J 6.2. What is the current business strategy of your firm?
   (Single choice.)

   1) Creating new products for new potential markets
   2) Improving upon products to sustain current market shares
   3) Marketing and distribution of products
   4) Combining innovation and enhancement in market competitiveness
   5) Lowering production costs

J 7. What was the initial employment model of the firm?
   (Interviewer, show card J 7. Single choice.)

   1) Trying to minimize employees' wage costs
   2) Maintaining a long-term friendly relationship through a two-way
      commitment with employees
   3) Attracting the very best talents in the industry
   4) Cooperative team building

J 8. Does your firm have the same employment model today?
   (If yes, go to J 9.)

   1) Yes _____   2) No _____

J 8.1. In what year did you change your initial model?   Year _____

J 8.2. What is your current employment model?
   (Interviewer, show card J 7. Single choice.)

   1) Trying to minimize employees' wage costs
   2) Maintaining a long-term friendly relationship through a two-way
      commitment with employees
   3) Attracting the very best talents in the industry
   4) Cooperative team building

J 9. Currently, how important are the following items for your firm to attract managerial and technical talents?

(Please check ✓ the corresponding answer. Single choice for each row.)

	Not important	Important	Most important
Salary & benefits			
Attractive work			
Social relations at work			.

J 10. Currently, how important are the following items for your firm in selecting managerial and technical talents?

(Please check ✓ the corresponding answer. Single choice for each row.)

	Not important	Important	Most important
Skills			
Potentials			
Fit with the organization's culture			
Social ties to management			

J 11. Currently, how important are the following items for your firm in coordinating managerial and technical talents?

(Please check ✓ the corresponding answer. Single choice for each row.)

	Not important	Important	Most important
Direct supervision			
Peer control			
Firm regulations and rules			

J 12. On a 7-point scale, where 1 = very little and 7 = very much, please circle the number best describing the extent to which your firm has utilized guanxi connections with competitors.

1—2—3—4—5—6—7

Social Status of Entrepreneurs

K 1. Imagine social status like a ladder on a scale from 1 to 10, with 1 the lowest and 10 the highest. Where do you think private entrepreneurs would be ranked by ordinary people?

(Show card K 1. Single choice.)

Rank _____

K 2. Where would you think your firm ranks within your own industry?
Rank _____

K 3. What is the annual income you receive from this company (including firm dividends and bonuses)? Please check ✓ the appropriate category.

(Interviewer, show card K 3. Single choice.)

1) Less than ¥100,000
2) ¥100,000<¥250,000
3) ¥250,000<¥500,000
4) ¥500,000<¥750,000
5) ¥750,000<¥1,000,000
6) ¥1,000,000<¥1,500,000
7) ¥1,500,000<¥2,000,000
8) More than ¥2,000,000

L 1. Thanks very much for your time in participating in our survey! Before we finish, we have one more question. If professors from our research team would like to interview you within the year, would you participate?

(Please write down the reaction of the respondent.)

1) Will   2) Will not   3) We will see.

(Please record the CEO interview time length on the first page. Start the clock again for the CFO interview.)

FIRM SURVEY to Be Answered by Chief Financial Officer

Questionnaire ID: _____

Firm name: _____

Respondent name: _____

Date of interview: Year _____ Month _____ Day _____

Industry classification: _____

Firm address: _____

City: _____

E-mail contact of respondent: _____

Located in industrial development park/district? 1) Yes ____   2) No ____

Interviewer name:

   1) Main interviewer _____

   2) Secondary interviewer _____

Interview length: _____ minutes

Interviewee agrees to be recorded? 1) Yes _____   2) No _____

Financial Information

A 1. Please provide this information for your firm for the following three fiscal years.

(If the firm has not been established for all three years, please write NA for the years before the founding of the firm. The same rule applies hereafter.)

	2005	2004	2003
Value of your total assets (in ¥10,000)			

A 2. What was the founding registered capital of this firm?

_____ ¥10,000

B 1. What was the average number of total employees (including contractual employees) in your firm for the following three years?

	2005	2004	2003
Average number of employees			

B 2. What percentage of your employees are college graduates? _____ %

B 3. Please provide the following information for your firm (in ¥10,000) for these three years.

(If a firm does not contribute to these funds, please record "0.")

	2005	2004	2003
Total annual wages			
Retirement pension fund			
Health insurance			
Unemployment insurance			
Employee general insurance			
Other insurance			

C 1. Please provide the total sales and exports information (in ¥10,000) for the firm for the following three years.

(Enter "0" if a firm did not export in a specific year. Enter NA if the firm was founded later.)

	2005	2004	2003
Value of total sales (products and services, including exports)			
Value of total exports (products and services, including sales to export agencies)			

D 1. Please report the total production costs for your firm for the following three years, as either a percentage of total sales or the actual figure (In ¥10,000).

	2005	2004	2003
Total costs of production			

Check ✓ one of the following:

_____ Reported as % of sales

_____ Reported as figures

E 1. Please report the value of new investments in fixed assets made by the firm in the following three years. *Report actual figure (in ¥10,000). Where investments were not made, please enter "0."*

	2005	2004	2003
Total new investments in fixed assets			

E 2. What is the average depreciation time (in years) of your new investments in fixed assets? _____ years

F 1. Please estimate the total annual amount (in ¥10,000) of travel and entertainment costs of this firm for the following three years.

	2005	2004	2003
Total travel and entertainment costs			

Firm Structure

G 1. How many subsidiaries (branch factories, sales, or service outlets) does your firm have in China? _____

G 2. Does your firm belong to a business group?
   (If no, go to H 1.)

   1) Yes _____   2) No _____

G 2.1. Please name the business group. _____

G 2.2. What percentage of your sales are from business with other firms in the same business group? _____ %

G 2.3. What percentage of supplies come from other firms in the same business group? _____ %

Ownership

H 1. What percentage of your firm's shares are owned by each of the following categories?

	Percentage of shares (%)
Senior management or their family members	
Other domestic individuals	
Domestic institutional investors	
Domestic state-owned firm	
Domestic private firm	
Domestic collective firm	
Domestic banks	
Foreign individuals	
Foreign institutional investors	
Foreign firms	
Foreign banks	
National/central government	
Provincial government	
Municipal/county government	
Other government, including cooperatives and collectives	
Total	100%

H 2. What percentage of shares does your largest shareholder hold?

_____ %

H 3. If any, what is the percentage of shares held by overseas Chinese, including Hong Kong, Macau, and Taiwan investors?
   (Enter 0 if there is none.)

_____ %

H 4. Has the company changed the ownership structure since 2003?
(If no, go to I 1.)

1) Yes _____   2) No _____

H 4.1. In what year did your firm's ownership structure change to the current one?

1) 2003
2) 2004
3) 2005
4) 2006

H 4.2. What percentage of your firm's shares were owned by each of the following categories before this change?

	Percentage of shares (%)
Senior management or their family members	
Other domestic individuals	
Domestic institutional investors	
Domestic state-owned firm	
Domestic private firm	
Domestic collective firm	
Domestic banks	
Foreign individuals	
Foreign institutional investors	
Foreign firms	
Foreign banks	
National/central government	
Provincial government	
Municipal/county government	
Other government, including cooperatives and collectives	
Total	100%

Firm Performance

I 1. What were your company's profits (in ¥10,000) during the last three years?

	2005	2004	2003
After-tax profits			
Earnings before interest payments and taxes			

J 1. Including all subsidiaries, what were your company's total liabilities during the last three years?

	2005	2004	2003
Total liabilities (in ¥10,000)			

Competition / Market Position

K 1. How much money would it take to establish a new firm exactly like your current firm? _____ ¥10,000

Tax

L 1. How much tax did you pay in the following fiscal years?

	2005	2004	2003
Total tax (in ¥10,000)			

L 2. Does your firm benefit from any tax exemption programs?

1) Yes _____   2) No _____

Finance

M 1. For the year 2005 and the founding year, what percentage of total capital was externally financed?

   (If "0," skip M 2.)

	2005	Founding year
Proportion of external finance		

M 2. For these years, please identify the proportion of sources of your external finance.

	2005	Founding year
Domestic commercial bank		
Foreign-owned commercial bank		
Investment funds / state subsidy		
Trade exportation tax reimbursement		
Loans from family and relatives		
Loans from friends		
Loans from business partners		
Other informal sources (e.g., money lenders, informal bank, pawn shop)		
Others		
Total	100%	100%

M 2.1. What was the total amount of external finance in 2005?

   _____ ¥10,000

M 3. Are you using supplier credit (i.e., accounts payable) to purchase your inputs?

   (If no, go to M 3.2.)

   1) Yes _____   2) No _____

M 3.1. What percentage of your firm's inputs are purchased on credit? _____ %

M 3.2. Is it offered to you by your suppliers? 1) Yes _____ 2) No _____

Payment Conditions / Customer Credit

N 1. On average, what percentage of your monthly sales are

1) paid before delivery _____ %
2) paid at delivery _____ %
3) sold on credit _____ %
Total 100 %

(Please go back to record the CFO interview time length.)

(English translation from Chinese original)

Questionnaire ID: _____

Firm name: _____

Respondent name: _____

Date of interview: Year _____   Month _____   Day _____

Industry classification: _____

Firm address: _____

City: _____

The firm is located in (circle):

    1) City
    2) County
    3) Town
    4) Village

E-mail contact of respondent: _____

Located in industrial development park/district?   1) Yes ____   2) No ____

Interviewer name:

    1) Main interviewer _____

    2) Secondary interviewer _____

Interview length: _____ minutes

Interviewee agrees to be recorded?   1) Yes _____   2) No _____

Personal Background

A. Have you personally been interviewed already in the first wave
of this survey?

(If yes, proceed with A 6.)

   1) Yes_____   2) No _____

A1. Gender

   1) Male _____   2) Female _____

A2. When were you born?   Year _____

A3. What is your birthplace?

   _____ province _____ city/county   zip code _____

A4. Under which *hukou* were you born?   1) Rural ____   2) Urban ____

A5. Did your parents ever own or operate a private business?

   1) Yes_____   2) No _____

A8. In which year did you take up the position of general manager / CEO in
this firm?   _____

A 11.1. Have you ever worked as the manager of a state-owned enterprise?

   1) Yes _____   2) No _____

A 12. Did you yourself ever have a cadre position in government office?
   (If no, go to A 6.)

   1) Yes _____   2) No _____

A 12.1. Please indicate at which government level you have worked.
(Single choice.)

1) Provincial/ministerial
2) Bureau/municipal
3) County/division
4) Township/department

A 6. What is the highest education level you reached?
(Please show card A 6. Single choice.)

0) No formal education
1) Primary school
2) Junior high school
3) Vocational school / high school
4) Junior college
5) Undergraduate education at home
6) Undergraduate education abroad
7) Master's degree at home
8) Master's degree abroad
9) Doctoral degree at home
10) Doctoral degree abroad

A 6.1. How many years of formal schooling have you received? ____

A 7. Have you received any specialized professional training?
(If no, go to A 9.)

1) Yes _____   2) No _____

A 7.1. Which training did you receive?
(Multiple choices possible.)

1) MBA
2) eMBA
3) Public administration
4) Other—please specify the most important

A 9. Are you today one of the owners of this firm?
(If no, go to A 9.5.)

1) Yes _____   2) No _____

A 9.1. Are you the biggest shareholder of the firm?

1) Yes _____   2) No _____

A 9.1.1. What percentage of shares do you own?   _____ %

A 9.1.2. Of your total personal wealth, what percentage can be attributed to the value of your part of this firm?   _____ %

A 9.2. Are you a founder of the firm?
(If no, go to A 11.)

1) Yes _____   2) No _____

A 9.2.1. What was the most important reason that you first started this firm?
(Single choice. Show card.)

1) Was in bad with the leader of previous organization
2) Previously my abilities were not fully utilized
3) To have more income
4) To expand or diversify prior private firm operations (if you had started another firm before this one)
5) No job, unemployed
6) Job was unstable
7) Wanted to leave farm work
8) Other (please specify)

A 9.2.2. Has someone else's experience in founding and running a business motivated you to start your own business?   1) Yes ____   2) No ____

A 9.2.3. What were the sources of start-up capital for this firm?
(Show card.)

	Percent of initial investment
Founders' own money	
Loans from family members	
Loans from friends	
Loans from acquaintances	
Loans from local government	
Domestic bank loan	
Informal credit association (money lenders, informal bank, pawn shop)	
Other	

A 9.3. Is this the first firm you have founded?
(If yes, go to A 11.)

1) Yes _____   2) No _____

A 9.4. How many firms did you start before? _____
(Go to A 11 after respondent answers.)

A 9.5. Were you hired by the owners?   1) Yes _____   2) No _____

A 9.6. When was the first CEO recruited, to the best of your knowledge?

Year _____

A 11. Please give us information on your last two jobs before becoming owner/CEO of this firm.

(Show card. If they have never worked before, write NA.)

	Period (year to year)	Occupation	Did your job include any management work? If yes, what was your job level?	Organization	Sector	Annual income you received in the year you left this job (including bonuses) (¥10,000)
		1) Technical personnel 2) Sales/marketing personnel 3) Accounting/ finance 4) Administrative officer 5) Enterprise director 6) Ordinary worker 7) Retail service staff 8) Farmer 9) Military personnel 10) Unemployed 11) Other	1) Non-management 2) Ordinary manager 3) Middle-level manager 4) High-level manager	1) Research institution 2) Higher education institution 3) Party / government organization 4) State-owned enterprise 5) Red hat firm 6) Collective enterprise 7) Private enterprise 8) Individual business 9) Rural collective household enterprise 10) Foreign-invested joint venture 11) Other	1) Same industry as current enterprise 2) Different manufacturing industry than current enterprise 3) Retail 4) Wholesale 5) Agriculture 6) Other	
Most recent	from|_|_|_|_| to |_|_|_|_|					
Job before last job	from|_|_|_|_| to |_|_|_|_|					

A 13. Do any of your relatives have a cadre position in government office?
(If no, go to A 15.)

1) Yes _____   2) No _____

A 13.1. Please indicate the highest cadre rank of your relatives.
(Single choice.)

1) Provincial/ministerial *(bu)*
2) Bureau *(ting/ju)*
3) Division *(chu)*
4) Departments *(ke)*

A 15. In a typical month, how much time do you spend on events, conferences, etc. organized by professional/occupational groups or other business
associations where you meet other entrepreneurs and managers?

_____ hours

A 16. Are you today a Chinese Communist Party member?
(If no, go to A 17.)

1) Yes _____   2) No _____

A 16.1. In which year did you join the party?   _____

A 16.2. What is your current position in the party? *(Interviewer: Don't read
the choices. Circle the corresponding answer directly after the inquiry.)*
1) Party Committee Secretary
2) Party Committee Deputy Secretary
3) Party Committee Member
4) General Party Branch Secretary
5) General Party Branch Deputy Secretary
6) General Party Branch Committee Member
7) Party Branch Secretary
8) Party Branch Deputy Secretary
9) Party Branch Committee Member
10) Regular Party Member

A 16.3. Have you previously held a position in the party? *(Interviewer: Don't read the choices. Circle the corresponding answer directly after the inquiry and indicate period.)*

    1) Party Committee Secretary   ____ year to ____

    2) Party Committee Deputy Secretary   ____ year to ____

    3) Party Committee Member   ____ year to ____

    4) General Party Branch Secretary   ____ year to ____

    5) General Party Branch Deputy Secretary   ____ year to ____

    6) General Party Branch Committee Member   ____ year to ____

    7) Party Branch Secretary   ____ year to ____

    8) Party Branch Deputy Secretary   ____ year to ____

    9) Party Branch Committee Member   ____ year to ____

    10) Regular Party Member   ____ year to ____

A 17. Now I want to ask you how much you trust different types of people. On a scale of 1 to 5, where 1 means very distrustful and 5 means very trustful, how much do you trust the people in these categories? *(Show card A 17.)*

Shopkeeper	
Teachers	
Local government officials	
Banking staff	
Central government officials	
Strangers	
Your own suppliers	
Police	
Your own customers	
Judges and staff of courts	
Entrepreneurs/businessmen	
Your own employees	

A 18. We would like to understand better your personal network. We are not interested in particular names or people, but we would like to get some general information. (*Show card.*)

	(1)	(2)	(3)	(4)	(5)	(6)	(7)	(8)
	How many of these persons do you know personally? *(If respondent answers zero, go to column 6.)*	Please tell us now more about the person whose assistance you would be most likely to seek. What is the relationship of this person to you? 1) Family member 2) Relative 3) Friend 4) Friend of a friend 5) Classmate 6) Co-worker 7) Neighbor 8) Other	How long have you known this person? 1) Less than a year 2) 1 to 5 years 3) More than 5 years 4) N.A.	How often do you usually talk to this person, on average? 1) Almost every day 2) At least once a week 3) At least once a month 4) Less than once a month	Do you need to offer incentives or gifts to enlist the help of this person? 1 Yes 0 No *(After answers, go to A 19.)*	If you are not personally acquainted with any of the listed officials, whose assistance would you seek if you needed it? 1) Family member 2) Relative 3) Friend 4) Friend of a friend 5)Classmate 6) Co-worker 7) Neighbor 8) Other	Would this person directly know one of the listed officials? 1 Yes 2 No	Do you need to offer incentives or gifts to enlist the help of these people? 1 Yes 2 No
Cadres in Party Committee at county/division government level								
Cadres in Party Committee at municipal (or above) government level								

A 19. Thinking about your five most valuable business acquaintances, please list the *nature of your relationship*.

(Multiple choices possible; check ✔ all that apply.) (Show card.)

Most important contacts	Contact is your supplier	Contact is your customer	Contact is a competitor	Joint purchase of material (buyer collective)	Mutual lending, if needed	Joint technology deveopment / technical problem solving	Mutual assistance with sales or marketing/ cooperative distribution channel	Recom-mendation / introduction of new customers	Mutual information sharing concerning market development (for instance, price, new market trends such as goods in high demand, etc.)	Information sharing concerning government regulation (such as taxation, standards, etc.)
1										
2										
3										
4										
5										

A 20. Informal lending *(Multiple choices possible.)*

Assume Lao Zhang in your local business community is approached by a business acquaintance Lao Li to help him out with a short-term loan for an investment. Lao Li knows that Lao Zhang's company is doing fine, and that Lao Zhang could afford to lend. Knowing your local business community, what would happen if Lao Zhang still would not grant Lao Li the requested loan? *(Interviewer, show card. Please note: if the respondent has chosen option 1 and also other options, remind him/her that option 1 means nothing will happen and cross out option 1 and mark X on this question.)*

1) Nothing will happen.
2) Lao Li would tell others about his experience.
3) Lao Li would in the future also not lend to Lao Zhang.
4) There will be a material change in the business relations between Lao Zhang and Lao Li (for instance less trading, etc.).
5) Other people besides Lao Li would also treat Lao Zhang differently.

A 21. Helping others to start a firm *(Multiple choices possible.)*

Assume a longtime employee Lao Li wants to start his own firm and asks his employer Lao Zhang for advice and assistance. Lao Zhang was always content with Lao Li and appreciated Lao Li's work. In spite of their good relationship, Lao Zhang refuses to assist or to support Lao Li's decision in any way. Knowing your local business community, what would happen? *(Interviewer, show card. Please note: if the respondent has chosen option 1 and also other options, remind him/her that option 1 means nothing will happen and cross out option 1 and mark X on this question.)*

1) Nothing will happen.
2) Lao Li would tell others about Lao Zhang's strict position.
3) Lao Li would seek to hurt Lao Zhang's business (for instance, lure away customers, etc.).
4) There would be a material change in the personal relationship between Lao Zhang and Lao Li (no future business, information sharing, etc.).
5) Other people besides Lao Li would also treat Lao Zhang differently.

A 22. Information on parents' last job.

(Show card.)

	Highest level of formal education	Occupation before retirement (or current job)	Organization
	1) No formal education 2) Primary school 3) Junior high school 4) Vocational school / high school 5) Junior college 6) Undergraduate education 7) Master's degree and above	1) Technical personnel 2) Sales / marketing personnel 3) Accounting / finance 4) Administrative officer 5) Enterprise director 6) Ordinary worker 7) Retail service staff 8) Farmer 9) Military personnel 10) Unemployed 11) Other	1) Research institution 2) Higher education institution 3) Party / government organization 4) State-owned enterprise 5) Red hat firm 6) Collective enterprise 7) Private enterprise 8) Individual business 9) Rural collective household / enterprise 10) Foreign-invested joint venture 11) Other
Father			
Mother			

INFORMATION ABOUT THE FIRM

(Interviewer, please check whether this firm has participated in the first wave of this survey. If yes, proceed with B 7.)

1) Yes _____   2) No _____

B 1. In which year was the firm registered as a private firm? _____

B 2. Did the firm exist before it registered as a private firm?

(If no, go to B 3.)

1) Yes _____   2) No _____

B 2.1. In which ownership form did the firm exist before?
(Interviewer, show card B 2.1. Single choice.)

1) State-owned enterprise
2) Urban collective-owned enterprise
3) Rural collective-owned enterprise
4) Private firm
5) Other (please specify) _____

B 3. In the year the firm was registered as a private enterprise, how many investors were there?   _____ persons

B 4. What was the total number of full-time paid employees when the firm started?   _____ persons

B 5. What were the annual sales in the year the firm started?

_____ ¥10,000

B 6. Under which legal status was the private firm founded?
(Interviewer, show card B 6. Single choice.)

1) Sole ownership enterprise
2) Joint ownership enterprise
3) Limited liability corporation
4) Shareholding corporation Ltd.
5) Subsidiary/division of a domestic enterprise
6) Other (please specify) _____

B 7. Has there been a change in legal status since the founding of the private firm?
(If no, go to B 8.)

1) Yes _____   2) No _____

B 7.2. In which year did the last legal change take place?   _____

B 7.3. Which legal status does the firm currently have?
(Interviewer, show card B 6. Single choice.)

1) Sole ownership enterprise
2) Joint ownership enterprise

3) Limited liability corporation

4) Shareholding corporation Ltd.

5) Subsidiary/division of a domestic enterprise

6) Other (please specify) _____

B 8. Is your firm listed on a stock market (domestic or international)?

1) Yes _____   2) No _____

B 9. Before being registered as a private firm, did this firm ever operate as a red hat firm?

1) Yes ____   Please indicate the period: from year ____ to year ____

2) No _____

B 10. Assume an unexpected investment opportunity came up. Where would you turn to borrow money? Rank the three most likely sources. *(Show card.)*

1) Domestic commercial bank

2) Foreign-owned commercial bank

3) Investment funds / state subsidy

4) Trade exportation tax reimbursement

5) Loans from family and relatives

6) Loans from friends

7) Loans from business partners

8) Other informal sources (money lenders, informal bank, pawn shop, etc.)

9) Other

B 11. Assume Lao Li gives Lao Zhang an informal loan to finance further investment in Lao Zhang's company. When the repayment of the loan is due, Lao Zhang fails to pay the money back to Lao Li. Assume further that Lao Zhang refuses to repay Lao Li "in kind." In your local business community, what would you expect to happen? *(Interviewer, show card. Please note: if the respondent has chosen option 1 and also other options, remind him/her that option 1 means nothing will happen and cross out option 1 and mark X on this question.)*

1) Nothing will happen.

2) Lao Li would tell others (business friends, customers, suppliers) about this experience.

3) Lao Li would try to cover his losses (for instance, by taking away materials or goods from Lao Zhang).

4) There will be a material change in the quality of business relations between Lao Li and Lao Zhang (no further business, information sharing, etc.).

5) Other people besides Lao Li would also respond to Lao Zhang's behavior (for instance, no future lending, only cash transactions, or no more business transactions).

Governance

C 1. Do any of the shareholders of the firm currently also hold management positions in the firm?

(If no, go to C 2.)

1) Yes _____   2) No _____

C 1.1. How many shareholders currently hold such positions?

_____

C 1.2. What percentage of shares are currently held by those shareholders in the management positions?   _____ %

C 2. Do you have shareholder meetings in your firm?

1) Yes _____ How many such meetings are held per year? _____
2) No_____

C.3. Do you have a board of directors in your firm?

(If no, go to C 5.)

1) Yes _____   2) No _____

C 3.1. How many members does the board of directors have?   _____

C 3.2. Does the board of directors have independent members?

1) Yes _____   2) No _____

C 3.6. Are you also the chairman of the board?   1) Yes ____   2) No ____

C 3.7. How many directors also hold ownership shares in other firms you are doing business with?   _____ persons

C 3.8. How many directors hold parallel official positions (board members, board of trustees, management positions, etc.) in other firms you are doing business with?   _____ persons

C 5. Since the founding of the firm as a private firm, has there been any change in the position of the CEO?   1) Yes ____   2) No ____

Supplier Relations

D 1. In 2008, what percentage of material inputs and supplies for your firm (including all subsidiaries) were

Purchased from domestic sources	
Purchased through imports	
Total	100%

D 2. What is the ownership type of your largest supplier?

1) State-owned enterprise
2) Collective-owned enterprise
3) Private-owned firm
4) Foreign (wholly owned) enterprise
5) Joint venture enterprise
6) Cooperation enterprise
7) Other (please specify)

D 3. Please provide information on your most important input.

Name of the input	Total number of suppliers you use for this input

D 4.1. Thinking about your current main supplier for your main input (listed above), may we ask some questions concerning this relationship?
(Show card.)

Indicate whether the supplier was introduced to you through one of the following channels (single choice): 1) Family 2) Relatives 3) Friends 4) Business acquaintances 5) Not introduced through personal recommendation	How long (no. of years) has your relationship with the supplier existed?	Does this supplier offer trade credit to you? 1 Yes 2 No→D 4.2	Do you buy on credit? 1 Yes 2 No→ D 4.2	If you buy on credit, number of days before supplier will urge you to pay	If the supplier charges an interest rate, please indicate the rate.	What is the average number of days before supplier imposes penalties?

D 4.2. Did you have the same supplier as your main supplier for your main input in the founding year of the firm?
(If yes, skip to D 5.)

1) Yes _____   2) No _____

D 4.2. About the main supplier for your main input in the founding year of the firm, may we ask some questions concerning this relationship?
(Show card.)

Indicate whether the supplier was introduced to you through one of the following channels *(single choice)*: 1) Family 2) Relatives 3) Friends 4) Business acquaintances 5) Not introduced through personal recommendation	How long (number of years) has your relationship with the supplier existed?	Is trade credit offered to you? 1 Yes 2 No→D 5	Do you buy on credit? 1 Yes 2 No→D 5	If you buy on credit, number of days before supplier will urge you to pay	If the supplier charges an interest rate, please indicate the rate.	What is the average number of days before supplier imposes penalties?

D 5. On a 7-point scale (from very little to very much), please circle the number best describing the extent to which your firm has utilized guanxi connections with suppliers.

1—2—3—4—5—6—7

D 6. Where are your company's important suppliers located? Please give the percentage for the following locations:

1) Within the same locality as your company   ___ %

2) Within the same region as your company   ___ %

3) Within China but not within the same province   ___ %

4) Overseas (including Hong Kong, Macau, and Taiwan)   ___ %

D 7. Do relatives of the owners of your company own any of the suppliers of your company's production materials?   1) Yes _____   2) No _____

D 8. Have you had disputes with suppliers, such as a delay, suspension of payment, return shipment or cancellation of future shipments between 2006 and 2008?
(If no, go to D 9.)

1) Yes _____   2) No _____

D 8.1. If yes, how many disputes? _____

D 8.2. How does your firm generally handle disputes with your suppliers? *(Show card D 8.2. Single choice.)*

    1) Ignore

    2) Try your best to negotiate, and work it out between you two

    3) Bring the matter to local government or administrative authorities

    4) Go to court / file a lawsuit

    5) Utilize personal connections to resolve

    6) Other means (please specify) _____

D 8.3. How many disputes did you resolve through court between 2006 and 2008? _____

D 9. If one of your suppliers deceives another firm, would you find out?

    1) Yes _____   2) No _____

D 10. What percentage of your total supply volume (value) is based on written contracts with your suppliers? _____ %

D 11. What would you base your decision on, before choosing a new supplier of a crucial input material?
(Interviewer, show card D 11. Single choice.)

    1) Just rely on my own experience

    2) Good reputation according to long-term business partner

    3) Good reputation according to information from business administration

    4) Good reputation according to information from friends and family

    5) The quality, price, and the supply time of the product

    6) Other (please specify) _____

D 12. Delivery on time *(Multiple choices possible.)*

Assume Lao Zhang delivers supplies to Lao Li with a substantial delay. As a consequence, Lao Li is losing a contract with one of his customers. Assume further Lao Zhang refuses to cover Lao Li's losses. In your local business community, what would you expect to happen? *(Interviewer, show card. Please*

note: if the respondent has chosen option 1 and also other options, remind him/her
that option 1 means nothing will happen and cross out option 1 and mark X on
this question.)

1) Nothing will happen.
2) Lao Li would tell others (business friends, customers, suppliers) about this experience.
3) Lao Li would try to cover his losses in future transactions with Lao Zhang (for instance, by negotiating a better price on future deals, etc.).
4) There will be a material change in the quality of business relations between Lao Zhang and Lao Li (no further business, information sharing, etc.).
5) Other people besides Lao Li would also respond to Lao Zhang's business practice (for instance, reduce or cut business with Lao Zhang).

D 13. Maintaining quality *(Multiple choices possible.)*

Assume Lao Zhang has delivered (knowingly) supplies of inferior quality to Lao Li and refuses to fix the problem. In your local business community, what would you expect to happen? *(Interviewer, show card. Please note: if the respondent has chosen option 1 and also other options, remind him/her that option 1 means nothing will happen and cross out option 1 and mark X on this question.)*

1) Nothing will happen.
2) Lao Li would tell others (business friends, customers, suppliers) about this experience.
3) Lao Li would try to cover his losses in future transactions with Lao Zhang (for instance, by no payment on future deals, etc.).
4) There will be a material change in the quality of business relations between Lao Zhang and Lao Li (no further business, etc.).
5) Other people besides Lao Li would also treat Lao Zhang differently (for instance, reduce or cut business with Lao Zhang).

D 14. Timely payment *(Multiple choices possible.)*

Assume Lao Li has delivered goods to Lao Zhang according to the specifications of a contract in a timely manner, but after a reasonable period, Lao Zhang still has not paid for the goods. In your local business community, what would you expect to happen? *(Interviewer, show card. Please note: if the respondent has chosen option 1 and also other options, remind him/her that option 1 means nothing will happen and cross out option 1 and mark X on this question.)*

1) Nothing will happen.
2) Lao Li would tell others (business friends, customers, suppliers) about this experience.
3) There will be a material change in the quality of business relations between Lao Zhang and Lao Li (no further business, etc.).
4) Other people besides Lao Li would also treat Lao Zhang differently (for instance, reduce or cut off business with Lao Zhang).

Customer Relations

E 1. What is the major market for your main product? *(Show card.)*

1) Your city
2) Your province
3) China
4) Overseas (export)

E 2. Approximately what percentage of your firm's domestic sales in 2008 were to each of the following?
(Show card.)

1) The government	_____ %
2) State-owned enterprise	_____ %
3) Multinationals located in China	_____ %
4) Your parent company or affiliated subsidiaries	_____ %
5) Large domestic private firms (those with 300+ workers)	_____ %
6) Small private firms or individuals	_____ %
7) Other (please specify)	_____ %

E 3. Do you socialize with customers in order to secure a major contract?

1) Yes _____ What percentage of the contract value would you usually spend on banquets, gifts, travel costs, etc.? _____ %
2) No _____

E 4. What percentage of your sales are to return customers?

_____ %

E 5. How many of your customers do you know in person (such that you would recognize them on the street and stop for a chat)? (Give proportion.)

_____ %

E 6. On a 7-point scale (from very little to very much), please give us the number best describing the extent to which your firm currently utilizes guanxi connections with buyers.

_____

1—2—3—4—5—6—7

E 7. On average, how long has your firm done business with customers in your main business line?

1) Less than 1 year
2) 1 year to less than 2 years
3) 2 years to less than 3 years
4) 3 years to less than 4 years
5) 4 or more years

E 8. Measured by sales, where are the purchasers of the products in your main business line located? (Give proportion.)
(Show card.)

1) Within the same locality as your company _____ %
2) Within the same province or municipality as your company _____ %
3) Within China but not within the same province _____ %
4) Overseas (including Hong Kong, Macau, and Taiwan) _____ %

E 9. Did you have business disputes with customers between 2006 and 2008?
(If no, go to E 10.)

1) Yes _____   2) No _____

E 9.1. If yes, how many disputes? _____

E 9.2 How does your firm generally handle disputes with your customers? *(Show card D 8.2. Single choice.)*

1) Ignore
2) Try your best to negotiate, and work it out between you two
3) Bring the matter to local government or administrative authorities
4) Go to court / file a lawsuit
5) Utilize personal connections to resolve
6) Other means (please specify) _____

E 9.3. How many disputes did you resolve through court between 2006 and 2008? _____

E 10. What percentage of your total sales volume (value) is based on written contracts with your customers? _____ %

▶ *Resurvey firms skip E 11 and go directly to E 12.*

E 11. Did your firm find the first customer through social contacts?

1) Yes_____   2) No_____

If so, please specify the nature of the connection. *(Single choice.)*
1) Family and relatives
2) Friend
3) Acquaintance

E 12. Did the firm find its currently most important (largest sales) customer through social networks?

1) Yes_____   2) No_____

If so, please specify the nature of the connection. *(Single choice.)*
1) Family and relatives
2) Friend
3) Acquaintance

E 15.1. Sales growth rate in 2008: _____

E 15.2. Net profit growth rate in 2008: _____

E 17. Assume that two persons, Lao Zhang and Lao Li, have maintained a trusting business relationship over the years. Suddenly, Lao Li actively tries to lure away clients of Lao Zhang. In your local business community, what consequences would you expect?

(Interviewer, show card. Multiple choices possible. Please note: if the respondent has chosen option 1 and also other options, remind him/her that option 1 means nothing will happen and cross out option 1 and mark X on this question.)

1) Nothing will happen.
2) Lao Zhang will tell others (clients and others) about his experience.
3) Lao Zhang will try to also lure clients away from Lao Li to cover the loss.
4) There will be a material change in the quality of the business relation between Lao Zhang and Lao Li (for instance, less information sharing, etc.).
5) Others would also treat Lao Li differently.

E 18. What do you expect from others? Rank the following from 1 to 7, where 1 = strongly disagree and 7 = strongly agree. *(Show card.)*

I believe that most of my business acquaintances provide business advice to others.	1—2—3—4—5—6—7	
I believe that most of my business acquaintances would lend money to others if they want to found their own business.	1—2—3—4—5—6—7	
I believe that most of my business acquaintances would pass on customer requests to others in case they cannot take the order themselves.	1—2—3—4—5—6—7	
I believe that most of my business acquaintances would inform others if someone they know commits any form of malfeasance in doing business.	1—2—3—4—5—6—7	
I believe that most of my business acquaintances would help others out with (idle) machinery / technology in case a business friend had a major technical problem and would otherwise risk losing a contract.	1—2—3—4—5—6—7	

Labor

F 1. What proportion of your total staff is in each of these categories?
   (Show card.)

Management staff	Technical staff	Unskilled labor	Other	Total
				100%

F 2. Which channels do you use on average to hire labor in these categories?
Please provide percentages for the period from 2006 to 2008.
   (Show card.)

	Management staff	Technical staff	Unskilled labor
Direct applications			
Human resources exchange center			
Employment services			
Post ads			
Temporary work			
Through family or relatives			
Through friends			
Through acquaintances			
From previous enterprise before transformation of ownership			
Chain recruitment (workers recommend their friends and acquaintances)			
Other (please specify)			
Total	100%	100%	100%

Innovation

G 1. Has your firm (including all subsidiaries) undertaken the following initiatives between 2006 and 2008? *(Show card.)*

	Undertaken? 1 Yes 2 No	In case you had collaborators, indicate type of collaboration: 1 Research institute 2 University 3 Other firm 0 No collaborators *(Multiple choices possible.)*
New patent approved		
Introduced a new product		
Upgraded an existing product line		
Discontinued at least one product (not production) line		
Agreed to a new joint venture with a foreign partner		
Obtained a new licensing agreement		
Outsourced a major production activity that was previously conducted in-house		
New production process improvements		
New management techniques		
New quality controls in production		

G 1.2. If you introduced new products between 2006 and 2008, what percentage of total sales value came from these new products in 2008?
   (If none was introduced, enter NA here.)

_____ %

G 1.3. During the last three years (2006 to 2008), how important were any of the following as a source of ideas or information for new and improved products, processes, or services? Indicate the three most important ones. *(Show card.)*

    1) Customers/clients

    2) Suppliers

    3) From within the business (e.g., employees, own R&D department)

    4) From other domestic business in the same industries

    5) From other domestic business in other industries

    6) From overseas business / international firms

    7) Industry association or private enterprise association

    8) Books and journals from science/industry/trade

    9) Conferences or trade fair

    10) Central/local government assistance services

    11) Universities, research institutes, research consultants or services

    12) Technical, industry, or service standards

    13) Banks, accountants, or financial consultants

    14) Others (please specify) _____

G 2. Does your firm currently conduct its own R&D activities / have an R&D department?

    1) Yes _____ What is your firm's annual budget for R&D activities?
                      _____ ¥10,000

    2) No

G 3. Does your firm hold any patents (for products or technology)?
    (If no, go to H 1.)

    1) Yes _____   2) No _____

G 3.1. If yes, how many patents do you currently hold?   _____

G 3.2. If yes, please specify the number of patents in each category:
Patents for inventions   _____
Design patents (on an ornamental design for functional items) _____
Utility models   _____

INSTITUTIONAL ENVIRONMENT

Government Connections

H 1. Between 2006 and 2008, did your firm receive any of the following forms of formal or informal assistance *(show card)* from a national, regional, or local government agency or government official who assisted you to

	Yes	No
Obtain bank loans		
Identify foreign investors		
Locate foreign technology to license		
Identify potential foreign clients		
Identify potential foreign customers		
Identify domestic clients		
Get land use rights		
Obtain discounts for renting buildings, machinery, etc.		
Obtain tax benefits		
Other (please specify) _____		

H 2. Do or did you have a government position?
   (If no, go to H 3.)

   1) Yes _____   2) No _____

H 2.1. What level of government position do or did you hold?
   (Check ✓ the corresponding answer.)

Rank	Now	Earlier
Provincial/ministerial level or higher		
Bureau level		
Division level		
Department level or lower		

H 3. Are you *currently* a member of the following organizations?
   If yes, since when? *(Show card.)*

	1 Yes 2 No	If yes, since what year?
People's Congress		
CPPCC (Chinese People's Political Consultative Conference)		
All-Commerce Association		
Association of private entrepreneurs		
Industrial association (guild)		
Other (please specify)		

H 5. Do or did any shareholders other than yourself (if you hold any shares) have a government position?   1) Yes _____   2) No _____

H 6. Is there a CCP organization within your firm?

   1) Yes _____   2) No _____

H 7. Have you regularly funded the party's activities between 2006 and 2008?

   1) Yes _____ And the average annual sum you have set aside for such
      funding was _____ ¥10,000.
   2) No _____

H 8. Does the firm currently have a labor union?

    1) Yes _____   2) No _____

H 10. Is your firm occasionally asked by government agencies and local administration to provide information on economic and social development?

    1) Yes _____ How many requests do you receive annually? _____
    2) No _____

H 12. On a 7-point scale, where 1 = very little and 7 = very much, please circle the number best describing the extent to which you and your firm currently utilize guanxi connections with different government authorities. *(Show card.)*

With various levels of political government	1—2—3—4—5—6—7
With industrial authorities	1—2—3—4—5—6—7
With other government authorities, such as taxation bureaus, banks, industrial and commercial administrative bureaus, and the like	1—2—3—4—5—6—7

Organization

J 1. Does your current firm development follow any organizational blueprint? *(If no, go to J 2.)*

    1) Yes _____   2) No _____

J 1.1. Where do you look to develop the organizational blueprint? *(Interviewer, show card J 1.1. Multiple choices possible.)*

    1) Owners'/founders' ideas
    2) Professional management staff
    3) Firm management educational and training programs
    4) Self-study/books
    5) Mimicking successful national firms
    6) Mimicking successful international firms

7) Learning from own failures

8) Learning from failures of other firms

9) Professional consultants

10) Others

J 2. Please tell us about the current formalization degree of your company organization. *(Show card.)*

	Regulations within the firm *Check ✓ if yes*	Year of implementation or institutionalization
Formal, written organizational rules		
Formal, written job descriptions		
Formal, written performance assessments		
Formal, written pay scale		
Formal, written promotion procedures		
External financial auditing of books		
International certification (including ISO 9000, 9001, 9002, 9003, or 9004)		

J 3. Please tell us about any major internal organizational changes in your firm between 2006 and 2008.

Type of change	*Check ✓ if yes*	Year of the change
Change in business mission		
Division/department restructuring		
Implementation of new technology		
Mergers		
Major collaborations		
Adjustments in firm scale		
Outsourcing		
New management programs such as total quality management, re-engineering		
Other (please specify)		

J 4. In general, for how many years do you try to plan in advance in terms of strategic/organizational development of your firm?

(Single choice.)

1) No development plan
2) 1-month to 4-month plan
3) 4-month to 1-year plan
4) 1-year to 3-year plan
5) 5-year or longer

▶ *Resurvey firms, skip J 5 and J 6 and go to J 6.2.*

J 5. What was the initial business strategy when your firm was founded?

(Single choice. Show card.)

1) Creating new products for new potential markets and improving upon products to sustain current market shares
2) Marketing and distribution of products
3) Combining innovation and enhancement in market competitiveness
4) Lowering production costs

J 6. Does your firm have the same business strategy today?

(If yes, go to J 12.)

1) Yes _____   2) No _____

J 6.2. What is the current business strategy of your firm?

(Show card. Single choice.)

1) Creating new products for new potential markets
2) Improving upon products to sustain current market shares
3) Marketing and distribution of products
4) Combining innovation and enhancement in market competitiveness
5) Lowering production costs

J 12. On a 7-point scale, where 1 = very little and 7 = very much, please circle the number best describing the extent to which your firm currently utilizes guanxi connections with competitors.

1—2—3—4—5—6—7

Social Status and Norms of Entrepreneurs

K 1. Imagine social status like a ladder on a scale, with 1 the lowest and 10 the highest. Where do you think private entrepreneurs would be ranked by ordinary people? *(Show card K 1. Single choice.)*

Rank _____

K 2. Where would you think your firm ranks within your own industry?

Rank _____

K 2.1. What do you think others expect from you? Rank the following from 1 to 7, where 1 = strongly disagree and 7 = strongly agree. *(Show card.)*

I believe that most of my business acquaintances who are important to me expect me to provide business advice.	1—2—3—4—5—6—7
I believe that most of my business acquaintances who are important to me expect me to lend money to others if they would like to found a firm.	1—2—3—4—5—6—7
I believe that most of my business acquaintances who are important to me expect me to pass on customer requests, in case I cannot take the order myself.	1—2—3—4—5—6—7
I believe that most of my business acquaintances who are important to me expect me to inform them if someone I know commits any malfeasance in doing business.	1—2—3—4—5—6—7
I believe that most of my business acquaintances who are important to me expect me to help them out with (idle) machinery / technology in case they have a major technical problem and would otherwise risk losing a contract.	1—2—3—4—5—6—7

K 3. What is the current annual income you receive from this company (including firm dividends and bonuses)? Please check ✓ the appropriate category.

(Interviewer, show card K 3. Single choice.)

1) Less than ¥50,000
2) ¥50,000 < ¥100,000
3) ¥100,000 < ¥150,000
4) ¥150,000 < ¥200,000
5) ¥200,000 < ¥250,000
6) ¥250,000 < ¥375,000
7) ¥375,000 < ¥500,000
8) ¥500,000 < ¥750,000
9) ¥750,000 < ¥1,000,000
10) ¥1,000,000 < ¥1,500,000
11) ¥1,500,000 < ¥2,000,000
12) more than ¥2,000,000

K 4. Was anyone inspired by your business and experience to found a firm?

1) Yes _____ How many? _____ Among these, how many are family members _____, relatives _____, friends and acquaintances (employees, neighbors, etc.) _____?
2) No _____

L 1. Thanks very much for your time in participating in our survey! Before we finish, we have one more question. If professors from our research team would like to interview you within the year, would you participate?

(Please write down the reaction of the respondent.)

1) Will   2) Will not   3) We will see.

(Please record the CEO interview time length on the first page. Start the clock again for the CFO interview.)

FIRM SURVEY to Be Answered by Chief Financial Officer

Questionnaire ID: _____

Firm name: _____

Respondent name: _____

Date of interview: Year _____   Month _____   Day _____

Industry classification: _____

Firm address: _____

City: _____

E-mail contact of respondent: _____

Located in industrial development park/district?   1) Yes ____   2) No ____

Interviewer name:

   1) Main interviewer _____

   2) Secondary interviewer _____

Interview length: _____ minutes

Interviewee agrees to be recorded?   1) Yes _____   2) No _____

Financial Information

A 1. Please provide this information for your firm for the following four fiscal years. (Market value means the value if you transfer your firm to others.) *(If the firm has not been established for all three years, please write NA for the years before the founding of the firm. The same rule applies hereafter.)*

	2008	2007	2006	Founding year
Book value of your total assets (in ¥10,000)				
Market value of your total assets (in ¥10,000)				

▶ *If the firm is being resurveyed, skip A 2 and go to A 3 directly.*

A 2. What was the founding registered capital of this firm?
_____ ¥10,000

A 3. Please provide this information for your firm for the following four fiscal years. (Market value means the value if you transfer your firm to others.)

	2008	2007	2006	Founding year
Book value of your total equity (total assets − total liabilities) (in ¥10,000)				
Market value of your total equity (total assets − total liabilities) (in ¥10,000)				

A 4. Please provide this information for your firm for the following four fiscal years.

	2008	2007	2006	Founding year
Value of your total working capital (in ¥10,000)				

B 1. What was the average number of total employees (including contractual employees) in your firm for the following three years?

	2008	2007	2006
Average number of employees			

B 2. What percentage of your employees are college graduates? _____ %

B 3. Please provide this information for your firm for the following three years. *(If a firm does not contribute to these funds, please record "0.")*

	2008	2007	2006
Total annual wages (in ¥10,000)			
Total annual insurance (in ¥10,000)			

C 1. Please provide the total sales and exports information (in ¥10,000) for the firm for the following three years. *(Enter "0" if the firm did not export in a specific year. Enter NA if the firm was founded later.)*

	2008	2007	2006	Founding year
Value of total sales (products and services, including exports)				
Value of total exports (products and services, including sales to export agencies)				

D 1. Please report the total production costs for your firm for the following three years, as either a percentage of total sales or the actual figure (in ¥10,000).

	2008	2007	2006
Total costs of production			

Check ✓ one of the following:

_____ Reported as % of sales   _____ Reported as figures

E 1. Please report the value of new investments in fixed assets made by the firm in the following three years. *Report actual figure (in ¥10,000). Where investments were not made, please enter "0."*

	2008	2007	2006
Total new investments in fixed assets			

F 1. Please estimate the total annual amount (in ¥10,000) of travel and entertainment costs of this firm for the following three years.

	2008	2007	2006
Total travel and entertainment costs			

Firm Structure

G 1. How many subsidiaries (branch factories, sales, or service outlets) does your firm currently have in China?

_____

G 2. Does your firm belong to a business group?

1) Yes _____ Please name the business group. _____
2) No _____

Ownership

H 1. What percentage of your firm's shares are currently owned by each of the following categories? *(Show card.)*

	Percentage of shares (%)
Senior management or their family members	
Other domestic individuals	
Domestic institutional investors	
Domestic state-owned firm	
Domestic private firm	
Domestic collective firm	
Domestic banks	
Foreign individuals	
Foreign institutional investors	
Foreign firms	
Foreign banks	
National/central government	
Provincial government	
Municipal/county government	
Other government, including cooperatives and collectives	
Total	100%

H 2. What percentage of shares does your currently largest shareholder hold?

_____ %

▸ *Resurvey firms, skip H 4 and go to I 1.*

H 4. Has the company changed the ownership structure since 2005?
(If no, go to I 1.)

1) Yes _____   2) No _____

H 4.1. In what year did your firm's ownership structure change to the current one?

1) 2006
2) 2007
3) 2008

H 4.2. What percentage of your firm's shares were owned by each of the following categories before this change?
(Show card.)

	Percentage of shares (%)
Senior management or their family members	
Other domestic individuals	
Domestic institutional investors	
Domestic state-owned firm	
Domestic private firm	
Domestic collective firm	
Domestic banks	
Foreign individuals	
Foreign institutional investors	
Foreign firms	
Foreign banks	
National or central government	
Provincial government	
Municipal or county government	
Other government, including cooperatives and collectives	
Total	100%

Firm Performance

I 1. What were your company's profits (in ¥10,000) during the last three years?

	2008	2007	2006	Founding year
After-tax profits				
Earnings before interest payments and taxes				
Retained earnings (profit that is not distributed to the owners)				

J 1. Including all subsidiaries, what were your company's total liabilities (in ¥10,000) during the last three years?

		2008	2007	2006	Founding year
Total liabilities					
Of which	Long-term liabilities (more than 12 months)				
	Short-term liabilities (less than 12 months				

Competition / Market Position

K 1. How much money would it currently take to establish a new firm exactly like your current firm? _____ ¥10,000

Tax

L 1. How much tax did you pay in the following fiscal years?

	2008	2007	2006
Total tax (in ¥10,000)			

L 2. Does your firm currently benefit from any tax exemption programs?

   1) Yes _____   2) No _____

Finance

M 1. For the year 2008 and the founding year, what percentage of total capital was externally financed?

	2008	Founding year
Proportion of external finance		

M 2. For these years, please identify the proportion of sources of your external finance. *(Show card.)*

	2008	Founding year
Domestic commercial bank		
Foreign-owned commercial bank		
Investment funds / state subsidy		
Trade exportation tax reimbursement		
Loans from family and relatives		
Loans from friends		
Loans from business partners		
Other informal sources (money lenders, informal bank, pawn shop, etc.)		
Others		
Total	100%	100%

M 2.1. What was the total amount of external finance in 2008?

_____ ¥10,000

M 2.2. What was the total amount of external finance at the end of the founding year?   _____ ¥10,000

M 3. Are you using supplier credit (i.e., accounts payable) to purchase your inputs?
(If no, go to M 3.2.)

1) Yes _____   2) No _____

M 3.1. What percentage of your firm's inputs were purchased on credit in 2008?

_____ %

M 3.2. Is it offered to you by your suppliers?   1) Yes ____   2) No ____

M 3.3. What percentage of your firm's inputs were purchased on credit in your founding year? _____ %

Payment Conditions / Customer Credit

N 1. On average, what percentage of your monthly sales are

    1) paid before delivery   _____ %

    2) paid at delivery   _____ %

    3) sold on credit   _____ %

    Total   100 %

(Please go back to record the CFO interview time length.)

List of Interviewees

To protect our interviewees, in the list that follows we do not provide names or any information that would allow identification of specific participants.

Interview number	Date	Gender	Location	Position
1	9 Jun 2005	M	Shanghai	Chairman of the Board
2	12 Jun 2005	M	Shanghai	Venture capitalist
3	13 Jun 2005	M	Shanghai	Owner and CEO
4	14 Jun 2005	M	Shanghai	Deputy CEO
5	14 Jun 2005	M	Hangzhou	Municipal Section Chief
6	15 Jun 2005	M	Shanghai	Director (shareholder) and Deputy General Manager
7	16 Jun 2005	M	Shanghai	Group of government officials
8	16 Jun 2005	M	Hangzhou	CEO; Chairman of the Board; Party Secretary
9	17 Jun 2005	F	Shanghai	Researcher, Director
10	21 Jun 2005	M	Hangzhou	CEO
11	21 Jun 2005	M	Hangzhou	Chairman of the Board
12	23 Jun 2005	M	Hangzhou	CEO
13	23 Jun 2005	M	Hangzhou	CEO
14	24 Jun 2005	M	Hangzhou	Chief Legal Consultant
15	24 Jun 2005	M	Hangzhou	Government official
16	25 Jun 2005	M	Hangzhou	Government official
17	25 Jun 2005	M	Hangzhou	Professor
18	27 Jun 2005	M	Shanghai	Professor

Interview number	Date	Gender	Location	Position
19	27 Jun 2005	M	Shanghai	Manager
20	25 Oct 2005	M	Beijing	Government official
21	26 Oct 2005	M	Hangzhou	General Manager
22	26 Oct 2005	M	Hangzhou	Chairman of the Board
23	27 Oct 2005	M	Hangzhou	General Manager
24	27 Oct 2005	M	Hangzhou	General Manager
25	28 Oct 2005	M	Hangzhou	Founder and CEO
26	31 Oct 2005	M	Hangzhou	Party Secretary of Hangzhou
27	1 Oct 2005	M	Hangzhou	Company owner
28	1 Nov 2005	M	Hangzhou	CEO
29	1 Nov 2005	M	Hangzhou	Partner/CEO
30	2 Nov 2005	M	Hangzhou	Company owner
31	2 Nov 2005	M	Hangzhou	Chairman of the Board
32	3 Nov 2005	M	Hangzhou	Company owner
33	3 Nov 2005	M	Hangzhou	Government official
34	4 Nov 2005	M	Hangzhou	Government official
35	7 Nov 2005	M	Hangzhou	General Manager
36	7 Nov 2005	M	Hangzhou	Vice-Rector
37	8 Nov 2005	M	Hangzhou	Company owner
38	8 Nov 2005	M	Hangzhou	CEO / Chairman of the Board
39	9 Nov 2005	M+F	Hangzhou	Government officials
40	9 Nov 2005	M	Hangzhou	Government official
41	10 Nov 2005	M	Hangzhou	Government official
42	10 Nov 2005	M	Hangzhou	General Manager
43	11 Nov 2005	F	Hangzhou	President
44	11 Nov 2005	M	Hangzhou	Partner/CEO
45	14 Nov 2005	M	Hangzhou	President
46	14 Nov 2005	M	Hangzhou	Asset Manager
47	15 Nov 2005	M	Hangzhou	Deputy Director
48	15 Nov 2005	M	Hangzhou	Deputy Director
49	16 Nov 2005	F	Hangzhou	President
50	16 Nov 2005	M	Hangzhou	General Manager
51	17 Nov 2005	M	Hangzhou	Professor
52	17 Nov 2005	M	Hangzhou	President and General Manager
53	28 Apr 2008	F	Wenzhou	CEO and owner
54	28 Apr 2008	M	Wenzhou	CEO and owner
55	29 Apr 2008	M	Wenzhou	CEO and owner
56	29 Apr 2008	M	Wenzhou	Deputy CEO and partner
57	29 Apr 2008	M	Wenzhou	CEO and owner
58	30 Apr 2008	M	Wenzhou	CEO and owner
59	5 May 2008	M	Ningbo	Manager and owner's uncle

Interview number	Date	Gender	Location	Position
60	5 May 2008	M	Ningbo	CEO and owner
61	6 May 2008	F	Ningbo	Owner's wife
62	6 May 2008	M	Ningbo	CEO and owner
63	7 May 2008	M	Ningbo	Deputy CEO
64	7 May 2008	M	Ningbo	CEO and owner
65	8 May 2008	M	Ningbo	CEO and owner
66	10 May 2008	M	Yongkang	CEO and owner
67	11 May 2008	M	Yongkang	CEO and owner
68	12 May 2008	M	Shanghai	Government official
69	13 May 2008	M	Shanghai	CEO and owner
70	13 May 2008	M	Shanghai	Venture capitalist
71	14 May 2008	M	Danyang	CEO and owner
72	25 Aug 2008	M	Shanghai	Venture capitalist
73	3 Dec 2009	M	Shanghai	Manager
74	3 Dec 2009	F	Shanghai	Professor
75	4–5 Dec 2009	M	Danyang	CEO and owner
76	4–5 Dec 2009	M	Danyang	Manager
77	7 Dec 2009	M	Changzhou	CEO and owner
78	7 Dec 2009	M	Changzhou	CEO and owner
79	8 Dec 2009	M	Changzhou	CEO and owner
80	8 Dec 2009	M	Changzhou	CEO and owner
81	9 Dec 2009	M	Changzhou	CEO and owner
82	9 Dec 2009	M	Changzhou	CEO and owner
83	10 Dec 2009	M	Changzhou	CEO and owner
84	10 Dec 2009	M	Changzhou	CEO and owner
85	11 Dec 2009	M	Changzhou	CEO and owner
86	28 May 2010	F	Shanghai	Professor
87	2 Jun 2010	M	Nanjing	Deputy CEO and owner
88	2 Jun 2010	M	Nanjing	CEO
89	3 Jun 2010	M	Nanjing	General Secretary
90	3 Jun 2010	M	Nanjing	CEO
91	4 Jun 2010	M	Nanjing	General Secretary
92	4 Jun 2010	M	Nanjing	CEO
93	7 Jun 2010	M	Nantong	CEO
94	7 Jun 2010	M	Nantong	CEO
95	8 Jun 2010	M	Nantong	CEO
96	8 Jun 2010	M	Nantong	Chairman of the Board
97	9 Jun 2010	M	Nantong	Chairman
98	9 Jun 2010	M	Nantong	Department Director
99	10 Jun 2010	M	Nantong	CEO
100	10 Jun 2010	M	Nantong	CEO
101	11 Jun 2010	M	Nantong	CEO
102	11 Jun 2010	M	Nantong	CEO
103	10 Jan 2011	M	Ningbo	CEO and owner
104	10 Jan 2011	M	Ningbo	CEO and owner

Interview number	Date	Gender	Location	Position
105	11 Jan 2011	F	Ningbo	CEO and owner
106	11 Jan 2011	M	Ningbo	CEO and Chairman of the Board
107	12 Jan 2011	M	Ningbo	CEO and owner
108	13 Jan 2011	M	Ningbo	Deputy CEO
109	13 Jan 2011	M	Ningbo	Production Manager
110	14 Jan 2011	M	Ningbo	CEO and owner
111	14 Jan 2011	M	Ningbo	CEO and owner

Notes

1. Where Do Economic Institutions Come From?

1. Justin Yifu Lin, "The Household Responsibility System in China's Agricultural Reform: A Theoretical and Empirical Study," *Economic Development and Cultural Change* 36 (1988): S199–224; Susan L. Shirk, *The Political Logic of Economic Reform in China* (Berkeley: University of California Press, 1993); Theodore Groves, Yongmiao Hong, John McMillan, and Barry Naughton, "Autonomy and Incentives in Chinese State Enterprises," *Quarterly Journal of Economics* 109 (1994): 183–210; Barry Naughton, *Growing Out of the Plan: Chinese Economic Reform, 1978–1993* (Cambridge: Cambridge University Press, 1995); Jean C. Oi, "Fiscal Reform and the Economic Foundations of Local State Corporatism in China," *World Politics* 45 (1992): 99–126; Gabriella Montinola, Yingyi Qian, and Barry R. Weingast, "Federalism, Chinese Style: The Political Basis for Economic Success," *World Politics* 48 (1995): 50–81.

2. Jeffrey Sachs, "Poland and Eastern Europe: What Is to Be Done?" in *Foreign Economic Liberalization: Transformation in Socialist and Market Economies,* ed. Andreas Koves and Paul Marer (Boulder, CO: Westview Press, 1991), 235–246; Stanley Fischer, "Russia and the Soviet Union Then and Now," in *The Transition in Eastern Europe:* Vol. 1, *Country Studies,* ed. Olivier J. Blanchard, Kenneth A. Froot, and Jeffrey D. Sachs (Chicago: University of Chicago Press, 1994), 221–258; Peter Murrell, "The Transition According to Cambridge, Mass.," *Journal of Economic Literature* 33 (March 1995): 164–178.

3. World Bank, Development Indicators, http://data.worldbank.org.ludwig.lub .lu.se/news/2010-GNI-income-classifications (accessed July 9, 2011).

4. Ibid.

5. See Victor Nee, "Social Inequalities in Reforming State Socialism: Between Redistribution and Markets in China," *American Sociological Review* 56 (1991): 267–282; Dennis Tao Yang, "Urban-Biased Policies and Rising Income Inequality in China," *American Economic Review: Papers and Proceedings* 89 (April 1999): 306–310. In a global perspective, it has been argued that world income inequality peaked late in the twentieth century, as thereafter income inequality between countries declined. This has been attributed in part to the rise of East Asian economies, especially China. See Glenn Firebaugh, *The New Geography of Global Income Inequality* (Cambridge, MA: Harvard University Press, 2003).

6. Shaohua Chen and Martin Ravillion, "China Is Poorer Than We Thought, But No Less Successful in the Fight against Poverty," *The World Bank: Policy Research Working Paper* 4621 (2008). According to China's national poverty line, the poverty headcount ratio is even down to 2.8 percent. See World Bank, World Development Indicators, http://data.worldbank.org.ludwig.lub.lu.se/country/china (accessed July 9, 2011).

7. It should be noted that China's stock-listed firms no longer exclusively represent partially privatized state-owned companies. By 2010, more than 25 percent of the companies listed at China's stock exchanges were purely nonstate corporations. See *Annual Report of Non-State-Owned Economy in China, No. 5 (2007–2008)* (Beijing: Social Sciences Academic Press, 2008), 157. Also, the average share of state ownership in stock-listed companies declined dramatically since the establishment of China's stock markets in the early 1990s. The Shanghai Stock Exchange reports that tradable shares had reached 78 percent of total equity by 2011. See Shanghai Stock Exchange, *Fact Book 2011*, 94, http://www.sse.com.cn/sseportal/en/pages/p1005/p1005_content/factbook_us2011.pdf (accessed September 4, 2011). Shenzhen Stock Exchange reports a somewhat lower share of 68 percent of tradable equity. See Shenzhen Stock Exchange, *Fact Book 2010*, 3, http://www.szse.cn/main/files/2011/04/18/935296451656.pdf (accessed September 4, 2011).

8. Data refer to the official classification system published in China's *State Statistical Yearbooks* and to enterprises with registered annual revenue of more than ¥5 million from principal business. State Statistical Bureau, *China Statistical Yearbook 2009* (Beijing: China Statistics Press, 2010), table 14-1. With inclusion of foreign-funded companies and companies with funds from Hong Kong, Taiwan, and Macau, the respective private-sector share in total industrial output equals 30 percent; the share of state-owned firms reaches 12 percent.

9. For the helping-hand perspective, refer to Timothy Frye and Andrei Shleifer, "The Invisible Hand and the Grabbing Hand," *American Economic Review: Papers and Proceedings* 87 (1997): 131–155. For studies exploring local state corporatism, refer to Oi, "Fiscal Reform"; Jean C. Oi, "The Role of the

Local State in China's Transitional Economy," *China Quarterly* 144 (1995):
1132–1150; and Andrew Walder, "Local Government as Industrial Firms:
An Organizational Analysis of China's Transitional Economy," *American
Journal of Sociology* 101 (1995): 263–301. The developmental state perspective
is reflected in Marc Blecher, "Developmental State, Entrepreneurial State:
The Political Economy of Socialist Reform in Xinji Municipality and
Guanghan County," in *The Chinese State in the Era of Economic Reform: The
Road to Crisis,* ed. Gordon White (Houndsmill: Palgrave Macmillan, 1991),
265–291; Jane Duckett, *The Entrepreneurial State in China: Real Estate and
Commerce Departments in Reform Era Tianjin* (London: Routledge, Chapman
& Hall, 1998).

10. Yasheng Huang, for example, argues that although Chinese institutions
    were far from the standards of advanced industrial economies, the direction
    of formal institutional change may have been a sufficiently credible political
    signal to jump-start private entrepreneurial activities. Huang admits that
    his study does not provide empirical evidence to support his conjecture.
    However, in his view the security of the proprietor (in contrast to the
    security of the property) may have provided sufficient incentives to start up
    private businesses without formal property rights protection. Yasheng
    Huang, *Capitalism with Chinese Characteristics: Entrepreneurship and the
    State* (Cambridge: Cambridge University Press, 2008).

11. Too often, government restrictions left researchers with little alternative
    but to use research sites, respondents, and data provided by government
    officials. With small, nonrandom convenience samples, it is impossible to
    draw general inferences about the population. Moreover, these studies often
    do not address how ordinary citizens responded to emergent opportunities
    for private business, and the strategies they developed to deal with the
    uncertainties of a rapidly changing institutional environment. See Marc
    Blecher and Vivienne Shue, *Government and Economy in a Chinese County*
    (Stanford, CA: Stanford University Press, 1996); Jean C. Oi, *Rural China
    Takes Off: Institutional Foundations of Economic Reform* (Berkeley: University
    of California Press, 1999).

12. Robert Ellickson points out that in the legal realist tradition, it is not the
    letter of the law that economic actors look to, but how the law is actually
    practiced. For example, if entrepreneurs see that the local government is not
    enforcing the seven-employee size limitation, then they will act accordingly
    and ignore the law. Comments at the Conference on Endogenous Institutional
    Change, Lund University, Sweden, October 1, 2011.

13. Susan H. Whiting, *Power and Wealth in Rural China: The Political Economy
    of Institutional Change* (Cambridge: Cambridge University Press, 2000);
    Kellee Tsai, *Capitalism without Democracy: The Private Sector in Contemporary
    China* (Ithaca, NY: Cornell University Press, 2007); David L. Wank,
    Commodifying Communism: Business, Trust, and Politics in a Chinese City

(Cambridge: Cambridge University Press, 1999). None of these ambitious studies employed a random sample of informants.

14. Douglass C. North, *Understanding the Process of Economic Change* (Princeton, NJ: Princeton University Press, 2005), 57.
15. Douglass C. North, *Structure and Change in Economic History* (New York: Norton, 1981), 32. North's theory of institutional change has been extended to explain departures from state socialism. See Victor Nee and Peng Lian, "Sleeping with the Enemy: A Dynamic Model of Declining Political Commitment in State Socialism," *Theory and Society* 23 (1994): 253–297. An irreversible pattern of declining factor productivity and economic performance in centrally planned economies in the 1970s and 1980s, coupled with the dynamic technological and economic progress in established market economies, pressured the elites of China, Eastern Europe, and Russia to initiate economic reforms.
16. Merton J. Peck and Thomas J. Richardson, *What Is to Be Done? Proposals for the Soviet Transition to the Market* (New Haven, CT: Yale University Press, 1992).
17. See Oliver E. Williamson, "Credible Commitments: Using Hostages to Support Exchange," *American Economic Review* 73 (1983): 519–540. In Ellickson's interpretation of the "legal centralist" perspective, "the state functions as the sole creator of operative rules of entitlement among individuals." Robert C. Ellickson, *Order without Law* (Cambridge, MA: Harvard University Press), 4.
18. Recent scholarship, however, suggests that it was not uncommon in the Industrial Revolution for rural household production to develop into capitalist factories, as in China after the start of economic reform. See Joel Mokyr, *The Enlightened Economy: An Economic History of Britain 1700–1850* (New Haven, CT: Yale University Press, 2009).
19. A study of the Yangzi delta from 1350 to 1988 underscores that even in a highly commercialized region, peasant commodity production persisted through to the modern era in its traditional form. Huang argues that commercialization in China did not pave the way to modern capitalism, but instead gave rise to "involution," defined as growth without development wherein the total output expands, but at the cost of diminished marginal returns. Philip Huang, *The Peasant Family and Rural Development in the Yangzi Delta, 1350–1988* (Stanford, CA: Stanford University Press, 1990).
20. Alan P. L. Liu, "The 'Wenzhou Model' of Development and China's Modernization," *Asian Survey* 32 (1992): 696–711; Kristin Parris, "Local Initiative and National Reform: The Wenzhou Model of Development," *China Quarterly* 134 (1993): 242–263.
21. Government regulations on township and village enterprises also allowed the formation of quasi-private "alliance enterprises" *(lianying hezuo qiye)*. By 1985,

4 percent of the so-called township village enterprises were registered as alliance enterprises. State Statistical Bureau, *China Statistical Yearbook 2003* (Beijing: China Statistics Press, 2004), 447. See also "Guowuyuan guanyu Chengzhen feinongye geti Jingji ruogan zhengcexing Guiding" [Political regulations of the State Council on the non-agrarian, urban individual economy], *Zhonghua Renmin Gongheguo* (September 25, 1981), 493–497; "Guanyu kaichuang shedui Qiye xin jumian de Baogao" [Report to create a new situation for commune and brigade companies, March 1, 1984]; *Zhongguo Nongye Nianjian 1985* [Yearbook of China's agriculture] (Beijing: Nongye Chubanshe, 1985), 450.

22. Thomas P. Lyons, "Economic Reform in Fujian: Another View from the Villages," in *The Economic Transformation of South China: Reform and Development in the Post-Mao Era*, Cornell East Asia Series No. 70, ed. Thomas Lyons and Victor Nee (Ithaca, NY: Cornell University East Asia Program, 1994), 141–168. For an account of informal norms safeguarding entrepreneurs from looting and predation, see Yusheng Peng, "Kinship, Networks and Entrepreneurs in China's Transitional Economy," *American Journal of Sociology* 105 (2004): 1045–1074.

23. See *Zhongguo Nongye Nianjian 1989* [Yearbook of China's agriculture] (Beijing: Nongye Chubanshe, 1989), 555–557.

24. Only the 1999 constitutional amendment eventually recognized the private sector as an "important" part of the economy.

25. Dali L. Yang, *Remaking the Chinese Leviathan: Market Transition and the Politics of Governance in China* (Stanford, CA: Stanford University Press, 2004), 152.

26. Tao Chen, Sheming Li, Bisheng Zhang, and Cai Bai, "Guanzu jiasu fazhan geti siying Jingji de Diaocha ji zhengce Cuoshi Jianyin" [Investigation of the fast development of individual and private enterprise and suggestions for political measures and instruments], *Jingyi Yanjiu Cankao* (July 8, 1993): 42–52.

27. "The Privately-Run Enterprises," *China News Analysis* 1382 (April 1, 1989): 7. Only a small group of firms with production technologies utilizing waste water, fumes, and other waste products as input material were eligible to receive tax reduction. See "Zhonghua Renmin Gongheguo siying Qiye Suodeshui zanxing Tiaoli" [China's temporary regulations on income taxation of private companies] promulgated on June 25, 1988, *Zhonghua Renmin Gongeheguo Guowuquan Gongbao* [Bulletin of the State Council] (July 25, 1988): 490.

28. Jianwei Bai, "Excessive Tax on Private Enterprises," in *Ningxia Ribao* (September 1, 1994): 2, translation in *JPRS-CAR-94-053* (November 8, 1994): 48; Xinxin Li, "Gaige Kaifanghou de Zhongguo siying Jingji" [China's private economy after the reform and opening], *Jingji Yanjiu Cankao* (December 1, 1994): 2–16; Zhongguo shekeyuan ruankeyuan yanjiu ketizu, "Siying

Jingji fazhan Yanjiu" [Analysis of the development of the private economy], *Jingji Yanjiu Cankao* (September 12, 1995): 11.

29. Whiting, *Power and Wealth in Rural China.*
30. Huang, *Capitalism with Chinese Characteristics.*
31. Cited in Bangguo Wu, "Several Questions Concerning the Reform and Development of State-Owned Enterprises," *Chinese Economy* 30 (2): 30. In a similar vein, in 1999 Jiang Zemin asserted the central government's policy to "ensure the preservation and increase the value of state enterprises and continuously increase the strength and control power of the state-owned economy." See *Foreign Broadcast Information Service,* FBIS-CHI-1999-0805, 3.
32. In the first half of 2003, for instance, even in Beijing the value of unexecuted civil and economic rulings was twice as large as the value of enforced rulings. See "Business: Winning Is Only Half the Battle: China's Courts," *Economist* (March 26, 2005): 84. See also Mark Findlay, "Independence and the Judiciary in the PRC: Expectations for Constitutional Legality in China," in *Law, Capitalism and Power in Asia,* ed. Kanishka Jayasuriya (London: Routledge, 1999), 281–299; Scott Wilson, "Law Guanxi: MNCs, State Actors, and Legal Reform in China," *Journal of Contemporary China* 17 (2008): 25–51; Barbara Krug, Nathan Betancourt, and Hans Hendrischke, "Rechtsprechung und Vertragsgestaltung in China: Die Folgenlosigkeit des neuen Insolvenz-gesetzes aus vertragstheoretischer Sicht," *Neue Zuercher Zeitung,* March 16, 2011, http://www.nzz.ch/nachrichten/wirtschaft/aktuell/rechtsprechung _und_vertragsgestaltung_in_china_als_heikler_parcours_fuer_auslaendische _firmen_1.9909790.html (accessed March 20, 2011).
33. See Economic Freedom Component Scores 2011; Heritage Foundation, http://www.heritage.org/index/explore (accessed July 21, 2011).
34. World Bank, http://www.doingbusiness.org/rankings (accessed July 9, 2011).
35. "When institutions are identified with politically devised rules or efficient contracts, institutional change is considered to result from an exogenous shift in the interests or knowledge of the political actors who set the rules or the efficient contracts." And "identifying institutions with politically devised rules . . . restricts them to outcomes of the political process." Avner Greif, *Institutions and the Path to the Modern Economy: Lessons from Medieval Trade* (Cambridge: Cambridge University Press, 2006), 9–10.
36. Joseph A. Schumpeter, *Theorie der wirtschaftlichen Entwicklung: Nachdruck der 1. Auflage von 1912* (Berlin: Duncker & Humblot, [1912] 2006).
37. For instance, the establishment of China's two stock exchanges in Shanghai and Shenzhen, which were initially designed to almost exclusively list large-scale state-controlled corporations, and intensified industrial policy measures supporting the buildup of powerful state conglomerates signaled

an illiberal move in central government policies. See Huang, *Capitalism with Chinese Characteristics.*

2. Markets and Endogenous Institutional Change

1. *Annual Report of Non-State-Owned Economy in China, No. 5 (2007–2008)* (Beijing: Social Sciences Academic Press, 2008), 76.
2. Victor Nee, "A Theory of Market Transition: From Redistribution to Markets in State Socialism," *American Sociological Review* 54 (1989): 663–681; Victor Nee, "The Emergence of a Market Society: Changing Mechanisms of Stratification in China," *American Journal of Sociology* 101 (1996): 908–949.
3. Victor Nee, "Organizational Dynamics of Market Transition: Hybrid Forms, Property Rights, and Mixed Economy in China," *Administrative Science Quarterly* 37 (1992): 1–27.
4. William J. Baumol, *Entrepreneurship, Management and the Structure of Payoffs* (Cambridge, MA: MIT Press, 1993).
5. Friedrich A. Hayek, "Competition as a Discovery Procedure," in *New Studies in Philosophy, Politics, Economics and the History of Ideas,* by Friedrich A. von Hayek (Chicago: University of Chicago Press, 1978); Harrison C. White, *Markets from Networks: Socioeconomic Models of Production* (Princeton, NJ: Princeton University Press, 2002).
6. Avinash K. Dixit, *Lawlessness and Economics: Alternative Modes of Governance* (Princeton, NJ: Princeton University Press, 2004), 3.
7. The development of the private enterprise economy in Vietnam has likewise involved extensive bottom-up dynamics. De novo entrepreneurs, lacking effective legal rights, relied on ad hoc strategies that built on close-knit communities to enable market entry and firm survival. See John McMillan and Christopher Woodruff, "Interfirm Relationships and Informal Credit in Vietnam," *Quarterly Journal of Economics* 114 (1999): 1285–1320; and Annette Miae Kim, *Learning to Be Capitalists: Entrepreneurs in Vietnam's Transition Economy* (Oxford: Oxford University Press, 2008). A study of private start-up firms in Poland, Slovakia, Romania, Russia, and Ukraine shows that social networks in communities there also contributed to entrepreneurial success in the context of weak legal institutions. John McMillan and Christopher Woodruff, "Private Order under Dysfunctional Public Order," *Michigan Law Review* 98 (2000): 2421–2458.
8. See Appendix 2, Interview 23. For the role of informal norms in established legal systems, see Stewart Macaulay, "Non-Contractual Relations in Business: A Preliminary Study," *American Sociological Review* 28 (1963): 55–67; Marc Galanter, "Justice in Many Rooms: Courts, Private Ordering, and Indigenous Law," *Journal of Legal Pluralism* 19 (1981): 1–47.
9. Susan H. Whiting, *Power and Wealth in Rural China: The Political Economy of Institutional Change* (Cambridge: Cambridge University Press, 2000).

10. Chinese courts based their assessment on the weakly defined concept of "smuggling" (as specified in China's Criminal Law, Article 118), which could be applied to long-distance transfer of goods with the purpose of resale. Smugglers faced a sentence of up to ten years or even the death penalty. See Zi Ye, "The Sword Hanging above Private Owners: Limitations in the Development of the Private Economy in Mainland China," *Kaifang* (August 18, 1993), 39–41, translated in *JPRS-CAR-93-088* (December 14, 1993), 40.

11. George C. Homans, *Social Behavior: Its Elementary Forms* (New York: Harcourt Brace Jovanovich, [1961] 1974), 76.

12. Michael Taylor, *The Possibility of Cooperation* (Cambridge: Cambridge University Press, 1987); Jon Elster, *The Cement of Society: A Study of Social Order* (Cambridge: Cambridge University Press, 1989); James S. Coleman, *Foundations of Social Theory* (Cambridge, MA: Harvard University Press, 1990).

13. Pamela E. Oliver, "Formal Models of Collective Action," *Annual Review of Sociology* 19 (1993): 274; Gerald Marwell and Pamela E. Oliver, *The Critical Mass in Collective Action* (Cambridge: Cambridge University Press, 1993).

14. Elinor Ostrom, *Governing the Commons: The Evolution of Institutions for Collective Action* (Cambridge: Cambridge University Press, 1990).

15. Lisa Bernstein, "Opting Out of the Legal System: Extralegal Contractual Relations in the Diamond Industry," *Journal of Legal Studies* 21 (1992): 115–152.

16. Robert Ellickson, *Order without Law* (Cambridge, MA: Harvard University Press, 1991).

17. Douglass C. North, *Structure and Change in Economic History* (New York: Norton, 1981); Douglass C. North, *Institutions, Institutional Change and Economic Performance* (Cambridge: Cambridge University Press, 1990). For an account of the rise of market society and modern capitalism in England, see Karl Polanyi, *The Great Transformation: The Political and Economic Origins of Our Time* (Boston: Beacon Press, 1944). Polanyi focuses on the interaction between the state and society in the construction of self-regulating markets. His historical analysis remains at the macro level in its treatment of the state and society as though these are unitary actors. He overlooks micro-level mechanisms embedded in networks and norms.

18. Hernando de Soto, *The Mystery of Capital: Why Capitalism Triumphs in the West and Fails Everywhere Else* (New York: Basic Civitas Books, 2000).

19. Robert Axelrod, "An Evolutionary Approach to Norms," *American Political Science Review* 80 (1986): 1106. See also H. Peyton Young, "The Economics of Convention," *Journal of Economic Perspectives* 10 (1996): 105–122. In a similar vein, it is argued that the growth of Atlantic trade after 1500 helped merchant groups push for institutional changes that would constrain the power of the monarchy and protect their property rights. See Daron Acemoglu, Simon Johnson, and James Robinson, "The Rise of Europe:

Atlantic Trade, Institutional Change, and Economic Growth," *American Economic Review* 95 (2005): 546–579.

20. Edward Stringham, "The Extralegal Development of Securities Trading in Seventeenth-Century Amsterdam," *Quarterly Review of Economics and Finance* 43 (2003): 321–344.

21. Peter M. Garber, *Famous First Bubbles* (Cambridge, MA: MIT Press, 2000), 23.

22. Avner Greif, *Institutions and the Path to the Modern Economy: Lessons from Medieval Trade* (Cambridge: Cambridge University Press, 2006), 25; Victor Nee and Sonja Opper, "Bureaucracy and Finance," *Kyklos* 6Z (2009): 293–315.

23. Edward L. Glaeser, Rafael La Porta, Florencio Lopez-de-Silanes, and Andrei Shleifer, "Do Institutions Cause Growth?" *Journal of Economic Growth* 9 (2004): 271–303. These researchers emphasize the role of human capital as a source of economic growth. However, they do not address the question of how long-term business relations and contracts are organized and sustained in the absence of state-mandated rules. Since Scully's first cross-national study on the correlation between institutional quality and economic growth, a broad empirical literature has confirmed the importance of government in providing state-mandated rules for economic growth. See Gerald W. Scully, "The Institutional Framework and Economic Development," *Journal of Political Economy* 96 (1988): 652–662. Others show that countries characterized by weak rule of law, pervasive corruption, and predatory political elites are likely to remain poor and locked in persistent underdevelopment. See, for instance, Philip Keefer and Stephen Knack, "Why Don't Poor Countries Catch Up? A Cross-National Test of an Institutional Explanation," *Economic Inquiry* 35 (1997): 590–601; Paolo Mauro, "Corruption and Growth," *Quarterly Journal of Economics* 110 (1995): 681–713. Good institutions not only correspond with higher productivity but also increase economic growth by facilitating trade with other countries. See Robert E. Hall and Charles I. Jones, "Why Do Some Countries Produce So Much More Output per Worker than Others?" *Quarterly Journal of Economics* 114 (1999): 83–116; David Dollar and Aart Kraay, "Institutions, Trade, and Growth," *Journal of Monetary Economics* 50 (2003): 133–162. Institutional quality may even trump geography and trade in explaining country growth. See Dani Rodrik, Arvind Subramanian, and Francesco Trebbi, "Institutions Rule: The Primacy of Institutions over Geography and Integration in Economic Development," *Journal of Economic Growth* 9 (2004): 131–165. However, these studies do not provide convincing evidence that formal property rights protection precedes economic growth.

24. Greif, *Institutions and the Path to the Modern Economy,* 19 and 30.

25. David Stark and Victor Nee, "Towards an Institutional Analysis of State Socialism," in *Remaking the Economic Institutions of Socialism,* ed. Victor Nee and David Stark (Stanford, CA: Stanford University Press, 1989), 14–15.

26. Mary C. Brinton and Victor Nee, eds., *The New Institutionalism in Sociology* (New York: Russell Sage Foundation, 1998); W. Richard Scott, *Institutions and Organizations* (Thousand Oaks, CA: Sage, 2001).

27. Homans, *Social Behavior,* 68.

28. John McMillan, *Reinventing the Bazaar* (New York: Norton, 2002), 6.

29. Ibid., 6.

30. Harrison C. White, *Markets from Networks: Socioeconomic Models of Production* (Princeton, NJ: Princeton University Press, 2002), 9.

31. Harrison C. White, "Where Do Markets Come From?" *American Journal of Sociology* 87 (1981): 518. For signaling theory, refer to George Akerlof, "The Economics of Caste and of the Rat Race and Other Woeful Tales," *Quarterly Journal of Economics* 90 (1976): 599–617; Michael A. Spence, *Market Signaling: Informational Transfer in Hiring and Related Screening Processes* (Cambridge, MA: Harvard University Press, 1974).

32. Oliver E. Williamson, *The Economic Institutions of Capitalism* (New York: Free Press, 1985); Avner Greif, "Contract Enforceability and Economic Institutions in Early Trade: The Maghribi Traders' Coalition," *American Economic Review* 83 (1993): 525–549; Avner Greif, "Cultural Beliefs and the Organization of Society: A Historical and Theoretical Reflection on Collectivist and Individualist Societies," *Journal of Political Economy* 102 (1994): 912–950.

33. W. Richard Scott, *Institutions and Organizations* (Thousand Oaks, CA: Sage Publications, 2001), 196, figure 8.1. See also Victor Nee and Paul Ingram, "Embeddedness and Beyond: Institutions, Exchange and Social Structure," in Brinton and Nee, *New Institutionalism in Sociology,* 19–45; Lauren B. Edelman, "Legal Ambiguity and Symbolic Structures: Organizational Mediation of Civil Rights Law," *American Journal of Sociology* 97 (1992): 1531–1576; Lauren Edelman, Christopher Uggen, and Howard S. Erlanger, "The Endogeneity of Legal Regulation: Grievance Procedures as Rational Myth," *American Journal of Sociology* 105 (1999): 406–454; Frank R. Dobbin, John R. Sutton, John W. Meyer, and W. Richard Scott, "Equal Opportunity Law and the Construction of Internal Labor Markets," *American Journal of Sociology* 99 (1993): 396–427.

34. The institutional mechanisms are distal, as opposed to the proximate mechanisms at the micro and meso levels of individuals and networks. Institutional mechanisms encompass the deeper causes because they shape the incentive structure for organizations and individuals, and thereby the contexts in which proximate mechanisms operate. The institutional-level mechanisms posited by economists and sociologists, despite differences in behavioral assumptions and conceptual language, are not as far apart as is commonly perceived. See Victor Nee, "The New Institutionalisms in Economics and Sociology," in *The Handbook of Economic Sociology,* ed. Neil J. Smelser and Richard Swedberg (New York and Princeton, NJ: Russell Sage Foundation and Princeton University Press, 2005), 49–74.

35. Robert K. Merton, *Social Theory and Social Structure* (New York: Free Press, 1968).

36. We assume that actors are rational in that they make decisions according to cost-benefit criteria. However, we do not see humans as the narrowly self-interested *Homo economicus* of neoclassical economics, possessing perfect information and unbounded cognitive capacity. Instead, they use rule-of-thumb heuristics based on the information currently available to them. See Barnaby Marsh, "Heuristics as Social Tools," *New Ideas in Psychology* 20 (2002): 49–57.

37. Ellickson, *Order without Law,* 167.

38. We thank Woody Powell for bringing this point to our attention. Experimental research confirms that subjects prefer to learn to cooperate rather than not cooperate in repeated public good games. See R. Mark Isaac, James Walker, and Arlington W. Williams, "Group Size and the Voluntary Provision of Public Goods: Experimental Evidence Utilizing Large Groups," *Journal of Public Economics* 54 (1994): 1–36.

39. H. Peyton Young, *Individual Strategy and Social Structure: An Evolutionary Theory of Institutions* (Princeton, NJ: Princeton University Press, 2001); Young, "Economics of Convention."

40. George C. Homans, *The Human Group* (New York: Harcourt, Brace, 1950); Mitchel Abolafia, *Making Markets: Opportunism and Restraint on Wall Street* (Cambridge, MA: Harvard University Press, 1996); William Foote Whyte, *Street Corner Society: The Social Structure of an Italian Slum* (Chicago: University of Chicago Press, 1943); Chester I. Barnard, *The Functions of the Executive* (Cambridge, MA: Harvard University Press, 1968); Truman F. Bewley, *Why Wages Don't Fall during a Recession* (Cambridge, MA: Harvard University Press, 1999).

41. This is shown in a tit-for-tat model effectively simulating the operation of network mechanisms. See Robert Axelrod, *The Evolution of Cooperation* (New York: Basic Books, 1984).

42. Russell Hardin, *Trust and Trustworthiness* (New York: Russell Sage Foundation, 2004).

43. Peter Blau, *The Dynamics of Bureaucracy,* 2nd ed. (Chicago: University of Chicago Press, 1955).

44. Quoted in Homans, *Social Behavior,* 343.

45. Harrison C. White, *Identity and Control: A Structural Theory of Social Action* (Princeton, NJ: Princeton University Press, 1992).

46. Charles Tilly, *Identities, Boundaries, and Social Ties* (Boulder, CO: Paradigm, 2005).

47. Michael Macy, personal communication, June 21, 2011.

48. Victor Nee, "Norms and Networks in Economic and Organizational Performance," *American Economic Review: Papers and Proceedings* 88 (1998): 86.

49. Mancur Olson, *The Rise and Decline of Nations: Economic Growth, Stagflation, and Social Rigidities* (New Haven, CT: Yale University Press, 1982).

50. For an analysis of opposition norms in response to external sanctions, see Douglas D. Heckathorn, "Collective Sanctions and Compliance Norms: A Formal Theory of Group-Mediated Social Control," *American Sociological Review* 55 (1990): 366–384.

51. Roger V. Gould, *Insurgent Identities: Class, Community, and Protest in Paris from 1848 to the Commune* (Chicago: University of Chicago Press, 1995).

52. Janos Kornai, "The Affinity between Ownership Forms and Coordination Mechanisms: The Common Experience of Reform in Socialist Countries," *Journal of Economic Perspectives* 4 (1990): 131–147.

53. Thomas Schelling, *Micromotives and Macrobehavior* (New York: Norton, 1978).

54. Greif, *Institutions and the Path to the Modern Economy*, 31.

55. Coleman, *Foundations of Social Theory*.

56. We see this social dynamic in the explosion of protest movements in Muslim societies stretching from the Mediterranean rim of North Africa to the Middle East. Once the tipping point is reached, opposition norms driving the social movements become self-reinforcing, as government repression declines in effectiveness as more and more protestors join the movement.

57. Francis Fukuyama, *Trust: The Social Virtues and the Creation of Prosperity* (New York: Free Press, 1996); Greif, *Institutions and the Path to the Modern Economy*.

58. Alejandro Portes and Julia Sensenbrenner, "Embeddedness and Immigration: Notes on the Social Determinants of Economic Action," *American Journal of Sociology* 98 (1993): 1320–1350; Homans, *Social Behavior*.

59. In a related line of argument, China's successful transition is in part accredited to the destruction of vested interest in the administration during the Cultural Revolution. See Mancur Olson, *Power and Prosperity: Outgrowing Communist and Capitalist Dictatorship* (New York: Basic Books, 2000).

60. North, *Institutions, Institutional Change and Economic Performance*.

61. Experimental, game-theoretic, and empirical research show that frequent social interaction in relationships cements commitment and informal constraints limiting malfeasance. See Edward J. Lawler and Jeongkoo Yoon, "Commitment in Exchange Relations: Test of a Theory of Relational Cohesion," *American Sociological Review* 61 (1996): 89–108; Robert Axelrod and William D. Hamilton, "The Evolution of Cooperation," *Science* 211 (1981): 1390–1396; Ernst Fehr and Klaus M. Schmidt, "A Theory of Fairness, Competition, and Cooperation," *Quarterly Journal of Economics* 114 (1999): 817–868; McMillan and Woodruff, "Interfirm Relationships"; Paul R. Milgrom, North, and Weingast, "The Role of Institutions in the Revival of Trade: The Law Merchant, Private Judges, and the Champagne Fairs,"

Economics and Politics 2 (1990): 1–23; Karen Clay, "Trade without Law: Private-Order Institutions in Mexican California," *Journal of Law, Economics, and Organization* 13 (1997): 202–231; Greif, "Contract Enforceability."

62. The dynamics of social norm diffusion has been modeled as a coordination game, in which the rate of the spread of a social innovation depends on three factors: the network topology, the relative payoff gain of the innovation compared to the status quo, and the rationality of economic agents. Innovations spread faster the higher the advance is relative to the status quo, and the more people are clustered in small localized groups. See H. Peyton Young, "The Dynamics of Social Innovation," *Proceedings of the National Academy of Science,* forthcoming. An alternative approach shows that innovations spread fastest in low-dimensional networks dominated by geographic proximity. See Andrea Montanari and Amin Saberi, "The Spread of Innovations in Social Networks," *Proceedings of the National Academy of Science* 107 (2010): 20196–20201.

63. Sebastian Heilmann, "Der chinesische Aktienmarkt: Staatliche Regulierung im Wandel," *Asien* 80 (2001): 25–41.

64. Victor Nee and Sijin Su, "Institutional Foundations of Robust Economic Performance: Public Sector Industrial Growth in China," in *Industrial Transformation in Eastern Europe in the Light of the East Asian Experience,* ed. Jeffrey Henderson (Houndmills: Macmillan, 1998), 174.

65. Wolfgang Jamann and Thomas Menkhoff, *Make Big Profits with Small Capital* (Munich: Minerva, 1988), 183.

66. Quoted in John McMillan and Christopher Woodruff, "The Central Role of Entrepreneurs in Transition Economies," *Journal of Economic Perspectives* 16 (2002): 153.

67. See Appendix 2, Interview 37.

68. White, *Markets from Networks.*

69. For a fine-grained case study of a similar process of self-reinforcing endogenous institutional change in the commercialization of science research at Stanford University, see Jeannette A. Colyvas and Walter W. Powell, "Roads to Institutionalization: The Remaking of Boundaries between Public and Private Science," *Research in Organizational Behavior* 27 (2006): 305–353.

70. See Appendix 2, Interview 21.

71. William A. Byrd and Qingsong Lin, *China's Rural Industry: Structure, Development, and Reform* (Washington, DC: World Bank Publication, 1990).

72. *Report on the Development of China's Private Enterprises No. 6. 2005* (Beijing: Social Sciences Academic Press, 2005), 229–232.

73. China's industry associations are government sponsored and not private business associations. They are usually staffed by active or former government officials. However, these associations often develop an independent voice and lobby for institutional change in support of the economic interests of their

members. The All China Federation of Industry and Commerce (ACFIC), for instance, actively lobbied for better protection of private enterprises and freedom from harassment. See Margaret M. Pearson, *China's New Business Elite: The Political Consequences of Economic Reform* (Berkeley: University of California Press, 1997); Scott Kennedy, *The Business of Lobbying in China* (Cambridge, MA: Harvard University Press, 2005).

74. Andrew Atherton, "From 'Fat Pigs' and 'Red Hats' to a New Social Stratum: The Changing Face of Enterprise Development Policy in China," *Journal of Small Business and Enterprise Development* 14 (2008): 640–655.

75. For data from 2009, see *China Statistical Yearbook 2010* (Beijing: China Statistics Press), table 14-1. For data from 1978, see Zhonghe Guo, "Wo Guo geti, siying Qiye Jianxi" [A brief analysis of China's individual and private firms], *Jingji Yanjiu Cankao* (February 13, 1993): 28. Skeptics as to the actual size of the private enterprise economy tend to also include partially privatized stock-listed firms in the category of state-owned or state-controlled company. However, even if all "shareholding corporations" were included in the broader category of state-owned and state-controlled companies, the combined gross production share would not exceed private industrial production.

76. *Annual Report of Non-State-Owned Economy in China, No. 5 (2007–2008)*, 94.

77. See ibid., 233. Already by 1999, traditional state-owned companies represented only 50 percent of China's large and medium-size companies. Gary Jefferson, Albert G. Z. Hu, Xiaojing Guan, and Xiaoyun Yu, "Ownership, Performance, and Innovation in China's Large- and Medium-Size Industrial Enterprise Sector," *China Economic Review* 14 (2003): 95.

78. See U.S. Census Bureau, http://www.census.gov/econ/smallbus.html (accessed May 26, 2011).

79. Gabriela Montinola, Yingyi Qian, and Barry Weingast, "Federalism Chinese Style: The Political Basis for Economic Success in China," *World Politics* 48 (1995): 50.

80. Ronald Coase, "The Institutional Structure of Production," *American Economic Review* 82 (1992): 714.

81. Douglass C. North, "Economic Performance through Time," *American Economic Review* 84 (1994): 366.

82. Montinola, Qian, and Weingast, "Federalism Chinese Style"; Whiting, *Power and Wealth in Rural China;* Kellee Tsai, *Capitalism without Democracy: The Private Sector in Contemporary China* (Ithaca, NY: Cornell University Press, 2007).

83. Douglass C. North and Robert Thomas, *The Rise of the Western World: A New Economic History* (Cambridge: Cambridge University Press, 1973).

3. The Epicenter of Bottom-Up Capitalism

1. See Appendix 2, Interview 13.
2. Adi Ignatius, "Jack Ma," *Time* magazine, April 30, 2009, http://www.time
   .com/time/specials/packages/article/0,28804,1894410_1893837_1894188,00
   .html (accessed May 15, 2009).
3. The Yangzi delta region covers sixteen municipalities in three provinces:
   Wuxi, Nanjing, Yangzhou, Zhenjiang, Changzhou, Nantong, and Suzhou in
   Jiangsu Province; Hangzhou, Huzhou, Shaoxing, Taizhou, Wenzhou, Ningbo,
   Zhoushan, and Jiaxing in Zhejiang Province; and Shanghai Municipality.
4. Philip Huang, *The Peasant Family and Rural Development in the Yangzi Delta,
   1350–1988* (Stanford, CA: Stanford University Press, 1990), 260–263.
5. Ibid., 263.
6. Debin Ma, "Economic Growth in the Lower Yangzi Region of China in
   1911–1937: A Quantitative and Historical Analysis," *Journal of Economic
   History* 68 (2008): 356.
7. Calculation based on provincial gross industrial output values provided by
   China Data Online, Michigan University, China Data Center.
8. Zhejiang Association for International Exchange of Personnel, April 22, 2007.
9. Jinchuan Shi, Yanjun Huang, Sijiang He, and Gujun Yan, *Zhong xiao jinrong
   Jigou yu zhong xiao Qiye fazhan Yanjiu—yi Zhejiang Wenzhou, Taizhou Diqu
   wei Lie* [The development of small and medium-size financial institutions
   and enterprises—taking Zhejiang's regions of Wenzhou and Taizhou as
   examples] (Hangzhou: Zhejiang daxue chubanshe, 2003).
10. By 1999, the gross output value of foreign manufacturing firms in
    Guangdong Province was nearly five times higher than the respective
    output in Zhejiang Province. *China Statistical Yearbook 2000* (Beijing:
    China Statistics Press, 2000), table 13-5.
11. Huang, *Peasant Family,* 25.
12. Alan P. L. Liu, "The 'Wenzhou Model' of Development and China's
    Modernization," *Asian Survey* 32 (1992): 696–711; Kristin Parris, "Local
    Initiative and National Reform: The Wenzhou Model of Development,"
    China Quarterly 134 (1993): 242–263; Susan H. Whiting, *Power and Wealth
    in Rural China: The Political Economy of Institutional Change* (Cambridge:
    Cambridge University Press, 2000).
13. Jean C. Oi, "Fiscal Reform and the Economic Foundations of Local State
    Corporatism in China," *World Politics* 45 (October 1992): 99–126.
14. Nationwide, TVEs received about ¥96 billion of credit in 1989. This was
    about thirty times the amount of credit available for individual and private
    firms in the same year, and more than ten times the total value of registered
    capital of private firms. *China Statistical Yearbook 1990* (Beijing: China Statistics
    Press, 1990); *China Statistical Yearbook 2004* (Beijing: China Statistics Press,
    2004).

15. Yasheng Huang, *Capitalism with Chinese Characteristics: Entrepreneurship and the State* (Cambridge: Cambridge University Press, 2008), 264; Jianjun Zhang, "Marketization, Class Structure, and Democracy in China: Contrasting Regional Experiences," *Democratization* 14 (2007): 425–445.

16. Huang, *Capitalism with Chinese Characteristics,* 82.

17. *Statistical Yearbook 2003* (Beijing: China Statistics Press, 2003), 447; Shahid Yusuf, Kaoru Nabeshima, and Dwight H. Perkins, *Under New Ownership: Privatizing China's State-Owned Enterprises* (Stanford, CA: Stanford University Press, 2006).

18. See Appendix 2, Interview 53.

19. Bureau of Industry and Commerce.

20. Liu, "'Wenzhou Model.'"

21. Kellee Tsai, *Back Alley Banking: Private Entrepreneurs in China* (Ithaca, NY: Cornell University Press, 2002).

22. Huang, *Capitalism with Chinese Characteristics;* Parris, "Local Initiative and National Reform."

23. Liu, "'Wenzhou Model.'"

24. Tsai, *Back Alley Banking.*

25. Calculation based on data from *Wenzhou Statistical Yearbook 1999* (Beijing: China Statistics Press, 1999), 277, and *Wenzhou Statistical Yearbook 2004* (Beijing: China Statistics Press, 2004), 30.

26. Zhang, "Marketization"; Tetsushi Sonobe, Dinghuan Hu, and Keijiro Otsuka, "From Inferior to Superior Products: An Inquiry into the Wenzhou Model of Industrial Development in China," *Journal of Comparative Economics* 32 (2004): 542–563.

27. Parris, "Local Initiative and National Reform"; Shi, Huang, He, and Yan, *Zhong xiao jinrong Jigou.*

28. Liu, "'Wenzhou Model'"; Zhang, "Marketization"; William MacNamara, "How to Get Ahead in Wenzhou," *Far Eastern Economic Review* 169 (2006): 32–37.

29. Liu, "'Wenzhou Model.'"

30. Ningbo Municipal People's Government, http://english.ningbo.gov.cn/art /2010/3/29/art_87_310152.html (accessed July 23, 2011).

31. Godfrey Firth, "Critical Eye on Ningbo," *China Business Review* 32 (2005): 32–35.

32. Dali L. Yang, *Remaking the Chinese Leviathan: Market Transition and the Politics of Governance in China* (Stanford, CA: Stanford University Press, 2004).

33. Jacques Gernet, *Daily Life in China on the Eve of the Mongol Invasion, 1250–1276* (Stanford, CA: Stanford University Press, 1962).

34. Sally Sargeson and Jianjun Zhang, "Reassessing the Role of the Local State: A Case Study of Local Government Interventions in Property Rights Reform in a Hangzhou District," *China Journal* 42 (1999): 77–99.

35. The ranking is based on factors like market size, transportation infrastructure, quality of labor force, business costs, and success in attracting private investment.

36. Peter MacInnis and Ruji Ma, "Nanjing Set Its Sights on 2000," *China Business Review* January–February 1995.

37. Yang, *Remaking the Chinese Leviathan.*

38. *China Statistical Yearbook 2003* (Beijing: China Statistics Press, 2003), 204.

39. *Nantong Statistical Yearbook 2007,* 447 and 470, accessed via China Data Online, http://chinadataonline.org/.

40. Whiting, *Power and Wealth in Rural China.*

41. Deborah S. Davis, "Self-Employment in Shanghai: A Research Note," *China Quarterly* 157 (March 1999): 22–43.

42. Huang, *Capitalism with Chinese Characteristics.*

43. The city government of Shanghai formally excluded private firms from bids in the Pudong Development Zone. See Xinxin Li, "Development of the Private Economy: Problems and Countermeasures," *Jingji Yanjiu* 1994, in *JPRS-CAR-94-001* (October 1994): 48.

44. If, for instance, the goal was to interview fifteen pharmaceutical companies in Shanghai, it was assumed that a pool of 7×15 (105) companies would suffice to generate fifteen completed interviews. Given a total number of 683 pharmaceutical companies falling into our sampling frame in Shanghai, every sixth (that is, 683/105) company listed in the firm register was drawn into the sampling pool (based on a randomly drawn starting number, this would include for instance firms #3, #9, #15 . . .).

45. I.e., (1) private firm legal status, (2) that the company was founded at least three years ago, and (3) that the company had a minimum of ten employees.

46. MSR originally was the survey research unit of the Shanghai Academy of Social Sciences. After we began our study, MSR privatized and is now registered as the Shanghai Yihong Business Consulting Co., Ltd.

47. The ratio between completed interviews and the total number of contacted firms is 28.1 percent in Shanghai, 16.1 percent in Nanjing, 36.9 percent in Nantong, 35.0 percent in Changzhou, 16.1 percent in Hangzhou, 26.9 percent in Wenzhou, and 35.6 percent in Ningbo.

48. Among 175 studies published in the years 1975, 1985, and 1995 in top-tier academic journals in management and behavioral studies, there is a norm value of 35.5 percent +/–13.3 for surveys involving top management, whereas mean values in non-Western societies tend to be lower. See Yehua Baruch, "Response Rate in Academic Studies—A Comparative Analysis," *Human Relations* 52 (1999): 421–438.

49. The number of employees is not a perfect cross-sector measure of size, but it is at least a transparent indicator. Alternatively using production value, the total number of medium and large firms would be somewhat larger.

50. Some performance measures serve as outcome variables to explore the impact of different strategic and behavioral choices of the entrepreneurs. Other measures serve as control variables to avoid confounding effects when it comes to the analysis of micro-strategies.

51. These training workshops included detailed discussions of the survey modules, trial interviews, and role-play situations that helped to standardize interviewer behavior. Most importantly, the interviewers were trained to refrain from providing additional information and leading statements that might have influenced responses by the interviewee. Role-play situations were conducted to highlight inappropriate responses or behavior during the interview process, such as value statements of approval or disapproval by the interviewer. Detailed written material specifying procedural and behavioral guidelines to be honored during the interview process was taken to the field. To assure proper implementation of the survey, the team supervisor maintained close contact with all interviewers in the field, held daily team meetings, and also made follow-up phone calls with each interviewee to assure that the interviews were conducted at a high-quality level and to the interviewee's satisfaction. The authors were in close contact with the team supervisors during the whole survey process.

52. The data sets and complete questionnaires are available at http://www.enterprisesurveys.org/.

53. The sample covers the following cities: Beijing, Tianjin, Benxi, Dalian, Changchun, Harbin, Chengdu, Shanghai, Hangzhou, Wenzhou, Guangzhou, Shenzhen, Jiangmen, Nanchang, Zhenzhou, Wuhan, Changsha, Nanning, Guiyang, Chongqing, Kunming, Xian, and Lanzhou.

54. Robert Cull and L. Colin Xu, "Institutions, Ownership, and Finance: The Determinants of Profit Reinvestment among Chinese Firms," *Journal of Financial Economics* 77 (2005): 117–146.

4. Entrepreneurs and Institutional Innovation

1. Douglass C. North and Barry R. Weingast, "Constitutions and Commitment: The Evolution of Institutions Governing Public Choice in Seventeenth-Century England," *Journal of Economic History* 49 (1989): 824.

2. Gregory Clark, "The Political Foundations of Modern Economic Growth: England, 1540–1800," *Journal of Interdisciplinary History* 26 (1996): 588.

3. Joel Mokyr, "Entrepreneurship and the Industrial Revolution in Britain," in David Landes, Joel Mokyr, and William J. Baumol, eds., *The Invention of Enterprise* (Princeton, NJ: Princeton University Press, 2010), 188–189.

4. Winifred B. Rothenberg, "The Emergence of a Capital Market in Rural Massachusetts, 1730–1838," *Journal of Economic History* 45 (1985): 781–808.

5. Ibid., 806.

6. Ibid., 782.

7. Joseph A. Schumpeter, *Theorie der wirtschaftlichen Entwicklung: Nach. 1. Auflage von 1912* (Berlin: Duncker & Humblot, [1912] 2006), 147. Translation by Sonja Opper.

8. Joseph A. Schumpeter, *Kapitalismus, Sozialismus und Demokratie* (Tübingen: A. Francke Verlag, [1942] 2005), 214. Translation by Sonja Opper.

9. Ibid., 137, 214, and 226.

10. Schumpeter, *Theorie der wirtschaftlichen Entwicklung*, 187.

11. Schumpeter, *Kapitalismus, Sozialismus und Demokratie*, 215.

12. David C. McClelland, *The Achieving Society* (Princeton, NJ: Van Nostrand, 1961).

13. Peter Kilby, *Entrepreneurship and Economic Development* (New York: Free Press, 1971).

14. Richard Swedberg, "The Social Science View of Entrepreneurship," in *Entrepreneurship*, ed. Richard Swedberg (New Delhi: Oxford University Press, 2000), 7–44.

15. Robert M. Solow, "On Macroeconomic Models of Free-Market Innovation and Growth," in *Entrepreneurship, Innovation, and the Growth Mechanism of the Free-Enterprise Economies*, ed. Eytan Sheshinksi, Robert J. Strom, and William J. Baumol (Princeton, NJ: Princeton University Press, 2007), 16.

16. Paul M. Romer, "Increasing Returns and Long-Run Growth," *Journal of Political Economy* 94 (1986): 1002–1038; Philippe Aghion and Peter Howitt, *Endogenous Growth Theory* (Cambridge, MA: MIT Press, 1998).

17. William J. Baumol, *The Free-Market Innovation Machine: Analyzing the Growth Miracle of Capitalism* (Princeton, NJ: Princeton University Press, 2002).

18. Solow, "On Macroeconomic Models," 18.

19. Social scientists have examined endogenous institutional change in a wide range of institutional contexts using the case study method. These studies provide fine-grained accounts of how economic and organizational actors construct in local contexts the institutional arrangements needed to capture gains from trade and to secure legitimacy for the new organizational practices. See Howard E. Aldrich and Martha Martinez, "Entrepreneurship as Social Construction: A Multi-Level Evolutionary Approach," in *Handbook of Entrepreneurship Research*, ed. Zoltan J. Acs and David B. Audretsch (Berlin: Springer, 2003), 359–399; Jeanette A. Colyvas and Walter W. Powell, "Road to Institutionalization: The Remaking of Boundaries between Public and Private Science," *Research in Organizational Behavior* 27 (2006): 305–353; Avner Greif and David D. Laitin, "A Theory of Endogenous Institutional Change," *American Political Science Review* 98 (2004): 633–652.

20. Max Weber, *The Protestant Ethic and the Spirit of Capitalism*, [1904] 2006). Translation by Talcott Parsons (New York: Scribner, 1930).

21. Ibid., 54–55.

.oid., 67–68.

4. Ibid., 69.

25. See Appendix 2, Interview 66.

26. See ibid., Interviews 71 and 75.

27. Data based on 2000 Population Census; *China Statistical Yearbook 2004* (Beijing: China Statistics Press, 2004).

28. Frank H. Knight, *Risk, Uncertainty and Profit* (Boston: Houghton Mifflin, 1921), 225.

29. Ibid., 226.

30. See Appendix 2, Interview 67.

31. Richard E. Kihlstrom and Jean-Jacques Laffont, "A General-Equilibrium Entrepreneurial Theory of Firm Formation Based on Risk Aversion," *Journal of Political Economy* 87 (1979): 719–748.

32. Håkan Holm, Sonja Opper, and Victor Nee, "Entrepreneurs under Uncertainty: An Economic Experiment," Scandinavian Working Paper Series in Economics 2012: 4; Daniel Ellsberg, "Risk, Ambiguity, and the Savage Axioms," *Quarterly Journal of Economics* 75 (1961): 643–669.

33. Zhonghe Guo, "Wo Guo geti siying Qiye Jianxi" [A brief analysis of China's individual and private firms], *Jingji Yanjiu Cankao* (1993): 24–34; *China Statistical Yearbook 1981* (Beijing: China Statistics Press, 1981).

34. Dwight H. Perkins, *Market Control and Planning in Communist China* (Cambridge, MA: Harvard University Press, 1966); Susan L. Shirk, "The Politics of Industrial Reform," in *The Political Economy of Reform in Post-Mao China*, ed. Elizabeth J. Perry and Christine Wong (Cambridge, MA: Harvard University Press, 1985), 195–221. During the pre-reform period, investment in heavy industry was between 5.6 times (in the first five-year plan from 1952 to 1957) and 11.7 times (between 1963 and 1965) as high as in light industry. Based on *China Statistical Yearbook 1993* (Beijing: China Statistics Press, 1993).

35. Wm. Theodore de Bary, "On Top of 'Bottom-Up Development,'" manuscript, Department of East Asian Languages and Culture, Columbia University, 2011. See also "Confucianism in the Early Tokugawa Period," *Sources of Japanese Tradition*, vol. 3, ed. Ryusaku Tsunoda, Wm. Theodore de Bary, and Donald Keene (New York: Columbia University Press, 1958), 28–41, 66–67, 256; Wm. Theodore de Bary, *Neo-Confucian Orthodoxy and the Learning of the Mind and Heart* (New York: Columbia University Press, 1981), 189–215.

36. See Appendix 2, Interview 13.

37. See ibid., Interview 12.

38. See ibid., Interview 42.

39. Interview conducted by Horizon Ltd. in Hangzhou on June 23, 2005.

40. See Appendix 2, Interview 42.

41. See ibid., Interview 100.

42. See ibid., Interview 13.

43. See ibid., Interview 72.

44. See ibid., Interview 69.

45. See ibid., Interview 21.

46. See ibid., Interview 100.

47. Xinxin Li, "Gaige kaifanghou de Zhongguo sying Jingji" [China's private economy after the reform and opening], *Jingji Yanjiu Cankao* (December 1, 1994): 2–16.

48. See Appendix 2, Interview 54.

49. See ibid., Interview 53.

50. See ibid., Interview 10.

51. See ibid., Interview 65.

52. See ibid., Interview 53.

53. See ibid., Interview 56.

54. See ibid., Interview 62.

55. See ibid., Interview 101.

56. See ibid., Interview 63.

57. *Zhejiang Ribao*, July 27, 2009.

58. Alfred **R.** Oxenfeldt, *New Firms and Free Enterprise: Pre–War and Post–War Aspects* (Washington, DC: American Council on Public Affairs, 1943); see also Ivan H. Light, *Ethnic Enterprise in America: Business and Welfare among Chinese, Japanese, and Blacks* (Berkeley: University of California Press, 1968).

59. First, government-mandated interest rate ceilings do not allow banks to flexibly adjust interest rates to accommodate the higher business risks involved in loans to start-up firms. Second, the Loan Guarantee Law (1995) specifies a high mandatory self-funding rate of 60 percent. Also, bank rules do not accept private homes or factory buildings as collateral for loans, and in any case, many entrepreneurs rent their factory buildings and machinery. See Huang, *Capitalism with Chinese Characteristics*. Finally, banks generally reject natural persons as guarantors of business loans. The regulatory environment of state-owned banking has meant that the financial market remains one of China's least liberalized markets. See Susan H. Whiting, *Power and Wealth in Rural China: The Political Economy of Institutional Change* (Cambridge: Cambridge University Press, 2000). Aggregate lending data confirm the precariousness of private sector access to formal credit. In 2007, only a percentage point increase from 1984. State-owned bank lending to private firms was even lower, with approximately 0.7 percent of total loans granted to private firms or self-employed entities. See *China Statistical Yearbook, 2005* (Beijing: China Statistics Press, 2008); *China Financial Statistics (1949–2005)* (Beijing: China Finance Press, 2007).

60. *China Financial Statistics (1949–2005)* (Beijing: China Finance Press, 2007).

...id Yusuf, Kaoru Nabeshima, and Dwight H. Perkins, *Under New Ownership: Privatizing China's State-Owned Enterprises* (Stanford, CA: Stanford University Press, 2006).

62. Although the law explicitly called for the provision of local financial support and service systems to assist the founding and development of small and medium-size enterprises, local implementation remains weak. See Andrew Atherton, "From 'Fat Pigs' and 'Red Hats' to a New Social Stratum: The Changing Face of Enterprise Development Policy in China," *Journal of Small Business and Enterprise Development* 14 (2008): 640–655.

63. Pei, *China's Trapped Transition*, 116.

64. In responding to the global economic crisis, when a rapid decline in global consumer demand was affecting all sectors of the industrial economy, the central government in 2008 announced a massive economic stimulus program of $585 billion. Relative to China's gross national product, the stimulus program was the largest of the major economies. The government channeled the stimulus money to state-owned banks, which in turn extended a torrent of low-interest credit to local governments to support mega-infrastructure projects and to state-owned enterprises. Support for private firms, in contrast, came primarily in the form of a promise to fight discrimination against them—for instance, in the form of the so-called three disorders *(san luan),* the arbitrary collection of fees, fines, and expenses by city and township government authorities, a practice still fairly common. In addition, the government reduced registration fees and administrative fees for newly founded private firms, and called for a broader specification of acceptable collateral in loans to private firms. *Renmin Ribao,* August 2, 2009. Notwithstanding these measures, private firms still are virtually excluded from direct support in the form of preferential access to low-interest loans, despite official figures showing that small and medium-size firms employed 75 percent of China's workers and produced 68 percent of the gross industrial product in 2008. Jason Leow, "Small Chinese Firms Struggle to Tap Banks," *Wall Street Journal* (May 14, 2009), A9.

Though private firms sought economic stimulus money, state-owned banks routinely rejected their loan applications. Instead, the massive economic stimulus provided a huge subsidy to local governments and large state-owned enterprises and public corporations. Not surprisingly, stimulus money has strengthened the state-owned and state-controlled firms, which have used credit lines for investments in the Shanghai and Shenzhen stock exchanges and for strategic acquisitions, ranging from buying promising domestic private firms to purchasing shares of foreign corporations and mines at prices heavily discounted by deflationary pressure from the global economic crisis.

65. Leow, "Small Chinese Firms."

66. Houyi Zhang, *Zhongguo de siying Jingji yu siying Qiyezhu* [China's private firm economy and company owners] (Beijing: Zhishi Chubanshe, 1995), 385.

67. Shadow loans and off-balance-sheet bank lending have soared recently, as they provide borrowers with more flexible loan procedures and offer lenders a higher rate of return than traditional savings accounts. Since September 30, 2011, however, China's Banking Regulatory Commission has tightened control over this type of informal lending to bring down inflation. See Linglin Wei, "China Cracks Down on Informal Lending," *Wall Street Journal*, October 15, 2011. http://online.wsj.com/article/SB10001424052970 20400230457663005047138610.html (accessed October 17, 2011).

68. See Appendix 2, Interview 65.

69. See ibid., Interview 32.

70. See ibid., Interview 21.

71. A survey conducted in Jiangsu and Zhejiang Provinces suggests that by the year 2000, private sources provided 76 percent of total private firm capital. See Pei, *China's Trapped Transition*, 116. In Wenzhou, the estimated volume of informal sources of finance surpassed ¥100 billion in 2000, a sum larger than the total savings and deposits of Wenzhou's state-owned banks. See Kellee Tsai, *Capitalism without Democracy: The Private Sector in Contemporary China* (Ithaca, NY: Cornell University Press, 2007), 176.

72. Frederik Balfour and Dexter Roberts, "The Leak in China's Banking System," *Business Week* (November 15, 2004): 67.

73. Leow, "Small Chinese Firms."

74. Kellee Tsai, *Back Alley Banking: Private Entrepreneurs in China* (Ithaca, NY: Cornell University Press, 2002).

75. See Appendix 2, Interview 27.

76. See ibid., Interview 21.

77. See ibid., Interview 37.

78. See ibid., Interview 37.

79. See ibid., Interview 23.

80. See ibid., Interview 101.

81. Leow, "Small Chinese Firms."

5. Legitimacy and Organizational Change

1. William C. Kirby, "China Unincorporated: Company Law and Business Enterprise in Twentieth-Century China," *Journal of Asian Studies* 54 (1995): 56.

2. Partnership companies and limited liability companies were not clearly defined. See Yi-Min Lin, *Between Politics and Markets: Firms, Competition, and Institutional Change in Post-Mao China* (Cambridge: Cambridge University Press, 2001), 29.

3. Susan Young, "Wealth but Not Security: Attitudes towards Private Business in China in the 1980s," *Australian Journal of Chinese Affairs* 25 (1991): 123.

4. The Central Committee Document no. 1 (1983) established shareholding cooperatives with at least two shareholders as a legitimate organizational

form. See Susan H. Whiting, "The Regional Evolution of Ownership Forms: Shareholding Cooperatives and Rural Industry in Shanghai and Wenzhou," in *Property Rights and Economic Reform in China,* ed. Jean C. Oi and Andrew G. Walder (Stanford, CA: Stanford University Press, 1999), 171–200.

5. Susan H. Whiting, *Power and Wealth in Rural China: The Political Economy of Institutional Change* (Cambridge: Cambridge University Press, 2000); Kellee Tsai, *Capitalism without Democracy: The Private Sector in Contemporary China* (Ithaca, NY: Cornell University Press, 2007).

6. Whiting, "Regional Evolution of Ownership Forms"; Jean Oi, *Rural China Takes Off: Institutional Foundations of Economic Reform* (Berkeley: University of California Press, 1999).

7. Whiting, "Regional Evolution of Ownership Forms."

8. For a detailed review of the case, refer to Huang, *Capitalism with Chinese Characteristics,* 69–72.

9. *Report on the Development of China's Private Enterprises No. 6, 2005* (Beijing: Social Sciences Academic Press, 2005), 246.

10. Paul DiMaggio and Walter W. Powell, "The Iron Cage Revisited: Institutional Isomorphism and Collective Rationality in Organizational Fields," *American Journal of Sociology* 48 (1983): 149.

11. William A. Klein and John C. Coffee, Jr., *Business Organization and Finance: Legal and Economic Principles,* 10th ed. (New York: Foundation Press, 2007).

12. Howard E. Aldrich and Martin Ruef, *Organizations Evolving* (London; Thousand Oaks, CA: Sage, 1999).

13. Victor Nee, "Organizational Dynamics of Market Transition: Hybrid Forms, Property Rights, and Mixed Economy in China," *Administrative Science Quarterly* 37 (1992): 1–27.

14. John W. Meyer and Brian Rowan, "Institutionalized Organizations: Formal Structure as Myth and Ceremony," *American Journal of Sociology* 83 (1977): 340–363; DiMaggio and Powell, "Iron Cage Revisited"; W. Richard Scott, *Institutions and Organizations* (Thousand Oaks, CA: Sage, 2001); Michael T. Hannan and John Freeman, *Organizational Ecology* (Cambridge, MA: Harvard University Press, 1989).

15. Arthur L. Stinchcombe, "Organizations and Social Structure," in *Handbook of Organizations,* ed. James G. March (Chicago: Rand-McNally, 1965), 153–193.

16. Young, "Wealth but Not Security."

17. Howard E. Aldrich and C. Marlene Fiol, "Fools Rush In? The Institutional Context of Industry Creation," *Academy of Management Review* 19 (1994): 645–670.

18. Elisabeth Clemens, "Organizational Repertoires and Institutional Changes: Women's Groups and the Transformation of U.S. Politics, 1890–1920," *American Journal of Sociology* 98 (1993): 755–798.

19. Jitendra V. Singh, Robert J. House, and David J. Tucker, "Organizational Change and Organizational Mortality," *Administrative Science Quarterly* 31 (1986): 587–611.

20. Mark Suchman, "Managing Legitimacy: Strategic and Institutional Approaches," *Academy of Management Review* 20 (1995): 571–610; Aldrich and Ruef, *Organizations Evolving.*

21. Glenn R. Carroll, "A Sociological View on Why Firms Differ," *Strategic Management Journal* 14 (1993): 237–249.

22. Jacques Delacroix and Hayagreeva Rao, "Externalities and Ecological Theory: Unbundling Density Dependence," in *Evolutionary Dynamics of Organizations,* ed. Joel A. C. Baum and Jitendra V. Singh (Oxford: Oxford University Press, 1994), 255–268.

23. A study of footwear production in the United States between 1940 and 1989 illustrates how geographically concentrated industries allow a higher level of tacit learning. See Olav Sorenson and Pino G. Audia, "The Social Structure of Entrepreneurial Activity: Geographic Concentration of Footwear Production in the United States, 1940–1989," *American Journal of Sociology* 106 (2000): 424–461.

24. Michael T. Hannan and John Freeman, "Where Do Organizational Forms Come From?" *Sociological Forum* 1 (1986): 50–72.

25. Sonja Opper, *Zwischen Political Governance und Corporate Governance: Eine institutionelle Analyse chinesischer Aktiengesellschaften* (Baden-Baden: Nomos Verlagsgesellschaft, 2004); Donald C. Clarke, "Corporate Governance in China: An Overview," *China Economic Review* 148 (2003): 494–507.

26. On the importance of political interests in shaping national corporate goverance systems, see Neil Fligstein, *The Transformation of Corporate Control* (Cambridge, Mass,: Harvard University Press, 1990).

27. Victor Nee and Sonja Opper, "On Politicized Capitalism," in *On Capitalism,* ed. Victor Nee and Richard Swedberg (Princeton, NJ: Princeton University Press, 2007), 93–127.

28. Doug Guthrie, *Dragon in a Three-Piece Suit: The Emergence of Capitalism in China* (Princeton, NJ: Princeton University Press, 1999).

29. Not until the 2006 revision of the Company Law were the capital requirements substantially reduced, to ¥30,000 for LLCs with more than one shareholder, and to ¥100,000 for LLCs with only one shareholder. This single-person LLC was introduced then, as a new legal form.

30. Baoshu Wang and Hui Huang, "China's New Company and Securities Law: An Overview and Assessment," *Australian Journal of Corporate Law* 19 (2006): 229–242.

31. All the more so as legalization of companies operating as natural persons lagged behind. The first "Partnership Enterprise Law" was not passed until 1997 (later amended in 2007), followed by the "Sole Proprietorship Enterprise Law" in 2000. The initial taxation rules, however, reinforced the

disadvantaged position of companies operating as natural persons. According to the Partnership Law, for instance, the partnership was taxed as an enterprise, and the individual partners were taxed again on their income. Implications and liabilities in case of bankruptcy remained unclear.

32. *Report on the Development of China's Private Enterprises No. 6, 2005* (Beijing: Social Sciences Academic Press, 2005), 246.
33. See Appendix 2, Interview 77.
34. See ibid., Interview 79.
35. See ibid., Interview 107; Lisa A. Keister, *Chinese Business Groups: The Structure and Impact of Interfirm Relations during Economic Development* (Oxford: Oxford University Press, 2000).
36. See ibid., Interview 84.
37. See ibid., Interview 83.
38. See ibid., Interview 77.
39. We cannot rule out some reverse endogeneity. Individuals with higher status assessments may simply choose to incorporate instead of running a single-proprietor business.
40. Meyer and Rowan, "Institutionalized Organizations."
41. Victor Nee, Sonja Opper, and Sonia Wong, "Developmental State and Corporate Governance in China," *Management and Organization Review* 3 (2007): 19–53.
42. See Appendix 2, Interview 77.
43. See ibid., Interview 81.
44. See ibid., Interview 79.
45. See ibid., Interview 85.
46. See ibid., Interview 80.
47. See ibid., Interview 46.

6. Industrial Clusters and Competitive Advantage

1. Michael Porter, *The Competitive Advantage of Nations* (London: Macmillan, 1990).
2. For discussion of similar patterns of adaptive and flexible craft production in Germany, Italy, and Japan, see Michael Piore and Charles Sabel, *The Second Industrial Divide* (New York: Basic Books, 1984).
3. See Appendix 2, Interview 66.
4. For a case study of the rise of the garment cluster in Zhili Township in Zhejiang Province, see Belton M. Fleisher, Dinghuan Hu, William McGuire, and Xiaobo Zhang, "The Evolution of an Industrial Cluster in China," working papers from Ohio State University, Department of Economics, No. 09-05 (2009).
5. See Appendix 2, Interview 100.
6. Zhenming Sun and Martin Perry, "The Role of Trading Cities in the Development of Chinese Business Cluster," *International Business Research* 1 (2008): 69–81.

7. Paul Krugman, "Increasing Returns and Economic Geography," *Journal of Political Economy* 99 (1991): 483–499. In the United States as of the 1990s, 380 industrial clusters employed 57 percent of the total workforce, producing 61 percent of national output. See Stuart A. Rosenfeld, "United States: Business Clusters," in *Networks of Enterprises and Local Development,* ed. OECD (Paris: Organization for Economic Cooperation and Development, Territorial Development Service, 1996).

8. Others have pointed to a different causal sequence. Despite the ubiquitous spread of industrial clusters for almost all industries, there is little indication that entrepreneurs consistently choose their location based on factor endowments or transportation costs. See Glenn Ellison and Edward L. Glaeser, "Geographic Concentration in U.S. Manufacturing Industries: A Dartboard Approach," *Journal of Political Economy* 105 (1997): 889–927. Instead, studies on entrepreneurship find that entrepreneurs tend to invest locally in their home environment. See George Katona and James N. Morgan, "The Quantitative Study of Factors Determining Business Decisions," *Quarterly Journal of Economics* 66 (1952): 67–90; Eva Mueller and James N. Morgan, "Locational Decisions of Manufacturers," *American Economic Review: Papers and Proceedings,* 52 (1962): 204–217; Arnold C. Cooper and William C. Dunkelberg, "Entrepreneurial Research: Old Questions, New Answers and Methodological Issues," *American Journal of Small Business* 1 (1987): 11–23. In a study of the development of manufacturing clusters in the United States from 1972 to 1992, dynamic analysis indicates that the stability of industrial clusters does not result from a larger inflow of new firms searching for favorable production conditions. In fact, firm start-ups would have been sufficiently dispersed to reduce geographic concentration. Instead, the stability of industrial clusters can be linked to lower rates of firm closure than observed in other locations, a finding current economic theory cannot fully account for. See Guy Dumais, Glenn Ellison, and Edward L. Glaeser, "Geographic Concentration as a Dynamic Process," *Review of Economics and Statistics* 84 (2002): 193–204.

9. AnnaLee Saxenian, *Regional Advantage: Culture and Competition in Silicon Valley and Route 128* (Cambridge, MA: Harvard University Press, 1994), 44.

10. Ibid. See also Walter W. Powell, Kenneth W. Koput, and Laurel Smith-Doerr, "Interorganizational Collaboration and the Locus of Innovation: Networks of Learning in Biotechnology," *Administrative Science Quarterly* 41 (1996): 116–145; Toby E. Stuart and Joel M. Podolny, "Local Search and the Evolution of Technological Capabilities," *Strategic Management Journal* 17 (1996): 21–38; Joel M. Podolny, Toby E. Stuart, and Michael T. Hannan, "Networks, Knowledge, and Niches: Competition in the Worldwide Semiconductor Industry, 1984–1991," *American Journal of Sociology* 102 (1996): 659–689.

11. Alfred Marshall, *Principles of Economics,* 8th ed. (London: Macmillan, 1920), 225.

12. Michael Storper and Anthony J. Venables, "Buzz: Face-to-Face Contact and the Urban Economy," *Journal of Economic Geography* 4 (2004): 352.

13. Edward L. Glaeser, "The Future of Urban Research: Nonmarket Interactions," *Brookings-Wharton Papers on Urban Affairs* 1 (2000): 104. See also Edward Glaeser and Joshua D. Gottlieb, "The Wealth of Cities: Agglomeration Economies and Spatial Equilibrium in the United States," *Journal of Economic Literature* 47 (2009): 983–1028.

14. Brian Uzzi, "The Sources and Consequences of Embeddedness for the Economic Performance of Organizations: The Network Effect," *American Sociological Review* 61 (1996): 176. See also John Humphrey and Hubert Schmitz, "Trust and Interfirm Relations in Developing and Transition Economies," *Journal of Development Studies* 34 (1998): 32–61; Khalid Nadvi, "Shifting Ties: Social Networks in the Surgical Instrument Cluster of Sialkot, Pakistan," *Development and Change* 30 (1999): 143–177.

15. Harrison C. White, *Markets from Networks: Socioeconomic Models of Production* (Princeton, NJ: Princeton University Press, 2002), 7.

16. See Appendix 2, Interview 90.

17. See ibid., Interview 37.

18. Tetsushi Sonobe, Dinghuan Hu, and Keijiro Otsuka, "From Inferior to Superior Products: An Inquiry into the Wenzhou Model of Industrial Development in China," *Journal of Comparative Economics* 32 (2004): 542–563.

19. The players in a niche with access to a more diverse set of activities and more experience at working together are better able to locate themselves in information-rich positions. See Powell, Koput, and Smith-Doerr, "Interorganizational Collaboration."

20. See Appendix 2, Interview 23.

21. Industries with higher dependence on trade credit realize higher growth rates in countries with weaker financial institutions. See Raymond Fisman and Inessa Love, "Trade Credit, Financial Intermediary Development, and Industry Growth," *Journal of Finance* 58 (2003): 353–374.

22. See Appendix 2, Interview 92.

23. See ibid., Interview 100.

24. Mitchell Petersen and Raghuram Rajan, "Trade Credit: Theories and Evidence," *Review of Financial Studies* 10 (1997): 661–691.

25. Robert Cull, L. Colin Xu, and Tian Zhu, "Formal Finance and Trade Credit during China's Transition," *Journal of Financial Intermediation* 18 (2009): 173–192.

26. Case studies have emphasized the importance of trade credit in China's industrial clusters. See Zuhui Huang, Xiaobo Zhang, and Yunwei Zhu, "The Role of Clustering in Rural Industrialization: A Case Study of the Footwear

Industry in Wenzhou," *China Economic Review* 19 (2008): 409–420; Jianqing Ruan and Xiaobo Zhang, "Finance and Cluster-Based Industrial Development in China," *Economic Development and Cultural Change* 58 (2009): 143–164. A quantitative study using national census data from 1995 and 2004 confirms that clustering is indeed accompanied by a more frequent use of trade credit, which helps reduce reliance on external finance. Clustering also helps create more nonstate establishments in the same location. See Cheryl Long and Xiaobo Zhang, "Cluster-Based Industrialization in China: Financing and Performance," *Journal of International Economics* 84 (2011): 112–123.

27. Stewart Macaulay, "Non-Contractual Relations in Business: A Preliminary Study," *American Sociological Review* 28 (1963): 62.

28. Ibid.

29. Camille Schuster, "How to Manage a Contract in China," *Business Credit* 107 (2005): 69.

30. Patricia Pattison and Daniel Herron, "The Mountains Are High and the Emperor Is Far Away: Sanctity of Contract in China," *American Business Law Journal* 40 (2003): 459–510.

31. See Appendix 2, Interview 38.

32. Our findings are consistent with a study of private companies in Nanjing and Shanghai conducted between 2002 and 2004 reporting that 92.8 percent of the interviewed firms typically rely on direct negotiations to resolve a business dispute. See Donald Clarke, Peter Murrell, and Susan Whiting, "The Role of Law in China's Economic Development," in *China's Great Transformation,* ed. Loren Brandt and Thomas G. Rawski (Cambridge: Cambridge University Press, 2008), 375–428.

33. See Appendix 2, Interview 87.

34. When asked about this in a slightly more general form, 74 percent of respondents in Shanghai and Nanjing (2002–2004) believed that other firms would learn about potential business disputes with suppliers. Clarke, Murrell, and Whiting, "Role of Law."

35. See Appendix 2, Interview 92.

36. See ibid., Interview 97.

37. See ibid., Interview 102.

38. See ibid., Interview 100.

39. The extent to which producers rely on local suppliers is only weakly negatively correlated (−0.07) with firm size (measured by total assets).

40. See Appendix 2, Interview 92.

41. See ibid., Interview 100.

42. See ibid., Interview 110.

43. Compared to their collective and state-owned competitors, private entrepreneurs typically show a much higher commitment to liberal markets and competition. This is confirmed by national statistics documenting the

attitudes of firm managers over time. In 2001, for instance, 44 percent of managers running nonstate companies perceived China's accession to the WTO as beneficial for their individual firm development. In contrast, only 31 percent of public firm managers welcomed China's increasing market integration with the global economy. Lan Li, *Zhongguo Qiyejia Chengzhan 15 Nian* [15 years' growth of Chinese entrepreneurs], Vol. 1 (Beijing: China Machine Press, 2009), 77.

44. "Producers learn and are pressured to huddle together as an industry such that their key cues come from their fellow producers who face the same opaque diversity of buyers and who offer differentiated products filling distinct niches." White, *Markets from Networks*, 7.

45. See Appendix 2, Interview 87.

46. See ibid., Interview 93.

47. See ibid., Interview 90.

48. Donald N. Sull, *Made in China* (Cambridge, MA: Harvard Business School Press, 2005), 137.

49. See Appendix 2, Interview 102.

50. See ibid., Interview 97.

7. The Development of Labor Markets

1. Victor Nee and Su Sijin, "Institutional Change and Economic Growth in China: The View from the Villages," *Journal of Asian Studies* 49 (1990): 3–25.

2. *China Statistical Yearbook 2007* (Beijing: China Statistics Press, 2007), table 13-6.

3. Justin Yifu Lin, "The Household Responsibility System in China's Agricultural Reform: A Theoretical and Empirical Study," *Economic Development and Cultural Change* 36 (1988): S199–224; John McMillan, John Whalley, and Lijing Zhu, "The Impact of China's Economic Reforms on Agricultural Productivity Growth," *Journal of Political Economy* 97 (1989): 781–807.

4. Jeffrey R. Taylor, "Rural Employment Trends and the Legacy of Surplus Labour, 1978–1986," *China Quarterly* 116 (1986): 736–766; Fang Tian and Fatang Lin, *Zhongguo Renkou Qianyi* [Population migration in China] (Beijing: Zhishi chubanshe, 1986).

5. This allowed an annual cereal production of only 233 pounds to 815 pounds per person. See *China Statistical Yearbook 2008* (Beijing: China Statistics Press, 2008), 473, 481.

6. Ching Kwan Lee, *Against the Law: Labor Protests in China's Rustbelt and Sunbelt* (Berkeley: University of California Press, 2007), 209.

7. Zhonggong Yanjiu, *Zhongguo Renkou yu jiuye Wenti* [China's population and employment problems] (Taibei, 1986).

8. Douglas Heckathorn, "Respondent-Driven Sampling II: Deriving Valid Population Estimates from Chain-Referral Samples of Hidden Populations," *Social Problems* 49 (2002): 11–34.

9. Douglas S. Massey, "Understanding Mexican Migration to the United States," *American Journal of Sociology* 92 (1987): 1372–1403.

10. Zun Tang, "Network Contingencies: Hiring and Job Search in China's Transitional Labor Market," unpublished PhD diss., Department of Sociology, Cornell University, 2007.

11. Douglas S. Massey, Joaquin Arango, Graeme Hugo, Ali Kouaouci, Adela Pellegrino, and J. Edward Taylor, *Worlds in Motion: Understanding International Migration at the End of the Millennium* (New York: Oxford University Press, 1998).

12. Tang, "Network Contingencies."

13. John Knight and Lina Song, *Towards a Labour Market in China* (Oxford: Oxford University Press, 2005), 174.

14. Andrew Scheineson, "China's Internal Migrants," *Council on Foreign Relations* (May 14, 2009), http://www.cfr.org/china/chinas-internal-migrants/p12943 (accessed July 27, 2011).

15. *China Labour Statistical Yearbook 2007* (Beijing: China Statistics Press, 2007), 301.

16. See Appendix 2, Interview 19.

17. See ibid., Interview 87.

18. See ibid., Interview 101.

19. William L. Parish, Xiaoye Zhe, and Fang Li, "Nonfarm Work and Marketization of the Chinese Countryside," *China Quarterly* 143 (1995): 697–730.

20. Li Ma, "The Making of the Chinese Working Class: Rural Migrants in Shanghai," unpublished PhD diss., Department of Sociology, Cornell University, 2010.

21. Baker & McKenzie, "China Employment Law Update," June 2011, http://www.bakermckenzie.com/files/Publication/0d7fe52e-7987-4a63-9bc4-fa21db8be2a8/Presentation/PublicationAttachment/0928b376-b7a9-43a3-8f34-071019dcf3af/nl_china_chinaemploymentlawupdate_jun11.pdf (accessed June 27, 2011).

22. Harry J. Holzer, "Hiring Procedures in the Firm: Their Economic Determinants and Outcomes," *National Bureau of Economic Research Working Paper* No. 2185 (1987); Karen E. Campbell and Peter V. Marsden, "Recruitment and Selection Processes: The Organizational Side of Job Searches," in *Social Mobility and Social Structure,* ed. Ronald L. Breiger (Cambridge: Cambridge University Press, 1990), 59–79.

23. See Appendix 2, Interview 96.

24. See ibid., Interview 32.

25. See ibid., Interview 90.

26. See ibid., Interview 22.

27. Albert Rees and George P. Shultz, *Workers in an Urban Labour Market* (Chicago: University of Chicago Press, 1970).

28. Mark Granovetter, *Getting a Job: A Study of Contacts and Careers* (Cambridge, MA: Harvard University Press, 1974), 11.

29. Acquiring *ex ante* information through social networks on potential candidates to recruit to positions requiring job-specific knowledge is consistent with transaction cost reasoning.

30. See Appendix 2, Interview 23.

31. See ibid., Interview 21.

32. Holzer, "Hiring Procedures in the Firm"; Curtis J. Simon and John T. Warner, "Matchmaker, Matchmaker: The Effect of Old Boy Networks on Job Match Quality, Earnings, and Tenure," *Journal of Labor Economics* 10 (1992): 306–330.

33. Technology-intensive companies in our survey—those that maintain R&D departments (42 percent) and those that already hold at least one patent (26 percent)—rely more on market recruitment of managers. We repeated the analysis reported in Table 7.2 using two-stage least-squares regressions, with R&D department and patent holdings as instruments for formal recruitment. The results paralleled those reported in Table 7.2, suggesting no need to change our conclusions.

34. Http://wenda.tiany.cn (accessed September 10, 2010). Similarly, safety provisions for workers in private firms are below those for workers in state-owned enterprises. See Lee, *Against the Law.*

35. In a large-scale survey conducted by the Ministry of Labor in four major cities in 1996, 42 percent even wanted to work as long as possible in their current job. Only 9 percent were very dissatisfied. Knight and Song, *Towards a Labour Market in China,* 101. Detailed case studies in Beijing and the provinces of Zhejiang, Shaanxi, and Guangdong provide a similar picture.

36. In general, "the strategy of exploiting the specific investments of incumbent employees is effectively restricted to circumstances where (1) firms are of fly-by-night kind, (2) firms are playing end-games, and (3) intergenerational learning is negligible." Oliver E. Williamson, *The Economic Institutions of Capitalism* (New York: Free Press, 1985), 261.

37. Leslie Chang, *Factory Girls: From Village to City in a Changing China* (New York: Spiegel & Grau, 2009).

38. Ibid.

39. Victor Nee, Jimy M. Sanders, and Scott Sernau, "Job Transitions in an Immigrant Metropolis: Ethnic Boundaries and Mixed Economy," *American Sociological Review* 59 (1994): 849–872.

40. See Appendix 2, Interview 67.

41. Rebecca Matthews, *Where Do Labor Markets Come From? The Emergence of Urban Labor Markets in the People's Republic of China,* unpublished PhD

diss., Department of Sociology, Cornell University, 1998, 93; see also Rebecca Matthews and Victor Nee, "Gender Inequality and Economic Growth in Rural China," *Social Science Research* 29 (2000): 606–632.

42. Respondents could choose between four different types of employment models: (1) trying to minimize employees' wage costs; (2) maintaining a long-term friendly relationship through a two-way commitment with employees; (3) attracting the very best talents in the industry; (4) cooperative team building.

43. See Appendix 2, Interview 107.

44. See ibid., Interview 103.

45. See ibid., Interview 109.

46. Lan Li, *Zhongguo Qiyejia Chengzhan 15 Nian* [15 years' growth of Chinese entrepreneurs], Vol. 2 (Beijing: China Machine Press, 2009), 282.

47. See Appendix 2, Interview 104.

48. See ibid., Interview 107.

49. See ibid., Interview 108.

50. See ibid., Interview 103.

51. For comparison, the monthly minimum wage in Shanghai was ¥690, in Zhejiang between ¥490 and ¥670, and in Jiangsu between ¥400 and ¥690 as of June 2006; see data from China Labor Watch, documented at http://www.zhongguogongren.org/clw20100810/oldwebsite/2006 %20Editorials/07-24-2006%20Minimum%20Wage%20Chart.htm (accessed July 27, 2011).

52. Friedrich Engels, *The Condition of the Working-Class in England in 1844* (London: George Allen & Unwin, 1892).

53. The "Tentative Regulations on the Collection and Payment of Social Insurance Premiums" enacted by order of the State Council, No. 259.

54. Only recently have various cities started to implement mandatory insurance for nonresidents also. Shanghai, for instance, offers social insurance to non-Shanghai-resident employees under the age of forty-five, in case they hold a professional technical title (regulation issued on June 12, 2009). See Human Rights Watch, "Slow Movement," http://www.hrw.org/node/87265 (accessed July 27, 2011).

55. Calculated based on data from *Shanghai Statistical Yearbook 2007* (Beijing: China Statistics Press, 2007), 42, and *China Statistical Yearbook 2006* (Beijing: China Statistics Press, 2006), table 23-40.

56. See Appendix 2, Interview 107.

57. The World Bank Investment Climate Survey conducted in 2003 by the National Bureau of Statistics.

58. See Appendix 2, Interview 104.

59. See ibid., Interview 107.

60. See ibid.

61. Paul DiMaggio and Walter W. Powell, "The Iron Cage Revisited: Institutional Isomorphism and Collective Rationality in Organizational Fields," *American Journal of Sociology* 48 (1983): 147–160.

62. See Mark A. Huselid, "The Impact of Human Resource Management Practices on Turnover, Productivity, and Corporate Financial Performance," *Academy of Management Journal* 38 (1995): 635–672; John W. Meyer, *World Society: The Writings of John W. Meyer,* ed. Georg Krücken and Gili S. Drori (Oxford: Oxford University Press, 2009); Paul N. Gooderham, Odd Nordhaug, and Kristen Ringdal, "Institutional and Rational Determinants of Organizational Practices: Human Resource Management in European Firms," *Administrative Science Quarterly* 44 (1999): 507–531; Doug Guthrie, *Dragon in a Three-Piece Suit: The Emergence of Capitalism in China* (Princeton, NJ: Princeton University Press, 1999).

63. See Appendix 2, Interview 32.

64. In the early phase of development, employment relations in private firms were generally based on oral agreement. After three decades of central labor allocation, bilateral contracts between employer and employee had neither a tradition nor a legal foundation. For urban residents, the government's central labor allocation system provided lifelong employment (the so-called iron rice bowl) in state-owned and collective enterprises. Individual work units did not have the right to choose individual employees, nor were individual pay or employment conditions subject to bilateral agreements. The lack of formal employment contracts and legal protection of labor relations continued well beyond the first decade of economic reform. Although in 1986 the central government gave managers of state-owned enterprises the right to recruit workers on the basis of their skills and work experience, these firms only gradually adopted formal labor contracts as a routine governance arrangement of the employment relationship. According to the 1986 regulation, only firms that sought to hire new employees had to use labor contracts of a limited duration. This led to a gradual shift to reliance on contract-based labor. By 1995, when the first national Labor Law required the general adoption of bilateral labor contracts, only 40 percent of the workforce in state-owned enterprises had shifted to the new contract system. It took another five years for state-owned firms to fully institute contract-based employment relations for all workers.

65. See Appendix 2, Interview 97.

66. Forty-one percent of the respondents believe that "salary and benefits" are "very important" to attract talent. In contrast, only 20 percent and 2 percent feel that "attractive work" and "social relations at work" are important.

67. Donald N. Sull, *Made in China* (Cambridge, MA: Harvard Business School Press, 2005), 113.

68. See Appendix 2, Interview 109.

69. See ibid., Interview 108.
70. See ibid., Interview 105.
71. Sull, *Made in China,* 155.

8. Institutions of Innovation

1. Philippe Aghion and Rachel Griffith, *Competition and Growth: Reconciling Theory and Evidence* (Cambridge, MA: MIT Press, 2005).
2. Joseph A. Schumpeter, *Capitalism, Socialism and Democracy,* 2nd ed. (London: Allen and Unwin, [1942] 1947), 83. See also William J. Baumol, Robert E. Litan, and Carl J. Schramm, *Good Capitalism, Bad Capitalism and the Economics of Growth and Prosperity* (New Haven, CT: Yale University Press, 2007); Joyce Appleby, *The Relentless Revolution: A History of Capitalism* (New York: Norton, 2010).
3. William J. Baumol, *The Free-Market Innovation Machine: Analyzing the Growth Miracle of Capitalism* (Princeton, NJ: Princeton University Press, 2002); Eytan Sheshinski, Robert J. Strom, and William J. Baumol, eds., *Entrepreneurship, Innovation, and the Growth Mechanism of the Free-Enterprise Economies* (Princeton, NJ: Princeton University Press, 2007).
4. Organisation for Economic Co-operation and Development (OECD), *China in the World Economy: The Domestic Policy Challenges* (Paris: OECD, 2002), 403.
5. Victor Nee, Jeong-han Kang, and Sonja Opper, "Entrepreneurial Action: Market Transition, Property Rights, and Innovation," *Journal of Institutional and Theoretical Economics* 166 (2010): 397–425.
6. See Appendix 2, Interview 35.
7. See ibid., Interview 11.
8. See ibid., Interview 111.
9. See ibid., Interview 12.
10. See ibid., Interview 54.
11. See ibid., Interview 103
12. By 2005, when we visited the sprawling suburban plant, Shanghai Maple had evolved into a modern corporate governance structure led by a talented young professional manager, Xu Gang, the CEO who later led the firm's merger with Geely Automobile. Today Shanghai Maple Automobile (SMA) is a capital-intensive entrepreneurial venture heavily relying on skilled labor producing luxury brands as a subsidiary of the Geely Group, which recently acquired Volvo from GM.
13. *Statistics on Science and Technology Activities of Industrial Enterprises 2008* (Beijing: China Statistics Press, 2008), 81. The residual goes to foreign-invested companies and companies founded by investors from Macau, Taiwan, and Hong Kong.

14. For example, Lenovo computers, an offspring of the Chinese Academy of Sciences, was since its founding in 1984 sponsored and promoted by national R&D programs to become China's first global computer brand. Zhijun Ling, *The Lenovo Affair* (Singapore: John Wiley & Sons [Asia], 2005). For accounts of central and local government sponsorship of innovation and regional economic development favoring large state-owned enterprises, see Adam Segal, *Digital Dragon: High-Technology Enterprises in China* (Ithaca, NY: Cornell University Press, 2003); Dan Breznitz and Michael Murphree, *Run of the Red Queen: Government, Innovation, Globalization, and Economic Growth in China* (New Haven, CT: Yale University Press, 2011).

15. The residual R&D departments belong to domestic joint stock companies, limited liability companies of mixed ownership form, and foreign firms. *Statistics on Science and Technology Activities of Industrial Enterprises 2008* (Beijing: China Statistics Press, 2008), 25.

16. *China Statistical Yearbook 2009* (Beijing: China Statistics Press, 2009), 831.

17. AnnaLee Saxenian, *Regional Advantage: Culture and Competition in Silicon Valley and Route 128* (Cambridge, MA: Harvard University Press, 1994), 113. See also AnnaLee Saxenian, *The New Argonauts: Regional Advantage in a Global Economy* (Cambridge, MA: Harvard University Press, 2006); Rob Koepp, *Clusters of Creativity: Enduring Lessons on Innovation and Entrepreneurship from Silicon Valley and Europe's Silicon Fen* (West Sussex, England: John Wiley, 2002).

18. Michael J. Piore and Charles F. Sabel, *The Second Industrial Divide: Possibilities for Prosperity* (New York: Basic Books, 1984); Brian Uzzi, "The Sources and Consequences of Embeddedness for the Economic Performance of Organizations: The Network Effect," *American Sociological Review* 61 (1996): 674–698; Francesco Ramella and Carlo Trigilia, "Firms and Territories in Innovation: Lessons from the Italian Case," Cornell University, Center for the Study of Economy and Society, working paper no. 55 (2010).

19. Michael Polanyi, *The Tacit Dimension* (Garden City, NY: Doubleday Anchor, 1967), 4.

20. Jason Owen-Smith and Walter W. Powell, "Knowledge Networks as Channels and Conduits: The Effects of Spillovers in the Boston Biotechnology Community," *Organization Science* 15 (2004): 7.

21. David C. Mowery, *International Collaborative Ventures in U.S. Manufacturing* (Cambridge, MA: Ballinger, 1988); Francisco Javier Olleros and Roderick J. MacDonald, "Strategic Alliances: Managing Complementarity to Capitalize on Emerging Technologies," *Technovation* 7 (1988): 155–176.

22. Walter W. Powell, Kenneth W. Koput, and Laurel Smith-Doerr, "Interorganizational Collaboration and the Locus of Innovation: Networks of Learning in Biotechnology," *Administrative Science Quarterly* 41 (1996): 116–145.

23. See Appendix 2, Interview 75.

24. Geert Duysters, Jojo Jacob, Charimianne Lemmens, and Jintian Yu, "Internationalization and Technological Catching Up of Emerging Multinationals: A Comparative Case Study of China's Haier Group," *Industrial and Corporate Change* 18 (2009): 325–349.

25. Qingrui Xu, Ling Zhu, Gang Zheng, and Fangrui Wang, "Haier's Tao of Innovation: A Case Study of the Emerging Total Innovation Management Model," *Journal of Technology Transfer* 32 (2007): 27–47.

26. See Appendix 2, Interview 93.

27. See ibid., Interview 55.

28. Harrison C. White, *Markets from Networks: Socioeconomic Models of Production* (Princeton, NJ: Princeton University Press, 2002).

29. See Appendix 2, Interview 30.

30. See ibid., Interview 35.

31. See ibid., Interview 35.

32. See ibid., Interview 79.

33. Joseph A. Schumpeter, *Theorie der wirtschaftlichen Entwicklung: Nachdruck der 1. Auflage von 1912* (Berlin: Duncker & Humblot, [1912] 2006), 89.

34. See Andrew H. van de Ven, "Central Problems in the Management of Innovation," *Management Science* 32 (1986): 590–607.

35. Ronald Burt, *Brokerage and Closure: An Introduction to Social Capital* (Oxford: Oxford University Press, 2005), 65.

36. Joel M. Podolny, "Networks as the Pipes and Prisms of the Market," *American Journal of Sociology* 107 (2001): 33–60; Bruce Kogut, "The Network as Knowledge: Generative Rules and the Emergence of Structure," *Strategic Management Journal* 21 (2000): 405–425; Matthew S. Bothner, "Competition and Social Influence: The Diffusion of the Sixth Generation in the Global Computer Industry," *American Journal of Sociology* 108 (2003): 1175–1210.

37. See Appendix 2, Interview 76.

38. Few firms can afford to internalize in a stand-alone department the technical knowledge required for innovations that are at the frontier of different scientific fields. In the United States too, the complex and expanding sources of scientific and technical expertise required in biotechnology research (for example) are rarely available in one firm. Because such expertise is widely dispersed in universities and in other firms, biotechnology firms must rely on cooperative ventures in often far-flung R&D networks. Small, dedicated biotechnology firms simply lack the resources and in-house expertise to conduct their own R&D to develop new products. In such instances, because the locus of innovative activity is embedded in interfirm networks, the boundaries between firms and research universities become blurred, which in turn promotes timely and effective diffusion of new technologies.

39. See Appendix 2, Interview 65.

40. See ibid, Interview 32.
41. Legal rules meeting international standards for intellectual property rights protection are now in place; however, the enforcement of such rules is rare and the expected fines in cases of enforcement are too small to pose an effective deterrent.
42. See Appendix 2, Interview 90.
43. See ibid., Interview 87.
44. Gary P. Pisano, Weijian Shan, and David Teece, "Joint Ventures and Collaboration in the Biotechnology Industry," in *International Collaborative Ventures in U.S. Manufacturing,* ed. David Mowery (Cambridge, MA: Ballinger, 1988), 183–222; Michael Porter and M. Fuller, "Coalitions and Global Strategy," in *Competition in Global Industries,* ed. Michael Porter (Boston, MA: Harvard Business School Press, 1986), 315–344; John Hagedoorn, "Understanding the Rationale of Strategic Technological Partnering: Interorganizational Modes of Cooperation and Sectoral Differences," *Strategic Management Journal* 14 (1993): 371–385.
45. See Appendix 2, Interview 78.
46. See Ronald Burt, "Structural Holes and Good Ideas," *American Journal of Sociology* 110 (2004): 349–399.
47. See Appendix 2, Interview 105.
48. Strategic alliances are widely used by firms worldwide to promote R&D cooperation. See John Hagedoorn and Joseph Schankenraad, "The Effect of Strategic Technology Alliances on Company Performance," *Strategic Management Journal* 15 (1994): 291–309; Weijian Shan, Gordon Walker, and Bruce Kogut, "Interfirm Cooperation and Startup Innovation in the Biotechnology Industry," *Strategic Management Journal* 15 (1994): 387–394; Kathleen M. Eisenhardt and Claudia B. Schoonhoven, "Resource-Based View of Strategic Alliance Formation: Strategic and Social Effects of Entrepreneurial Firms," *Organizational Science* 7 (1996): 136–150; Ranjay Gulati, "Alliances and Networks," *Strategic Management Journal* 19 (1998): 293–317; Toby E. Stuart, "Network Positions and Propensities to Collaborate: An Investigation of Strategic Alliance in a High-Technology Industry," *Administrative Science Quarterly* 43 (1998): 668–698; Toby E. Stuart, "Interorganizational Alliance Formation in a High-Technology Industry," *Strategic Management Journal* 43 (2000): 668–698; Gautam Ahuja, "Collaboration Networks, Structural Holes, and Innovation: A Longitudinal Study," *Administrative Science Quarterly* 45 (2000): 425–455.
49. See Appendix 2, Interview 81.
50. See ibid., Interview 108.
51. See ibid., Interview 94.
52. See ibid., Interview 32.
53. See ibid., Interview 94.
54. See ibid., Interview 79.

55. Jiapeng Wang, "BYD Signs Electric Auto Agreement with Daimler," *Caixin Online,* April 3, 2010, http://english.caixin.cn/2010-03-04/100122662.html (accessed August 10, 2010); Fangfang Li, "Daimler Drives to Take Advantage of Prospects," *China Daily Online,* http://www.chinadaily.com.cn/bizchina /2011-03/07/content_12130727.htm (accessed July 28, 2011).

56. National statistics indicate that by 2006 joint ventures invested ¥27.4 billion in R&D (compared to only ¥2.1 billion in 1995). See *China Statistical Yearbook on Science and Technology 2007* (Beijing: China Statistics Press, 2007), 127; *China Statistical Yearbook on Science and Technology 1996* (Beijing: China Statistics Press, 1996), 137.

57. See Appendix 2, Interview 103.

58. Powell, Koput, and Smith-Doerr, "Interorganizational Collaboration," 120–121.

59. China Entrepreneur Survey 1997, Lan Li, *Zhongguo Qiyejia Chengzhan 15 Nian* [15 years' growth of Chinese entrepreneurs], Vol. 1 (Beijing: China Machine Press, 2009), 445.

60. Li, *Zhongguo Qiyejia Chengzhan 15 Nian,* 504.

61. Lan Li, *Zhongguo Qiyejia Chengzhan 15 Nian* [15 years' growth of Chinese entrepreneurs], Vol. 2 (Beijing: China Machine Press, 2009), 97.

62. National Bureau of Statistics of China 2004.

63. To avoid confounding the effects of ownership with market power, we include specific controls for market power. Reflecting assumptions on the role of monopoly power, a dichotomous variable indicates whether a firm's domestic market share is more than 10 percent. See Joseph A. Schumpeter, *Capitalism, Socialism and Democracy* (London: Allen and Unwin, [1942] 1947); Kenneth J. Arrow, "Economic Welfare and the Allocation of Resources for Invention," in *The Rate and Direction of Inventive Activity: Economic and Social Factors,* ed. Richard Nelson (Princeton, NJ: Princeton University Press, 1962), 609–626. We also control for perceived competition by listing the self-reported number of competitors in a firm's main market niche. Competition may have different effects on innovation in less and highly competitive markets; hence, we allow for a nonlinear relation and specify a square term of the number of competitors. See, for instance, Fredrick M. Scherer, "Market Structure and the Employment of Scientists and Engineers," *American Economic Review* 57 (1967): 524–531; Philippe Aghion, Nick Bloom, Richard Blundell, Rachel Griffith, and Peter Howitt, "Competition and Innovation: An Inverted-U Relationship," *Quarterly Journal of Economics* 120 (2005): 701–728. Lastly, we control whether firms participate in the export market.

64. In a first step, we recategorized the industry categories in the World Bank data into fifteen discrete industrial sectors that are consistent with industry categories in *China Data Online* and *China Labour Statistical Yearbook*s. Then we constructed the provincial-level measure of private-firm activities for each

of these sectors. We define private firms as companies not registered as state-owned or collective, including wholly foreign-owned and joint venture firms. To approximate the market share of private firms, we used industrial output values retrieved from *China Data Online* for manufacturing sectors, and for service-sector activities, we used employees' earnings provided by *China Labour Statistical Yearbook*s. We created this measure for the years 2000 and 2002, the former for the 2002 survey and the latter for the 2003 survey, and matched its values to each firm based on the firm's province and survey year in the World Bank data set.

65. The sector with the lowest mean private share in our sample is "traffic, transport and storage services" with 14 percent, and the sector with the highest mean value is "electrical appliance for daily use" with 92 percent.

66. Our results are consistent with earlier work exploring panel data covering China's 22,000 large and medium-size enterprises over the period from 1994 to 1999. Statistical analysis shows that private firms outperform state-owned and collective companies in terms of the proportion of new product sales in total sales. Only overseas and foreign companies report higher sales shares for newly introduced products. Gary Jefferson, Albert G. Z. Hu, Xiaojing Guan, and Xiaoyun Yu, "Ownership, Performance, and Innovation in China's Large- and Medium-Size Industrial Enterprise Sector," *China Economic Review* 14 (2003): 89–113.

67. Boston Consulting Group, "Innovation 2010: A Return to Prominence— And the Emergence of a New World Order," http://www.bcg.com/documents /file42620.pdf (accessed June 6, 2011).

9. Political Economy of Capitalism

1. Joel Mokyr, "Entrepreneurship and the Industrial Revolution in Britain," in *The Invention of Enterprise*, ed. David Landes, Joel Mokyr, and William J. Baumol (Princeton, NJ: Princeton University Press, 2010), 183–210.

2. Karl Polanyi, *The Great Transformation: The Political and Economic Origins of Our Time* (Boston: Beacon Press, 1944), 140.

3. Dali L. Yang, *Remaking the Chinese Leviathan: Market Transition and the Politics of Governance in China* (Stanford, CA: Stanford University Press, 2004), 18. The direction of regulatory reforms was clearly summarized by Vice Premier Li Lanqing: "Government should retreat from micromanaging a lot of things the government is incapable of doing. . . . The government should focus on macroeconomic issues, on setting the rules of the market, on effectively enforcing these rules as administrator and regulator." Cited in ibid., 257.

4. Donald Clarke, Peter Murrell, and Susan Whiting, "The Role of Law in China's Economic Development," in *China's Great Transformation*, ed. Loren Brandt and Thomas G. Rawski (Cambridge: Cambridge University Press, 2008), 420. This is in line with various studies on private firm development

emphasizing that the initial rise of private firms preceded formal regulation. See Alan P. L. Liu, "The 'Wenzhou Model' of Development and China's Modernization," *Asian Survey* 32 (1992): 696–711; Susan Young, "Wealth but Not Security: Attitudes towards Private Business in China in the 1980s," *Australian Journal of Chinese Affairs* 25 (1991): 115–137; Susan Young, *Private Business and Economic Reform in China* (Armonk, NY: M. E. Sharpe, 1995).

5. The theory of state and local finance has long stressed the disciplining effect of fiscal decentralization on government activities and the provision of public goods. Two mechanisms constrain predatory political interference in the economy under fiscal decentralization. First, under the assumption of factor mobility, a federalist system introduces competition among local governments, which increases opportunity costs of bailouts and any activities leading to inferior enterprise performance. If local government jurisdictions fail to provide a hospitable business environment, they face poor chances of attracting investors and entrepreneurs needed to enhance economic prosperity. Competition eventually limits discretionary authority, predatory behavior, and rent seeking. Second, fiscal decentralization may harden budget constraints of jurisdictions and provide incentives for efficiency-oriented local activities. Local governments compete to build a business environment favorable to private capital. See Barry Weingast, "The Economic Role of Political Institutions," *Journal of Law, Economics and Organization* 11 (1995): 1–31; Yingyi Qian and Gérard Roland, "Federalism and the Soft Budget Constraint," *American Journal of Economics* 88 (December 1998): 1143–1162.

6. Whiting, *Power and Wealth in Rural China*, 21. There is a statistically significant association between individual economic performance and promotion chances of provincial leaders between 1978 and 1995. See Hongbin Li and Li-An Zhou, "Political Turnover and Economic Performance: The Incentive Role of Personnel Control in China," *Journal of Public Economics* 89 (2005): 1743–1762.

7. Margaret Levi, *Of Rule and Revenue* (Berkeley and Los Angeles: University of California Press, 1989); Gabriella Montinola, Yingyi Qian, and Barry R. Weingast, "Federalism, Chinese Style: The Political Basis for Economic Success," *World Politics* 48 (1995): 50–81; Yingyi Qian and Barry R. Weingast, "Federalism as a Commitment to Preserving Market Incentives," *Journal of Economic Perspectives* 11 (1997): 83–92; David D. Li, "Changing Incentives of the Chinese Bureaucracy," *American Economic Review: Papers and Proceedings* 88 (1998): 393–397.

8. Profits dropped from ¥82.9 billion to ¥41.3 billion between 1994 and 1996. *China Statistical Yearbook 1997* (Beijing: China Statistics Press, 1997).

9. Data from *China Industry Economic Statistical Yearbook 2007* (Beijing: China Statistics Press, 2007), 23; *China Industry Economic Statistical Yearbook 2001* (Beijing: China Statistics Press, 2001), 11.

10. *China Statistical Yearbook 1997* (Beijing: China Statistics Press, 1997); *China Statistical Yearbook 2005* (Beijing: China Statistics Press, 2005).

11. Yifan Hu, Sonja Opper, and Sonia M. L. Wong, "Political Economy of Labor Retrenchment: Evidence Based on China's State-Owned Enterprises," *China Economic Review* 17 (2006): 281–299.

12. Peter Murrell, "How Far Has the Transition Progressed?" *Journal of Economic Perspectives* 10 (1996): 32.

13. Yi-min Lin, *Between Politics and Markets: Firms, Competition, and Institutional Change in Post-Mao China* (Cambridge: Cambridge University Press, 2001); Nan Lin, "Local Market Socialism: Local Corporatism in Action in Rural China," *Theory and Society* 24 (1995): 301–354; William L. Parish and Ethan Michelson, "Politics and Markets: Dual Transformations," *American Journal of Sociology* 101 (1996): 1042–1059; Katherine R. Xin and Jone L. Pearce, "Guanxi: Connections as Substitutes for Formal Institutional Support," *Academy of Management Journal* 39 (1996): 1641–1658; Xiaobo Lu, "Booty Socialism, Bureau-preneurs, and the State in Transition," *Comparative Politics* 32 (2000): 273–294; David L. Wank, *Commodifying Communism: Business, Trust, and Politics in a Chinese City* (Cambridge: Cambridge University Press, 1999); Andrew H. Wedeman, *From Mao to Market: Rent Seeking, Local Protectionism, and Marketization in China* (Cambridge: Cambridge University Press, 2003).

14. George J. Stigler, "The Theory of Economic Regulation," *Bell Journal of Economics and Management Science* 2 (1971): 3–21.

15. Iván Szelényi, *Urban Inequality under State Socialist Redistributive Economies* (London: Oxford University Press, 1983).

16. Joseph P. H. Fan, T. J. Wong, and Tianyu Zhang, "Politically Connected CEOs, Corporate Governance, and Post-IPO Performance of China's Newly Partially Privatized Firms," *Journal of Financial Economics* 84 (2007): 330–357.

17. Andrei Shleifer and Robert W. Vishny, "Politicians and Firms," *Quarterly Journal of Economics* 109 (1994): 995–1025.

18. Thomas B. Gold, Doug Guthrie, and David L. Wank, eds., *Social Connections in China: Institutions, Culture, and the Changing Nature of "Guanxi"* (Cambridge: Cambridge University Press, 2002); Doug Guthrie, *Dragon in a Three-Piece Suit: The Emergence of Capitalism in China* (Princeton, NJ: Princeton University Press, 1999).

19. Yanjie Bian, Xiaoling Shu, and John R. Logan, "Community Party Membership and Regime Dynamics in China," *Social Forces* 79 (2001): 805–841; Mike W. Peng and Yadong Luo, "Managerial Ties and Firm Performance in a Transition Economy: The Nature of a Micro-Macro Link," *Academy of Management Journal* 43 (2000): 486–501.

20. James S. Coleman, "Social Capital in the Creation of Human Capital," *American Journal of Sociology* 94 (1988): S98; Victor Nee and Sonja Opper, "Political Capital in a Market Economy," *Social Forces* 88 (2010): 2105–2135.

21. See Appendix 2, Interview 21.

22. Bruce J. Dickson, *Red Capitalists in China: The Party, Private Entrepreneurs, and Prospects for Political Change* (Cambridge: Cambridge University Press, 2003), 127.

23. Robin Kwong, "China's Billionaires Begin to Add Up," *Financial Times,* October 22, 2007. http://www.ft.com/intl/cms/s/0/a759c0de-809c-11dc-9f14-0000779fd2ac.html#axzz1gnmqlBr3 (accessed October 23, 2007).

24. Dickson, *Red Capitalists in China.*

25. Minxin Pei, *China's Trapped Transition: The Limits of Developmental Autocracy* (Cambridge, MA: Harvard University Press, 2006), 93.

26. See Appendix 2, Interview 23.

27. See ibid., Interview 32.

28. Yasheng Huang, *Capitalism with Chinese Characteristics* (Cambridge: Cambridge University Press, 2008), 165; Dali Ma and William L. Parish, "Tocquevillian Moments: Charitable Contributions by Chinese Private Entrepreneurs," *Social Forces* 85 (2006): 943–964.

29. See Appendix 2, Interview 42.

30. See ibid., Interview 24.

31. A provincial marketization index developed by China's National Economic Research Institute confirms that the product market scored highest in terms of liberalization across all provinces in the year 2006. According to the same index, factor markets are among the least liberalized. Gang Fan and Xiaolu Wang, *NERI Index of Marketization of China's Provinces 2009 Report* (Beijing: National Economic Research Institute, 2010), 13.

32. Tian Zhu, "China's Corporatization Drive: An Evaluation and Policy Implications," *Contemporary Economic Politics* 17 (1999): 530–539; Man-Kwong Leung and Vincent Wai-Kwong Mok, "Commercialization of Banks in China: Institutional Changes and Effects on Listed Enterprises," *Journal of Contemporary China* 9 (2000): 41–52; Hongbin Li, Lingsheng Meng, Qian Wang, and Li-An Zhou, "Political Connections, Financing and Firm Performance: Evidence from Chinese Private Firms," *Journal of Development Economics* 87 (2008): 283–299; Victor Nee and Sonja Opper, "On Politicized Capitalism," in *On Capitalism,* ed. Victor Nee and Richard Swedberg (Princeton, NJ: Princeton University Press, 2007), 93–127.

33. *China Statistical Yearbook 2009* (Beijing: China Statistics Press, 2009).

34. Robert Cull and L. Colin Xu, "Who Gets Credit? The Behavior of Bureaucrats and State Banks in Allocating Credit to Chinese State-Owned Enterprises," *Journal of Development Economics* 71 (2003): 533–559; Thomson Reuters Datastream.

35. The observed advantage of long-standing party members is robust in light of the inclusion of a broad set of variables that controls for firm size, time of founding, industrial sector, city, and individual characteristics of the founder, such as gender, age, origin, and education.

36. See Appendix 2, Interview 44.
37. See ibid., Interview 107.
38. Cheng Li, "Think National, Blame Local: Central-Provincial Dynamics in the Hu Era," *China Leadership Monitor* 17 (2006): 1–24.
39. See Appendix 2, Interview 28.
40. We cannot fully rule out, however, that donations to the party may be to show gratitude: following rather than preceding favorable treatment from government.
41. Andrew Walder, "Elite Opportunity in Transitional Economies," *American Sociological Review* 68 (2003): 899–916.
42. See Appendix 2, Interview 28.
43. Eric Helland and Michael Sykuta, "Regulation and the Evolution of Corporate Boards: Monitoring, Advising, or Window Dressing?" *Journal of Law and Economics* 47 (2004): 167–193.
44. Gordon Tullock, *The Economics of Special Privilege and Rent-Seeking* (Boston: Kluwer Academic Publishers, 1989).
45. Return on sales as an alternative measure produces similar results.
46. See Appendix 2, Interview 37.
47. The survey includes six typical fields of local government support (locating foreign technology, obtaining bank financing, and identifying foreign investors, foreign clients, foreign suppliers, and domestic clients). In these measures of political capital, it does not matter whether government assistance was provided through formal channels and procedures or rests on informal network-based support. We construct an index (ranging from 0 to 6) of government assistance received in all these fields. It should be noted that government assistance does not guarantee successful outcomes. In this sense, we are not running the risk of including a tautological independent variable. In sum, government support signals that the firm is on good terms with bureaucrats and politicians. It can also be interpreted as a signal of otherwise not explicitly revealed political capital. Pairwise correlation coefficients ranging from −0.01 to 0.23 confirm that these selected measures capture different dimensions of firm-based political capital.
48. To control for the greater heterogeneity of the sample, which includes not only different industries in manufacturing and the service sector but also different nonstate ownership forms, we include a set of control variables that also cover capital intensity, capital structure, and partial government ownership. To control for professional competence of firm managers and for the management's incentive structure, dummy variables indicate whether the CEO has a college education and management tenure and whether employment is based on an incentive contract. It should be noted that the survey does not provide information as to whether the manager is also one of the company owners. Regional control variables sort China into main regions (coastal,

central, northeast, northwest, and southwest). They also include measures of provincial marketization (NERI Index) and per capita GDP at the city level, to control for institutional and economic variation.

49. Daqing Qi, Woody Wu, and Zhang Hua, "Shareholding Structure and Corporate Performance of Partially Privatized Firms: Evidence from Listed Companies," *Pacific-Basin Finance Journal* 8 (2000): 587–610; Fan, Wong, and Zhang, "Politically Connected CEOs"; Li, Meng, Wang, and Zhou, "Political Connections, Financing and Firm Performance."

50. Wilfried R. Vanhonacker, David Zweig, and Siu Fung Chung, "Transnational or Social Capital? Returnees versus Local Entrepreneurs," in *China's Domestic Private Firms: Multidisciplinary Perspectives on Management and Performance,* ed. Anne S. Tsui, Yanjie Bian, and Leonard Cheng (Armonk, NY: M. E. Sharpe, 2006).

51. We considered three robustness issues to confirm the findings we report on the fungibility of political connections held by entrepreneurs in the Yangzi delta regional economy. We checked whether our OLS results were driven by outliers or predictor variables with high leverage. Robust regressions, however, generally confirmed our findings and did not indicate systematic advantages for firms with political connections. Reverse causality is a potential risk when using cross-sectional data sets. It is possible that political capital may have different effects depending on the firm's economic performance. For instance, political connections may be easier to activate for poorly performing firms facing bankruptcy, or alternatively, political capital might become more valuable for top performers thanks to the government's interest in cultivating national brands and global players. To mitigate the risk of reverse causality, we have experimented with different lagged performance measures (such as return on assets) as additional control variables, but our substantive findings remained unaffected. Our findings are confirmed for a subsample of loss-making firms. Theoretically, there is also a chance that firms that are performing weakly in the specified market settings respond by recruiting new CEOs with viable government ties. If such a selection effect actually existed, our estimation results would possibly not reveal positive effects of political capital. To rule out such concerns, we have explored whether our results still hold up if firms with recently recruited CEOs (we experimented with tenure of up to five years, three years, or one year) are excluded from the sample. Overall, however, our general findings were confirmed.

52. Dickie Mure, "Obituary: Rong Yiren, the 'Red Capitalists,'" *Financial Times.com,* October 28, 2005, http://www.ft.com/intl/cms/s/0/103cae12 -47d4-11da-a949-00000e2511c8.html#axzz1gnmqlBr3 (accessed October 29, 2005).

53. For comparative studies on political capital's fungibility, see Gil Eyal, Iván Szelényi, and Eleanor Townsley, *Making Capitalism without Capitalists:*

The New Ruling Elites in Eastern Europe (London: Verso Press, 1998); also Lawrence Peter King, *The Basic Features of Postcommunist Capitalism in Eastern Europe* (Westport, CT: Praeger, 2001).

54. "Tom Daschle's Washington," *Wall Street Journal,* February 4, 2009, http://online.wsj.com/article/SB123371143249046139.html (accessed February 4, 2009).

55. Janos Kornai, "The Affinity between Ownership Forms and Coordination Mechanisms: The Common Experience of Reform in Socialist Countries," *Journal of Economic Perspectives* 4 (1990): 131–147; Peter Evans, *Embedded Autonomy: States and Industrial Transformation* (Princeton, NJ: Princeton University Press, 1995); Victor Nee, "The Role of the State in Making a Market Economy," *Journal of Institutional and Theoretical Economics* 156 (2000): 64–88; Martin Ricketts, "Comment on 'The Role of the State in Making a Market Economy,'" *Journal of Institutional and Theoretical Economics* 156 (2000): 95–98; Siegwart M. Lindenberg, "A Market Needs a State: Securing Calculability and Market-Induced Values in China," *Journal of Institutional and Theoretical Economics* 156 (2000): 89–94.

10. Conclusion

1. Ernst Fehr and Urs Fischbacher, "Social Norms and Human Cooperation," *Trends in Cognitive Science* 8 (2004): 185.

References

Abolafia, Mitchel, *Making Markets: Opportunism and Restraint on Wall Street* (Cambridge, MA: Harvard University Press, 1996).

Acemoglu, Daron, Simon Johnson, and James Robinson, "The Rise of Europe: Atlantic Trade, Institutional Change, and Economic Growth," *American Economic Review* 95 (2005): 546–579.

Aghion, Philippe, Nick Bloom, Richard Blundell, Rachel Griffith, and Peter Howitt, "Competition and Innovation: An Inverted-U Relationship," *Quarterly Journal of Economics* 120 (2005): 701–728.

Aghion, Philippe, and Rachel Griffith, *Competition and Growth: Reconciling Theory and Evidence* (Cambridge, MA: MIT Press, 2005).

Aghion, Philippe, and Peter Howitt, *Endogenous Growth Theory* (Cambridge, MA: MIT Press, 1998).

Ahuja, Gautam, "Collaboration Networks, Structural Holes, and Innovation: A Longitudinal Study," *Administrative Science Quarterly* 45 (2000): 425–455.

Akerlof, George, "The Economics of Caste and of the Rat Race and Other Woeful Tales," *Quarterly Journal of Economics* 90 (1976): 599–617.

Aldrich, Howard E., and C. Marlene Fiol, "Fools Rush In? The Institutional Context of Industry Creation," *Academy of Management Review* 19 (1994): 645–670.

Aldrich, Howard E., and Martha Martinez, "Entrepreneurship as Social Construction: A Multi-Level Evolutionary Approach," in *Handbook of Entrepreneurship Research*, ed. Zoltan J. Acs and David B. Audretsch (Berlin: Springer, 2003), 359–399.

Aldrich, Howard E., and Martin Ruef, *Organizations Evolving* (London: Sage, 1999).

Annual Report of Non-State-Owned Economy in China, No. 5 (2007–2008) (Beijing: Social Sciences Academic Press, 2008).

Appleby, Joyce, *The Relentless Revolution: A History of Capitalism* (New York: Norton, 2010).

Arrow, Kenneth J., "Economic Welfare and the Allocation of Resources for Invention," in *The Rate and Direction of Inventive Activity: Economic and Social Factors,* ed. Richard Nelson (Princeton, NJ: Princeton University Press, 1962), 609–626.

Atherton, Andrew, "From 'Fat Pigs' and 'Red Hats' to a New Social Stratum: The Changing Face of Enterprise Development Policy in China," *Journal of Small Business and Enterprise Development* 14 (2008): 640–655.

Axelrod, Robert, *The Evolution of Cooperation* (New York: Basic Books, 1984).

———, "An Evolutionary Approach to Norms," *American Political Science Review* 80 (1986): 1095–1111.

Axelrod, Robert, and William D. Hamilton, "The Evolution of Cooperation," *Science* 211 (1981): 1390–1396.

Bai, Jianwei, "Excessive Tax on Private Enterprises," in *Ningxia Ribao* (September 1, 1994): 2, translation in *JPRS-CAR-94-053* (November 8, 1994): 48.

Baker & McKenzie, "China Employment Law Update," June 2011, http://www .bakermckenzie.com/files/Publication/0d7fe52e-7987-4a63-9bc4-fa21db8be2a8 /Presentation/PublicationAttachment/0928b376-b7a9-43a3-8f34-071019dcf3af /nl_china_chinaemploymentlawupdate_jun11.pdf (accessed June 27, 2011).

Balfour, Frederik, and Dexter Roberts, "The Leak in China's Banking System," *Business Week* (November 15, 2004): 67.

Barnard, Chester I., *The Functions of the Executive* (Cambridge, MA: Harvard University Press, 1968).

Baruch, Yehua, "Response Rate in Academic Studies—A Comparative Analysis," *Human Relations* 52 (1999): 421–438.

Bates, Robert H., *Beyond the Miracle of the Market: The Political Economy of Agrarian Development in Kenya* (Cambridge: Cambridge University Press, 1989).

Baumol, William J., *Entrepreneurship, Management, and the Structure of Payoffs* (Cambridge, MA: MIT Press, 1993).

———, *The Free-Market Innovation Machine: Analyzing the Growth Miracle of Capitalism* (Princeton, NJ: Princeton University Press, 2002).

Baumol, William J., Robert E. Litan, and Carl J. Schramm, *Good Capitalism, Bad Capitalism, and the Economics of Growth and Prosperity* (New Haven, CT: Yale University Press, 2007).

Bernstein, Lisa. "Opting Out of the Legal System: Extralegal Contractual Relations in the Diamond Industry." *Journal of Legal Studies* 21(1992): 115–157.

Bewley, Truman F., *Why Wages Don't Fall during a Recession* (Cambridge, MA: Harvard University Press, 1999).

Bian, Yanjie, Xiaoling Shu, and John R. Logan, "Community Party Membership and Regime Dynamics in China," *Social Forces* 79 (2001): 805–841.

Blau, Peter, *The Dynamics of Bureaucracy,* 2nd ed. (Chicago: University of Chicago Press, 1955).

Blecher, Marc, "Developmental State, Entrepreneurial State: The Political Economy of Socialist Reform in Xinji Municipality and Guanghan County," in *The Chinese State in the Era of Economic Reform: The Road to Crisis*, ed. Gordon White (Houndsmill: Palgrave Macmillan, 1991), 265–291.

Blecher, Marc, and Vivienne Shue, *Government and Economy in a Chinese County* (Stanford, CA: Stanford University Press, 1996).

Boston Consulting Group, "Innovation 2010: A Return to Prominence—And the Emergence of a New World Order," http://www.bcg.com/documents/file42620 .pdf (accessed June 6, 2011).

Bothner, Matthew S., "Competition and Social Influence: The Diffusion of the Sixth Generation in the Global Computer Industry," *American Journal of Sociology* 108 (2003): 1175–1210.

Breznitz, Dan, and Michael Murphree, *Run of the Red Queen: Government, Innovation, Globalization, and Economic Growth in China* (New Haven, CT: Yale University Press, 2011).

Brinton, Mary C., and Victor Nee, *The New Institutionalism in Sociology* (New York: Russell Sage Foundation, 1998).

Burt, Ronald, *Brokerage and Closure: An Introduction to Social Capital* (Oxford: Oxford University Press, 2005).

——, "Structural Holes and Good Ideas," *American Journal of Sociology* 110 (2004): 349–399.

"Business: Winning Is Only Half the Battle: China's Courts," *Economist* (March 26, 2005): 84.

Byrd, William A., and Qingsong Lin, *China's Rural Industry: Structure, Development, and Reform* (Washington, DC: World Bank Publication, 1990).

Campbell, Karen E., and Peter V. Marsden, "Recruitment and Selection Processes: The Organizational Side of Job Searches," in *Social Mobility and Social Structure*, ed. Ronald L. Breiger (Cambridge: Cambridge University Press, 1990), 59–79.

Carroll, Glenn R., "A Sociological View on Why Firms Differ," *Strategic Management Journal* 14 (1993): 237–249.

Chandler, Alfred D., Jr., *The Visible Hand: The Managerial Revolution in American Business* (Cambridge, MA: Harvard University Press, 1977).

Chang, Leslie, *Factory Girls: From Village to City in a Changing China* (New York: Spiegel & Grau, 2009).

Chen, Shaohua, and Martin Ravillion, "China Is Poorer Than We Thought, but No Less Successful in the Fight against Poverty," *The World Bank: Policy Research Working Paper* 4621 (2008).

Chen, Tao, Sheming Li, Bisheng Zhang, and Cai Bai, "Guanzu jiasu fazhan geti siying Jingji de Diaocha ji zhengce Cuoshi Jianyin" [Investigation of the fast development of individual and private enterprise and suggestions for political measures and instruments], *Jingyi Yanjiu Cankao* (July 8, 1993): 42–52.

China Financial Statistics (1949–2005) (Beijing: China Finance Press, 2007).

China Industry Economic Statistical Yearbook, various years (Beijing: China Statistics Press).

China Statistical Yearbook on Science and Technology, various years (Beijing: China Statistics Press).

Clark, Gregory, "The Political Foundations of Modern Economic Growth: England, 1540–1800," *Journal of Interdisciplinary History* 26 (1996): 563–588.

Clarke, Donald C., "Corporate Governance in China: An Overview," *China Economic Review* 148 (2003): 494–507.

Clarke, Donald C., Peter Murrell, and Susan Whiting, "The Role of Law in China's Economic Development," in *China's Great Transformation,* ed. Loren Brandt and Thomas G. Rawski (Cambridge: Cambridge University Press, 2008), 375–428.

Clay, Karen, "Trade without Law: Private-Order Institutions in Mexican California," *Journal of Law, Economics, and Organization* 13 (1997): 202–231.

Clemens, Elisabeth, "Organizational Repertoires and Institutional Changes: Women's Groups and the Transformation of U.S. Politics, 1890–1920," *American Journal of Sociology* 98 (1993): 755–798.

Coase, Ronald, "The Institutional Structure of Production," *American Economic Review* 82 (1992): 713–719.

Coleman, James S., *Foundations of Social Theory* (Cambridge, MA: Harvard University Press, 1990).

———, "Social Capital in the Creation of Human Capital," *American Journal of Sociology* 94 (1988): S95–120.

Colyvas, Jeannette A., and Walter W. Powell, "Roads to Institutionalization: The Remaking of Boundaries between Public and Private Science," *Research in Organizational Behavior* 27 (2006): 305–353.

Cooper, Arnold C., and William C. Dunkelberg, "Entrepreneurial Research: Old Questions, New Answers and Methodological Issues," *American Journal of Small Business* 1 (1987): 11–23.

Cull, Robert, and L. Colin Xu, "Institutions, Ownership, and Finance: The Determinants of Profit Reinvestment among Chinese Firms," *Journal of Financial Economics* 77 (2005): 117–146.

———, "Who Gets Credit? The Behavior of Bureaucrats and State Banks in Allocating Credit to Chinese State-Owned Enterprises," *Journal of Development Economics* 71 (2003): 533–559.

Cull, Robert, L. Colin Xu, and Tian Zhu, "Formal Finance and Trade Credit during China's Transition," *Journal of Financial Intermediation* 18 (2009): 173–192.

Davis, Deborah S., "Self-Employment in Shanghai: A Research Note," *China Quarterly* 157 (March 1999): 22–43.

de Bary, Wm. Theodore, "Confucianism in the Early Tokugawa Period," *Sources of Japanese Tradition*, vol. 3, ed. Ryusaku Tsunoda, Wm. Theodore de Bary, and Donald Keene (New York: Columbia University Press, 1958), 28–41, 66–67.

———, *Neo-Confucian Orthodoxy and the Learning of the Mind and Heart* (New York, Columbia University Press, 1981), 189–215.

————, "On Top of "Bottom-Up Development," manuscript, Department of East Asian Languages and Culture, Columbia University, 2011.

Delacroix, Jacques, and Hayagreeva Rao, "Externalities and Ecological Theory: Unbundling Density Dependence," in *Evolutionary Dynamics of Organizations*, ed. Joel A. C. Baum and Jitendra V. Singh (Oxford: Oxford University Press, 1994), 255–268.

de Soto, Hernando, *The Mystery of Capital: Why Capitalism Triumphs in the West and Fails Everywhere Else* (New York: Basic Civitas Books, 2000).

Dickson, Bruce J., *Red Capitalists in China: The Party, Private Entrepreneurs, and Prospects for Political Change* (Cambridge: Cambridge University Press, 2003).

DiMaggio, Paul, and Walter W. Powell, "The Iron Cage Revisited: Institutional Isomorphism and Collective Rationality in Organizational Fields," *American Journal of Sociology* 48 (1983): 147–160.

Dixit, Avinash K., *Lawlessness and Economics: Alternative Modes of Governance* (Princeton, NJ: Princeton University Press, 2004).

Dobbin, Frank R., John R. Sutton, John W. Meyer, and W. Richard Scott, "Equal Opportunity Law and the Construction of Internal Labor Markets," *American Journal of Sociology* 99 (1993): 396–427.

Dollar, David, and Aart Kraay, "Institutions, Trade, and Growth," *Journal of Monetary Economics* 50 (2003): 133–162.

Duckett, Jane, *The Entrepreneurial State in China: Real Estate and Commerce Departments in Reform Era Tianjin* (London: Routledge, Chapman & Hall, 1998).

Dumais, Guy, Glenn Ellison, and Edward L. Glaeser, "Geographic Concentration as a Dynamic Process," *Review of Economics and Statistics* 84 (2002): 193–204.

Duysters, Geert, Jojo Jacob, Charimianne Lemmens, and Jintian Yu, "Internationalization and Technological Catching Up of Emerging Multinationals: A Comparative Case Study of China's Haier Group," *Industrial and Corporate Change* 18 (2009): 325–349.

Edelman, Lauren B., "Legal Ambiguity and Symbolic Structures: Organizational Mediation of Civil Rights Law," *American Journal of Sociology* 97 (1992): 1531–1576.

Edelman, Lauren B., Christopher Uggen, and Howard S. Erlanger, "The Endogeneity of Legal Regulation: Grievance Procedures as Rational Myth," *American Journal of Sociology* 105 (1999): 406–454.

Eisenhardt, Kathleen M., and Claudia B. Schoonhoven, "Resource-Based View of Strategic Alliance Formation: Strategic and Social Effects of Entrepreneurial Firms," *Organizational Science* 7 (1996): 136–150.

Ellickson, Robert, *Order without Law* (Cambridge, MA: Harvard University Press, 1991).

Ellison, Glenn, and Edward L. Glaeser, "Geographic Concentration in U.S. Manufacturing Industries: A Dartboard Approach," *Journal of Political Economy* 105 (1997): 889–927.

Ellsberg, Daniel, "Risk, Ambiguity, and the Savage Axioms," *Quarterly Journal of Economics* 75 (1961): 643–669.

Elster, Jon, *The Cement of Society: A Study of Social Order* (Cambridge: Cambridge University Press, 1989).

Engels, Friedrich, *The Condition of the Working-Class in England in 1844* (London: George Allen & Unwin, 1892).

Evans, Peter, *Embedded Autonomy: States and Industrial Transformation* (Princeton, NJ: Princeton University Press, 1995).

Eyal, Gil, Iván Szelényi, and Eleanor Townsley, *Making Capitalism without Capitalists: The New Ruling Elites in Eastern Europe* (London: Verso Press, 1998).

Fan, Gang, and Xiaolu Wang, *NERI Index of Marketization of China's Provinces, 2009 Report* (Beijing: National Economic Research Institute, 2010).

Fan, Joseph P. H., T. J. Wong, and Tianyu Zhang, "Politically Connected CEOs, Corporate Governance, and Post-IPO Performance of China's Newly Partially Privatized Firms," *Journal of Financial Economics* 84 (2007): 330–357.

Fehr, Ernst, and Urs Fischbacher, "Social Norms and Human Cooperation," *Trends in Cognitive Science* 8 (2004): 185–190.

Fehr, Ernst, and Klaus M. Schmidt, "A Theory of Fairness, Competition, and Cooperation," *Quarterly Journal of Economics* 114 (1999): 817–868.

Findlay, Mark, "Independence and the Judiciary in the PRC: Expectations for Constitutional Legality in China," in *Law, Capitalism and Power in Asia*, ed. Kanishka Jayasuriya (London: Routledge, 1999), 281–299.

Firebaugh, Glenn, *The New Geography of Global Income Inequality* (Cambridge, MA: Harvard University Press, 2003).

Firth, Godfrey, "Critical Eye on Ningbo," *China Business Review* 32 (2005): 32–35.

Fischer, Stanley, "Russia and the Soviet Union Then and Now," in *The Transition in Eastern Europe*, Vol. 1, *Country Studies*, ed. Olivier J. Blanchard, Kenneth A. Froot, and Jeffrey D. Sachs (Chicago: University of Chicago Press, 1994), 221–258.

Fisman, Raymond, and Inessa Love, "Trade Credit, Financial Intermediary Development, and Industry Growth," *Journal of Finance* 58 (2003): 353–374.

Fleisher, Belton M., Dinghuan Hu, William McGuire, and Xiaobo Zhang, "The Evolution of an Industrial Cluster in China," working papers from Ohio State University, Department of Economics, No. 09-05 (2009).

Fligstein, Neil, *The Transformation of Corporate Control* (Cambridge, MA: Harvard University Press, 1990).

Frye, Timothy, and Andrei Shleifer, "The Invisible Hand and the Grabbing Hand," *American Economic Review: Papers and Proceedings* 87 (1997): 131–155.

Fukuyama, Francis, *Trust: Social Virtues and the Creation of Prosperity* (New York: Free Press, 1995).

Galanter, Marc, "Justice in Many Rooms: Courts, Private Ordering, and Indigenous Law," *Journal of Legal Pluralism* 19 (1981): 1–47.

Garber, Peter M., *Famous First Bubbles* (Cambridge, MA: MIT Press, 2000).

Gernet, Jacques, *Daily Life in China on the Eve of the Mongol Invasion, 1250–1276* (Stanford, CA: Stanford University Press, 1962).

Glaeser, Edward L., "The Future of Urban Research: Nonmarket Interactions," *Brookings-Wharton Papers on Urban Affairs* 1 (2000): 101–149.

Glaeser, Edward L., and Joshua D. Gottlieb, "The Wealth of Cities: Agglomeration Economies and Spatial Equilibrium in the United States," *Journal of Economic Literature* 47 (2009): 983–1028.

Glaeser, Edward L., Rafael La Porta, Florencio Lopez-de-Silanes, and Andrei Shleifer, "Do Institutions Cause Growth?" *Journal of Economic Growth* 9 (2004): 271–303.

Goffman, Erving, *Stigma: Notes on the Management of Spoiled Identity* (New York: Simon & Schuster, 1963).

Gold, Thomas B., Doug Guthrie, and David L. Wank, eds., *Social Connections in China: Institutions, Culture, and the Changing Nature of "Guanxi"* (Cambridge: Cambridge University Press, 2002).

Gooderham, Paul N., Odd Nordhaug, and Kristen Ringdal, "Institutional and Rational Determinants of Organizational Practices: Human Resources Management in European Firms," *Administrative Science Quarterly* 44 (1999): 507–531.

Gould, Roger V., *Insurgent Identities: Class, Community, and Protest in Paris from 1848 to the Commune* (Chicago: University of Chicago Press, 1995).

Granovetter, Mark, *Getting a Job: A Study of Contacts and Careers* (Cambridge, MA: Harvard University Press, 1974).

Greif, Avner, "Contract Enforceability and Economic Institutions in Early Trade: The Maghribi Traders' Coalition," *American Economic Review* 83 (1993): 525–549.

———, "Cultural Beliefs and the Organization of Society: A Historical and Theoretical Reflection on Collectivist and Individualist Societies," *Journal of Political Economy* 102 (1994): 912–950.

———, *Institutions and the Path to the Modern Economy: Lessons from Medieval Trade* (Cambridge: Cambridge University Press, 2006).

Greif, Avner, and David D. Laitin, "A Theory of Endogenous Institutional Change," *American Political Science Review* 98 (2004): 633–652.

Groves, Theodore, Yongmiao Hong, John McMillan, and Barry Naughton, "Autonomy and Incentives in Chinese State Enterprises," *Quarterly Journal of Economics* 109 (1994), 183–209.

"Guanyu kaichuang shedui Qiye xin jumian de Baogao" [Report to create a new situation for commune and brigade companies, March 1, 1984] in *Zhongguo Nongye Nianjian 1985* [Yearbook of China's agriculture] (Beijing: Nongye Chubanshe, 1985).

Gulati, Ranjay, "Alliances and Networks," *Strategic Management Journal* 19 (1998): 293–317.

Guo, Zhonghe, "Wo guo geti siying Qiye Jianxi" [A brief analysis of China's individual and private firms], *Jingji Yanjiu Cankao* (February 13, 1993): 24–34.

"Guowuyuan guanyu Chengzhen feinongye geti Jingji ruogan zhengcexing Guiding" [Political regulations of the State Council on the non-agrarian, urban individual economy], *Zhonghua Renmin Gongheguo* (September 25, 1981), 493–497.

Guseva, Alya, *Into the Red: The Birth of the Credit Card Market in Postcommunist Russia* (Stanford: Stanford University Press, 2008).

Guthrie, Doug, *Dragon in a Three-Piece Suit: The Emergence of Capitalism in China* (Princeton, NJ: Princeton University Press, 1999).

Hagedoorn, John, "Understanding the Rationale of Strategic Technological Partnering: Interorganizational Modes of Cooperation and Sectoral Differences," *Strategic Management Journal* 14 (1993): 371–385.

Hagedoorn, John, and Joseph Schankenraad, "The Effect of Strategic Technology Alliances on Company Performance," *Strategic Management Journal* 15 (1994): 291–309.

Hall, Robert E., and Charles I. Jones, "Why Do Some Countries Produce So Much More Output per Worker Than Others?" *Quarterly Journal of Economics* 114 (1999): 83–116.

Hannan, Michael T., and John Freeman, *Organizational Ecology* (Cambridge, MA: Harvard University Press, 1989).

———, "Where Do Organizational Forms Come From?" *Sociological Forum* 1 (1986): 50–72.

Hardin, Russell, *Trust and Trustworthiness* (New York: Russell Sage Foundation, 2004).

Hayek, Friedrich A., "Competition as a Discovery Procedure," in *New Studies in Philosophy, Politics, Economics and the History of Ideas*, by Friedrich A. von Hayek (Chicago: University of Chicago Press, 1978).

Heckathorn, Douglas D., "Collective Sanctions and Compliance Norms: A Formal Theory of Group-Mediated Social Control," *American Sociological Review* 55 (1990): 366–384.

———, "Respondent-Driven Sampling II: Deriving Valid Population Estimates from Chain-Referral Samples of Hidden Populations," *Social Problems* 49 (2002): 11–34.

Heilmann, Sebastian, "Der chinesische Aktienmarkt: Staatliche Regulierung im Wandel," *Asien* 80 (2001): 25–41.

Helland, Eric, and Michael Sykuta, "Regulation and the Evolution of Corporate Boards: Monitoring, Advising, or Window Dressing?" *Journal of Law and Economics* 47 (2004): 167–193.

Holm, Håkan, Sonja Opper, and Victor Nee, "Entrepreneurs under Uncertainty: An Economic Experiment," Scandinavian Working Paper Series in Economics 2012:4.

Holzer, Harry J., "Hiring Procedures in the Firm: Their Economic Determinants and Outcomes," *National Bureau of Economic Research Working Paper* No. 2185 (1987).

Homans, George C., *Social Behavior: Its Elementary Forms* (New York: Harcourt Brace Jovanovich, [1961] 1974).

Hu, Yifan, Sonja Opper, and Sonia M. L. Wong, "Political Economy of Labor Retrenchment: Evidence Based on China's State-Owned Enterprises," *China Economic Review* 17 (2006): 281–299.

Huang, Philip, *The Peasant Family and Rural Development in the Yangzi Delta, 1350–1988* (Stanford, CA: Stanford University Press, 1990).

Huang, Yasheng, *Capitalism with Chinese Characteristics: Entrepreneurship and the State* (Cambridge: Cambridge University Press, 2008).

Huang, Zuhui, Xiaobo Zhang, and Yunwei Zhu, "The Role of Clustering in Rural Industrialization: A Case Study of the Footwear Industry in Wenzhou," *China Economic Review* 19 (2008): 409–420.

Human Rights Watch, "Slow Movement," http://www.hrw.org/node/87265 (accessed July 27, 2011).

Humphrey, John, and Hubert Schmitz, "Trust and Interfirm Relations in Developing and Transition Economies," *Journal of Development Studies* 34 (1998): 32–61.

Huselid, Mark A., "The Impact of Human Resource Management Practices on Turnover, Productivity, and Corporate Financial Performance," *Academy of Management Journal* 38 (1995): 635–672.

Ignatius, Adi, "Jack Ma," *Time* magazine, April.30, 2009, http://www.time.com/time/specials/packages/article/0,28804,1894410_1893837_1894188,00.html (accessed May 15, 2009).

Isaac, R. Mark, James Walker, and Arlington W. Williams, "Group Size and the Voluntary Provision of Public Goods: Experimental Evidence Utilizing Large Groups," *Journal of Public Economics* 54 (1994): 1–36.

Jamann, Wolfgang, and Thomas Menkhoff, *Make Big Profits with Small Capital* (Munich: Minerva, 1988).

Jefferson, Gary, Albert G. Z. Hu, Xiaojing Guan, and Xiaoyun Yu, "Ownership, Performance, and Innovation in China's Large- and Medium-Size Industrial Enterprise Sector," *China Economic Review* 14 (2003): 89–113.

Katona, George, and James N. Morgan, "The Quantitative Study of Factors Determining Business Decisions," *Quarterly Journal of Economics* 66 (1952): 67–90.

Keefer, Philip, and Stephen Knack, "Why Don't Poor Countries Catch Up? A Cross-National Test of an Institutional Explanation," *Economic Inquiry* 35 (1997): 590–601.

Kennedy, Scott, *The Business of Lobbying in China* (Cambridge, MA: Harvard University Press, 2005).

Keister, Lisa A., *Chinese Business Groups: The Structure and Impact of Interfirm Relations during Economic Development* (Oxford: Oxford University Press, 2000).

Kihlstrom, Richard E., and Jean-Jacques Laffont, "A General-Equilibrium Entrepreneurial Theory of Firm Formation Based on Risk Aversion," *Journal of Political Economy* 87 (1979): 719–748.

Kilby, Peter, *Entrepreneurship and Economic Development* (New York: Free Press, 1971).

Kim, Annette Miae, *Learning to Be Capitalists: Entrepreneurs in Vietnam's Transition Economy* (Oxford: Oxford University Press, 2008).

King, Lawrence Peter, *The Basic Features of Postcommunist Capitalism in Eastern Europe* (Westport, CT: Praeger, 2001).

Kirby, William C., "China Unincorporated: Company Law and Business Enterprise in Twentieth-Century China," *Journal of Asian Studies* 54 (1995): 43–63.

Klein, William A., and John C. Coffee Jr., *Business Organization and Finance: Legal and Economic Principles,* 10th ed. (New York: Foundation Press, 2007).

Knight, Frank H., *Risk, Uncertainty and Profit* (Boston: Houghton Mifflin, 1921).

Knight, John, and Lina Song, *Towards a Labour Market in China* (Oxford: Oxford University Press, 2005).

Koepp, Rob, *Clusters of Creativity: Enduring Lessons on Innovation and Entrepreneurship from Silicon Valley and Europe's Silicon Fen* (West Sussex, England: John Wiley, 2002).

Kogut, Bruce, "The Network as Knowledge: Generative Rules and the Emergence of Structure," *Strategic Management Journal* 21 (2000): 405–425.

Kornai, Janos, "The Affinity between Ownership Forms and Coordination Mechanisms: The Common Experience of Reform in Socialist Countries," *Journal of Economic Perspectives* 4 (1990): 131–147.

Krug, Barbara, Nathan Betancourt, and Hans Hendrischke, "Rechtsprechung und Vertragsgestaltung in China: Die Folgenlosigkeit des neuen Insolvenzgesetzes aus vertragstheoretischer Sicht," *Neue Zuercher Zeitung,* March 16, 2011, http://www.nzz.ch/nachrichten/wirtschaft/aktuell/rechtsprechung_und _vertragsgestaltung_in_china_als_heikler_parcours_fuer_auslaendische _firmen_1.9909790.html (accessed March 20, 2011).

Krugman, Paul, "Increasing Returns and Economic Geography," *Journal of Political Economy* 99 (1991): 483–499.

Kwong, Robin, "China's Billionaires Begin to Add Up," *Financial Times.Com,* October 22, 2007, http://www.ft.com/intl/cms/s/0/a759c0de-809c-11dc-9f14 -0000779fd2ac.html#axzz1gnmqlBr3 (accessed October 23, 2007).

Lawler, Edward J., and Jeongkoo Yoon, "Commitment in Exchange Relations: Test of a Theory of Relational Cohesion," *American Sociological Review* 61 (1996): 89–108.

Lee, Ching Kwan, *Against the Law: Labor Protests in China's Rustbelt and Sunbelt* (Berkeley: University of California Press, 2007).

Leow, Jason, "Small Chinese Firms Struggle to Tap Banks," *Wall Street Journal* (May 14, 2009), A9.

Leung, Man-Kwong, and Vincent Wai-Kwong Mok, "Commercialization of Banks in China: Institutional Changes and Effects on Listed Enterprises," *Journal of Contemporary China* 9 (2000): 41–52.

Levi, Margaret, *Of Rule and Revenue* (Berkeley and Los Angeles: University of California Press, 1988).

Li, Cheng, "Think National, Blame Local: Central-Provincial Dynamics in the Hu Era," *China Leadership Monitor* 17 (2006): 1–24.

Li, David D., "Changing Incentives of the Chinese Bureaucracy," *American Economic Review, Papers and Proceedings* 88 (1998): 393–397.

Li, Fangfang, "Daimler Drives to Take Advantage of Prospects," *China Daily Online*, http://www.chinadaily.com.cn/bizchina/2011-03/07/content_12130727.htm (accessed July 28, 2011).

Li, Hongbin, Lingsheng Meng, Qian Wang, and Li-An Zhou, "Political Connections, Financing and Firm Performance: Evidence from Chinese Private Firms," *Journal of Development Economics* 87 (2008): 283–299.

Li, Hongbin, and Li-An Zhou, "Political Turnover and Economic Performance: The Incentive Role of Personnel Control in China," *Journal of Public Economics* 89 (2005): 1743–1762.

Li, Lan, *Zhongguo Qiyejia Chengzhan 15 Nian* [Fifteen years' growth of Chinese entrepreneurs], vols. 1 and 2 (Beijing: China Machine Press, 2009).

Li, Xinxin, "Development of the Private Economy: Problems and Countermeasures," *Jingji Yanjiu* 1994, in *JPRS-CAR-94-001* (October 1994): 48.

———, "Gaige Kaifanghou de Zhongguo siying Jingji" [China's private economy after the reform and opening], *Jingji Yanjiu Cankao* (December 1, 1994): 2–16.

Light, Ivan H., *Ethnic Enterprise in America: Business and Welfare among Chinese, Japanese, and Blacks* (Berkeley: University of California Press, 1968).

Lin, Justin Yifu, "The Household Responsibility System in China's Agricultural Reform: A Theoretical and Empirical Study," *Economic Development and Cultural Change* 36 (1988): S199–224.

Lin, Nan, "Local Market Socialism: Local Corporatism in Action in Rural China," *Theory and Society* 24 (1995): 301–354.

Lin, Yi-Min, *Between Politics and Markets: Firms, Competition, and Institutional Change in Post-Mao China* (Cambridge: Cambridge University Press, 2001).

Lindenberg, Siegwart M., "A Market Needs a State: Securing Calculability and Market-Induced Values in China," *Journal of Institutional and Theoretical Economics* 156 (2000): 89–94.

Ling, Zhijun, *The Lenovo Affair* (Singapore: John Wiley & Sons [Asia], 2005).

Liu, Alan P. L., "The 'Wenzhou Model' of Development and China's Modernization," *Asian Survey* 32 (1992): 696–711.

Long, Cheryl, and Xiaobo Zhang, "Cluster-Based Industrialization in China: Financing and Performance," *Journal of International Economics* 84 (2011): 112–123.

Lu, Xiaobo, "Booty Socialism, Bureau-preneurs, and the State in Transition," *Comparative Politics* 32 (2000): 273–294.

Lyons, Thomas P., "Economic Reform in Fujian: Another View from the Villages," in *The Economic Transformation of South China: Reform and Development in the Post-Mao Era*, Cornell East Asia Series No. 70, ed. Thomas Lyons and Victor Nee (Ithaca, NY: Cornell University East Asia Program, 1994), 141–168.

Ma, Dali, and William L. Parish, "Tocquevillian Moments: Charitable Contributions by Chinese Private Entrepreneurs," *Social Forces* 85 (2006): 943–964.

Ma, Debin, "Economic Growth in the Lower Yangzi Region of China in 1911–1937: A Quantitative and Historical Analysis," *Journal of Economic History* 68 (2008): 355–392.

Ma, Li, "The Making of the Chinese Working Class: Rural Migrants in Shanghai," unpublished PhD diss., Department of Sociology, Cornell University, 2010.

Macaulay, Stewart, "Non-Contractual Relations in Business: A Preliminary Study," *American Sociological Review* 28 (1963): 55–67.

MacInnis, Peter, and Ruji Ma, "Nanjing Set Its Sights on 2000," *China Business Review* January–February 1995.

MacNamara, William, "How to Get Ahead in Wenzhou," *Far Eastern Economic Review* 169 (2006): 32–37.

Macy, Michael W., "Backward-Looking Social Control." *American Sociological Review* 58 (1993): 819–836.

Marsh, Barnaby, "Heuristics as Social Tools," *New Ideas in Psychology* 20 (2002): 49–57.

Marshall, Alfred, *Principles of Economics*, 8th ed. (London: Macmillan, 1920), 225.

Marwell, Gerald, and Pamela E. Oliver, *The Critical Mass in Collective Action* (Cambridge: Cambridge University Press, 1993).

Massey, Douglas S., "Understanding Mexican Migration to the United States," *American Journal of Sociology* 92 (1987): 1372–1403.

Massey, Douglas S., Joaquin Arango, Graeme Hugo, Ali Kouaouci, Adela Pellegrino, and J. Edward Taylor, *Worlds in Motion: Understanding International Migration at the End of the Millennium* (New York: Oxford University Press, 1998).

Matthews, Rebecca, "Where Do Labor Markets Come From? The Emergence of Urban Labor Markets in the People's Republic of China," unpublished PhD diss., Department of Sociology, Cornell University, 1998.

Matthews, Rebecca, and Victor Nee, "Gender Inequality and Economic Growth in Rural China," *Social Science Research* 29 (2000): 606–632.

Mauro, Paolo, "Corruption and Growth," *Quarterly Journal of Economics* 110 (1995): 681–713.

McClelland, David C., *The Achieving Society* (Princeton, NJ: Van Nostrand, 1961).

McMillan, John, *Reinventing the Bazaar* (New York: Norton, 2002).

McMillan, John, John Whalley, and Lijing Zhu, "The Impact of China's Economic Reforms on Agricultural Productivity Growth," *Journal of Political Economy* 97 (1989): 781–807.

McMillan, John, and Christopher Woodruff, "The Central Role of Entrepreneurs in Transition Economies," *Journal of Economic Perspectives* 16 (2002): 153–170.

———, "Interfirm Relationships and Informal Credit in Vietnam," *Quarterly Journal of Economics* 114 (1999): 1285–1320.

———, "Private Order under Dysfunctional Public Order," *Michigan Law Review* 98 (2000): 2421–2458.

Merton, Robert K., *Social Theory and Social Structure* (New York: Free Press, 1968).

Meyer, John W., *World Society: The Writings of John W. Meyer,* ed. Georg Krücken and Gili S. Drori (Oxford: Oxford University Press, 2009).

Meyer, John W., and Brian Rowan, "Institutionalized Organizations: Formal Structure as Myth and Ceremony," *American Journal of Sociology* 83 (1977): 340–363.

Milgrom, Paul R., Douglass C. North, and Barry Weingast, "The Role of Institutions in the Revival of Trade: The Law Merchant, Private Judges, and the Champagne Fairs," *Economics and Politics* 2 (1990): 1–23.

Mizruchi, Mark S., and Joseph Galaskiewicz, "Network of Interorganizational Relations," *Sociological Methods and Research* 22 (1993): 46–70.

Mokyr, Joel, *The Enlightened Economy: An Economic History of Britain, 1700–1850* (New Haven, CT: Yale University Press, 2009).

———, "Entrepreneurship and the Industrial Revolution in Britain," in *The Invention of Enterprise,* ed. David Landes, Joel Mokyr, and William J. Baumol (Princeton, NJ: Princeton University Press, 2010), 183–210.

Montanari, Andrea, and Amin Saberi, "The Spread of Innovations in Social Networks," *Proceedings of the National Academy of Science* 107 (2010): 20196–20201.

Montinola, Gabriella, Yingyi Qian, and Barry R. Weingast, "Federalism, Chinese Style: The Political Basis for Economic Success," *World Politics* 48 (1995): 50–81.

Mowery, David C., *International Collaborative Ventures in U.S. Manufacturing* (Cambridge, MA: Ballinger, 1988).

Mueller, Eva, and James N. Morgan, "Locational Decisions of Manufacturers," *American Economic Review: Papers and Proceedings* 52 (1962): 204–217.

Mure, Dickie, "Obituary: Rong Yiren, the 'Red Capitalists,'" *Financial Times.com,* October 28, 2005, http://www.ft.com/intl/cms/s/0/103cae12-47d4-11da-a949 -00000e2511c8.html#axzz1gnmqlBr3 (accessed October 29, 2005).

Murrell, Peter, "How Far Has the Transition Progressed?" *Journal of Economic Perspectives* 10 (1996): 25–44.

———, "The Transition according to Cambridge, Mass," *Journal of Economic Literature* 33 (March 1995): 164–178.

Nadvi, Khalid, "Shifting Ties: Social Networks in the Surgical Instrument Cluster of Sialkot, Pakistan," *Development and Change* 30 (1999): 143–177.

Naughton, Barry. *Growing Out of the Plan: Chinese Economic Reform, 1978–1993* (Cambridge: Cambridge University Press, 1995).

Nee, Victor, "The Emergence of a Market Society: Changing Mechanisms of Stratification in China," *American Journal of Sociology* 101 (1996): 908–949.

———, "The New Institutionalisms in Economics and Sociology," in *The Handbook of Economic Sociology,* ed. Neil J. Smelser and Richard Swedberg (New York and Princeton, NJ: Russell Sage Foundation and Princeton University Press, 2005), 49–74.

———, "Norms and Networks in Economic and Organizational Performance," *American Economic Review: Papers and Proceedings* 88 (1998): 86.

———, "Organizational Dynamics of Market Transition: Hybrid Forms, Property Rights, and Mixed Economy in China," *Administrative Science Quarterly* 37 (1992): 1–27.

———, "The Role of the State in Making a Market Economy," *Journal of Institutional and Theoretical Economics* 156 (2000): 64–88.

———, "Social Inequalities in Reforming State Socialism: Between Redistribution and Markets in China," *American Sociological Review* 56 (1991): 267–282.

———, "A Theory of Market Transition: From Redistribution to Markets in State Socialism," *American Sociological Review* 54 (1989): 663–681.

Nee, Victor, and Paul Ingram, "Embeddedness and Beyond: Institutions, Exchange and Social Structure," in *The New Institutionalism in Sociology,* ed. Mary Brinton and Victor Nee (New York: Russell Sage Foundation, 1998), 19–45.

Nee, Victor, Jeong-han Kang, and Sonja Opper, "Entrepreneurial Action: Market Transition, Property Rights, and Innovation," *Journal of Institutional and Theoretical Economics* 166 (2010): 397–425.

Nee, Victor, and Peng Lian, "Sleeping with the Enemy: A Dynamic Model of Declining Political Commitment in State Socialism," *Theory and Society* 23 (1994): 253–297.

Nee, Victor, and Sonja Opper, "Bureaucracy and Finance," *Kyklos* 62 (2009): 293–315.

———, "On Politicized Capitalism," in *On Capitalism,* ed. Victor Nee and Richard Swedberg (Princeton, NJ: Princeton University Press, 2007), 93–127.

———, "Political Capital in a Market Economy," *Social Forces* 88 (2010): 2105–2133.

Nee, Victor, Sonja Opper, and Sonia Wong, "Developmental State and Corporate Governance in China," *Management and Organization Review* 3 (2007): 19–53.

Nee, Victor, Jimy M. Sanders, and Scott Sernau, "Job Transitions in an Immigrant Metropolis: Ethnic Boundaries and Mixed Economy," *American Sociological Review* 59 (1994): 849–872.

Nee, Victor, and Sijin Su, "Institutional Foundations of Robust Economic Performance: Public Sector Industrial Growth in China," in *Industrial Transformation in Eastern Europe in the Light of the East Asian Experience,* ed. Jeffrey Henderson (Houndmills: Macmillan, 1998), 167–187.

North, Douglass C., "Economic Performance through Time," *American Economic Review* 84 (1994): 359–369.

———, *Institutions, Institutional Change and Economic Performance* (Cambridge: Cambridge University Press, 1990).

———, *Structure and Change in Economic History* (New York: Norton, 1981).

———, *Understanding the Process of Economic Change* (Princeton, NJ: Princeton University Press, 2005).

North, Douglass C., and Robert Thomas, *The Rise of the Western World: A New Economic History* (Cambridge: Cambridge University Press, 1973).

North, Douglass C., and Barry R. Weingast, "Constitutions and Commitment: The Evolution of Institutions Governing Public Choice in Seventeenth-Century England," *Journal of Economic History* 49 (1989): 803–832.

Oi, Jean C., "Fiscal Reform and the Economic Foundations of Local State Corporatism in China," *World Politics* 45 (1992): 99–126.

———, "The Role of the Local State in China's Transitional Economy," *China Quarterly* 144 (1995): 1132–1150.

———, *Rural China Takes Off: Institutional Foundations of Economic Reform* (Berkeley: University of California Press, 1999).

Oliver, Pamela E., "Formal Models of Collective Action," *Annual Review of Sociology* 19 (1993): 274.

Olleros, Francisco Javier, and Roderick J. MacDonald, "Strategic Alliances: Managing Complementarity to Capitalize on Emerging Technologies," *Technovation* 7 (1988): 155–176.

Olson, Mancur, *Power and Prosperity: Outgrowing Communist and Capitalist Dictatorship* (New York: Basic Books, 2000).

———, *The Rise and Decline of Nations: Economic Growth, Stagflation, and Social Rigidities* (New Haven, CT: Yale University Press, 1982).

Opper, Sonja, *Zwischen Political Governance und Corporate Governance: Eine institutionelle Analyse chinesischer Aktiengesellschaften* (Baden-Baden: Nomos Verlagsgesellschaft, 2004).

Organisation for Economic Co-operation and Development (OECD), *China in the World Economy: The Domestic Policy Challenges* (Paris: OECD, 2002).

Ostrom, Elinor, *Governing the Commons: The Evolution of Institutions for Collective Action* (Cambridge: Cambridge University Press, 1990).

Owen-Smith, Jason, and Walter W. Powell, "Knowledge Networks as Channels and Conduits: The Effects of Spillovers in the Boston Biotechnology Community," *Organization Science* 15 (2004): 5–21.

Oxenfeldt, Alfred R., *New Firms and Free Enterprise: Pre-War and Post-War Aspects* (Washington, DC: American Council on Public Affairs, 1943).

Parish, William, and Ethan Michelson, "Politics and Markets: Dual Transformations," *American Journal of Sociology* 101 (1996): 1042–1059.

Parish, William L., Xiaoye Zhe, and Fang Li, "Nonfarm Work and Marketization of the Chinese Countryside," *China Quarterly* 143 (1995): 697–730.

Parris, Kristin, "Local Initiative and National Reform: The Wenzhou Model of Development," *China Quarterly* 134 (1993): 242–263.

Pattison, Patricia, and Daniel Herron, "The Mountains Are High and the Emperor Is Far Away: Sanctity of Contract in China," *American Business Law Journal* 40 (2003): 459–510.

Pearson, Margaret M., *China's New Business Elite: The Political Consequences of Economic Reform* (Berkeley: University of California Press, 1997).

Peck, Merton J., and Thomas J. Richardson, *What Is to Be Done? Proposals for the Soviet Transition to the Market* (New Haven, CT: Yale University Press, 1992).

Pei, Minxin, *China's Trapped Transition: The Limits of Developmental Autocracy* (Cambridge, MA: Harvard University Press, 2006).

Peng, Mike W., and Yadong Luo, "Managerial Ties and Firm Performance in a Transition Economy: The Nature of a Micro-Macro Link," *Academy of Management Journal* 43 (2000): 486–501.

Peng, Yusheng, "Kinship, Networks and Entrepreneurs in China's Transitional Economy," *American Journal of Sociology* 105 (2004): 1045–1074.

Perkins, Dwight H., *Market Control and Planning in Communist China* (Cambridge, MA: Harvard University Press, 1966).

Petersen, Mitchell, and Raghuram Rajan, "Trade Credit: Theories and Evidence," *Review of Financial Studies* 10 (1997): 661–691.

Piore, Michael J., and Charles F. Sabel, *The Second Industrial Divide: Possibilities for Prosperity* (New York: Basic Books, 1984).

Pisano, Gary P., Weijian Shan, and David Teece, "Joint Ventures and Collaboration in the Biotechnology Industry," in *International Collaborative Ventures in U.S. Manufacturing,* ed. David Mowery (Cambridge, MA: Ballinger, 1988), 183–222.

Podolny, Joel M., "Networks as the Pipes and Prisms of the Market," *American Journal of Sociology* 107 (2001): 33–60.

Podolny, Joel M., Toby E. Stuart, and Michael T. Hannan, "Networks, Knowledge, and Niches: Competition in the Worldwide Semiconductor Industry, 1984–1991," *American Journal of Sociology* 102 (1996): 659–689.

Polanyi, Karl, *The Great Transformation: The Political and Economic Origins of Our Time* (Boston: Beacon Press, 1944).

Polanyi, Michael, *The Tacit Dimension* (Garden City, NY: Doubleday Anchor, 1967).

Porter, Michael, *The Competitive Advantage of Nations* (London: Macmillan, 1990).

Porter, Michael, and M. Fuller, "Coalitions and Global Strategy," in *Competition in Global Industries,* ed. Michael Porter (Boston: Harvard Business School Press, 1986), 315–344.

Portes, Alejandro, and Julia Sensenbrenner, "Embeddedness and Immigration: Notes on the Social Determinants of Economic Action," *American Journal of Sociology* 98 (1993): 1320–1350.

Powell, Walter W., Kenneth W. Koput, and Laurel Smith-Doerr, "Interorganizational Collaboration and the Locus of Innovation: Networks of Learning in Biotechnology," *Administrative Science Quarterly* 41 (1996): 116–145.

"The Privately-Run Enterprises," *China News Analysis* 1382 (April 1, 1989): 7.

Qi, Daqing, Woody Wu, and Zhang Hua, "Shareholding Structure and Corporate Performance of Partially Privatized Firms: Evidence from Listed Companies," *Pacific-Basin Finance Journal* 8 (2000): 587–610.

Qian, Yingyi, and Gérard Roland, "Federalism and the Soft Budget Constraint," *American Journal of Economics* 88 (December 1998): 1143–1162.

Qian, Yingyi, and Barry R. Weingast, "Federalism as a Commitment to Preserving Market Incentives," *Journal of Economic Perspectives* 11 (1997): 83–92.

Ramella, Francesco, and Carlo Trigilia, "Firms and Territories in Innovation: Lessons from the Italian Case," Cornell University, Center for the Study of Economy and Society, Working Paper No. 55 (2010).

Rees, Albert, and George P. Shultz, *Workers in an Urban Labour Market* (Chicago: University of Chicago Press, 1970).

Report on the Development of China's Private Enterprises No. 6, 2005 (Beijing: Social Sciences Academic Press, 2005).

Ricketts, Martin, "Comment on 'The Role of the State in Making a Market Economy,'" *Journal of Institutional and Theoretical Economics* 156 (2000): 95–98.

Rodrik, Dani, Arvind Subramanian, and Francesco Trebbi, "Institutions Rule: The Primacy of Institutions over Geography and Integration in Economic Development," *Journal of Economic Growth* 9 (2004): 131–165.

Romer, Paul M., "Increasing Returns and Long-Run Growth," *Journal of Political Economy* 94 (1986): 1002–1038.

Rosenfeld, Stuart A., "United States: Business Clusters," in *Networks of Enterprises and Local Development*, ed. OECD (Paris: Organization for Economic Cooperation and Development, Territorial Development Service, 1996).

Rothenberg, Winifred B., "The Emergence of a Capital Market in Rural Massachusetts, 1730–1838," *Journal of Economic History* 45 (1985): 781–808.

Ruan, Jianqing, and Xiaobo Zhang, "Finance and Cluster-Based Industrial Development in China," *Economic Development and Cultural Change* 58 (2009): 143–164.

Ruef, Martin, *The Entrepreneurial Group: Social Identities, Relations, and Collective Action* (Princeton, NJ: Princeton University Press, 2010).

Sachs, Jeffrey, "Poland and Eastern Europe: What Is to Be Done?" in *Foreign Economic Liberalization: Transformation in Socialist and Market Economies*, ed. Andreas Koves and Paul Marer (Boulder, CO: Westview Press, 1991), 235–246.

Sargeson, Sally, and Jianjun Zhang, "Reassessing the Role of the Local State: A Case Study of Local Government Interventions in Property Rights Reform in a Hangzhou District," *China Journal* 42 (1999): 77–99.

Saxenian, AnnaLee, *The New Argonauts: Regional Advantage in a Global Economy* (Cambridge, MA: Harvard University Press, 2006).

———, *Regional Advantage: Culture and Competition in Silicon Valley and Route 128* (Cambridge, MA: Harvard University Press, 1994).

Scheineson, Andrew, "China's Internal Migrants," *Council on Foreign Relations* (May 14, 2009), http://www.cfr.org/china/chinas-internal-migrants/p12943 (accessed July 27, 2011).

Schelling, Thomas, *Micromotives and Macrobehavior* (New York: Norton, 1978).

Scherer, Fredrick M., "Market Structure and the Employment of Scientists and Engineers," *American Economic Review* 57 (1967): 524–531.

Schoonhoven, Claudia Bird and Elaine Romanelli (eds.), *The Entrepreneurship Dynamic: Origins of Entrepreneurship and the Evolution of Industries* (Stanford, CA: Stanford Business Books, 2001).

Schumpeter, Joseph A., *Capitalism, Socialism and Democracy*, 2nd ed. (London: Allen and Unwin, [1942] 1947).

——, *Theorie der wirtschaftlichen Entwicklung: Nachdruck der 1. Auflage von 1912* (Berlin: Duncker & Humblot, [1912] 2006).

Schuster, Camille, "How to Manage a Contract in China," *Business Credit* 107 (2005): 69–70.

Scott, W. Richard, *Institutions and Organizations: Ideas and Interests* (Thousand Oaks, CA: Sage, 2001).

Scully, Gerald W., "The Institutional Framework and Economic Development," *Journal of Political Economy* 96 (1988): 652–662.

Segal, Adam, *Digital Dragon: High-Technology Enterprises in China* (Ithaca, NY: Cornell University Press, 2003).

Shan, Weijian, Gordon Walker, and Bruce Kogut, "Interfirm Cooperation and Startup Innovation in the Biotechnology Industry," *Strategic Management Journal* 15 (1994): 387–394.

Shanghai Statistical Bureau, *Shanghai Statistical Yearbook 2007* (Beijing: China Statistics Press, 2007).

Sheshinski, Eytan, Robert J. Strom, and William J. Baumol, eds., *Entrepreneurship, Innovation, and the Growth Mechanism of the Free-Enterprise Economies* (Princeton, NJ: Princeton University Press, 2007).

Shi, Jinchuan, Yanjun Huang, Sijiang He, and Gujun Yan, *Zhong xiao jinrong Jigou yu zhong xiao Qiye fazhan Yanjiu—yi Zhejiang Wenzhou, Taizhou Diqu wei lie* [The development of small and medium-size financial institutions and enterprises—taking Zhejiang's regions of Wenzhou and Taizhou as examples] (Hangzhou: Zhejiang daxue chubanshe, 2003).

Shirk, Susan L., *The Political Logic of Economic Reform in China* (Berkeley: University of California Press, 1993).

——, "The Politics of Industrial Reform," in *The Political Economy of Reform in Post-Mao China,* ed. Elizabeth J. Perry and Christine Wong (Cambridge, MA: Harvard University Press, 1985), 195–221.

Shleifer, Andrei, and Robert W. Vishny, "Politicians and Firms," *Quarterly Journal of Economics* 109 (1994): 995–1025.

Simon, Curtis J., and John T. Warner, "Matchmaker, Matchmaker: The Effect of Old Boy Networks on Job Match Quality, Earnings, and Tenure," *Journal of Labor Economics* 10 (1992): 306–330.

Simon, Herbert A., *Models of Man: Social and Rational* (New York: John Wiley & Sons, 1957).

——, "Organizations and Markets," *Journal of Economic Perspectives* 5 (1991): 25–44.

Singh, Jitendra V., Robert J. House, and David J. Tucker, "Organizational Change and Organizational Mortality," *Administrative Science Quarterly* 31 (1986): 587–611.

Solow, Robert M., "On Macroeconomic Models of Free-Market Innovation and Growth," in *Entrepreneurship, Innovation, and the Growth Mechanism of the Free-Enterprise Economies,* ed. Eytan Sheshinksi, Robert J. Strom, and William J. Baumol (Princeton, NJ: Princeton University Press, 2007), 15–19.

Sonobe, Tetsushi, Dinghuan Hu, and Keijiro Otsuka, "From Inferior to Superior Products: An Inquiry into the Wenzhou Model of Industrial Development in China," *Journal of Comparative Economics* 32 (2004): 542–563.

Sorenson, Olav, and Pino G. Audia, "The Social Structure of Entrepreneurial Activity: Geographic Concentration of Footwear Production in the United States, 1940–1989," *American Journal of Sociology* 106 (2000): 424–461.

Spence, Michael A., *Market Signaling: Informational Transfer in Hiring and Related Screening Processes* (Cambridge, MA: Harvard University Press, 1974).

Stark, David, and Victor Nee, "Towards an Institutional Analysis of State Socialism," in *Remaking the Economic Institutions of Socialism,* ed. Victor Nee and David Stark (Stanford, CA: Stanford University Press, 1989).

State Statistical Bureau, *China Labour Statistical Yearbook 2007* (Beijing: China Statistics Press, 2007).

————, *China Statistical Yearbook,* various years (Beijing: China Statistics Press).

Statistics on Science and Technology Activities of Industrial Enterprises 2008 (Beijing: China Statistics Press, 2008).

Stigler, George J., "The Theory of Economic Regulation," *Bell Journal of Economics and Management Science* 2 (1971): 3–21.

Stinchcombe, Arthur L., "Organizations and Social Structure," in *Handbook of Organizations,* ed. James G. March (Chicago: Rand-McNally, 1965), 153–193.

Storper, Michael, and Anthony J. Venables, "Buzz: Face-to-Face Contact and the Urban Economy," *Journal of Economic Geography* 4 (2004): 351–370.

Stringham, Edward, "The Extralegal Development of Securities Trading in Seventeenth-Century Amsterdam," *Quarterly Review of Economics and Finance* 43 (2003): 321–344.

Stuart, Toby E., "Interorganizational Alliance Formation in a High-Technology Industry," *Strategic Management Journal* 43 (2000): 668–698.

————, "Network Positions and Propensities to Collaborate: An Investigation of Strategic Alliance in a High-Technology Industry," *Administrative Science Quarterly* 43 (1998): 668–698.

Stuart, Toby E., and Joel M. Podolny, "Local Search and the Evolution of Technological Capabilities," *Strategic Management Journal* 17 (1996): 21–38.

Suchman, Mark, "Managing Legitimacy: Strategic and Institutional Approaches," *Academy of Management Review* 20 (1995): 571–610.

Sull, Donald N., *Made in China* (Cambridge, MA: Harvard Business School Press, 2005).

Sun, Zhenming, and Martin Perry, "The Role of Trading Cities in the Development of Chinese Business Cluster," *International Business Research* 1 (2008): 69–81.

Swedberg, Richard, "The Social Science View of Entrepreneurship," in *Entrepreneurship*, ed. Richard Swedberg (New Delhi: Oxford University Press, 2000), 7–44.

Szelényi, Iván, *Urban Inequality under State Socialist Redistributive Economies* (London: Oxford University Press, 1983).

Tang, Zun, "Network Contingencies: Hiring and Job Search in China's Transitional Labor Market," unpublished PhD diss., Department of Sociology, Cornell University, 2007.

Taylor, Jeffrey R., "Rural Employment Trends and the Legacy of Surplus Labour, 1978–1986," *China Quarterly* 116 (1986): 736–766.

Taylor, Michael, *The Possibility of Cooperation* (Cambridge: Cambridge University Press, 1987).

Tian, Fang, and Fatang Lin, *Zhongguo Renkou Qianyi* [Population migration in China] (Beijing: Zhishi chubanshe, 1986).

Tilly, Charles, *Identities, Boundaries, and Social Ties* (Boulder, CO: Paradigm, 2005).

"Tom Daschle's Washington," *Wall Street Journal*, February 4, 2009, http://online.wsj.com/article/SB123371143249046139.html (accessed February 4, 2009).

Tsai, Kellee, *Back Alley Banking: Private Entrepreneurs in China* (Ithaca, NY: Cornell University Press, 2002).

———, *Capitalism without Democracy: The Private Sector in Contemporary China* (Ithaca, NY: Cornell University Press, 2007).

Tullock, Gordon, *The Economics of Special Privilege and Rent-Seeking* (Boston: Kluwer Academic Publishers, 1989).

Uzzi, Brian, "The Sources and Consequences of Embeddedness for the Economic Performance of Organizations: The Network Effect," *American Sociological Review* 61 (1996): 674–698.

van de Ven, Andrew H., "Central Problems in the Management of Innovation," *Management Science* 32 (1986): 590–607.

Vanhonacker, Wilfried R., David Zweig, and Siu Fung Chung, "Transnational or Social Capital? Returnees versus Local Entrepreneurs," in *China's Domestic Private Firms: Multidisciplinary Perspectives on Management and Performance*, ed. Anne S. Tsui, Yanjie Bian, and Leonard Cheng (Armonk, NY: M. E. Sharpe, 2006).

Walder, Andrew, "Elite Opportunity in Transitional Economies," *American Sociological Review* 68 (2003): 899–916.

———, "Local Government as Industrial Firms: An Organizational Analysis of China's Transitional Economy," *American Journal of Sociology* 101 (1995): 263–301.

Wang, Baoshu, and Hui Huang, "China's New Company and Securities Law: An Overview and Assessment," *Australian Journal of Corporate Law* 19 (2006): 229–242.

Wang, Jiapeng, "BYD Signs Electric Auto Agreement with Daimler," *Caixin Online*, April 3, 2010, http://english.caixin.cn/2010-03-04/100122662.html (accessed August 10, 2010).

Wank, David L., *Commodifying Communism: Business, Trust, and Politics in a Chinese City* (Cambridge: Cambridge University Press, 1999).

Weber, Max, *The Protestant Ethic and the Spirit of Capitalism*. Translation by Talcott Parsons (1904; New York: Scribner, [1930] 2006).

Wedeman, Andrew H., *From Mao to Market: Rent Seeking, Local Protectionism, and Marketization in China* (Cambridge: Cambridge University Press, 2003).

Wei, Linglin, "China Cracks Down on Informal Lending," *Wall Street Journal*, October 15, 2011, http://online.wsj.com/article/SB10001424052970204002304576630050471382610.html (accessed October 17, 2011).

Weingast, Barry, "The Economic Role of Political Institutions," *Journal of Law, Economics and Organization* 11 (1995): 1–31.

Wenzhou Statistical Bureau, *Wenzhou Statistical Yearbook*, various years (Beijing: China Statistics Press).

White, Harrison C., *Identity and Control: A Structural Theory of Social Action* (Princeton, NJ: Princeton University Press, 1992).

———, *Markets from Networks: Socioeconomic Models of Production* (Princeton, NJ: Princeton University Press, 2002).

———, "Where Do Markets Come From?" *American Journal of Sociology* 87 (1981): 517–547.

Whiting, Susan H., *Power and Wealth in Rural China: The Political Economy of Institutional Change* (Cambridge: Cambridge University Press, 2000).

———, "The Regional Evolution of Ownership Forms: Shareholding Cooperatives and Rural Industry in Shanghai and Wenzhou," in *Property Rights and Economic Reform in China*, ed. Jean C. Oi and Andrew G. Walder (Stanford, CA: Stanford University Press, 1999), 171–200.

Whyte, William Foote, *Street Corner Society: The Social Structure of an Italian Slum* (Chicago: University of Chicago Press, 1943).

Williamson, Oliver E., "Credible Commitments: Using Hostages to Support Exchange," *American Economic Review* 73 (1983): 519–540.

———, *The Economic Institutions of Capitalism* (New York: Free Press, 1985).

Wilson, Scott, "Law Guanxi: MNCs, State Actors, and Legal Reform in China," *Journal of Contemporary China* 17 (2008): 25–51.

Wu, Bangguo, "Several Questions Concerning the Reform and Development of State-Owned Enterprises," *Chinese Economy* 30 (1997): 6–47.

Xin, Katherine R., and Jone L. Pearce, "Guanxi: Connections as Substitutes for Formal Institutional Support," *Academy of Management Journal* 39 (1996): 1641–1658.

Xu, Qingrui, Ling Zhu, Gang Zheng, and Fangrui Wang, "Haier's Tao of Innovation: A Case Study of the Emerging Total Innovation Management Model," *Journal of Technology Transfer* 32 (2007): 27–47.

Yang, Dali L., *Remaking the Chinese Leviathan: Market Transition and the Politics of Governance in China* (Stanford, CA: Stanford University Press, 2004).

Yang, Dennis Tao, "Urban-Biased Policies and Rising Income Inequality in China," *American Economic Review: Papers and Proceedings* 89 (April 1999): 306–310.

Ye, Zi, "The Sword Hanging above Private Owners: Limitations in the Development of the Private Economy in Mainland China," *Kaifang* (August 18, 1993), 39–41, translated in *JPRS-CAR-93-088* (December 14, 1993), 40.

Young, H. Peyton, "The Dynamics of Social Innovation," *Proceedings of the National Academy of Science*, forthcoming.

———, "The Economics of Convention," *Journal of Economic Perspectives* 10 (1996): 105–122.

———, *Individual Strategy and Social Structure: An Evolutionary Theory of Institutions* (Princeton, NJ: Princeton University Press, 2001).

Young, Susan, *Private Business and Economic Reform in China* (Armonk, NY: M. E. Sharpe, 1995).

———, "Wealth but Not Security: Attitudes towards Private Business in China in the 1980s," *Australian Journal of Chinese Affairs* 25 (1991): 115–137.

Yusuf, Shahid, Kaoru Nabeshima, and Dwight H. Perkins, *Under New Ownership: Privatizing China's State-Owned Enterprises* (Stanford, CA: Stanford University Press, 2006).

Zhang, Houyi, *Zhongguo de siying Jingji yu siying Qiyezhu* [China's private firm economy and company owners] (Beijing: Zhishi Chubanshe, 1995).

Zhang, Jianjun, "Marketization, Class Structure, and Democracy in China: Contrasting Regional Experiences," *Democratization* 14 (2007): 425–445.

Zhonggong Yanjiu, *Zhongguo Renkou yu jiuye Wenti* [China's population and employment problems] (Taibei, 1986).

Zhongguo Nongye Nianjian [Yearbook of China's agriculture], various years (Beijing: Nongye Chubanshe).

Zhongguo shekeyuan ruankeyuan yanjiu ketizu, "Siying Jingji fazhan Yanjiu" [Analysis of the development of the private economy], *Jingji Yanjiu Cankao* (September 12, 1995): 11.

Zhu, Tian, "China's Corporatization Drive: An Evaluation and Policy Implications," *Contemporary Economic Politics* 17 (1999): 530–539.

Index

Page numbers in italics refer to figures and tables.

Shareholders, 120–126
Shareholding cooperatives, 111, 377–378n4
Silicon Valley comparisons, 48, 199–200
Smuggling, 362n10
Social capital, 234, 236
Social insurance, 181–183, 387nn53–54
Social Insurance Law, 181
Social learning, 86–88, 204, 206–209
Social mechanisms: embedded in
    networks, 8–10, 15, 21, 23, 31, 40, 146,
    366n61; definition of institutions and,
    18; market expansion and, 34–36, 39;
    survey and, 68; social learning as,
    86–88, 204, 206–209; learning on the
    job as, 89–92; mutual assistance as,
    92–96, 103–104, 206–207; relationship-
    based lending as, 102–103; reputation
    as screening device as, 104–105, 150;
    community sanctions as, 105–106, 149;
    isomorphism as, 113–119; industrial
    clusters and, 132–144; personalized
    exchange as, 136–139, 148–149; multi-
    plex networks as, 139–140; collaborative
    purchasing/marketing as, 141; informa-
    tion exchange as, 141–143, 148–149,
    206–207, 382n19, 383nn32,34; short-
    term finance and, 143–144; labor
    migration and, 165–167; innovation
    and, 199–220, 225, 259–260
Social norms: and institutional change,
    14–17, 20, 23–32, 74–75, 259–263,
    366n61; cooperation and, 15, 262;
    maintaining, 21–23; identities and,
    22–23; and deviation, 27, 29–30;
    network diffusion of, 31, 367n62;
    innovation and, 77–78, 225. *See also*
    Business norms; Cooperation norms
Social rewards and punishment, 21–22,
    366n61
Sociological institutionalism, 17
Sole-proprietor companies, 109–110, *117*
Sole Proprietorship Enterprise Law,
    379–380n31
Spatial concentration. *See* Industrial
    clusters *(chanye jiqun)*

Standards, industry, 204
Stanford, Leland, 257
State-mandated rules: private enterprise
    and, 4, 5; endogenous institutional
    change and, 12, 16, 17, 20, 23–32, 39
State-owned enterprises: reform and, 1, 5,
    7, 10, 38–39; decline of, 3, 38, 228–231,
    232; as industrial base, 49, 58, 60;
    favoritism and, 96–97; modern
    enterprise system and, 114–115;
    industrial clusters and, 135, 139,
    151–153, 155–156; labor and, 163, 166,
    168, 179–181; innovation and, 198–199,
    220–222; asset privatization and,
    246–247. *See also* Township- and
    village-run enterprises (TVEs)
Stimulus money, economic crisis and,
    97–98, 376n64
Stock exchanges: business norm develop-
    ment and, 17; Chinese, 32–33,
    356nn7–8, 360–361n37
Strategic alliances, 211–213, 215, 392n48
Suppliers: industrial clusters and, 132–133,
    141, 143; production chains *(chanyelian),*
    132–133; switching, 145; private net-
    works of, 151–155; innovation and, 203
Survey, Yangzi delta. *See* Yangzi delta
    survey
Suzhou, 58, 60
Suzhou-Nantong Yangzi Bridge, 60

Tax system, 6, 359n27
Technology development. *See* Innovation
Tianjin, 47
Township- and village-run enterprises
    (TVEs): Sunan (southern Jiangsu)
    model of, 49; decline and privatization
    of, 49–50; Changzhou and, 59; doing
    business with, 151, 155–156; asset
    privatization and, 246; state credit and,
    369n14
Trade credit, 143–144, 373n27, 382n21,
    382–383n26
Trade fairs, 138–139, 158, 203–204
Training, on-the-job, 89–92